Mafia Raj

The Rule of Bosses in South Asia

• Lucia Michelutti • Ashraf Hoque •
• Nicolas Martin • David Picherit•
• Paul Rollier • Arild E. Ruud •
• Clarinda Still •

SPEAKING TIGER

SPEAKING TIGER BOOKS LLP
125A, Ground Floor, Shahpur Jat, near Asiad Village,
New Delhi 110049

First published by Stanford University Press, 2019
This edition first published in India by Speaking Tiger Books, 2023

Reprinted and published by arrangement with Stanford University Press

ISBN: 978-93-5447-619-8

10 9 8 7 6 5 4 3 2 1

Printed at Chaman Enterprises, New Delhi

Lucia Michelutti is Professor of Anthropology at the University College London.

Ashraf Hoque is Associate Professor in the Department of Anthropology at the University College London.

Nicolas Martin is Assistant Professor in Indian/South Asian Studies at the Asien-Orient-Institut of the University of Zurich.

David Picherit is Research Fellow at the French National Centre for Scientific Research.

Paul Rollier is Assistant Professor in South Asian Studies at the University of St. Gallen.

Arild E. Ruud is Professor of South Asia Studies at the University of Oslo.

Clarinda Still is Research Associate at the University College London.

CONTENTS

ACKNOWLEDGMENTS

The research for this book was funded by the European Research Council "An Anthropological Study of Muscular Politics in South Asia" (AISMA/284080) and the Economic and Social Research Council "Political Cultures in South Asia" (ES/I036702). There are many people to thank for help with this project. We are especially grateful for the intellectual engagement and inspiration we have enjoyed with all the members of the research program "Democratic Cultures" (https://www.ucl.ac.uk/democratic-cultures). Many ideas and nuances would have not have emerged without this larger collaboration: many thanks to Thomas Blom Hansen, Paul Brass, David Gellner, Barbara Harriss-White, Sondra Hausner, Beatrice Jauregui, Hassan Javid, Morten Koch Andersen, Sanjay Kumar, Sanjay Kumar Pandey, Satendra Kumar, Norbert Peabody, Anastasia Piliavsky, Indrajit Roy, Andrew Sanchez, and Tone Sissener. We are especially grateful to the members of the Advisory Group for their support and advice throughout the project: John Dunn, Peter Evans, David Gilmartin, Jonathan Parry, Pamela Price, John Sidel, and Steven Wilkinson.

We also thank many others who made their own contributions as readers, interlocutors, friends, and research assistants: Daniela Berti, Zahid Choudhury, John Dickey, Srinivas Dusi, Rebecca Empson, Chris Fuller, Katy Gardener, Laurent Gayer, John Harriss, Martin Holbraad, Mozahid Islam, David Jackman, Nida Kirmani, Angelika Malinar, Mobasser Monem, Ignatius Prabhakar, Maksud Ibna Rahmam, Sumathi Rajesh, Ladi Shah, K. Satyanaryana, AbuBakar Siddique, Edward Simpson, Johnathan Spencer, Gilles Tarabout, Milan Vaishnav, Federico Varese, Gilles Verniers, Jeff Witsoe, Zulfiqar Ali Shah, and the late Naeem Shakir.

In India, Pakistan, and Bangladesh we accrued many debts toward our in loco partners without whom this research would have not been possible: in India, the Center for the Studies of Development Societies and the University of Madras in Chennai; in Pakistan, the Lahore University of Management Sciences; and in Bangladesh, the University of Dhaka.

A special thanks goes to the project manager Pascale Searle, whose help and support has been invaluable.

Some of this material has been presented at seminars in Zurich, Oxford, Madison, Sussex, Paris, Sylhet, Lahore, and London. We are grateful to our hosts and interlocutors on those occasions. We organized three memorable writing workshops, one in Sylhet in Bangladesh, one in Lahore, and another in Bergen. Much of the argument of this book has been shaped by the discussions on those occasions.

We also record our appreciation to three anonymous readers for their constructive comments. We thank the staff at Stanford University Press, not least the series editor Thomas Blom Hansen, for making the publishing process of this book an enjoyable experience.

Finally, we thank those members of our own families who have had to put up with our long fieldwork trips and disappearances for workshops and conferences. Lucia thanks Oliver, Matilda, and Iolanda Heath for their constant support, encouragement, and patience throughout this adventure. She also thanks Rosalba Luongo and Zoe Josephine Payne for taking care of the girls with love while she was in the field for extended periods of time. Grazie! Ash extends his warm gratitude to his family and friends, who supported him throughout the project, especially his partner, Rosie, whose tolerance and loyalty were unparalleled. Finally, he thanks his late mother, who sadly passed away during the production of this book. Her prayers and encouragement, however, remain immutable. Nicolas thanks Emily and Clemente for accompanying him to the Punjab for fifteen months. David thanks warmly Marion Delpeu, as well as Anaëlle and Anouk Picherit (the last being born just before the 2014 elections) for their support and patience. Arild thanks Elisabet, Sandra, Marius, and Mathea for patiently accommodating to weird interests. Paul thanks Benedetta.

Clarinda thanks David Owen, Hazel Still, and Gaby Jacoby Owen for all their support and Saul, Xanthe, and Liza (the latter two of whom were born during the course of the project).

Last, we thank the bosses of this book for sharing with us their lives and thoughts.

MAFIA RAJ

INTRODUCTION

UNDERSTANDING THE RULE OF BOSSES IN SOUTH ASIA

ON A WINTER'S NIGHT in 2010, Lahore's most notorious don was ambushed in the parking lot outside Lahore's airport and shot six times. Tipu Truckonwala, "the truck owner," had just returned from Dubai where, fearing for their lives, he had relocated his wife and children. His three bodyguards and two drivers died immediately, and Tipu passed away two days later in the hospital, surrounded by local politicians and his armed strongmen. Markets closed for the day, and his funeral procession drew thousands of Lahoris who paid their respect to the underworld don. His death brought an end to the twenty-year feud between his family and another Kashmiri clan, the Butts of Gowalmandi, a feud that had claimed the lives of dozens since the murder of Tipu's father in 1994. Armed with Kalashnikovs and riding motorbikes, the warring gunmen targeted their victims on the streets or outside courts and hospitals. Alternatively, the family elders had their rivals killed in staged police encounters through the intercession of corrupt police officers. Besides real estate and truck transportation, Tipu's family was allegedly involved in smuggling, car theft, narcotics, extortion, gambling, begging rings, and arms trafficking and had contacts with the highest echelons of the state. At the same time, just like his rivals, Tipu ran an unofficial *dera* (den) at his truck depot, where he would receive plaintiffs from all over town: families seeking mediation in land disputes; policemen eager for a rapid transfer; mothers seeking the release of their sons from police custody; poor residents begging him to have the local administration repair a water pipe in the neighborhood. In the popular imagination, Tipu and his rivals are the quintessential Lahori dons, part of the city's "top ten": dreaded yet sometimes admired figures at the interstice between competing formal and informal codes of law and sovereignty.

The romantic, mythical, and phantasmagorical dimensions of the outlaw have long been recognized as central to the power enjoyed by Robin Hood–type gangsters who are often portrayed as figures of popular resistance à la Eric Hobsbawm.[1] Occasionally in India, these extraordinary individuals are also transformed into "hero gods," such as Veerappan the notorious South Indian sandalwood and ivory smuggler. On October 18, 2004, Veerappan was killed by the police in a gun battle. He had been a fugitive for twenty years and was allegedly responsible for the deaths of 180 policemen and state officials and the kidnapping of politicians and movie stars; he was the epitome of the feared charismatic gangster. Supported by a tribal population and local nationalist political parties, the "jungle cat" came to be revered as a demigod; worshipped in religious rituals; and immortalized in TV serials, movies, novels, comic books, and songs. Today, he even has global marketing power, as witnessed by the "deep, dangerous and intoxicating *Smuggler's Soul*" perfume (created by Lush, a global biocosmetic company) that bears his image on the label.[2] The allure of Veerappan and Tipu is not an exception in South Asia, where strongmen are all too often feared and loved and are an integral part of political landscapes.

Overall, insofar as these outlaws overlap with the state, they often resemble not so much Hobsbawm's social bandits but rather what scholars of strongmen and mafias have characterized as "violent entrepreneurs," defined loosely as individuals who use private (and state) force as means of social control and economic accumulation.[3] Throughout this book we use the term "boss" to refer to these mafia-esque characters.[4] These are ultimately individuals "who make themselves respected."[5] By asserting personal mastery and living on the fringe of "normal structures," they often also come to possess quasi-magical powers and charismatic authority.[6] Today, boss myths are often spread through contemporary media and movies. These are worlds where it is difficult to distinguish between art and life: they no longer imitate each other but appear to have merged. Here "film stars cross over from their fantasy world into politics to emerge as powerful figures guiding the destiny of millions."[7] To capture this complex reality, this book provides an anthropological framework to examine the workings of bosses *in action* in seven locations in India, Pakistan, and Bangladesh. Our approach is explicitly ethnographic and grounded in lived experiences.[8] We situate "the figure of the boss" analytically, and through that concept we theorize what we call "the art of bossing."[9] We argue that such an "art" form is a potent relational mode of power and economic accumulation symptomatic of the current age. Understanding the microlevel dynamics of "the rule of bosses" nuances our knowledge of power and authority in South Asia, the broader anthropological study of criminal-political formations, and the lure of the strongman in other parts of the world.

SOVEREIGNTY AND FORCE IN SOUTH ASIA

Historically, power and leadership across South Asia have been associated with the use of coercion and brute force, with kings portrayed as valiantly ruthless sword-bearing rulers.[10] After independence, Nehru was appalled to find that politicians in Congress in the North Indian state of Uttar Pradesh had, in his own words, "violated every single one of the 511 paragraphs in the criminal code."[11] As discussed by Hansen and Stepputat, "The incompleteness, tentativeness, and fragmented nature of colonial states and the excessive forms of violence they frequently visited on their subject populations have structured postcolonial states in profound ways."[12] The legacy of a fragmented society and the practices of indirect rule under the British Raj are reflected in a myriad of de facto sovereigns.[13] Today, "muscular" styles remain a persistent feature of South Asian political economic landscapes and electoral democracies.

In India, 34 percent of current elected Members of Parliament (MPs) are said to have criminal histories.[14] In Pakistan, the international focus on religious extremism and state militarization has diverted attention from the fact that many acts of terror (kidnapping, bombing, murder, and threats) are often connected to struggles between local political interests in a nation where politicians commonly manage their constituencies like personal fiefdoms.[15] In Bangladesh, while the clampdown on crime and corruption during the 2007–8 emergency regime was aimed at creating a cleaner political environment, over the past few years extralegal political activities have reportedly been on the rise and are often instigated by actors within the ruling party.[16] Public concern with the "criminalization of politics" in the region goes far beyond anxieties about endemic nepotism or the mismanagement of public funds. Many criminal politicians are accused not just of embezzlement but also of burglary, kidnapping, and murder. The observed political and economic landscapes, then, appear not only as corrupt but also as highly violent spheres.[17]

In this environment, gangster politicians have increasingly become popular models of authority and public conduct, not only for politicians but also for businessmen and ambitious youth. In addition, the myth of the boss contributes to inspiring and legitimizing numerous real-life strongmen who coexist, overlap, and compete to control resources and people.[18] Referred to by the terms *goonda*, *dabang*, *mastan*, *badmash*, "mafia don," or "godfather," these individuals are an integral part of everyday social, political, and economic life in the region. Today, their power and authority are played out against a backdrop of rapid economic growth and an increasing scramble for economic resources. Alongside the manipulation of later forms of capitalism, competitive electoral politics (and their rising costs) are the pillars of the construction of decentralized fiefdoms headed by powerful bosses.[19] Systematic corruption, violence, and accumulation of wealth lie at the heart of bosses' systems of governance, popularly known in the region as "Mafia Raj," "Goonda Raj" or "Mastangiri," that is, mafia or criminal rule. These systems, which use force to accelerate the path toward power and wealth, share similarities with the *Caciques* and *Caudillos* of

Latin America, the Mafiosi in Italy, urban political machines in the United States, and today's gangster politicians and mafia-like systems in Brazil, Bulgaria, Indonesia, Jamaica, Nigeria, the Philippines, Russia, Thailand, and Turkey.[20]

MAFIA RAJ

"Mafia" has now become an indigenous South Asian term and a folk concept.[21] In South Asia, the Italian words *mafia* or *mafioso* are increasingly used not only by the media but also in everyday vernacular conversation. In its South Asian usage, the term refers to organized crime in general. More often than not, however, it is employed to refer to business enterprises that seek to monopolize particular trades through extralegal and violent means, and crucially to refer to political protection (e.g., alcohol mafia, water mafia, coal mafia, land mafia). It is this intertwining of crime, business, and politics that is popularly referred to as mafia or Mafia Raj.[22] The latter term first gained currency in India, together with the hypothesis of a "criminalization of politics," following the disclosure in 1993 of a government report detailing the reach of a growing nexus between politicians, the bureaucracy, and mafia organizations in the country. According to the report, these organizations had acquired enough political patronage and "muscle and money power" to "operate with impunity" and to run "a parallel government, pushing the state apparatus into irrelevance." "Even the members of the judicial system," the report reads, "have not escaped the embrace of the mafia."[23] In reality, there is no such thing as a singular and well-defined mafia. Instead, there are varieties of mafia-like systems that have their own characteristics and whose morphology greatly differs from the prototypical and cinematographic Sicilian Cosa Nostra. Such a mythical mafia does not in fact exist in Italy either. Currently on trial in a major scandal involving crime syndicates in the government of the city of Rome, the Italian boss Massimo Carmierati theorized contemporary amorphous and variegated mafia systems as the "world in between." In a tapped phone conversation with his henchman, he explains: "It is all about the 'world in between' theory, mate. You see, up above us are the living and below us are the dead and then there is us, in the middle . . . and that's a world in between where everybody and everything can meet."[24]

These in-between worlds are not the mafia represented in the romanticized image of Don Corleone but rather are amorphous configurations of bosses able to expand their range of action, not just with weapons but mainly through political influence and economic investments. These systems do not have rigid vertical and hierarchical structures; their boundaries and memberships are shifting and volatile and are thus difficult to characterize as discrete organizations. "The world in between" is the zipper between legality and illegality. It is the world where "the upper world," made up of white-collar workers, business, and institutions, and the "world below," composed of varieties of criminal bosses and musclemen, meet and produce "proto-mafia" systems of governance rather than traditional organized criminal organizations.

THE ART OF BOSSING

Despite increased public concern about a growing overlap between the criminal, the political, and the economic spheres, the South Asian world in between remains underresearched. Mafia Raj, whose modus operandi is so vividly described in fiction, movies, TV, press, and social media, remains mostly absent in academia. India, Pakistan, and Bangladesh are rarely the focus of international literature on organized crime, mafias, and gangs.[25] In the region, historians and social anthropologists have commonly focused on studying colonial notions of "thuggery," "the dacoit," and "the criminal tribe/caste." These studies have widely explored the conditions under which a distinctly modern notion of crime took shape in colonial South Asia.[26] Yet the contemporary mafia-like boss and, more generally, the daily management and spectacle of criminal (political) sovereignty have not received equal scrutiny. Thus, the analysis of "power among the powerful" is missing from the growing literature on the anthropology of statehood, democracy, and local political economies.[27]

To address this gap, this book examines the everyday workings of bosses' realpolitik across seven sites in India, Pakistan, and Bangladesh. We ask, How do bosses command and aspire to command? What exactly do they do? What are the contexts in which they operate? These may be straightforward questions, but they have rarely been asked and never systematically studied in this way. In the following pages, readers have the opportunity to meet bosses at different stages of their careers and with different degrees of influence and personal power. Our focus is on "Middle" India, Pakistan, and Bangladesh, on small and *mofussil* (provincial) towns often neglected by anthropologists specializing in South Asia, who instead tend to focus on metro-cities or villages.[28] We seek to illustrate bosses' struggle for personal sovereignty and their recurrent cinematographic self-legitimizing mythologies, as well as how these fearless and beloved figures transgress and/or reinforce social norms; how they display masculine prowess through murder, rape, beatings, and racketeering; how they make money through legitimate and illegitimate businesses; how they collaborate with (or avoid) the police; how they use caste, lineage, brotherhood, and class to acquire capital and to fight elections; how they bluff their strength; how they create intimate bonds with followers, subjects, and citizens; and how they are obeyed, tolerated, or rejected.

Our gallery of portrayals include "the Legend," a gangster Robin Hood–turned–regional hero in South India; "the Rookie," an emerging political *mastan* (enforcer) with a muscular and artistic background in peri-urban Bangladesh; "Lady Dabang," a mistress-cum-estate developer–turned–small-town political boss in provincial North India; "the Henchman," a low-caste party boss who through muscle and theatrics is challenging caste hierarchies and seeking a dignified life for himself and his family; "the Adjudicators," a constellation of small-time influential bosses who run a private *dera* and seek to administer justice in their respective neighborhoods and markets in a Pakistani city; "the Bluffer," a self-appointed boss who through bluff and mimicry captures popular fantasies of power and bossism in the Indian Punjab; and "the Godfather," a Machiavellian elected don in a provincial town in Bangladesh. Except for "the Bluffer" all the characters have extensive criminal records; they are accused of murder, attempted murder, kidnapping, racketeering, fraud, money laundering, or a combination of these.

Thus, our intimate portrayals document "real people doing real things,"[29] which cumulatively help us map the art of bossing. Robert Dahl pointed out in a seminal article that "in the English language power is an awkward word, for unlike 'influence' and 'control' it has no convenient verb form."[30] By using the term "bossing," we wish to capture the processual nature of "doing power" and the manners in which, as Richard Sennett suggested, "authority can become a process, a making, breaking, a remaking of meanings. It can be visible and legible."[31] More specifically, we conceptualize "the art of bossing" as the performance of personal sovereignty.[32] This art form refers to the violent, criminal, business, and "democratic" tactics and strategies that some men (seldom women) deploy to *control* people and resources to pursue a better life for themselves, their families, and, at times, their communities. Enacting personal sovereignty requires a capacity for violence and for making money, repeated acts of give and take, figurations and mythologies. We show how these ingredients are put together, joined, mixed, and packaged and how such an art brings political-economic authority into existence. Importantly, we document the uncontrollable nature of such processes and the perpetual instability of bosses' power. Bossing requires the constant juggling of legitimacy and illegitimacy and demands an ability to thrive financially in opaque Mafia Raj worlds, where rules are suspended and moral uncertainty reigns.[33] In this volatile environment "the will *to boss*" needs to be performed, invented, and bluffed on a daily basis. These are worlds where even representations are animated figures. Acting like a boss and behaving like a boss are sometimes the same thing, and other times not. Either way, performances contribute to creating material and tangible chains of command, predation, and control over resources and, perhaps more important, over people's lives.

This grounded approach to the art of bossing allows us to depart from an abstract Foucauldian analysis of sovereign power and modern government.[34] By putting flesh and blood on abstract name tags (the godfather, the *dabang*, the *mastan*, the *badmash*) and grounding the available statistics and discourses on crime in real-life processes, this book seeks to shift attention away from power as it occurs in discourses and institutions toward power as it is held by people in particular contexts. Ultimately, our case studies illustrate that power is not principally dispersed or diffused but can be highly concentrated, possessed, and wielded. They illustrate that individuals can be active agents of power, not just their point of application and/or effect, and, importantly, that their sources of "boss authority" have multiple and uncontrollable origins. Bossing does not have a unique ontology. We start by analytically situating the figure of the boss and outline how such a tool allows us to conceptualize the art of bossing against the backdrops of a variety of Mafia Raj, each with its own political economies and aesthetic figurative power.

THE FIGURE OF THE BOSS

As use of the term "boss" suggests, the book stresses the often "curiously underrated role of violence and coercion [and mafia-related business 'methods'] in local strongmen's rule" in South Asia and beyond.[35] Collective violence, community riots, or armed conflicts in the region are the subject of a growing and sophisticated body of literature.[36] However, routinized, individualized forms of violence and criminal forms of intimidation in the economic spheres, which are at the heart of systems of governance such as bossism, while acknowledged, remain underanalyzed.

The seductive and puzzling appeal of strongmen has fascinated anthropologists for a long time. In the 1960s, the so-called big man debate led by Marshall Sahlins, Maurice Godelier, and Marilyn Strathern produced important theoretical developments in the study of power, leadership, and personhood.[37] In South Asia, however, as Matt Mines convincingly pointed out, the role played by personal uniqueness, volition, achievement, and prowess has been understudied and overlooked. Mines traced this gap to the influence of Louis Dumont and his argument that Western notions of the individual based on equality and freedom were absent from Indian society.[38] More than thirty years have now passed since Mines's provocative statement, but we still know precious little about the role played by individual agency in capturing, responding to, challenging, or exploiting existing power structures and changing cultures of authority. More generally, we lack an ethnographic analysis that pays equal attention to personalized forms of power, criminal formations, and the democratic game through which even a man of humble origins can become a man of importance, a leader of men.[39] We also lack ethnographies of how personal sovereignty is lived and how models of authority are transforming across kinship, religious, economic, and political domains. We need such analysis to complement excellent studies on the criminalization of politics in South Asia, as the recent one by Milan Vaishnav. His work on elected criminal politicians provides unique insights into the ways in which crime pays in Indian politics and beyond, but it does not address the cultures that surround the criminal politician.[40] It should be noted that when studying bossism, not only are the state, democracy, capitalism, violence, and the law at issue but also notions of kingship, honor and masculinity, charisma and myth, patronage, friendship, family and kinship, caste sovereignties and territorial dominance, trust and faith, and widespread sociocultural imaginaries of power. Violent self-interest and profit-driven individual actions are frequently embedded in the local social fabric. However, the relationality of bossism should be not viewed as embedded in pregiven mythical bonds between the individual Robin Hood strongman and his or her adoring followers but rather as the product of hard quotidian work. This is work that is shaped (yet not determined) by specific sociocultural and economic situations and institutional milieus. In short, to understand the workings of the art of bossing, emphasis should be placed both on the individual and the system. Both agency and structural perspectives are necessary to understand this form of power, its performativity, and its multiple sources of illegitimacy/legitimacy.

The concept of the "figure" allows us to pursue such a complex task. The protagonists of this book are not only real people; they are also figures: individuals who stand out from the humdrum of everyday life and thus give voice to social forms larger than themselves. Figures, as Barker, Harms, and Lindquist remind us, operate as "symbols that embody the structures and feeling associated with larger, seemingly impersonal conditions of a particular time."[41] Hence, the concept of the "historically situated figure" differs widely from the sociological concept of the social type (such as the "charismatic leader," "big man," "chief," or "social bandit") primarily developed as a disembodied and ahistorical tool of classification. Thus, the concept of "the figure of the boss" (rather than the boss as an ideal type) provides us with insights into the ethos of (criminal) power that are at once highly particular but also recognizably general. It allows us to understand bosses as historically situated figures, with predecessors but fundamentally emerging from a particular socioeconomic, cultural, and political development of the modern republics and market economies of South Asia. At each of our sites we had the opportunity to meet a "henchman," a "godfather," an "adjudicator," or a "bluffer" and also had to contend with the overarching presence of local mythical social bandits and the globalized myth of the mafia-style boss. Thus, we could have opted to write a book focusing exclusively on godfathers at the apex of their power or on criminals-turned-heroes. However, by providing snapshots of bosses across the spectrum, from the fledgling entrepreneur to the established don, we aim to produce an analysis that does not attempt to typify existing forms of bossism comprehensively but instead provides insights into the processual nature of bossism and its experiential dimension.[42]

Most significantly for our study, by commandeering notions of force, governance, justice, and control of black economies, the bosses of this book inherently upset the neat boundaries between the legal and the illegal, state actor and nonstate actor, democratic and undemocratic, formal and informal economies, and legitimate and illegitimate violence. Thus, the figure of the boss provides (1) a unique road map for studying the particular ethos of personal sovereignty that characterizes settings where criminals cannot be distinguished from legitimate authorities and the official economy; (2) a key methodological vantage point from which to study interpenetrations (or the absence thereof) between the underworld and the institutional spheres empirically; and (3) an entry point to document the "fictional realities" of systems of Mafia Raj not as purely illusionary constructions but as realities in their own right.[43] Such figurations, we argue, not only have the capacity to produce social geographies of fear but are also crucial in shaping conversions of force and legitimacy and in forging the intimate bonds, complicities, or opportunistic partnerships that connect bosses to their populations.[44]

Studying the figural power of the boss and Mafia Raj allows us to explore how such figurative qualities are recognized both in our settings and globally. In today's world, thanks to the Hollywood and South Asian movie industries and streaming, the boss has become a powerful cross-cultural archetype: a "cultural persona."[45] Mapping the role of transcultural mythologies of power and everyday local and transregional business relations helps us unravel how localized arts of bossing are intertwined with local, regional, and global production systems in different ways. It also helps us shed light on a global appreciation for leaders who cultivate a bosslike attitude and the idea that business acumen and cinematographic entertainment can provide a template for modern mass populist politics. The current success of strongmen leaders like Recap Tayyip Erdogan, Narendra Modi, Vladimir Putin, and Donald Trump points to the scalability of the logics of the art of bossing in a world where the economy increasingly governs politics and fictional realities increasingly occupy center stage in the making of charismatic forms of authority. The provision of protection, the redistribution of material goods, and/or the use of coercion are usually viewed by scholars of bossism as the building blocks of strongmen's authority;[46] however, this book shows how the cultivation of "the figural" through a variety of scripts and performances is also a powerful (and often underexplored) tool to create and reproduce fear, admiration, and ultimately authority. Bosses' opaque moralities and their figural entertainment, whether considered appealing or offensive, are a compelling force, as they have the capacity to fascinate and seduce people across generations, classes, and nations.

What Does It Take to Be a Boss?

The academic use of the term "boss" originates in studies of urban politics in the late nineteenth- and early twentieth-century United States. In this literature the paradigmatic boss is an individual who acquires power by achieving monopolistic or quasi-monopolistic control over an area's coercive and economic resources.[47] The boss is usually defined as a person who claims for himself (it is normally a man) the rights to discipline and punish, protect, tax, and represent local populations. In their pioneering study on leadership and influence in South Asia, Price and Ruud highlight that the first moral imperative of bosses is to gain and maintain personal dominance over their establishment. Bosses may incorporate elements of the fixer and middleman or of the hustler.[48] But what primarily characterizes them is that they command (or aspire to command) specific jurisdictions, such as networks of people, party machines, labor unions, neighborhoods, villages, trades and businesses, bazaars, wards or assembly constituencies, small towns, temples-cum-*akhara* (wrestling schools), or *deras* and criminal organizations. *This command is what defines them. Bosses do not only want to make money; they want to rule.* Hence, bossing is the capacity to run people, resources, and situations; to give orders and be obeyed; and to be in control.

The aspiration to command requires investing in a special set of resources that are not necessarily available to illegal entrepreneurs, patrons, brokers, or individual criminals. A crucial resource is to be able to make credible threats of violence. As the following chapters illustrate, the exemplar boss is an individual who possesses "the ability to kill, punish, and discipline with impunity,"[49] one who relies on the use or threat of force to protect illegal economic activities and to administer justice and achieve social control and economic accumulation.[50] However, bosses do not rely exclusively on brute force when bossing. Violence is necessarily coupled with legal and illegal entrepreneurship, charisma and persuasion, the cultivation of personal mythologies (or the ability to fake them), rules and honor, kinship networks, intelligence, acting skills, professional legal and financial advice, and critically, collusion with political and administrative resources.

The domain of the political is central to the activities of contemporary mafia-like bosses. To run and protect their economic activities (legal and illegal), bosses tend to develop symbiotic relations with the state—and in the process they sometimes become "gangster-politicians." When such individuals and their entourage become part of state institutions and appropriate economic and financial resources of the state, we witness the formation of what the Italian sociologist

Armao calls "mafia-owned democracies."[51] These are systems of governance where "[even] the official is illegal,"[52] where nested criminal official actors replace the state as the privileged partners of capitalism. In today's world the most successful bosses increasingly "combine the local dimension of territorial control [plundering or appropriation often through party machine networks] with the global dimension of the transnational markets."[53] These are original systems of political and economic governance where not only criminals, businessmen, and politicians meet but also where the public becomes implicated as clients, customers, and voters.

How Bosses Govern and Make Money

Many studies show that later globalized forms of capitalism are fertile ground for growing corruption, the criminalization of politics, and the politicization of criminals.[54] In *Globalization and Its Discontents*, Stiglitz writes that "in contrast to what it was supposed to do, privatization has made matters so much worse that in many countries today privatization is jokingly referred to as 'briberization.'"[55] A great deal of the new business opportunities created by economic liberalization and deregulation still require the backing of the state to succeed. In India, as Chandra highlighted, "The state's control over resources in the new economy has relocated in three ways—(1) through its control over entry into formerly reserved sectors; (2) through its influence over the supply of inputs, including land, raw materials, and credit; and (3) through its creation of new regulations while abolishing old ones."[56] In this process, new industries, new rules, new networks, and considerably higher stakes have been created. The preliberalization state used to control sectors such as mining, oil, and gas and highly regulated sectors such as media and land—the basic resource par excellence through what is known as the "permit-license-quota Raj."[57] These resources had to be reallocated. The scramble to acquire these areas of the economy and new profitable parts of the state is at the heart of the criminal-political configurations that shape contemporary forms of bossism across the sites studied in this book. Writing about the 1990s, Kochanek states that "in India, businessmen function largely behind the scenes to protect their interests. In Pakistan, businessmen become politicians. In Bangladesh politicians are often businessmen."[58] It seems that now in all three countries, we witness, in varying degrees, violent entrepreneurship fusing with politics and the state. Officially elected bosses are a legitimate element in the democratic state. And at the same time, they are violent entrepreneurs who work within the state and divert public funds and/or manipulate the laws for private gains.

Varieties of Bossism

Intreccio (intertwinement) is the term often used by Italian scholars of mafia to make sense of those systems of political and economic governance in which it has become increasingly difficult to separate legality and illegality. This term captures how the relation between crime and the state is *not* a structural and functional alliance: "*Intreccio* is more than a metaphor for the elements that compose this alliance—it is a reality in itself. In fact, as when fibers that are closely woven together become a new thread, one whose original strands cannot be differentiated, so too does the intertwinement between the Mafia and the state constitute a reality that is more than the sum of its parts."[59] In South Asia, such entities are popularly referred to using vernacular terminologies such as "Mafia Raj" (in India and Pakistan) or "Mastangiri" and "Mastanocracy" (in Bangladesh). These regimes represent localized manifestations of the mafia-owned democracy phenomena.[60] Thus, they are not simple assemblages of "criminalized nexuses" or "networks" or "parallel states," but rather they are systems of political economic governance in their own right where criminals, businessmen, and politicians work together to create an environment that fits their needs.

These realities contrast with the available literature that portrays strongmen as separate from the state, as antistate figures and/or running "parallel states," as figures that undermine the legitimacy of the state, or as rebellious "social bandits."[61] In South Asia, institutional vacuums[62] are said to have produced and consolidated "shadow networks" that exist simultaneously with the state but remain "phenomenologically different, each representing distinct forms of authority and politico-economic organization."[63] Alternatively, the boss is described as occupying the realms of nonformal sovereignties and commandeering the infrapowers of brokerage.[64] Barbara Harriss-White referred to India's informal assemblage of agents (fixers, advisers, political workers, crooks, contractors, etc.) and formal state agents acting in an informal capacity as a "shadow state."[65] Yet the bosses we researched often integrate or aspire to integrate with institutional structures and are frequently unsatisfied with merely fixing, mediating, or acting informally. Significantly, as the word "raj" (rule, reign, government) in Mafia Raj suggests, these figures and their criminal-political formations aspire to rule. Bosses often seek elected offices to attain not only power and capital but also official authority and a position of formal command.

Recent anthropological work on various forms of sovereignty in Colombia, Jamaica, and Russia have documented similar realities and theoretically attempt to conceive informal power as intrinsic to the concept of governance. For example, Jaffe shows that systems of bossism in Jamaica should be understood as part of "hybrid states," as political formations in which criminal dons and elected officials co-govern urban spaces through public-private partnerships.[66] Exploring the nature of paramilitarism in Colombia, Aldo Civico shows that "rather than an erosion, absence or even failure of the state, the intertwinement between illegal actors and the state is an extension of the state's sovereignty into spaces that are produced as an exteriority that still lives in a natural condition. . . . [This intertwinement] represents an extension of the state's power, not its diminution."[67]

Similarly, studies of vigilante groups in different parts of the world suggest that, however critical of the state they may seem, these private law enforcers often play into the hands of institutional actors.[68] Sidel's comparative study of bossism in Indonesia, the Philippines, and Thailand also made a related argument by showing how the subordination of the state to elected officers creates the conditions for the emergence, survival, and success of local strongmen.[69] Hence, it is often the strength of local states, rather than their weaknesses, that underpins bosses' personal sovereignty. Yet the South Asian case pushes these arguments even further as it presents instances of direct conversions of violent entrepreneurs into political actors. Such cases are reported as fairly rare in other parts of the world.[70] The following chapters document the growing competition to perform the roles of the state and the everyday varieties of Mafia Raj that are proliferating. Crucially, such regimes show that "globalization is not only compatible with statehood; it has actually fueled the desire for it."[71]

"You're Not My Boss!": Fantasies of Power and Authority

Integral to our argument is the role of the fantastic power of the self-made entrepreneurial criminal boss.[72] Media forms, such as advertising, cinema, radio, newspapers, and digital social networks, help generate and glamorize bosses' aspirational spirit and craving for power by propagating and valorizing consumer capitalism and ideologies of individual empowerment. The media thus becomes crucial to understanding the art of and the aesthetics of Mafia Raj.[73] Drawing on culturally entrenched templates of revolutionary social bandits, contemporary novels, the press, TV series, and movies often romanticize the boss as a champion of the people and a provider of local justice whose acts of violence are motivated by a deep sense of honor and order.[74] So the boss may transgress and transcend the law. But in doing so, he often reiterates its necessity and thereby enhances the power of the state. One example is the recent Telugu movie *Gabbar Singh* (2012). Its hero is an unpredictable, individualistic, transgressive, maverick policeman who teaches corrupt state officials and politicians the virtues of a true leader, with much blood spilled along the way. It is no coincidence that the movie's protagonist is Pavan Kalyan, an actor who has recently entered politics and is a contender for the position of chief minister in future elections.[75]

Gruesome violence is often central to these narratives of crime, heroism, and statehood. For instance, the excessive shedding of blood in Bangladeshi action movies or the luridly sensationalist covers of early twentieth-century Urdu detective novels provide a dystopian image of local society to its viewers and readers.[76] The phenomenal popularity of the crime genre in South Asia since the late nineteenth century suggests that there is a rich repertoire of attitudes and fantasies surrounding bosses, criminals, policemen, and detectives. For instance, detective and crime novels in Hindi and Urdu (*jasusi naval/upanyas*) arguably constitute one of the most popular and widely circulated form of commercial fiction in north India and Pakistan since the late nineteenth century.[77] In contrast to their Western equivalent, Hindi-Urdu detective stories tend to be driven by traditional notions of honor and masculinity and imbued with a supernatural atmosphere.[78] But the detective in these cheap paperback novels has given way to the investigative journalist exposing crime on Indian TV news programs: "a more violent, avenging figure, suggesting almost a criminalization of the detective-hero."[79] Quite tellingly in these narratives the role of police investigation is always marginal.[80] As the identity of the criminal is seldom in question, there is no need to investigate or to assemble clues and evidence to solve a crime because the protagonist inhabits a world where corruption and mafia criminality are neither mysterious nor concealed. On the contrary, everybody knows and hence everybody is implicated. The issue, then, is not to establish the identity of the culprit; the culprit, in a sense, is everybody. In the prototypical Mafia Raj the legitimate state protectors—the police, the prosecutors, and the judges—are all part of the racket. The paradigmatic boss depends for his survival on selective enforcement of the law and on "the tacit consent and studied ignorance" of the authorities.[81] As the famous North Indian mafia don D. P. Yadav once said in an interview, "I don't care if there are 500 cases against me. I will continue to fight for my self-respect. . . . First we should establish 'apradhi kaun hai?' [Who is criminal?] Who is the real mafia? I am making a film on the subject called Mafia Kaun? [Who is the mafia?]. The police and the administration will be exposed."[82] As Vincente Rafael's study of criminal figures in Southeast Asia concisely explains, the question of the identity of the criminal and of what actually constitutes a crime must always be supplemented with the question, In whose eyes and under what "conditions of looking" do crimes and criminals appear?[83]

Personal Mastery and Charisma

Extortion, intimidation, and beatings at the hands of a variety of enforcers constitute an integral part of everyday life in South Asia. Bosses "protect," control, and run neighborhoods, markets, business groups, and political parties by reproducing and enforcing conditions of economic and political insecurity. They are often the source of violence as well as the provider of protection from the violence they mete out. Thus, they are perceived as criminals and are objects of public revulsion and fear but nevertheless are also tolerated and even admired. But why? The simple answer is that *personal mastery being rare, it has auratic qualities and commands respect.*[84] The personal sovereignties of South Asian bosses are played out in uncertain times and fields where (semi)illegality and organized criminal syndicates brush against each other. These are seductive contact zones that are saturated with suspicion and secrecy but also vitality and the hope for a better future.[85] It is this power of the self-made entrepreneurial boss with all his capacity to excite, politicize, and even entertain that provides charisma to these figures. In our settings bosses are often admired because they are successful self-made men (and occasionally women) who ambitiously dare to take risks; manage to accumulate wealth; and build a better life for themselves, their families, their clients, and their associates. They are admired for their determination and their claim to reestablish order. They are also admired because they *appear* to challenge and reject caste and class barriers, gender roles, family hierarchies, and inequalities. But it is their apparent ability to defy and escape death and be above the law that ultimately endows them with an aura of extraordinariness.

These mythologies of power create hopes and dreams of individual self-determination and draw on shared imaginaries of popular emancipation and desire for freedom. Thus, bosses' ostensible declarations of independence through charismatic improvisation and pragmatic complicities give voice to widespread cultural values of defiance, pride, respectability, and self-worth and promise to transform the way authority is experienced daily. In turn, these emergent mythologies of power vernacularize ideas and practices of democracy and the economy in new ways and help produce systems of mafia-owned democracies. Such transformations are creating a fissure between authority and legitimacy. In his book *Authority*, Richard Sennett compellingly argues that in the modern age, "the independent ones" are people who are able to command respect. These are autonomous figures who, contrary to their paternalistic predecessors, do not have to express (or to pretend to) care for others to get power. These are leaders who are given power even if they are doubted to be legitimate.[86] Sennett argues that it is precisely such "illegitimacy" that has the capacity to *arouse* bonds of charismatic authority.[87]

In India, changing patterns of authority are said to have been prompted by the emergence of bosses' culture.[88] Thomas Blom Hansen documented how such changes began to be felt by the late 1980s. By that time, old forms of patronage—the donor-servant ideal—and the values attached to it had been adapted to and transformed by democracy and new economies. "India's democratic revolution gradually undermined the idiom and practices of *ma-baap'ism* [paternalism/patronage]," and "in Bombay of the 1980's, the so-called *dada culture*, which enjoys a long history in Bombay and other Indian cities as a popular model of authority and power, acquired new prominence as a style of public and political conduct, as *dadaism*."[89] Throughout the book, we show a tension between authority and legitimacy, paternalistic and autonomous styles of power. We show how bossism creates opportunities and room for "ways of life" for a variety of individuals and groups who aspire to be independent,[90] from laborers working in the sand or "quarry mafia" to drivers in transportation companies to successful estate developers. However, such "(in)dependents" do not often have rights within the system. The fear of being excluded from and/or denied access to a livelihood, employment, social protection, or lucrative business opportunities is an efficient "peaceful" deterrent. Violent repression is seldom used. The threat of violence and economic opportunism are what keep the system working and perpetuating itself.

MEETING THE BOSS

The project on which this book is based was born, in part, by frustration with the lack of academic writing on "actual bossing" in South Asia and a general lack of anthropological works on practitioners of violence and crime. In anthropology, what is generally widely studied are the effects of violence on victims and subalterns and/or discourses about criminalization.[91] As Dennis Rodgers pointed out, "Even the most cursory review of the relevant literature underscores the fact that the number of anthropologists who have directly participated within violent groups or with violent individuals is small compared to the number of researchers who have investigated violence from the perspective of those who suffer it."[92] In a similar vein, this "anthropology of suffering," as Joel Robbins famously described it, seems to have also marginalized the study of force as a form of power *in action* and, importantly, how power operates in flesh and blood among the powerful.[93]

To study powerful bosses and criminal formations anthropologically, and to study them comparatively and as a team, has demanded its own methods of research. This section provides an overview of such methods and approaches and fleshes out some of the challenges we encountered (as individuals and as a team) while conducting the research. Fieldwork, writing, and publishing in anthropology tend to be an individual affair.[94] However, we carried out multisited ethnographic work in collaboration with each other, not only at the completion of field research but more so during the course of the study. While the merits of such a collaborative ethnographic approach have already been demonstrated, few anthropologists have yet achieved this during the field research stage.[95] This approach, we argue, has the advantage of tackling the perennial problem of *post factum* comparison by facilitating the production of a common "ethnographic archive." The project comprises seven major ethnographic studies.[96] The research sites were chosen keeping the regional balance in mind, as well as the expertise of the researchers in the selected settings. Such knowledge, together with our long-term engagement, personal contacts, and networks of trust in the areas under study, made the team particularly well equipped to tackle a difficult topic of research.[97] During the fieldwork, we interacted and maintained regular communication, frequently discussed our findings, and added new lines of inquiry and categories of informants to our research, which enabled us to coordinate our research questions and examine emerging hypotheses. Importantly, it allowed us to pay attention to issues of internal validity within the study: patterns and outliers could be observed as findings were collected across the sites. Overall, the challenge was to maintain the freedom and flexibility of individual ethnographic research projects while collecting data that allowed us to jointly develop analytical empirical concepts, such as "the figure of the boss." This tool enabled us to identify and explain commonalities among seven very distinctive contexts while at the same time highlighting the nature of the differences across these sites and the similarities with comparable situations in the rest of the world.

Participant observation was the main research method. Studying the figure of the boss anthropologically involved careful documentation of the relevant sociocultural ground and the political systems and economies that made such figures *stand out* in the particular moment we were conducting fieldwork. Long-term anthropological fieldwork in the domains of family life, devotional practice, leisure, and work provided us with important insights into local cultures of leadership, criminality, and politics, as well as into the workings of "mafia methods" that often remain impenetrable for institutional analysis methods.

Each of us shadowed a boss or a cast of bosses in their daily life and studied their "will to boss." We mapped their territories, areas of domination, spheres of interest, and jurisdictions. We followed them during election campaigns or appearances in court. We observed their styles of self-presentation, rhetoric, and the sites where they chose to gather support or to perform. These spaces included caste or business association meetings, religious festivals, bazaars, *deras*, wrestling arenas, university campuses, hotels, lodges and night clubs, commemoration ceremonies, and sports events. Besides relying heavily on participant observation, we conducted research work in the field of economics. It became increasingly obvious that this was necessary to contextualize and understand the ways the bosses accumulated capital and the nature of the economies in which they operate.[98] Collecting economic evidence and mapping the patterns of local "black" economies are not easy tasks. While bosses were often ready to talk openly about their murders and show off their prowess by recounting unsavory episodes of their careers, the topic of money remained an extremely sensitive one. It was difficult for us to obtain data on the political economies of gangs, groupings, and mafias. For example, assessing how much henchmen are paid or how rewards are redistributed among associates in criminal enterprises involves questions that often remained not fully answered.

We used multiple sources of information to map bossism as a form of governance. We interviewed members of the bosses' families, gang members, enemies, rivals, businessmen, criminal lawyers, crime reporters, accountants, doctors, police investigators, astrologists, priests, and the residents of the spaces where bosses operate. The interviews were generally conducted in Bangla, Hindi, Punjabi, Telugu, or Urdu and less frequently in "pure" English. It should be noted that in many of our sites, a mix of Telugu and English, or Hindi and English, and so on was the norm. English was often employed to describe the performance of strongmen. Where possible, we drew on a variety of written literature and visual documentation, including bosses' personal archives (letters, accounts, autobiographies, and diaries), press archives, official publications, police and court documents, political party publications, ongoing blogs, Facebook postings, videos, and movies. Movies, fiction, and social media are indeed creating criminal-political styles that previously did not exist in our settings and enable an imaginary of a certain type of boss to emerge. We also watched dozen of gangster movies and read criminal and detective novels and local press crime and political articles for this purpose.

The methodological issues of the dangers anthropologists face while in the field are seldom discussed. As Sluka stated, "The world is not becoming a safer place for the pursuit of anthropological fieldwork, but perhaps for that very reason, there is more need now for such research than there has ever been before. We can meet this challenge, but we should do so rationally by considering the dangers involved as methodological issues in their own right."[99]

We minimized the risks in each of our sites by exploring criminal-political formations indirectly, as much as possible. This was possible because fortunately for us criminal politics is for the most part a topic of everyday conversation in South Asia and discussed in great detail by local and national newspapers and other media. Democracy in our selected areas is often highly violent in its workings. Many prominent and successful political bosses openly operate on the border between the legal and the illegal, and some brag about their criminal acts. Thus, in a number of settings democratic politics gave visibility to bosses' activities and allowed us to shadow them and their entourage in public or semipublic domains (such as at daily *darbars* at their residences or party meetings or rallies).[100] In short, in many instances the political world provided us with a relatively safe entry point into the world of illegality. However, in situations where criminality and formal politics remained more compartmentalized, such as in Lahore, gaining access to these figures proved to be more difficult. We also avoided focusing on large-scale international organized criminal activities such as arms trafficking, the heroin trade, or organ theft and their impact on politics.

Many of us witnessed mafia methods in action, such as electoral violence, the orchestration of riots or acts of revenge, and the collection of protection money. We listened to men and women openly and frankly discussing the murders, attempted murders, or kidnappings they had carried out. This exposure undoubtedly presents important ethical and emotional challenges. Researching the workings of bossism can often be a stressful affair. In this regard, working interactively was a vital source of intellectual inspiration and moral support. When studying bossism, common problems associated with ethnographic fieldwork are intensified because the uncertainty that characterizes muscular governance means that local people mistrust strangers more than usual. Systems of Mafia Raj are environments marked by high levels of criminal, political, and daily social violence and "cultures of impunity" that required us to be constantly alert to threats to our own physical safety and, crucially, to the ways in which our research could imperil our informants or local collaborators. In many ways, during our research, we had to deal with the very same uncertainties and the volatile environments that mark the lives of our informants. Like the people we studied, we had to learn to keep ourselves safe. In the process we learned about complicities, protection, and the duplicitous form of relations that typify the "rule by *goondas*," worlds in which the police and the judiciary are compromised and delegitimized and justice is often commodified.

Importantly, we also had to learn about seduction and what it means to become part of bosses' figural power and local fictional realities. Studying powerful criminal actors is said to present a peculiar power dynamic that renders anthropologists particularly vulnerable to what Robben terms "ethnographic seduction."[101] In short "by being 'won over' or 'seduced' by our informants, we [anthropologists] may risk legitimizing their claims to morality, virtue, or honor at the expense of more critical perspectives."[102] Throughout our fieldwork, we had to question ourselves and reflect on the seduction we were experiencing in the process of gaining gain favor with or access to the bosses themselves.[103] We asked ourselves time and again if we were buying into the narrative of the violent honorable self-made bosses, if we were victims of their charismatic improvisation and seduced by a world characterized by risk and injustice but also extreme vitality. Soon it became clear that the question was not how to avoid seduction but rather how to investigate it as a critical part of the bossism itself.

Contrary to Robben, who believes that seduction can hamper the critical perspective of the anthropologist, we think that it is precisely by being seduced that we could move backstage to watch bosses' public performances and share their intimate spaces and family lives. While exposing us to the possibility of being fooled and deceived by them, it also allowed us to begin to understand why people in the locality may be lured in. We witnessed bosses crying, shouting, loving, beating, eating, lying, or laughing. It is in these "offstage" spaces that we learned about the art of bossing and that we started to understand why ordinary people are appalled and fascinated by these characters. Being seduced, we argue, is part of participant observation. In the field we learned when and how to speak in front of bosses, when to keep silent, and how to deal with a multiplicity of actors: drivers, personal assistants (PAs), right-hand fellows, and bodyguards who were an integral part of bosses' entourages and who were often controlling our activities as researchers. We were constantly overwhelmed by rumors, accusations, lies, silences, warnings, and tricks and became part of the "figuralities" of the bosses we studied.

Crucially, without their protection and blessings we would have not been able to conduct the research safely. Being seduced (albeit with a critical distance) allowed us to circulate among different bosses, "companies," party machines, and businesses in the area under study. Such mobility is critical if one wishes to map the systemic nature of bossism. When studied systematically, what superficially can appear as chaotic, episodic, or random violent appropriations instead are established (and certainly not disorganized) systems of criminal entrepreneurship and organized violence. It is the production of such a type of knowledge and its exposure that may make research in this field potentially dangerous rather than the actual fieldwork itself.[104] The problem we encountered is how to go about documenting (and writing about) realities that are often known to everybody but that need to stay "undocumented." Documentation transforms public secrets into non-secrets and exposes what Herzfeld famously conceptualized as "cultural intimacy."[105] We wish to make it clear that we are not detectives and are not collecting evidence of crimes, trying to establish who is a criminal and what is criminal. What we hope our account provides is a "thick description" of bossism that hints at some of the continuities between crime and statehood in the localities under study to ultimately show how the lives of millions of people in South Asia are shaped by these systems of muscular economic governance on a daily basis.

THE STRUCTURE OF THE BOOK

The book asks three simple questions: How do bosses command and aspire to command in contemporary India, Pakistan, and Bangladesh?

What exactly do they do? What are the contexts in which they operate? Chapter 1 starts to answer these questions by mapping in detail the peculiar South Asian backdrop against which the bosses of this book stand out as figures of bossism in the first decade of the twenty-first century. It illustrates the criminal-political economies at the heart of Mafia Raj; how vernacularized ideas and practice of democracy are used to pursue mafia-like businesses; the role of party machines in forging bosses' careers; and the multiple sources of protection that bosses need to cultivate to obtain and maintain impunity. We also explore how "the art of making do" (*jugad*) transmogrifies into the "art of bossing" and how informal economy brushes with organized crime.

With the groundwork established in the Introduction and first chapter, the following seven chapters illustrate ethnographically how bosses perform their personal sovereignties in the course of everyday life. The chapters focus on the specificity of the local scenarios and the varieties of configuration of Mafia Raj that we (as ethnographers) individually encountered in our fieldsites. We meet bosses at different stages of their careers and with different scales of personal power. The author name that appears with each chapter is the individual who carried out the research. However, as previously discussed, it has been a collaborative effort to shape the chapters into their final form. Thus, despite the author name given of the first page of each chapter, this book is not an edited collection but a co-authored volume.

Set in provincial Bangladesh against the background of sprawling criminal activities from smuggling to money laundering and drugs, Chapter 2, "The Rookie," shows how a well-educated young man uses his actor's skills and capacity for violence to become a *mastan* with a longer-term project to become an elected political "godfather." It describes a young entrepreneur at the very start of his career and the difficulties he encounters establishing his will to boss. Chapter 3, "The Bluffer," is set in rural Indian Punjab. It features a lower-caste self-appointed boss who through bluffs and hustling, and by portraying himself as a Robin Hood who steals from corrupt politicians to provide for the poor, is trying to carve out for himself some authority in the local ecology of power. During this process he is profiting by siphoning off state resources and acting as a vote contractor. His performances illustrate how the fantasy of the boss is deeply shaping the lives of ordinary people across South Asia and inspiring a craving for power. Chapter 4, "The Henchman," analyzes the volatile role of aides and associates in the management of bossism in Andhra Pradesh, South India. It shows that henchmen are bosses in their own right and the way that they rule over their "jurisdictions." It also highlights how factionalism, class, and caste dynamics shape bossism hierarchies and how bosses control people or resources by subcontracting coercive control to their henchmen and runners. Chapter 5, "The Adjudicators," is set in Pakistan and examines bosses as adjudicators in Lahore's working-class neighborhoods. A variety of small-time and influential bosses are presented to capture the distinctive appeal of extralegal forms of adjudication. The chapter illustrates how these men draw on popular fantasies of power rooted in the ideal of the "genteel gangster" to become informal adjudicators and to discipline through their capacity to kill with relative impunity. Contrary to other cases presented in this book, this chapter suggests that, depending on the political environment in which they operate, criminal formations in South Asia may also strive to maintain a distance from electoral politics. Chapter 6, "Lady Dabang," explores the rise of a town boss in what is popularly viewed as an extremely misogynist and muscular political world but is also one of the most vibrant laboratories of Indian democracy since independence: the state of Uttar Pradesh. It unravels the transition from traditional protectors to contemporary mafia-style bosses (*dabang*). The story brings to light the masculine character of bossism and the way women navigate through muscular and macho systems of governance and, in the process, develop particular bossing styles and statecraft techniques to enhance their authority. Returning to Bangladesh, in Chapter 7, "The Godfather," we meet "the Godfather," a typical figure in Bangladesh's politics. The chapter is about an elected MP who is well known for his use of brutality and extortion to bolster his position and intimidate opponents and for his unsavory associates. He has used this combination of the licit and the illicit with success to the extent that he is now the unquestioned boss of his hometown of eight hundred thousand inhabitants located southeast of Dhaka. Chapter 8, "The Legend," takes up again in the South Indian state of Andhra Pradesh and examines the creation of a "boss-hero." Known as "the Legend," Ravi is the exemplar Robin Hood figure who steals from his opponents and from the state and gives back to his own people. Born into the violent factional politics of the southern region of Andhra Pradesh, he was the deadly rival of a man in the opposing caste and the opposition party. Ravi's assassination in 2005 immortalized him as an icon of the Telugu Desam Party, and his widow upholds his political legacy in her ministerial position in the state cabinet today.

These seven chapters cumulatively show how the art of bossing is a mix of intimidation, extortion, and protection; legitimate and illegitimate businesses; and electoral politics coupled with traditional and new ideas of honor, masculinity, and hero mafia cultures and figurations, which are at the heart of bosses' capacity to command. The bosses of this book show that there is a fine line between being perceived as a protector (and provider) and a racketeer. Negotiating this distinction in competitive democratic contexts is an art in itself.[106] The Conclusion sums up what we learned about the art of bossing and what we could learn in the future by focusing analytically on the figures of bossism. We argue that this prism has the potential to bridge fields of inquiry that have generally been studied and theorized separately, such as democracy, the state, business, violence, and crime. Such a holistic approach offers the possibility of further understanding the ways violence, coercion, crime, and money are embedded in social relations and how such relations contribute to creating charismatic forms of authority in South Asia and beyond. Ultimately, our goal is for this work to be read and used in a number of different ways. Readers who are not interested in academic debates might read the seven ethnographic chapters to gain a sense of how bossism works *in practice* in the everyday life of South Asians and get a feel for its proximity to the lives of millions of ordinary people across the subcontinent.

CHAPTER 1

BACKDROPS

> I don't want to be a product of my environment.
> I want my environment to be a product of me.
>
> —Frank Costello, *The Departed*, 2006[1]

THIS CHAPTER maps out the backdrops against which the stories of "the Rookie," "the Bluffer," "the Henchman," "the Adjudicators," "Lady Dabang," "the Godfather," and "the Legend" unfold. We provide the reader with a comparative panoramic view of the current sociopolitical and economic scenarios that animate bosses' actions and preview how such broader dynamics will be enriched in the ethnographic chapters. Importantly, we show that such backdrops are not static, pregiven environments but are dialectically created by bosses' themselves. India, Pakistan, and Bangladesh offer particularly useful points of comparison for understanding the economic and political transformations that are creating opportunities for bosses' careers to thrive.[2] These three countries share a British colonial past and its historical, cultural, and political legacy; their criminal laws still follow British legal tradition, and all three countries inherited a first-past-the-post electoral system. The British Raj was divided into India and Pakistan in 1947, and in 1971 Bangladesh was created out of East Pakistan. Despite many historical links, the political environment of the three countries diverged notably in the postcolonial era with the emergence of democracy in India, intermittent "authoritarianism" in Pakistan, and what has been termed "confrontational democracy" in Bangladesh.[3] Nevertheless, such different trajectories have produced all manifestations of the modern figure of the boss.

While singling out historical and cultural specificities, our collaborative work points to a number of parallels across these three countries and beyond. Scholarly work on South Asia usually tends to be centered on India or focused on specific in-country issues. The result is that common regional practices and the effects of more globalized trends often remain unexamined.[4] Yet we know that the global economy and later forms of capitalism are reshaping the relationships between markets and the state, and between democracy and individual citizens. The protagonists of this book are figures of these uncertain and dynamic times. We show that they live in worlds characterized by both extreme scarcity and excessive opulence. Their habitats are marked by political agonism, on the one hand, and unaccountable state institutions, on the other. Intense scrambles for resources are animated by violent forms of entrepreneurialism and cultures of criminality. The workings and the social consequences of such predatory regimes have hardly been documented to date.[5]

In the following sections we outline the nature of Mafia Raj political economies in India, Pakistan, and Bangladesh; their volatility and uncertainty; the extreme competitive and polarized nature of bosses' politics in the three countries; the role of political party machines in shaping varieties of "worlds in between"; and the cultures of impunity that allow bosses to operate "above the law." Eventually, we map how bosses create the backdrops to their actions and shape available opportunities. In many ways the bosses of this book are "itinerant," a term coined by Deleuze and Guattari, as their performances need to be tailored and adapted to "the continuous variations of variables" in their respective localities.[6] This requires agile and flexible chains of command that are capable of taking the opportunities created by the market and democracy.

MUSCULAR PREDATORY ECONOMIES

The bosses discussed in this book operate in environments where change has been occurring at a mind-boggling pace over the past two decades.

Their lives are part of wider transnational spheres and the global economy. They live in emerging urban megaregions that are growing up around cities such as New Delhi, Agra, Chandigarh, Chennai, Hyderabad, Bangalore, Dhaka, and Lahore. They live in what is often referred to as *mofussil*, or "Middle" India, Bangladesh, and Pakistan: the South Asia of small-town and peri-urban villages. These are settings where the divide between village and town, rural and urban, is no longer discernible. Over the past few decades, the informal economy in these regions has become increasingly interspersed with globally linked opportunities for making money. New transport infrastructures and expanding labor and land markets have reshaped local spaces and temporalities. These are zones where some of the world's most chaotic and polluted cities are located.[7] According to the 2017 figures, fifteen of the twenty most polluted places on the globe are in India, Pakistan, and Bangladesh, an indication of the abrupt and haphazard way in which new economies are taking root in the subcontinent.[8] Notably, they reflect their short-term ethos and extractive nature.

Predatory forms of capitalism are coupled with a delegitimation of state institutions and poor service delivery. The *Fragile States Index 2015*, which ranks countries from most to least fragile, ranked Pakistan number 13; Bangladesh, number 32; and India, number 69.[9] Despite scoring much higher than its neighbors, India was among the ten most deteriorated countries in 2015. Its apparent decline in this regard continues a trend that has lasted a decade.[10] India is, as we are often reminded, both the largest and one of the most robust parliamentary democracies in the world. However, with regard to service delivery and a whole range of other social indicators—child nutrition and mortality, maternal health, immunization, life expectancy, sanitation, literacy, standard of schooling—its performance has been widely judged as dismal and as significantly worse than that of many other countries with lower per capita income.[11] Likewise, when reviewing the Failed State Index's criterion "provision of public services," India does little better than Pakistan (7.9) and Bangladesh (8.1).[12]

However, while poverty persists and inequality is expanding, Middle South Asia is also home to an increasing number of people with spectacular amounts of money.[13] Pockets of extreme wealth are increasingly found in expanses of poverty and neglect. It should be highlighted that these are times when fortunes are made (and unmade) in one generation. In our settings, there are people who weigh their money rather than count it. Rumors about trucks carrying black money or the hijacking of such vehicles by criminals (or the police) are recurrent in our fieldsites. "Estimated at 40% of GDP ten years ago and growing, India's black economy is not marginal or confined to socially excluded people; it is central and involves prominent and socially powerful people too."[14] In Bangladesh, according to a 2011 Bangladesh government Ministry of Finance report, depending on your chosen method of calculation, the estimated underground economy is between 45 percent and 80 percent of the gross domestic product (GDP).[15] Similarly, in Pakistan there is no consensus among economists, and estimates range between 30 percent and 90 percent.[16] Estimates are difficult, as formal, informal, and black economies crisscross each other,[17] and it is precisely the regulations that abstractly delimit the boundaries of such economies that are exploited and manipulated to make a profit in Mafia Raj. Consider the case of sand mining, for example. Sand is considered a minor mineral under Indian law, and its extraction is governed by state rather than national laws. State governments have the power to make rules to prevent illegal mining and regulate the transportation and storage of sand.[18] They also have the power to make this form of mining legal, and if they do so, as many environmental activists are pressing for, the "sand mafia" would no longer be profitable.[19] To understand the political economy of bossism, one needs to look precisely at these "business relations" and partnerships that connect politicians, bureaucrats, entrepreneurs, and the police.[20] Such a complex network is often simplified when violent entrepreneurs are elected.

Informal Enterprises or Mafias?

Across South Asia there is a wealth of literature on fixers, brokers, and their vernacular cultures of entrepreneurship, some of which are linked in interesting ways to neoliberal discourses. In the 2000s the Indian government also began to use the term *jugad* (the indigenous "art of making do") as a means of advertising a type of homegrown spirit of ingenuity in India.[21] What remains deliberately hidden from view is that these often glorified neoliberal informal jobs require enforcement and participation in organized power syndicates and groups to operate. The case studies in this book show that there is a continuum between informal enterprise and what local people refer to as "mafias." The studies unravel everyday planning, tricks, risks, and showing off, as well as how they are tailored, amplified, and temporalized by the local interplay of the economy, force, electoral politics, and the law.[22] This takes the idea of the bricoleur and the art of making do to an entirely new level, a level not considered in any detail in the literature on entrepreneurs in South Asia yet widely explored in the work on violent cultures of entrepreneurship in Italy, Russia, and Southeast Asia. This is *jugad* but on a different scale, in a different sphere, and with different consequences, often as serious as life or death. We find Pine's study of the Camorra in Naples instructive for the South Asian case: "The art of making do is a speculative performance, the staging of a better life. Enacting it requires creative tactics for seizing opportunities and negotiating risks. Excessive speculation, however, can lead to violent determinations: the ad hoc art of making do has the potential to transmogrify into organized crime."[23] Our portrayals show how the art of making do can be transformed into the art of bossing. This is not an innocent art of finding a way around or getting by, but rather it is carving a path toward bossism as a mode of economic and political governance.[24]

As mentioned previously, privatization is fueling muscular economics and with it varieties of Mafia Raj. It is not a coincidence that the most iconic Mafia Raj in North India—Bihar, Jharkhand, Uttar Pradesh, and Andhra Pradesh—are also the regions that provide local political bosses with some of the greatest economic opportunities through land seizures, mining, industrial contracting, the construction industry, and racketeering.[25] In Bangladesh during the democratic era, neoliberal economic policies that had been put in place during the martial period by General Ziaur Rahman, founder of the Bangladesh Nationalist

Party (BNP), were accelerated. The democratic era witnessed a rise in the gross national product (GNP) as a result of neoliberal policies, especially from the mid-2000s onward, with an average annual growth rate of 6 percent. This period also coincides with the rise of muscle or "confrontational" politics between the two major political parties and their bonded clients vying for resources and patronage. In the case of Pakistan, decreasing returns in the industrial sector over the past few years, rather than economic liberalization, have led to massive investments in the real estate economy. This has been accompanied by a stark increase in land-grabbing operations (*qabza*), a lucrative activity that often sees the collusion of criminal bosses, bureaucrats, and elected politicians in the form of "*qabza* groups." The country's military has also become a key actor in these illegal forms of capital accumulation and in shaping localized systems of Mafia Raj.[26] Thus in many parts of the subcontinent, a twenty-first-century version of the American El Dorado is taking place: a *desi* (indigenous) Gold Rush.[27] The new gold is land, sand, stones, and other extractive materials.[28] Violence and collusion with the state are crucial for furthering the accumulation agendas of this type of venture capitalism.[29] Conversely, these new enterprises provide both black and legal money to finance political campaigns and thus create or consolidate criminal political formations.[30] It is this particular connection between profit and political influence that engenders criminality in politics and fuels political competition.[31]

Mafia Raj Recurrent Businesses

Such dynamics are exemplified by many of the bosses' business career trajectories presented in the following chapters. Across our fieldsites, it is often real estate and forms of predatory property accumulation that create the most profitable opportunities for violent political entrepreneurs: what Schneider and Schneider have called "mafia capitalism."[32] Land and property transactions are opening up new career paths that require the capacity to handle coercion, manage extralegal activities, and above all, play the game of politics.[33] In each of our settings, the so-called endless city spills into rural areas, making land prices skyrocket. This sprawl is increasingly happening in the subcontinent as real estate developers promote the image of a world-class lifestyle outside the traditional city. Many parts of the region are witnessing an unprecedented boom in agricultural land prices. The combination of stagnating agricultural income and rising consumerism means that people who were previously engaged in agriculture are increasingly becoming involved in a variety of other businesses and starting to think of themselves as enterprising subjects, as Gooptu describes them.[34] The rise of investment in land development is not a specifically South Asian phenomenon; it is seen worldwide.[35] The state-assisted scramble for land has been theorized by Harvey (2003, 2006) as "accumulation by dispossession." In South Asia, the stories of the Mumbai or Karachi mafias in the 1990s epitomize this trend.[36] Today violent land grabbing is also directly or indirectly shaping the careers of all the figures of bossism that we encounter in this book. In provincial North India, small-time developers are starting to become serious property moguls and are sending their children to train in business schools in the United States. The story of Paritala Ravi illustrates such a trajectory. "Lady Dabang" also started her career as a land grabber and often describes herself as a "property dealer." She is now a billionaire who controls the local "land mafia," owns property across the country, and runs in state elections. Lahore's bosses are active in *qabza* groups, informal partnerships specializing in the illegal appropriation of properties. In the Indian Punjab real estate investments are again the basis of criminal political careers of bosses. The career of the Bangladeshi godfather gained momentum when he successfully managed to expropriate the decaying inner-city area and transform it into a building site.

Besides real estate development, the typical violent extractive industries in which bosses are usually involved include mining sand, quarrying granite, and quarrying limestone for cement. They are also involved in the transportation business; hotel and restaurants; regulation of labor markets; commercialization of drugs; loan sharking, fraud, financial crimes, and extortion (collection of protection money [*goonda tax/hafta/chandabaazi*] or kidnapping). Protection, extortion, and enforcement are particularly attractive avenues because, as Letizia Paoli argues, they do not require high initial investments, they carry low management costs, and they are relatively low-risk investments, particularly where state protection is unreliable or inadequate.[37] Moreover, in today's world one does not even need real fighting abilities or any particular preparation: "No training, just balls," said an aspiring shooter in Lahore, or "You just need a pistol, courage, and to get involved in the *bhumi* [land] mafia." Our informants often pointed out that there was a growing demand for enforcers because the ballooning black economy requires tight governance by extralegal entities and has therefore given rise to a proliferation of private protection industries. Collecting debts or delayed payments is one of the services that enforcers often offer. The fear of losing property or of being cheated (typical features of uncertain political economies) further contributes to a sense of insecurity and the need for bosses to act as enforcers, protectors, and adjudicators.

In this context, businesses such as extortion become appealing career paths for working-class youth whose manual and industrial work has been economically and socially devalued by economic liberalization. According to Gooptu, economic liberalization produced a young generation focused on making money quickly, and extortion brings immediate rewards.[38] But it is not only the industry of extortion that provides quick short-term returns. Young unemployed men are increasingly becoming engaged in scams involving government programs, as epitomized by "the Bluffer."

THE LURE OF MUSCULAR POLITICS

"Muscular economics" lives in symbiosis with the agonistic world of "muscular politics." It has been said that what fascinates South Asian citizens with politics (and public authority) is "the sheer melodrama of it all, the ostentatiously performed agonism of the exchanges between political opponents, as well as the symbolic excess of South Asia's magical realist politicians—elephants and camels on the road to jail."[39] Others have pointed out that Indian democracy has survived and flourished because it was quickly seen to be the most effective system for achieving personal sovereignty and hence social mobility.[40] The market of politics provides economic and symbolic resources that are creatively used to expand personal assets and renegotiate the lives of communities.[41] A number of ethnographies trace processes of vernacularization of democracy and show how ordinary people (and different groups) are shaping ideas of democracy and adapting them to their needs.[42] Michelutti showed how members of the Yadav community think about, conduct, and legitimize muscular—and often illegal—politics in the North Indian "patronage democracy." Similarly, drawing on the vernacularization framework, Ruud illustrated that rural voters in Bangladesh find the rich, generous, experienced, and unscrupulous leader a more promising representative than the "clean," Gandhian-style candidate:

> The closer an MP candidate is to the supreme leader, the more promising middleman he will be for the constituency. The elected leader is a patron, who supplies patronage, and offers protection or services when needed. Special rules apply to the procedure by which these middlemen are chosen, a grand and rather festive occasion called "to vote." But in the eyes of our informants, "to vote" is not to ensure the representativity of the poor, but to ensure responsiveness towards the poor. Which party they end up voting for depends to some extent on the individual voter's calculation of a candidate's ability to be influential, to get things done.[43]

Thus, democracy is often about acquiring state control as well as personal power and wealth. Similarly, Witsoe shows how processes of vernacularization of democracy in Bihar have affected the way people imagine the state and how corruption is understood as power:

> Many people began to perceive state institutions as inherently corrupt sources of political patronage that, having long served to perpetuate upper-caste dominance, could now be used in the same way by a new class of political leaders to empower lower-caste groups. Within this context, corruption was tolerated, sometimes even celebrated, as a means to lower-caste empowerment.[44]

Likewise, Piliavsky reminds us that corruption is often not understood as the misappropriation of public office for private gain but rather as a patron's failure to fulfill his duties of protection and redistribution toward his clients.[45] This emerging ethnographic map of "democracy" highlights underlying processes of the commodification of politics. It shows that democracy is often uncoupled from the rule of law or notions of accountability. Hustling for a share of political money is viewed as a quick way to lay the foundations for a successful boss career. It may be true that few poor people actually become billionaires by setting up their own businesses or through private-sector careers, but there are real-life examples that show that a poor person can become a person of wealth and power by entering into politics, especially in India. The former chief minister of Uttar Pradesh, Mayawati; the current chief minister of West Bengal, Mamata Banerjee; and the current prime minister, Narendra Modi, are living incarnations of such success. The stories of "the Bluffer" and "Lady Dabang" show in particular how Mayawati is viewed as a prototypical successful boss. They admire her business and political acumen, her humble beginnings, her authoritarian style, and the fear that she instills. While campaigning and becoming a symbol of Dalit pride, she also managed to establish a successful partnership with rich businessmen in the construction industry. She used state machinery to seize land from farmers and provided legal force for such evictions. In return, businessmen provided her with capital and know-how. The profits were shared.[46]

Such visible moneymaking opportunities fuel a popular craving to enter into the business of power. Today, such "exemplar" careers of criminal political entrepreneurship are intensifying the "permanent performance" that is said to characterize South Asian politics.[47] As a result, in many of our settings there is no ordinary political-economic time but only states of perpetual agonistic political and economic competition.[48] Performances are said to mark exceptional events such as elections.[49] But because bosses' sovereignty is "always tentative and unstable," it depends on "repeated performance of violence and a 'will to rule.'"[50] Performance and theatrics are the hallmarks of bosses' worlds. Their time is permanently exceptional and hence deeply uncertain for both the actors involved and those experiencing the drama. By the same token, these zones of perpetual "exception" are highly seductive; they are characterized by risk, fear, and secrecy but also vitality and entrepreneurship. It is in these unstable but opportunity-rich arenas that bosses operate.

Fast Money and the Criminal-Political Game

The seven ethnographic chapters show how in today's South Asia a large number of people aspire to become bosses and eventually political bosses.[51] In many of our settings the criminal-political game is viewed as an opportunity for fast money, a launch pad to the dream life, and/or the moment to convert from a criminal career to a clean political one. In India and Bangladesh (less so in Pakistan), an entrepreneur, possibly of lower caste or class, through force and hustle is able to become a boss and then eventually an elected political leader. One of the recurrent comments we all heard in the field is, "Here everybody wants to be a boss." In Bangladesh, Jamal ("the Rookie") explains, "You know how some people want to become a doctor or an engineer, a pilot, or whatever? For me, even from then, I wanted to 'do politics' [*rajniti*]."

Politics in this context means to become wealthy and acquire kingly status. People move into "criminal work" and careers associated with muscular politics because of the high returns associated with such paths, not only for themselves but also for their families and at times their clans, caste, and communities. In some instances, as in the cases of "Lady Dabang" and "the Bluffer," they become involved in the industry of violence and crime because of unemployment and the need to survive.[52] A number, however, do not start to be enforcers and hustlers because of economic need. Mafias develop where there is wealth and where the state is not able to regulate the conflicts and opportunities that arise from such wealth, because much of this wealth is in the criminal/black economy. This pattern is clearly shown in the comparative material in East Asia, Italy, and Russia. Some of our informants also found themselves in violent industries purely by chance. Some happen to be born into feuds and are compelled to exact revenge on behalf of earlier generations. Some like "the Adjudicators" and "the Legend" rationalize their violent lives morally in terms of fate or protection of their honor. Others more directly weigh their life chances and rationally take the opportunity to convert violence into a profitable business.

For example, "Lady Dabang," a self-made woman in western Uttar Pradesh, says that the key to gaining confidence and freedom is violence; it is through fear, and by instilling uncertainty and insecurity, that one maintains power. Contrary to their parents who grew up thinking that avoiding risks was essential to making a secure and peaceful life, the new generation tries to achieve freedom and independence, if necessary, by using force. What they do not accept is being automatically part of others' social capital.[53] As a *dabang* in western Uttar Pradesh stated, "Today muscle is power. Earlier, only the son of the king could rule. Today everybody can rule. You need weapons to rule. Leaders need to have guns. Not everybody should have guns—only people with status. However, nowadays everyone who wishes can get guns and rule." The North Indian boss contrasts kingly authority with muscle and gun power in a world where sufficient force can leverage rule. The previous quotation is indicative of the spirit of the time. The general message that the protagonists of this book seem to have assimilated is that one should not wait for the state to help but should act in the here and now and get what needs to be taken, quickly.

Not many people believe that the government can solve their problems in the long term. Instead, they believe that by capturing parts of the state apparatus (by violent means if necessary), they can improve their lives. Aspiring bosses do not wait; they act promptly. They make decisions. Their lives are exciting; there is no place for wasting time and getting bored. These are characters who view the political-economic careers offered by Mafia Raj systems as platforms to improve their lives and as an opportunity to be part of a glamorous VIP melodrama. In *Capital: The Eruption of Delhi* Rana Dasgupta wonderfully captures how the hypercorrupted "new black money elites" (the economic godfathers and new South Asian oligarchs) are setting the tone—aesthetic, commercial, and ethical—for everyone else.[54] "Prince Moosa" of Bangladesh claimed to have US$7 billion in a Swiss account. He is famous for the diamond-encrusted soles of his shoes and luxurious palace in Dhaka. He once offered Britain's Labour Party £5 million as an election campaign donation.[55] Such individuals—who see themselves as above the law—personify an opulent oligarchical culture that ordinary people aspire to achieve or be part of.

The bosses in this book often embody a provincialized *desi* version of such predatory and lavish cultures. Increasingly, money determines success in life. Getting rich, and getting rich quickly, is the ethos. Violent self-interest and profit-driven sovereign acts are hence embedded in these new moral imaginations.[56] Our stories show the different ways people in various corners of the subcontinent live up to these models, cope with the pressure of uncertainty, strive for a good life, and make the decisions these pursuits entail. Their aim is to maximize their opportunities and gains while taking advantage of the current conditions.

Party Machines and Student Politics as Laboratories of Bosses' Careers

How do violent entrepreneurs enter (or fail to enter) into politics? What is the role of political party machines in shaping the art of bossing? In India, political parties are said to select violent entrepreneurs because they can self-finance and offer expertise in voter intimidation and violence.[57] This is also the case in Bangladesh.[58] Money power is crucial. Here the official limit when running for parliament is 15 lakh takas (US$20,000).[59] It is regularly reported that candidates spend much more, and almost one in four reports having spent more than 45 lakhs (US$55,000).[60] Most Bangladeshi politicians laugh at such figures and suggest that to run effectively for Parliament, one needs to spend 1–3 crore taka (US$120,000–360,000), although the figure varies considerably from case to case. In Bangladesh, enforcers, entrepreneurs, and politicians, along with members of the civil service and the police, form elaborate and delicate networks underpinned by mutual favors, money, and coercion.[61] In India, the Election Commission limit is 70 lakh (7 million) rupees (US$115,000) per campaign for a seat in the Lok Sabha. Nonetheless, candidates are said to spend fifty to one hundred times more in the hope of winning. In short, political parties and candidates have to break the rules in order to stand a chance of winning.[62] The use of money power is not only limited to MP (Member of Parliament) or MLA (Member of Legislative Assembly) elections but also to local elections. In the 2015 *panchayat* (village council) election in western Uttar Pradesh candidates reported having to spend 2.5 lakhs (US$10,000) on vote buying.

Money power goes hand in hand with muscle power. In India, according to Vaishnav, candidates with criminal indictments are twice as likely to win elections as their law-abiding counterparts.[63] This leads very frequently to political parties taking a shortcut by choosing candidates they think can win because they already have muscle power in the area. Similarly, in Pakistan, Martin reports that even Imran Khan, with his anticorruption agenda, was compelled to give local criminal strongmen candidacy to deliver votes to his Pakistan Tehreek-e-Insaaf party.[64] A candidate's criminal record is not made public in Pakistan as it is in India. Nevertheless, it is common knowledge that all political parties occasionally resort to fielding criminals to win elections; PPP (Pakistan People Party) with the Aman Committee in Karachi's Lyari neighborhood, or PML-N (Pakistan Muslim League [Nawaz]) with the pro-jihadi group Ahl-e-Sunnat Wal Jamaat (ASWJ) in Punjab for "seat-adjustment" before elections. It is also generally held that in Bangladesh the reason the Awami League lost the 1991 election against all expectations was that it did not choose candidates with sufficient "power of conviction," individuals who can muster resources (in particular, money and henchmen) at short notice.[65]

These ready-made "winning candidates" are increasingly individuals who have plenty of cash and muscle power, for example, as in the case of Uttar Pradesh. Until the early 1990s, typical MLAs would be drawn from the ranks of the old gentry, mostly the upper castes: they might be lawyers, doctors, or engineers or work in other professions. Today, these professions have been largely replaced by a new, broader category of entrepreneurs who dominate the local (often semi-cartelized) local economy: brick-kiln owners, builders, owners of cement factories, sand contractors, transportation businessmen, and so on.[66] Across India, changes in the occupational profile of the elected candidates and contestants reflect a change in caste background. The second democratic upsurge has brought lower castes to the forefront. The rise of political parties that vie for support from historically underprivileged groups has been accompanied by the rhetoric of equality and social justice. In this environment, *goondas* (gangsters) claiming to be able to deliver the state's economic and political resources to the people are increasingly attractive leaders. Crucially, there seems to be no stigma attached to a person with a criminal record once inducted into mainstream politics.

In Bangladesh, student politics and the confrontation between the two dominant party machines are the laboratory for bosses' careers. Bangladesh's political scenario is often described as a "partyarchy," a system in which the ruling party directs the administration, the police, schools, and budgets through its in loco political boss—the MP.[67] But the party machines are weak and underfunded and should be better understood as networks of strong local leaders rallying around a strong central supreme leader. Student politics within party machines are widely used as a platform to train as political bosses. The local enforcer, the *mastan*, is a crucial tool in the toolbox for the young student leaders that they continue to use extensively as they mature as leaders. "The archetypal *mastan* is young, urban, armed, and testosterone-charged. He acts officiously as the leader of the locality, pushing aside respected elders and appointed authorities. An upstart, he rules through fear, sometimes avenging wrongs but more often committing them himself."[68] In the first autocratic decades of independent Bangladesh *mastans* were signed up by political parties on a large scale and used to coerce votes; recruit, and manage gatherings, rallies, and protests; and generate money for the party. Today, in return for providing numbers for a demonstration, a meeting, or a skirmish with rival parties, student leaders are afforded some impunity to pursue their own interests, particularly if their party is in power. The ideal student boss, therefore, must have the charisma to attract supporters, entrepreneurial acumen, and a penchant for violence. He must also be able to fend off political rivals, even from his own party, as demonstrated by "the Rookie" and "the Godfather."[69] Crucially, when a young *mastan* is transformed into *kedar* (a rank-and-file party worker), he himself becomes a boss. Then he is not only supposed to be available when called on to "perform a riot," but he also needs to be a self-reliant cell that can provide money and resources to the party. An important parallel development in Bangladeshi experiences with Mastanocracy has been the sharp increase in the number of businessmen in Parliament. Early parliaments of the 1970s had a majority of representatives from the professional classes—lawyers, teachers, university professors—but since the 1990s, businessmen have been in the majority.[70]

Pakistan presents a similar pattern. In urban Pakistan, political parties traditionally outsourced the use of force to their student wings. Many established politicians started their careers as (violent) student leaders, orchestrating clashes with rival student wings for the control of university campuses. Crime penetrated university campuses mainly in the 1980s. Today, different developments are occurring across the country. Over the last decade, strong-arm politics has receded in urban Punjab, in contrast to parts of rural Punjab,[71] Karachi, Baluchistan, or Khyber Pakhtunkhwa, where political parties remain directly involved in warfare and organized crime (protection rackets). To a lesser extent, this was also the case in Punjab from the mid-1980s until the late 1990s. The 1985 non-party-based general elections saw an alliance of local politicians and strongmen, with the former relying on the latter for votes. The heroin trade in Lahore's Old City was also a point of contact between them and allowed a number of businessmen to move from drugs to politics. Furthermore, throughout the 1990s political parties actively used their affiliated student unions to gain political ground, resulting in violent clashes for the control of the city's campuses. In addition, the fact that some members of Islamist groups (e.g., Jamaat-ud-Dawa/Milli Muslim League, Lashkar-e-Jhangvi/ASWJ) now participate in parliamentary elections in the province suggests a degree of permeability among the political realm, sectarian militancy, and organized crime.

In Punjab, since the return of the Sharif brothers from exile in Saudi Arabia, however, we are witnessing less violent forms of association between crime and politics. After consecutive terms in office at the provincial level, the PML-N has been able to co-opt much of the provincial bureaucracy, allowing the party to exercise unprecedented power through administrative means (e.g., statutory regulatory orders) and the police force. The effectiveness of the PML-N clientelistic networks means that the party no longer has to rely on criminals and can, most of the time, avoid resorting to violence. The Lahore-based former prime minister Nawaz Sharif and his brother Shahbaz Sharif (now former chief minister of Punjab) are the mafia, so to speak. Rather than employ *goondas* and *badmashs*, the ruling PML-N now tends to rely on the police force to intimidate rivals or settle political scores. In this context, elected governments do not need to rely on criminal entrepreneurs as much as they did in the past.

Local party competition and the structure of local party machines affect the ways systems of "mafia-owned democracies" are organized. The nature of each party machine and its capacity to monopolize violence shape "various types of interaction between political actors and violent entrepreneurs as well as various modes of penetration of organized criminal violence within the political arena," as this book explores.[72] There now exist forms of "competitive Mafia Raj,"[73] such as the ones in Uttar Pradesh in North India and in Karachi, Pakistan.[74] These are highly violent forms of bossism triggered by the coexistence of multiple and competitive centers of power. In these settings, gangsters often enter directly into politics. Violence is, however, an expensive and dangerous commodity. Competitive Mafia Raj are often followed by periods of what we might call "pax mafiosa" during which criminals peacefully collude indirectly with the state, as in the Punjab in Pakistan, Andhra Pradesh in South India, or Bangladesh. Such configurations are always in flux and often cyclical. In a similar fashion, Armao characterizes Italy as a "consociational mafia-owned democracy": a regime based on cooperation between mafiosi, politicians, and entrepreneurs. However, Mexican democracy is conceptualized as a "centrifugal mafia-owned democracy" and characterized by strongly competitive behaviors between the various leaders involved and a much greater degree of violence than in the Italian situation.[75]

STATE, LAW, AND IMPUNITY

Ultimately, bosses' prosperity and survival depend on the law and its manipulation. Without law, crime does not pay. Every criminal aims to neutralize the long arm of the law whenever possible and make it subservient to his or her interests.[76] Thus, effectively manipulating the police, political protection networks, and lawyers is crucial for prosperity. This is equally the case for bosses from privileged backgrounds and newcomers. Impunity is not achieved by magic. As previously mentioned, in a prototypical Mafia Raj bosses collaborate with the police and the state and enter into politics to protect their criminal economic enterprises and ensure their own impunity. This reminds us that bosses operate in settings where the rule of law prevails on a formal level; they do not operate on the fringes of the state,[77] nor do they operate in formal "states of exception."[78] Being caught and going to jail are real possibilities for everybody—including powerful and established bosses. Several of our informants have been in jail, and many of them are implicated in a variety of criminal cases. Hence, the state in our settings is not absent; it is ever present. Even in Pakistan and Bangladesh, where the state is said not to have permeated society as deeply as in India, the security and judiciary apparatus retains a capacity to punish.[79] Some would argue that Pakistan and Bangladesh have in fact experienced a deeper reach of the state than India during periods of authoritarianism. Across the three countries going to court is part of the everyday life of bosses, as political conflicts are increasingly played out in court. At the same time, there are massive complaints about how the judicial process is being subjected to political pressure; courts are said to be increasingly politicized and accused of "judicial overreach."[80]

Our research bears witness to the fact that where bosses last over time, there are successful lawyers and well-bribed policemen and judges in their wake. Impunity and pardon can be bought in a variety of ways. Fieldwork in district courts showed that bail and detention are often treated as commodities. Police and judges are highly corrupt. If one wishes to file a First Information Report (FIR), money is usually offered even before being requested. In some places there is virtually a price list for bail, to halt a police investigation, or to stop a court case. The police (the official "protectors") are often referred to as the main extortionists in the justice system or, more accurately, the "justice business."[81] In short, district-level courtrooms are "auction houses," and this is a well-known "open secret."[82] Whatever happens, it will involve money changing hands. This is such a mundane and prosaic observation that in everyday life it passes as unremarkable. In Lahore people say, "Pulis shaitan ka dusra shakal hai" (the police force is the other face of Satan).

Extralegal Adjudication

How is impunity achieved outside the courtroom? In North India aligning oneself with the ruling party is a well-rehearsed tactic to avoid or delay prosecution. Changing party loyalty is indeed extremely common in North India, but less so in Bangladesh, where party loyalty is particularly praised and entrenched. In Pakistan, the very same legal system that delivers justice also conveniently creates loopholes that help bosses receive impunity. For example, in 1996 a law concerning "blood money" was introduced as part of the Islamization of Pakistan's criminal law. The heir of a victim of murder could now drop charges against the accused in exchange for monetary compensation (*diyat*).[83] As a result most murders are now treated as private offenses against the victim's legal heirs. This "privatization of criminal justice" means that convicted murderers are incarcerated only if they fail to meet the requested amount of blood money or to convince, or coerce, the heirs into accepting it,[84] which has had the effect of the powerful quite literally getting away with murder. Not surprisingly, the rates of homicide, honor killings, and acquittal have soared since the introduction of this law.

In North India, compensation and settlement out of court are common. Informally, blood money is often sanctioned by caste/community *panchayats* or by bosses who act as adjudicators. In the literature, much emphasis has been placed on the role of informal adjudication processes in enforcing caste- and gender-specific behavior such as honor killings ordered by *khap panchayats* (caste/clan village assemblies).[85] However, less attention has been devoted to investigating the adjudication of murders and violent crimes related to the local predatory economy (i.e., rampant land grabbing and estate developments, illegal stone and sand mining, extortion rackets, adulteration of products, and other fraudulent practices relating to a variety of products and services). In Bangladesh, court cases are also usually run in tandem with informal adjudication processes. In semirural areas, the courts and local village tribunals (*shalish*) and a variety of other brokers are involved in seeking justice. It is common knowledge that one needs to pay and have connections to evade, settle, or win a court case. What is less clear is who one needs to pay, how much, and how to make the payment. It is at this negotiating stage that bosses with criminal experience and muscular lawyers are indispensable. Across all our sites, bosses are essential because they know how to navigate the world of the law and the courts, as well as the multiple biddings that such processes entail. Acting as intermediaries between the police and the clients is often one of the platforms from which bosses' careers are launched. The law not only allows bosses facing criminal charges to maintain their positions of influence and rule with impunity but also creates the opportunity for them to enter into the justice "business" and become legitimate adjudicators and punishers. Their power is both reflected and enhanced by taking this supralegal position. Bosses' authority is often reflected in their role as judges. Bosses provide justice and security. This includes dispute resolutions and the protection of neighborhoods or business.

CHAPTER 2

THE ROOKIE

Ashraf Hoque

IN 2002, I attended a student cultural event at a provincial degree college in Bangladesh. My cousin's son, Jamal, was the organizer. I had never visited a Bangladeshi college previously, although I was acutely aware that they were sites for political battles—violent or otherwise. Jamal was the president of the Student Union Art and Culture Society. He was a thespian. He had been a much-lauded child actor who had regularly performed on the national stage. So when he invited me to attend a show that he had organized, I felt proud and honored and did not need much persuading. Prior to the event, family members had informed me that Jamal was a *neta* (political leader), a fact that seemed to amuse them. Admittedly, I also found this to be quite amusing. Jamal was shorter than even the average Bangladeshi. He was also baby-faced (and still is)—an image that complemented an incessantly jovial and somewhat mischievous demeanor. The notion that this short, childlike teenager who loved to sing and dance was some sort of political leader seemed quite bizarre. Furthermore, at home he was always quiet and respectful, almost meek. Definitely not someone you would associate with the highly charged, fiercely competitive, and often ruthless world of Bangladeshi student politics, I thought.

The event was held in the college auditorium. In between speeches (mostly political in nature) made by students and guest speakers, the large audience was treated with live music performed by a famous pop band that had traveled all the way from Dhaka—to the obvious (and very loud) delight of the young crowd. Aside from the headline act, there were comedy sketches, poetry recitals, and even a patriotic play to enjoy. Boys and girls in large mixed groups were swaying to the music, screaming in adoration, and being generally merry. About halfway through the show, I decided to venture outside for a cigarette. As I stood smoking, I noticed a group of young men across the college courtyard. They were looking at me quite intensely. Not thinking much of it, I continued smoking. In Bangladesh, one is not expected to smoke in front of anyone considered to be an "elder" (*murobbi*). In fact, this is considered highly disrespectful. More pertinently, in a college or university environment, the rules of where and when one smokes are subject to further stratification. A student in a lower-year group cannot smoke in view of any senior "brother" (*bhai*).[1] Often a student may be smoking on campus when, out of nowhere, a senior student appears. This is not a problem providing the former makes an overt effort to hide the cigarette or remove himself from the scene, thus demonstrating "respect" (*shomman*). Once this protocol is observed, the matter is settled and normalcy is resumed. On this occasion, however—completely ignorant of these dynamics—I was shamefully unaware of the serious faux pas that I had committed.

Having been raised in England, I had no idea of the typical behavioral conventions of a college campus in Bangladesh. I was aware, from my relatively Bangladeshi upbringing in diaspora, that smoking in front of familiar elders was a contemptuous cultural act. However, openly smoking in public—where one is anonymous—was socially accepted as far as I was aware at the time. I presumed, therefore, that having a cigarette in a public place such as college, and where most of the students were younger than I, would also be accepted. I was wrong.

A few minutes passed, but the gaze of the group of men remained fixed. It was at this point that I began to seriously consider the reasons for their stares. It was normal in Bangladesh to be stared at. Being able to outstare another person is almost a public rite of passage. Bangladeshis, especially Sylhetis, are particularly adept at recognizing a *Lon-*

doni[2]—the attire, the grooming, the foreign mannerisms. I was therefore accustomed to being "visually surveyed" in most places. On this occasion, I had presumed the same and carried on smoking. My suspicions were aroused less by the rather uncomfortable glaring than by the swagger of this group. They were dressed in leather jackets and jeans. They wore training shoes (most people wore sandals in the summer heat). Their hair was long and carefully styled. Raised sunglasses. Gold chains. This all alluded to the possibility that the group of men may have been of some significance. A moment later, one of them left the group and began walking toward me across the courtyard. As he approached, his group behind observed intently.

"Who are you?" he asked, when within distance.

"Who are *you*," I asked in retort.

"This is my college, and you are disrespecting it," his tone became more aggressive. At this point, a friend of Jamal's who, unbeknown to me, had been observing, interrupted the encounter: "This is Jamal's uncle from London; he's come to see the show."

The young man stalled into a moment of silence. His expression, sullen and affronted, endured as he then offered me his hand: "As-salam-wa-alaikum."

We exchanged brief, formulaic pleasantries before he returned to the group. I was then subtly ushered back into the auditorium by Jamal's friend.

"Those boys are senior Chhatra League," he informed me.[3] "Nobody smokes in front of them. Don't worry; you didn't know. Besides, you're *Jamal's* uncle."

The previous year, the Bangladesh Nationalist Party (BNP) had won the general elections, ousting the Awami League. At the time of the incident, the balance of power in the country had thus shifted to members and supporters of the BNP, who had by then consolidated their rule. Chhatra League had hitherto run the student union at this government college. Now, however, it had exchanged hands, with the BNP calling all the shots. Jamal was a member of the Bangladesh Jatiotabadi Dal (BJD), the student wing of the BNP. His relatively high position in the group had meant that he was a figure of authority on campus. Before this incident, I had no idea that this was the case. I found out later that the group of men held long-running enmities with the BJD in the area. They particularly disliked Jamal because of his fierce temper and propensity for violence. They also feared him. Jamal had been involved in a number of violent skirmishes in the local area, some of which had led to serious injuries. Some of those injuries were inflicted by Jamal. I found these revelations to be quite confusing and difficult to believe. My impression of Jamal was as a mild-mannered, gentle, and respectful young man. I had no idea that he was so heavily involved in the murky world of Bangladeshi student politics and an early-career practitioner of the "art of bossing."

In 2002, Jamal was well on course to become a "gangster politician." By 2014, he had been in and out of prison, was addicted to drugs and alcohol, unemployed, separated from his wife, disowned by half of his family, and clinically depressed.

ENTER THE *MASTAN*

In the years since the restoration of democracy in 1991, Bangladesh has witnessed the rise of a folk hero. But unlike most heroes the world over, the particular figure of the *mastan* has a necessary dark side. *Mastan* originates from the word *mast*, which translates loosely as "divine intoxication." Being *mast* is usually attributed to wandering minstrels, mystics, and ascetics to connote a connection with the otherworld—a place where worldly possessions, worries, and intrigues are redundant. A *mastan* was someone who fought his inner urges to resist the material, carnal temptations of the world. In a curious, if not ironic, twist of its origins, the figure of the *mastan* has an altogether different meaning in the cultural consciousness of contemporary Bangladesh. This *mastan* is no longer yearning for an elevated place in the next world, but in this one. He is no longer detached from the aspirations of material life, but very much a protagonist for it. He dresses well. He eats well. His leisurely pursuits are exclusive; his tastes, opulent. Such a lifestyle requires money, and lots of it. For this reason, all *mastans* possess a burning desire to generate wealth. In popular cinema, the *mastan* is portrayed as a working-class upstart, young, armed, and striving for his class interests. The *mastan* is violent, angry, and beset by a sense of injustice. He represents the frustrations of young people in a dysfunctional state, taking the law into his own hands, championing an amoral ideology of selfhood.[4] But perhaps the most important attribute that separates this *mastan* from his cultural predecessor is his firm commitment to the realm of politics, because in twenty-first-century Bangladesh, there is no better way of getting rich than becoming a politician.

Bangladesh's independence from Pakistan was the culmination of decades of cultural, political, and economic marginalization of the eastern wing in a geographically (and ethnically) fragmented country. Throughout the Pakistan period (and indeed during the struggle for independence from colonial rule) students were at the vanguard for the struggle for rights and recognition. In newly formed Pakistan, the Bengali Language Movement of 1952, instigated in defiance of moves to omit Bengali as a national language and the wholesale introduction of Urdu, provided the first in a series of bloody and often fatal flashpoints between Bengalis (mainly students) and the state apparatus on the road to cessation. Various student-led *hartals* (strikes) and noncooperation movements seeking social and economic parity followed in the short but tumultuous united Pakistan period, eventually leading to the general elections victory of Sheikh Mujibur Rahman, a Bengali and leader of the Awami League. When his overwhelming mandate was infamously denied by West Pakistan's political and military top brass, a spate of popular uprisings in the eastern wing—once again driven by students—ultimately led to the separation of East Pakistan and the creation of a new nation in 1971.

In independent Bangladesh, the student as the national icon and agent for idealistic change has survived. To a large degree, this is due to students' role in the nation's creation narrative. Their reputation was further enhanced, however, in the aftermath of self-rule. Student involvement in the all-party Gono Andolon (People's Movement) to restore democracy against the military dictatorship of Lt. Gen. H. M. Ershad in the late 1980s further entrenched the sacred place of student activism in Bangladeshi politics.[5] Prior to this, Bangladesh had endured fifteen years of military administration, first under Lt. Gen.

Ziaur Rahman (founder of the BNP), and then Ershad (founder of the Jaitiyo Party). Particularly under the latter's tenure, hundreds of students were arrested, tortured, and imprisoned for demanding free elections. A significant number, once again, gave their lives.

By the time Bangladesh had rid itself of authoritarian rule, the figure of the student reigned supreme as the quintessentially Bangladeshi symbol of virtue and justice. More than twenty-five years on, however, the student activist no longer stands in defiance of state power but seeks it for himself. Becoming a student activist is no longer about lofty idealism and democratic rights for all but an indefatigable and ruthless craving to be somebody, to become "the boss."

THE STORY OF JAMAL

So how does one get attracted to the world of student politics in the first place? How does one learn the art of bossing in this part of the world? Jamal, whose unwitting protection allowed me to smoke a cigarette in relative peace, began his career as an infant. He grew up at the homestead of his maternal grandfather. There, he completed his education up to (but not including) degree level. Jamal grew up not knowing his father. Due to a long-standing feud, which began when he was just a baby, his maternal uncles had prevented Jamal's mother from moving to her marital home. Consequently, Jamal had never met any member of his paternal family until he was in his late teens and, because his mother never remarried, remained an only child—unusual in Bangladesh, where most nuclear families are large. Growing up at one's *nanabari* (maternal homestead) attracts stigma. These children are derogatorily known as *boithol* (indolent and/or homeless), a title that remains with them into adulthood.

> Originally, everyone at my *nanabari* were Jamaat.[6] Their live-in tutor was even Jamaat. He was Shibir.[7] He was a teacher at Maulvi Bazaar College. He used to teach us. He took me and enrolled me in the Foolkuri Asar [Rosebud Community]. This was an organization set up by Jamaat for infants, but they never came out openly about it. It was part of the Jatiyo Shishoo-Kishoor Sangoton [National Children's Organization], set up initially by Ziaur Rah-

> man.[8] So I enrolled and partook in dramas, musicals—without music, [as] it was an Islamic-minded organization. Foolkuri Ashar was a famous organization in Bangladesh. It has a good reputation. Suppose in the Awami League they have the Awami Shilpo Gushti [Popular Artists' Family]—this is a cultural branch of the party. You know that in every aspect of life in Bangladesh there is the hand of politics. Even drivers of vehicles; there is an Awami League Drivers' Association, as well as a BNP one. A BNP Hawkers' Party, an Awami Hawkers' Party—they're still around. So I joined this organization; we were all small. I became an expert in drama. I used to love it. I performed in front of thousands of people—16 December, et cetera.[9] I was small, so everybody used to show me affection. Everybody liked me.
>
> When I was in Class 9 (fourteen or fifteen years old), I meet a few friends from Government Boys' School, which was a good school. I became friends with them and, gradually, got with their "side"—[their boss was] Zillu *bhai* [leader of a JCD faction in Maulvi Bazaar].[10] There was another [JCD] group called the George Group—we used to hear *mastan* stories about them. JCD was really strong in Maulvi Bazaar at the time. So, after spending time [socializing, *adda*] with them, I was introduced to their *boro* [big] *bhai*—Zillu *bhai*—this was about sixteen years ago now. Gradually I got to know everyone. At this time, BNP wasn't in government; there were various *hartals*, and vehicles were sabotaged [by us]. We got paid [to do this]—the opposition party has a separate source of income even if they're not in power [laughs]. I became really active.

Jamal's friends and family had thus first introduced him to politics. His maternal extended family were religiously conservative and supported the third party in Bangladeshi politics—the Islamist Jamaat-e-Islami. His talent for performing onstage gained him entry to a well-known national drama society, where he was exposed to Islamist propaganda from an early age. Curiously, he opted not to join Jamaat after graduating from high school. Instead, he was impressed by the glamour and notoriety of the JCD, in particular, their political *boro bhai* Zillu. His political debut, at the age of sixteen, involved participating in a violent street protest where he was paid by JCD organizers to vandalize property, as this act is not only a display of power to political opponents and the wider public,[11] but it also demonstrates an aspirant's willingness and devotion to internal party leaders at the local level. I asked Jamal what he thought were the reasons behind his recruitment:

> I was a good student, but I don't know why the party's senior *netas* used to pull me for some reason. They could profit from attracting someone from my *nanabari* to the JCD [as they were a prominent family in Maulvi Bazaar but supported Jamaat]—it would be a credit for them. They started pursuing me from then. After I got into college, I started to get into politics full-blown. Zillu *bhai* was very smart. He was articulate as well as a cadre. So as soon as I passed the SSC examinations,[12] they inducted me into the party: "Jamal, come and join the JCD with us; you have a good relationship with us."
>
> Then it seemed that my [maternal] cousin was pulling me to join Shibir. After being part of Foolkuri, I had developed good relations with Shibir. They used to take me to Sunamganj, Habiganj, et cetera to perform in Islamic theater. There are very few places in Sylhet where I didn't perform. They have a theater called Korthok Theater, and I was part of that too. As a result of this I became very popular in Maulvi Bazaar—everyone knew me. They used to know me in a good light. It's a small town, so it was easier for people to know each other. So I was confused as to whom to join: "Should I join Shibir or JCD?"
>
> I wanted to get into politics ever since I was young; I don't know why. You know how some people want to become a doctor or an engineer, a pilot, this and that? For me, even from then, I wanted to "do politics" [*rajniti*]. Do you know what my mother said to me? She said, "Do politics. Sheikh Mujib did it; big people have done it in the past, but don't get into politics and do anything bad." My mother used to say—in fact my [paternal] grandfather also said this to me—"Go to jail as a result of politics," as in "go to jail having fought for a good cause." "But don't get involved in any theft or corruption."
>
> I saw that BNP was quite powerful in Maulvi Bazaar. I tricked my cousin. I knew that I had protection from Shibir at home, so I joined JCD. As soon as I joined the party—I was only in my first year at college—I managed to secure a post. I was very temperamental when I was younger, and I think that played a part in me getting promoted. People were intimidated by

> my temperament, but I didn't realize that at the time. If I go to Maulvi Bazaar now, I could summon twenty boys immediately. I became the committee executive for the college drama society. I also produced a JCD campus magazine, *Amora Nobeen* [We Are New], which was received well widely.

At the onset of his political career, Jamal possessed all the critical attributes of an aspiring student leader. He came from a wealthy and respected family, but their support for Jamaat made them a target for infiltration by the mainstream political parties, who were frustrated by their previous lack of success in this regard. In Bangladesh, the patrilineage (*gushti*) one belongs to or associates with often determines political allegiances—particularly among conservative groups. According to Jamal, every member of his maternal family in Maulvi Bazaar supported Jamaat. His "defection" to the BNP, therefore, would undoubtedly arouse intrigue within the small-town community, hence boosting the party's local profile and undermining that of Jamaat. His recruitment would also appease the BNP "High Command" in other areas. Jamal was a talented youth. He was a good student, meaning he could secure a place at college, respect among his peers, and the patronage of well-meaning teachers. He was also talented in the arts—a writer, actor, and musician. Such arts are indeed deeply complementary with the art of bossing. They made him stand out. As an artist he soon gained figural power in his college. His figurality and skills could be utilized for party purposes—organizing functions, producing publications, and delivering confident public speeches. Jamal thus possessed the potential to become a boss. He was wealthy, locally well known, talented, and charismatic. Most significantly, however, his temperament also demonstrated an appetite for violence and subversion—crucial in the domain of Bangladeshi politics. His enthusiastic participation in an organized riot on his political debut further proved this fact. In addition, Jamal's personal ambitions chimed with the opportunity presented to him. He always wanted to be a politician, and his ever-increasing popularity among the who's who of local politics endeared him to the scene.

Jamal claims that although he certainly had a knack for subversive acts, such as physically intimidating political opponents, extorting rents from local businesses, and bribing law enforcement agents, he was a promising prospect for the BNP hierarchy primarily due to his social status and leadership skills. This made him an ideal leader in the perceptions of "educated" (*shikkito*) and, therefore, "respectable" (*shommani*) people who could relate to him and held him in high esteem. Jamal was thus a rare and prized asset for his political party—a leader. However, graduation to the rank of leader can be attained only once one is first fully assimilated as a *kedar* —a rank-and-file party worker. A *kedar* is not only called on to perform a riot when necessary,[13] but he is also to be a self-subsistent cell who can provide money and resources to the party.

There are two routes to a political career: *kedar-giri* and leadership. The former is associated with muscle and wealth; the latter, with personal charisma (*bektigoto bebohaar/taan*) and education (*shikka*). The most successful leaders possess a combination of all four. *Mastan-giri* (thuggery) is taught at the *kedar* level, from college onward. This is the foundational basis of a career in Bangladeshi politics. Because politics here is all about protection, a *kedar* must be able to build up a network of patronage to get things done. It is this ability to be a "broker" (*dalal*) that determines political credibility. The more money one has, the more commission one can offer for services. In this way a group or faction is created who work together on certain "business projects"—each taking a cut for their services. If people see that you are good at making money, they will vote for you, as this implies competence.

The formula to perform an effective art of bossing in this part of the world therefore comprises the ability to pragmatically muster muscle and wealth under the veneer of respectability—usually attained through successful entrepreneurship, ancestral pedigree, and formal education. Jamal was eager and demonstrated these attributes early on in his career. His party looked on in anticipation:

> I made money. I got a lot of business. The magazine was free, but people submit articles and editorials, don't they? The principal, people from Sylhet [City]—a lot of people—wanted to submit editorials. [They] wanted to show their face in the magazine. So they used to give X amount of money and re-

quest an article about them or by them. Some people used to try to submit the tiniest photograph and offer me fifteen thousand taka for it. But I used to initially refuse, saying, "No, no, no. I can't do that. That space is reserved for Zillu *bhai*," who was the boss. There were various ways of making the maximum profit. I used to make fifty to sixty thousand taka [approximately five hundred pounds] from each issue. I used to promote myself as well, including my name and photo in the issue. This is an alternative line into politics; do you understand what I mean? It's the path for poets or artists to enter the political scene.

So, after that, I developed an understanding with people within the college environment. Gradually I became popular at college—right through the spectrum—from seniors to juniors. We were the juniors at the time. Within a month, I became a well-known figure at the college. I can't really explain why. All the teachers, all the students, they all knew me. I won an improvisation [*prattonik*] competition at college as well. They picked subjects at random and expected us to perform the characters. Like, for example, a *mukti juddha* [freedom fighter], a peasant, a driver, a thug, a policeman. You were given two minutes to complete the performance. I competed against hundreds of entrants, in front of thousands of spectators. I never dreamed of winning it, but I did. I got to the last five, then the last three. Then I was number one! This was a combined competition, all the students from both the college and the national university. People said that I performed really well. I couldn't tell, obviously, but the spectators told me afterward that my performance was really good. I was amazed.

I became immediately popular throughout the college off the back of that. People would want to become my friend; they'd approach me when they saw me. When I used to walk by, people used to say, "Hey, Jamal, how are you?" One day, I went to the market with my uncle on a cycle rickshaw; from the moment we left the house, people were giving me *salams* [salutations]. God knows. I got that much respect from people; only God knows why. My uncle, he'd just come back from abroad. He went to my mum and said, "I must've lost my mind; this boy was greeted by everyone and his dog! I can't understand it. Why did all these people, young and old, give him *salams*?" So he said to me, "Okay, you want to do politics, that's fine. But you have make sure your studies don't suffer."

Jamal was a peri-urban middle-class student who was groomed to go all the way to the top of the political heap. His early activities saw him fast-tracked into official positions within the JCD. Most aspiring leaders, however, never quite progress from being an enforcer. They come from relatively poorer, lower-middle-class or peasant backgrounds. Some continue to make a reasonable living through providing muscle, numbers, and contacts to their political associates in return for patronage. For most, the career inevitably fades with the loss of youth, marriage, and the arrival of children.

Although Jamal managed to successfully graduate from the status of street-level enforcer to bona fide student leader and all the trappings that came with it, he retired from politics following his marriage, after which he consciously pursued a respectable, settled life. By this stage, his acting career had flourished and he had managed to secure regular employment in a number of television drama serials largely produced by Channel S, a private television channel based in Maulvi Bazaar financed by the British-Bangladeshi (*Londoni*) diaspora. Acting in "criminal" movies and TV series reflects a world in which fiction and reality are constantly blurred. Despite his intentions, remaining in Maulvi Bazaar proved difficult for Jamal. He was well known in political circles, and the temptation for "easy money" through criminal activity and quick access to drugs and alcohol became overwhelming. Jamal was addicted to Phensedyl—a highly addictive banned cough syrup smuggled into Bangladesh via India. His addiction was serious. He had been in and out of rehab clinics throughout his twenties. Maulvi Bazaar, located near the border with India and en route to Dhaka, was and remains a center for the illegal Phensedyl trade, largely coordinated by student leaders.

The road route between Maulvi Bazaar and Dhaka is vital for the smuggling of contraband, including cigarettes, alcohol, and drugs. Once safely in Dhaka, the products are sold in the burgeoning black market and are mainly consumed by addicts (mainly student activists-cum-gangsters) and VIPs (including film stars, ministers, and businessmen). The route is also a popular tributary for the transportation of large quantities of cash to be laundered in the capital. Although very few people claim seized cash from the police, it is widely reputed that most of this "dirty" cash belongs to Sylheti politicians and British-Bangladeshi businessmen laundering profits made in the United Kingdom.

As mentioned previously, this part of Bangladesh is linked to a wider transnational economy, particularly conjoined with Britain's economy. British-Bangladeshis are politically and economically active in Sylhet and have contributed to an economic boom in the area over the past few decades through providing sustained remittances to their Bangladeshi relatives.[14] *Londonis* are involved in a number of commercial sectors, including construction, retail, transportation, banking, and the exportation of fish and other fresh produce to Europe and North America. Due to high duty, a significant proportion of this money arrives in Bangladesh undeclared through a network of illegal transnational brokers known as "black-wallas" (Sylheti: *belek-ala*).

But it is not just foreign money being laundered. According to Jamal and others, most of the convoys to Dhaka consist of cash made by bureaucrats, government contractors, politicians, and high-ranking police officers from a range of spurious sources based at Sylhet City, the regional capital. Maulvi Bazaar and its hinterland are uniquely located on the border with a remote part of northeastern India and must be passed through either by rail or road to get to Dhaka from Sylhet City. The region is also one of the greatest sources of foreign capital (legal or otherwise) in the country. All this makes the area fertile ground for a thriving black economy.

For criminal entrepreneurs like Jamal, opportunities to capitalize were not missed. Prior to his marriage, he was heavily involved in the smuggling process. However, in addition to augmenting his political career/gangster reputation through collecting rents from smugglers and providing for his ever-growing entourage, getting involved in the smuggling nexus also meant a steady supply of drugs to feed his spiraling addiction:

> You are first introduced to it [Phensedyl] through your friends. Suppose I'm an activist and I'm getting a lot of attention and respect from political *boro bhais*. After you've passed your SSC, senior leaders tend to pay you a lot of attention. Do you understand? Affection, generosity, protection. So, natu-

rally, you will become attracted to them; you'll seek them out on campus, in the canteen; you'll go and sit with them. But even in the educational environment, they possess their own form of power. People know that this person is part of the JCD. Occasionally these guys will get information that a money-laundering [*hoondi*] convoy is passing through carrying hundreds of thousands of taka, so they go and hijack it. Thus, their pockets get lined with excessive amounts of cash. Now, can they show this money to their family? If he's from a good family, he won't let anyone know.

In Bangladesh, very few people are involved in *shontrashi* [criminality/terrorism] out of hunger. Do you understand? The people who are currently engaged in this are addicts. You'll discover that these addicts have been or still are associated with one political party or another. Go to Sylhet [City] now, and in every area there are twenty, thirty, fifty boys—most of them are addicted. There are so many areas like this.

Our neighboring country is India. It all comes from India. Our region is next to the border. That is why I can talk authoritatively about this. There are underground relationships between dealers on this side and suppliers on that side. They are the ones at the higher level. Occupying the middle ground are the agents [*dalal*] or "middlemen"—they go and collect from the other side and supply the dealers here, who occupy the lowest rung in the operation. So people like me would then go to dealers and buy the product.

Do you know how it gets to Dhaka? I know how; I've seen it. Dhaka is supplied through Brahmanbaria[15]—this is the hub from our part of the country. Every day, there are many businessmen who send cars packed with one hundred kilograms of cannabis, two thousand bottles of Phensedyl, and so on, to Dhaka. These items are then distributed within Dhaka.

Jamal's addiction had forced him to acquire cash through illicit means. Although he never admitted to being directly involved in hijacking vehicles containing black money, he did admit to supplying his own car to smugglers and arranging for their ease of passage through Maulvi Bazaar. He claims to have made hundreds of thousands of taka through these ventures, money that he could not disclose to his family out of fear of arousing suspicion of his activities. He spent the proceeds on fueling his addiction, buying clothes, and partying with his associates.

Consider this magazine. I took money from the leaders, took out ads. I kept the surplus. People want to make money like that, but most people don't get the opportunity. But because I was close to political leaders of a party that was in power, I could make money. I used to make money from the theater company as well. Even though it was in the cultural line [but did politics at the same time], I had a lot of power. So imagine I did a program with a budget of, say, fifty thousand taka [approximately five hundred pounds]. From this budget, I would request the principal for a grant of twenty thousand [approximately two hundred pounds]. I would invite chief guests, like the city mayor, who would give us five thousand. Then the *boro bhais* would raise money of around fifteen thousand [approximately one hundred fifty pounds]. I would also know other political leaders who would donate in return for being a guest speaker. They would usually be former college leaders who are now at the district level; they want to be seen and known among the new generation.

I asked Jamal if he had ample opportunities for business when his party was in power. He replied that he did.

For example, when I was vice chairman [JCD], a *boro bhai* came to me and said, "Why don't you get a lease for the city corporation motorcycles? [Obsolete government equipment such as computers, trucks, furniture, etc., are periodically auctioned by the municipality.] So I took ten thousand and a few friends and went to the city corporation and chose the bike of my choice. I announced to people there, "I want that bike," and because everybody knew that I was a cadre, no one bid for the bike. I bought the bike for seven thousand and sold it for twenty thousand on the same day. I could have done a lot more business using my party links if I had sufficient capital.

When the government used to extract sand from the riverbanks [for use in construction], senior party members would be granted opportunities to bid to the district commissioner [of police] for a lease. I requested to be a partner in the enterprise, but they wanted to give me a cut of the profits instead. They said, "You're a student; take the money." They didn't take me seriously. So they gave me ten thousand taka, and I went to Cox Bazaar [a seaside resort] with my friends!

There was a *mela* [fair] once, and my theater company performed. The

> JCD district organizer extorted money from the organizers and shared it out with party members. He gave me ten thousand taka. I was in the first or second year at the time, so, for me, that was a hell of a lot of money. See how kids become *noshto* [corrupt/maligned]?
>
> I had some bad friends; they used to do *chandabaazi* [racketeering]. So, say you built a building; they used to take money from the contractors. These friends used to give money to me as well. If they [the contractors] refused to pay, they'd get tortured in a cell. They'd take the *tikadar* (head contractor)—who was usually from outside districts and, therefore, was scared and kept quiet—to an isolated place and beat him up with sticks. I used to beat people like that too. When the BNP comes into power, money laundering increases in the country for some reason—I think maybe it's because there are a lot of *Londonis* in Maulvi Bazaar and Sylhet and they want to transfer money without paying tax.
>
> This one time I got information that a private hire driver had hijacked a car carrying black money. So I went to his house with a few friends and took him to a quiet place on top of a remote hill. Then we beat him with sticks. He told us that he didn't take the money, but it was the nephew of the *Londoni* man [whose money it was] that took it. The nephew had called the driver several times during the journey and wanted to know his whereabouts. After the hijacking, the driver went to the nephew's house and accused him of stealing his uncle's money and showed proof. The nephew gave the driver twelve lakhs [£12,000] to keep his mouth shut. I got one lakh [£1000] from the driver and shared it out with my friends.
>
> On another occasion, I got information that there was another heist worth eighty-five lakhs [approximately eighty thousand pounds] in Fechuganj. I knew the boys who did it. All of a sudden they had expensive clothes, phones, and [were] flashing cash. They got sixteen lakhs from that job. I demanded a cut too, so they all paid me two lakhs [approximately two thousand pounds].

Jamal's commitment to the lifestyle of a student activist–cum–mafia entrepreneur also led to various bouts of imprisonment. The most serious occurred in the mid-2000s when he was embroiled in an attempt-to-murder case. Jamal's JCD faction had engaged in a supremacy war with a rival faction from within their own party in Maulvi Bazaar. The conflict had culminated in the hospitalization of the faction leader, after he had been stabbed multiple times during an ambush organized by Jamal's faction, of which he was second in command. He was imprisoned for six months while awaiting trial. He was eventually acquitted on the grounds of lack of evidence after his family paid a substantial bribe to the district commissioner's office. Jamal promptly reentered the activist fold following his release from prison, as his addiction to Phensedyl reached its zenith. Spells in and out of rehab centers ensued before his father—by now fully reconciled with him—decided to arrange his marriage in an effort to lure him away from the lifestyle and ground him with responsibility. Leaving Maulvi Bazaar for Sylhet (sixty miles away) was the key condition to the marriage negotiations. Under duress, Jamal agreed to the terms and moved to Sylhet on a permanent basis, leaving his career as an actor and student activist behind. Despite this, his addiction to Phensedyl endured. His lifestyle eventually led to the estrangement of his wife, who opted to separate from him and return to her natal home with their infant son. At the onset of this research, Jamal was living on his own in a spare room in his paternal grandfather's home in Sylhet. He had created a network of activist friends in Sylhet and continued to maintain relations with his associates in Maulvi Bazaar, although by now his political activities had all but ceased. His networks ensured a regular stream of cash with which he funded his addiction.

Currently, Jamal is considering his future. He is fully aware of his potential as an emerging boss. He is also aware of the risks involved in pursuing such a career. According to him, politics is a "dirty game." Financial gain comes at an existential cost. He fears to be forever thought of as a *mastan*—a label that makes him simultaneously amused and resentful. Jamal's future is therefore uncertain. He is torn between the lure of easy money that a career in politics would yield and the respectability of more orthodox means of earning a livelihood. In addition, he is deeply regretful of how his life has unfolded and is eager to make amends. Jamal claims to be at a crossroads: between the next rung on the political ladder and the way out. Yet his desire to succeed in politics above all else is all too obvious:

> Politics is all that I know. I've been trained to expect to lead. Whatever I do, I have to lead. What should I do now? Maybe I should go abroad to work. Maybe I should try to be a good, honest leader. But that is impossible in Bangladesh.

MY ART IS POLITICS

The emergence of the gangster politician in Bangladesh has evolved from the twentieth-century tradition of student mobilization and street protest. The seminal moment in the recent history of the nation is its birth in 1971, after a brutal war of liberation that cost millions of lives. Students were instrumental throughout this formative chapter. They campaigned against the oppression of West Pakistani domination, which eventually led to the ultimately successful call for separation. Their legacy was further augmented in independent Bangladesh with the organization of recurring street protests, under the banner of the "People's Movement" for democracy, after two intervals of military dictatorship. After democracy was restored in 1990 came the entrance of the *mastan* into the Bangladeshi political scene. Political parties exploited the symbol of the student as an icon of national pride, the personification of Bangladeshi dignity and righteousness, to suit their partisan purposes. Street protests in this era became less concerned with higher political ideals and more engrossed in the display of vulgar force and intimidation. Student activism thus became professionalized. In exchange for partisan loyalty and muscle, young men (and increasingly women) were offered relative impunity from the law, a license to extort, and a lifestyle of glamour and excess. Depending on their suitability and scope of ambition, activists are promoted to leadership positions within their respective parties. Those candidates who further demonstrate high aptitude in the rigors of political life go on to become bona fide politicians and gain the endless bounties and excess that come with it.

Most activists, however, fail to graduate beyond the first rung of a political career and remain low-level enforcers until they eventually retire. There are a number of factors behind this. In addition to the ability to conjure muscle, a successful leader must give an impression of affluence and possess a "common touch." He must contain the necessary charisma to be able to relate to others—high and low—and retain the competence to deliver his objectives. As a rural laborer once remarked to me regarding Iliyas Ali, a leading yet controversial BNP politician who had mysteriously disappeared without trace in 2012:

> I think Iliyas Ali was a good man. I went to a few meetings and thought that the way he spoke was good and that he was okay. Suppose I'm sitting here with you today; I came here because I like the way you speak and your manners, and, because of that, I decided to come and sit with you.
>
> I came here, and after I came, you said, "Please have a seat," but if you'd said, "Leave from here!" and shown anger, in my mind—inside—I would've said, "No, he's not a good person." I wouldn't come again. You said, "Sit," and you're chatting to me; that's what I liked about Iliyas Ali when I attended his meetings; his manners [*bebohar*] are good, and he's a nice person.
>
> I met him once [at a meeting]. I shook his hand. There were a lot of people there, so I couldn't speak to him for long. It was rushed. Plus all the work he did in the union, and the other areas. I thought that was good, too. What if he took that money? Could anyone have done anything about that? No. But he didn't. Also, I spoke to people in other areas and asked people there, "Who gave this?," and they said it was Iliyas Ali. So I also found that he was good from [other] people's mouths.

Iliyas Ali came to prominence as a consequence of his instrumental role in the People's Movement in the 1980s as one of the leading University of Dhaka cadres opposing the military regime of Ershad. He has served multiple prison terms as a student activist. In his home province of Sylhet, he was known as the undisputed "chief [*sardar*] of *mastans*" in this period. As a Member of Parliament in the democratic era, Ali rose through the ranks and became one of the most popular politicians in the country, particularly in Sylhet, where supporters of all parties heralded him for his tireless development work and his vivacious yet uncompromising character. Ali encapsulated the archetypal modern Bangladeshi politician. He was brave (*shahoshi*), principled (*nitishil*), generous (*doyal*), powerful (*komotoshil*), and socially adept (*samajik*). Three years after his suspicious disappearance, political posters bearing his image remain a ubiquitous feature in towns and thoroughfares all over his home province. In the bazaars, folk songs eulogizing his life and achievements blare out to this day. His most ardent supporters believe he will return from "exile" stronger than ever and assume the leadership of the party. Curiously, they refuse outright to entertain the notion of his demise. In Sylhet, Iliyas Ali is the primary role model for aspiring student leaders. The reality is, however, that few will reach his heights, his mythical status. The majority will perish under the lure of addiction, the pressure of competition, and the failure to attract powerful patrons. The fact that Ali has vanished altogether—most probably due to his huge popular appeal and political successes—does not seem to deter emerging generations. Aspirational young Bangladeshis continue to dream of becoming a political boss and of the encompassing fame and endless fortune that comes with it. Becoming a gangster first is seemingly a small price to pay.

CHAPTER 3

THE BLUFFER

Nicolas Martin

Be quiet! If you aren't quiet you'll be losing out, not me. Listen to me quietly. Today I want to tell you that no one knows where your MNREGA money's going.[1] I also know that some of you aren't even being given job cards, but I'm here, and if you give me all the necessary documents, I'll go straight to the DDPO [district development and *panchayat* officer] and get you your card in less than an hour. But don't give anything to the thieves and thugs; beat them with your shoes. By the thirtieth of February [*sic*] this year I'll have got all of you your job cards.

I'm not fighting for my family. As I've already said in the past, I had a good job in the police, but I left so I could fight for you people. I was earning twenty thousand rupees and sending my two children to good schools, but I abandoned a life of comfort for your sake. And what will I do for you? I will raise MNREGA payments from one hundred eighty-four to one thousand rupees per day. I've already told Rahul Gandhi to do this. I've also signed and passed a form that entitles you to unemployment benefits from 2008 to 2012. I signed it. Here is the form for those of you who can read; I signed it and passed it. And what will you get? You'll get one hundred thousand rupees while you are sitting at home. No Block Development Officer and no *sarpanch* [elected village council head] can give you this, only me.

[Someone's phone rings.]

When I'm speaking, please turn your phones off.

I have been fighting on your behalf, and the government has already agreed to raise MNREGA daily wages from one hundred eighty-four to five hundred rupees. It has also agreed to give you one hundred thousand rupees in unemployment benefits, and I will ensure that they no longer merely provide you with one hundred days' guaranteed work, but with work throughout the year. I've also asked them to give you five-*bigha* [five-eighths acre] plots of land and government jobs. All the Balmikis in town have government jobs,[2] and I'm going to get all of you government jobs. MNREGA government servants get pensions worth twenty thousand rupees per month, and since you are also government servants for one hundred days per year, I also want you to get pensions. I've asked the government to provide you with a pension of three thousand rupees per month. On the eleventh we will go to Delhi to reiterate all of these requests.

If you follow my commands, one or two hundred buses will leave [our town] for Delhi. Those of you who don't come will lose out, but those who come will obtain the fruit of their struggle. I am not a leader; I am a *sevadaar* [social worker] and can only give you five minutes now because the public is waiting for me. Why are they waiting? Because if a leader is straight, no one can corrupt him, regardless of whether the chief minister himself approaches him, and people trust him. Now elections are coming, and leaders will come to your villages and homes to ask for votes. But what have they done for you? Did they give you job cards? No, you're unemployed. Go and see if I have a large mansion like your elected leaders. No! The public is with me because I am its servant. I have no desire for votes; you can vote for whomever you want. You can vote for Congress or for the Akali Dal; it's up to you. I'm not interested in votes; I want to fight for your rights. And if YOU won't fight for your rights, what is the point of your life? You might as well just die. If you don't follow me, your elected leaders in their mansions will stop the MNREGA scheme, just as they have stopped subsidized grain rations and the BPL [below poverty line] scheme.

Your children are walking around barefoot; I'm fighting for them so that they can wear shoes and go to school and have a future. So vote for whomever you want, but follow me. Only yesterday the police beat four Bazigar youths in Bharowal Kalan. The four innocents were intercepted by drunken police officers and beaten for no reason. But within five minutes, five hundred

> of my MNREGA workers blocked the main highway that crossed the village and locked up the offending police officers in the local *thana*. When I turned up, the SHO [station house officer], ASI [assistant sub-inspector of police], DSP [district superintendent of police], and all the other police officers were waiting for me. I then took them to my office, where they sat with me for two hours and begged me to release the officers. It was all in the papers; you can check for yourselves.

Sukhbir Singh, the "association minister" (*sangatthan mantri*)—an invented title—of the Punjab MNREGA union, gave this speech in a village in February 2014 when he was mobilizing new union members in the wake of the upcoming national elections. Sukhbir, a.k.a. "the minister," is a self-appointed boss who has created a space for himself in the contemporary Punjab Mafia Raj by bluffing through the use of local repertoires of authority. His bluffing shows how faking it can have real effects and create liminal forms of authority.[3] The bluff challenges the boundaries between the real and the imaginary, between fiction and reality, and shows how fantasies of bossism are deeply entrenched and reproduced across India, and South Asia more broadly. Crucially, Sukhbir's story highlights the importance of theatrics and illusion in the "art of bossing."

Only a few weeks earlier before giving this speech, Sukhbir had declared himself to be the leader of the MNREGA union and broke his ties with his mentor, Khushwant Singh. Both accused each other of corruption and of leading supporters astray. Sukhbir accused Khushwant of stealing Rs. 200,000 of union funds. Khushwant accused Sukhbir of spending party funds on his mistress and collaborator Ravinder Bibi, of forcefully occupying the local premises of the MNREGA union, and of stealing Rs. 8,000 from people's membership fees, among other things.

Sukhbir and Khushwant set up the MNREGA union to ensure people's right to MNREGA work, but it was also clear that their organization was the means through which they could pursue their personal ambition to establish themselves as bosses. Like the other characters described in this book, both of them are representative of the ethos of the times: an ethos according to which political power, influence, and wealth were inseparable. Moreover, like the political entrepreneurs described by scholars such as Jeffrey and Gooptu, they used *jugad* (the art of making do) to gain respect, influence, and resources both for themselves and for their followers. Sukhbir and Khushwant used the language of MNREGA rights activism and characterized their struggle as one against the powerful and the corrupt that were depriving the poor of their right to MNREGA work, but the truth was that they worked with the system rather than against it. On the latter score they resembled the Dalit nongovernmental organization (NGO) boss in Andhra Pradesh who sought to secure benefits for himself and his followers by working the system rather than by challenging it.

As in Andhra Pradesh and unlike in Uttar Pradesh, Punjabi Dalits have not managed to secure power through a political party such as the Bahujan Samaj Party (BSP). The Dalit vote is split between the Congress Party, the BSP, and, increasingly, the Sikh nationalist Shiromani Akali Dal (SAD). Traditionally, Dalits tended to view the SAD as the party of Jat Sikh farmers (the dominant caste in Punjab) and tended to support the ostensibly more secular and pro-poor Congress Party. However, in recent years the SAD has increasingly sought to reach out to Dalits through welfare schemes as well as through ad hoc patronage. The party appears to have recognized that Dalits, who form roughly a third of the population of the state, have become increasingly assertive and their demands can no longer be ignored. Many Jats resent this, falsely claiming that the government works only for Dalits and that the Dalits now rule the Punjab, but the truth is that a class of wealthy Jat Sikhs continues to monopolize both politics and business throughout rural Punjab.

While Dalits and their leaders have not gained a meaningful share of power and have effectively been co-opted by the major parties, it is nevertheless the case that they have been pressing to obtain a larger share of government resources, albeit in a fragmented, piecemeal, and sometimes opportunistic manner, as can be seen in the case of this small MNREGA union. Sukhbir and Khushwant's main achievement was to have helped a few hundred Scheduled Caste (SC, official designation given to former untouchables castes in India) members of their union obtain wage labor from the government under the MNREGA scheme and of having done so in the face of opposition from members of the dominant caste of Jat cultivators (many of whom were opposed to the scheme because they claimed that it made laborers lazy by paying them too much for little or no work at all).

However, to gain political capital with their followers and senior politicians, both Sukhbir Singh and Khushwant Singh boasted far greater achievements and influence than they could possibly have achieved or exerted. In fact, the extent to which they had successfully established themselves as bosses was precisely due to their ability to embellish and exaggerate their achievements, as well as to their ability to improvise and entertain. Both of them falsely told their audiences that they had single-handedly raised MNREGA wages across India from Rs. 150 to Rs. 184 daily and promised that they would soon further raise these wages to Rs. 500 and eventually up to Rs. 1,000. Both also claimed to have contacts in high places—they said they knew Sonia Gandhi, Rahul Gandhi, Manmohan Singh, and Mayawati—but denied that the other had any such contacts.[4] Both also claimed to have influence over the local administration and the police. Moreover, to impress the authorities and senior party leaders (from both the ruling SAD and the opposition Congress Party) and to get their attention and support, they greatly exaggerated the number of their followers, frequently claiming to have fifty thousand followers across the entire Punjab, when there were in fact no more than about five hundred concentrated in a single district. When making speeches during rallies, Sukhbir sometimes got carried away and claimed that his was an "all India" and sometimes that it was an "all world" union.

Unlike BSP leaders in Uttar Pradesh,[5] Khushwant and Sukhbir did not spend much time decrying the evils of the caste system, nor was their political agenda significantly focused on issues of dignity.[6] Instead they focused on rights issues—somewhat like the Mazdoor Kisan Shakti Sangathan (MKSS) in Rajasthan and other similar rights-based organizations—and on how corrupt politicians were depriving the poor of their rights and state entitlements. Although all of their roughly five hundred followers were SCs, they frequently claimed to be working for all of the poor regardless of their caste. Despite claiming to fight poverty and corruption on the basis of rights, the focus of their activities was in fact very narrow and centered almost exclusively on ensuring that people could get enrolled onto the MNREGA scheme. The most obvious reason was that brokering MNREGA work was relatively easy to do with limited financial and political resources; all that it required was literacy and knowledge of MNREGA rules and bureaucratic procedures. However, I also argue that by narrowly focusing on the implementation of the MNREGA scheme, they avoided the antagonism that may have arisen had they addressed thornier issues about the distribution of political power or village resources. Had they, for example, focused on issues of SC political representation at the *panchayat* (village council) level or the capture of the village common lands (*shamlaat zameen*) by wealthy Jats, they would have been much more likely to have antagonized members of the local political and economic establishment and invited the possibility of harassment at the hands of *goondas* (criminals) or even the police. Finally, I further suggest the fact that powerful politicians and brokers in the area considered Sukhbir to be a buffoon—because of his outlandish claims and demands—actually worked in his favor because it prevented him from being seen as a significant threat. Entertainment has been an important anthropological trope "for examining contestations of social hierarchy in everyday life, particularly with respect to humor, joking, and laughter."[7] Here humor and comedic entertainment were central to understanding the minister's enactment and creation of personal sovereignty. Entertainment figures such as street performers, magicians, clowns, criminals, or jokers have often been analyzed as occupying liminal spaces. Such perspective helps us understand "the protective benefits of entertainment value: entertainers have license to disobey rules."[8] Such a "protective" shield is an important ingredient in "the Bluffer" art of bossing.

Like other SC leaders around India, both Sukhbir and Khushwant were middle class and had worked for the government. Both were Ravidasias.[9] Khushwant had been in the army and now lived on his pension, real estate investments, and the proceeds of his political enterprise. Sukhbir, however, had been a low-ranking police officer and had left the service for reasons I mention later, but Khushwant was smoother and worldlier, perhaps because during his time in the army he had traveled all around India and encountered people from a variety of backgrounds and regions. He was also clearly wealthier. When I called him to organize a meeting, he offered to come meet me wherever I was and quickly turned up at the main hotel in Tehsil X in a ten-year-old Mercedes. He made a point of showing me his car and told me that he frequently drove it to Delhi. When I asked him how he could afford it, he said that he had prospered thanks to real estate investments—much like other characters described in this book. Sukhbir had a motorcycle but no car, and his home was only slightly larger than that of the average SC. Nevertheless, Sukhbir presented himself as an influential and forceful boss. He frequently invoked his police background and acted in an authoritarian and commandeering manner, a style of bossing that he had probably acquired during his years in the Punjab police. Moreover, he made a point of always wearing immaculate and starched *kurta pyjamas*, sporting a gold watch, and showing off his large Samsung mobile phone. In the photograph that adorned the entry to his headquarters in town, he wore a black turban, had a black-and-white silk foulard around his neck, and sported an upturned mustache in the style of Sikh police officers and army men. However, he did not engage in spectacular forms of violence, and unlike most of the other characters in this book, he never committed a murder.

Khushwant came to meet me that day because he thought I might be a journalist and because he knew that I had spent time with Sukhbir, his ex-associate and now rival. He therefore wanted to let me know his version of why the MNREGA union had split in two. That was the only time I met him, but I quickly realized that although there were differences in style between him and Sukhbir, the substance of their claims and discourse was the same, and at times even identical. Both of them presented themselves as influential, forceful, and worldly bosses while claiming to reject the trappings of power and posing as Robin Hood–like figures fighting the rich and mighty on behalf of the poor.

Khushwant, with his white Mercedes, was by far the smoother operator. Sukhbir's face was scarred and his nose broken and flattened like that of a professional boxer. He had a gruff, husky voice and the commanding attitude of a police officer, but Khushwant had a gentle face and a soft voice. Khushwant was keen on differentiating himself from Sukhbir, whom he described as a poor and uneducated thug who knew and possessed anything only thanks to him. He said that Sukhbir did not even own a winter coat when he first met him; Khushwant had bought him one and then paid all of Sukhbir's household expenses for months on end to allow him to do social work for the poor. When I mentioned that Sukhbir claimed that he was about to meet Rahul Gandhi in Delhi, Khushwant scoffed. He said that he himself had met "Rahul Ji" on several occasions but that Sukhbir had no idea about how to go about setting up an appointment with him. He said that Sukhbir did not know that to meet Rajul Gandhi, you had to book an appointment at least three months in advance. When I mentioned that I found some of Sukhbir's demands somewhat unrealistic, Khushwant agreed enthusiastically, but it turned out that his own demands were almost identical and as equally unrealistic as Sukhbir's. He too demanded a raise in MNREGA wages to Rs. 1,000 per day, unemployment compensation worth hundreds of thousands of rupees, Rs. 3,000 monthly as a pension, and five-*bigha* housing plots.[10] Even the story he told about himself was similar to Sukhbir's; Khushwant claimed that he could have easily opted for a life of indolent luxury and lived in a large air-conditioned mansion like other politicians, but he had chosen instead to brave the heat and the dust for the sake of the poor and their children.

On that day in February when Sukhbir gave the speech quoted earlier, he was searching for new supporters because his rupture with Khushwant had deprived him of more than half of what he called "his MNREGA workers." Sukhbir also had to find new supporters because some *sarpanches* had barred him from entering their villages and some of his followers had withdrawn their support because of widespread corruption allegations against him. Moreover, despite what he claimed in the speech, he was cultivating a vote bank for the upcoming elections. In this too he followed in the footsteps of Khushwant, who was also known to have sold votes to different political parties in the past but claimed to have nothing to do with party politics because it was dirty.

Sukhbir frequently pointed out that the business of votes had more to do with money than with ideology. Voters sometimes received money for their votes, and the middlemen who delivered blocks of votes to more senior politicians got even more money. But those who made the most money were the politicians who received people's votes. Most people took it for granted that to make money and to lead a VIP lifestyle, it was necessary to enter politics and that politics was increasingly corrupt and even criminalized. I elaborate on this point and thereby provide some of the background context within which Sukhbir was operating. This will help illustrate how Sukhbir drew on the image of the more powerful bosses who governed the Punjab. So while he claimed that he was fighting the system on behalf of the poor, his acts clearly indicated that he was seeking to establish himself within the very system he claimed to be fighting.

Under the SAD government in power until 2017, both journalists and academics frequently commented on the growing link between politics, business, and crime in the Punjab, and people frequently described the state as being under Goonda Raj much like Bihar was under its former chief minister, Lalu Yadav Prasad. People were concerned about the state's flourishing drug trade; widespread land grabbing, popularly held to be operating thanks to the patronage of senior SAD politicians; but also land grabs and the extortion of businessmen by ruling SAD politicians. More broadly, Gill discerns a sociological trend under which politics and business have become more intertwined than ever.[11] His research shows that rural politicians are increasingly involved in the moneylending, fertilizer and pesticide, hospitality, and real estate businesses and argues that whereas people used to meet politicians in party offices or in their rural residences, they now tend to meet them in their hotels or their business premises in town. This trend, he argues, reflects broader changes in the Punjab economy: whereas agriculture accounted for 58 percent of the Punjab's GDP in 1971, it accounted for only 24 percent in 2011. The wealthy farmers from the dominant Jat caste who traditionally controlled rural politics in the state have increasingly moved to towns, where they run a variety of businesses, educate their children in private schools, and lead highly consumerist lifestyles—buying flat-screen TVs, Land Cruisers, modern kitchen appliances, designer clothes, and the latest mobile phones. Because a farming income alone cannot sustain these levels of consumption, they have become involved in both business and politics. This is a trend that we have witnessed in all the sites where we conducted research for this book.

Gill, among others, indicates that the merging of politics and business (and crime) inevitably results in a conflict of interest whereby it is increasingly unclear whether politicians are furthering public interests or their own private business interests. This issue is widely discussed with reference to state-level political leaders, but it is equally relevant to political leaders lower down the ladder and even to small-time brokers like Sukhbir Singh and Khushwant Singh. At the very top we find that Sukhbir Badal's (the deputy chief minister and son of the chief minister) declared personal assets had risen from US$2.1 million in 2004 to US$16 million, but people suspect that this is nowhere close to the total of his undeclared assets. The word on the street is that Sukhbir Badal is competing to become richer than Mukesh Ambani, and there are rumors that, besides his substantial business interests in Punjab, he owns tens of thousands of acres in New Zealand. What is clear is that Sukhbir Badal, his sister, and his in-laws all have substantial stakes in the power, transport, hotel, and media sectors. More than half of the licenses for air-conditioned buses in the state belong to the Badal family, and Sukhbir Badal's sister has major stakes in a company that won a number of contracts from state-owned power enterprises. Sukhbir Badal also owns most major TV channels in the state, and he used them while in power to broadcast positive news about his government's performance.

The head of the constituency that I studied was likewise a phenomenally wealthy politician. He had family ties and significant business interests in the Punjab and North America. His elder brother owned hundreds of gas stations in the United States, and he owned, among other things, a lot of real estate and agricultural land, a flourishing mushroom business, and a successful IT company in Patiala. He even claimed to own a private jet, but I was never able to confirm whether this was true. Although not everyone had seen his private jet, almost everyone had seen his palatial four-story home equipped with elevators and a large underground parking lot housing a fleet of Mercedes and SUVs. Many of my informants exaggeratedly claimed that he was so rich that he had been able to spend Rs. 15 billion on his electoral campaign in 2012.

Of course, there is nothing new about the fact that politicians sometimes blur the line between public and private interests. What is probably new is the extent to which this is happening and that politicians openly pursue and flaunt riches, and also the extent to which they are either directly or indirectly involved in criminal activities. The image that most ordinary people now have of politicians, one that is propagated in Punjabi films, is of people with extraordinary wealth who live in vast mansions, travel in Mercedes with special license plates and flashing lights on top, and are escorted by armed police guards. What people most resent is that these politicians can get ahead by ignoring the rules that apply to ordinary mortals. Most emblematic of this, perhaps because it is most visible, is the fact that they use their flashing lights, special license plates, and police escorts to push traffic aside. Anyone who travels frequently in the Punjab has at some point been forced to make way, often aggressively, for the escorted convoy of some high-ranking politician or official. But this VIP culture is not restricted to senior politicians and has seeped its way into society so that low-ranking officers, village-level politicians, and even party thugs are also increasingly using special license plates and flashing lights to get ahead.

Of course, politicians and bureaucrats also get ahead of others in ways that are arguably far more damaging to public interests than jumping traffic. Most obvious is their widely reported use of political influence to gain government contracts and licenses, but also to steal public money, make land grabs, and traffic in drugs. According to statistics, 17 percent of provincial politicians in the Punjab have criminal records. Most notably, there are serious allegations that leading politicians in both the ruling SAD and the opposition Congress Party are involved in land grabbing, extortion rackets, and the state's flourishing trade in opiates. But this trend has also spread far beyond the leadership and has led to widespread concerns about the gangsterization of Punjabi culture, a trend popularly held to be discernible in Punjabi music videos in which young men dressed in leather jackets carry guns and drink in glamorous nightclubs with scantily clad women. Largely thanks to the patronage of higher-level politicians, *goondas* have thrived throughout the Punjab, and their numbers have allegedly increased. It is widely claimed, for example, that in the past there was one *goonda* in every *mohalla* (neighborhood) of every town, but now there are four. Between 2013 and 2014—during fieldwork—most people blamed these developments on the then ruling Shiromani Akali Dal. In Tehsil X, for example, the leading *goonda* was known to be closely associated with top-ranking SAD politicians in the state. This young man was called Gurbachan, was in his early thirties, and was granted impunity to operate a gambling den, traffic drugs, and capture disputed properties in exchange for doing the party's dirty work. The latter included distributing cash, alcohol, and drugs during elections; forcefully capturing polling booths; and threatening members of opposition political parties. Gurbachan could carry out all of these activities because the local MLA (Member of Legislative Assembly) had allegedly given the police clear instructions not to interfere with his activities.

Moreover, MLAs affiliated with SAD used the police to intimidate and harass political opponents. At the village level politicians used the police to file fake charges against the opponents of their local brokers, as well as against insubordinate villagers. SCs, as I have illustrated elsewhere,[12] were particularly vulnerable to such abuses of power and could easily be cowed into submission and prevented from exerting meaningful power at the *panchayat* level.

While these developments gave rise to widespread popular unease and fueled the rise of the anticorruption Aam Admi Party (AAP) in the state, it is interesting to note that people often seemed to both envy and admire powerful and wealthy politicians. Often in the very same breath that people from Tehsil X criticized the head of their constituency for corruption and high-handedness, they admiringly discussed the size of his residence, the number of expensive cars he owned, the vast sums of money that he spent on the 2012 MLA elections, his ability to bend rules and break laws on behalf of supporters, and even the cunning and power that he used to rig elections and harass and silence opponents. What both Sukhbir Singh and Khushwant Singh said and did clearly reflected this contradiction: they critiqued power and wealth as much as they sought and flaunted them by imitating the powerful.

Sukhbir was now in his late forties and had been doing *seva* (social work) for the ten years since he had left his police post. He had entered the force during the insurgency when recruitment was at its highest, but he claimed that he left of his own accord to do *seva*. People in his village gave a different account: they claimed that he was discharged because he frequently failed to show up for work and spent his time drinking and frequenting "loose" women. But he claimed, with great pathos, that he had left because he could not live in a world where small children went hungry. During rallies he often repeated this claim: he would point to children in the audience and say that he had given up a potentially lucrative career in the police so that children like them would not go to bed hungry and could get an education and have a future. He said that he could easily have lived like a VIP, traveling in expensive cars, resting in air-conditioned rooms, and rubbing shoulders with the powerful, but he had chosen instead to stay loyal to the common man (*aam admi*) and to work long hours regardless of the heat and dust.

But what exactly was the nature of Sukhbir's work, and how did he command people's allegiance? Sukhbir claimed that his work was to assist the poor and needy in all aspects of their lives, but his main focus was far more specific. Sukhbir's union was ostensibly set up to ensure that members of the SC obtained the one hundred days' work to which the government entitled them and that they were paid for it. But the union also helped him earn a comfortable livelihood and offered the prospect of political power and prestige.

As elsewhere throughout India, farmers were opposed to the MNREGA scheme because they claimed it raised the cost of labor by reducing its supply. Most Jat farmers also opposed it because they claimed that it failed to produce anything of value, but also because it made SCs even "lazier" than they already allegedly were. Why, they asked rhetorically, should SCs work in our fields if they can obtain Rs. 184 for doing nothing? So Jat farmers frequently failed to implement the MNREGA scheme and were able to do so because they generally controlled elected *panchayats*. In most cases, Jat *sarpanches* could afford to merely ignore the scheme's existence because many SCs appeared not to be aware of the exact procedures of how to enroll in it. But I also heard of cases in which Jat-dominated *panchayats* actively opposed the MNREGA scheme and refused to implement it despite SC demands. Members of the union often claimed that Jats refused to implement the scheme so that SCs would continue sweeping cow dung for them and so that wealthy Jat farmers could continue lending money to them with interest.

When *panchayats* did make the effort to run the MNREGA scheme, they sometimes did so to derive political and monetary benefits. Sukhbir and Khushwant told me that in the brief period before direct bank payments to MNREGA workers were instituted, *sarpanches* used to steal a significant proportion of the MNREGA funds in their care. With the advent of direct bank payments this was no longer possible, and *sarpanches* allegedly had even less reason to implement the scheme, but they nevertheless found new ways to exploit it. SCs in several villages told me that *sarpanches* and their close associates placed only factional supporters on the MNREGA muster roll, and some even put their farm servants on it to save money on wages. Others told me that *sarpanches* would sign them up only if they agreed to pay the *sarpanches* half the money that had been disbursed into their bank accounts. In other cases, the deal was that the *sarpanch* would get half the money in exchange for listing MNREGA workers as present when they were in fact working elsewhere or at home resting. One Jat *sarpanch* explained that his rival, the ex-*sarpanch*, would accompany MNREGA workers to the bank and then directly collect his dues from them.

Unlike the Jats, the landless laborers who were predominantly SC greatly appreciated the MNREGA work scheme and were therefore receptive to Sukhbir when he not only offered to enroll them but also to fight abuse and corruption in the scheme and extend its scope and depth. They appreciated the scheme because it helped them earn money during periods of low demand for labor, it allowed women and the elderly to make some money, and it offered what was regarded as easy work. Moreover, elderly men and women who could no longer do heavy labor could often do MNREGA work because it tended to be comparatively light. In most cases, MNREGA workers cleared weeds and leveled short stretches of country roads, and the pace of work was often leisurely. Those in charge of checking work progress often did not take their duties very seriously, if at all, and workers could take long rests and even abscond.

Most of Sukhbir's claims about what he had done and could do for people were at best open to doubt, but the one thing he could truly take credit for was his ability to obtain MNREGA work for people. Sukhbir possessed the basic knowledge of the MNREGA scheme necessary to help people obtain job cards. *Sarpanches*, for reasons outlined earlier, were not inclined to tell villagers about what the scheme entitled them to or to help them do the substantial paperwork necessary to obtain these entitlements. Moreover, some *sarpanches* made access to MNREGA work contingent on political loyalty and support. Sukhbir, once he had collected the Rs. 200 membership fee, helped people fill out the forms and open the bank accounts necessary for enrollment on the MNREGA scheme; and when *sarpanches* refused to place people on the MNREGA worker list, he organized rallies in front of the Tehsil X headquarters, or blocked roads, until the block development officer (BDO) approved his proposed list of MNREGA workers. In villages with deep factional rifts, this frequently resulted in two separate groups of MNREGA workers doing different types of work: the *sarpanch*'s group and the one organized by Sukhbir Singh, sometimes with the cooperation of the rival village faction.

But Sukhbir also used his basic literacy and knowledge of MNREGA rules, procedures, and institutions to exploit less knowledgeable villagers. Sukhbir kept trying to impress people with his extensive knowledge and use of official documents; he was often successful because he worked with SCs who had only the basic rudiments of literacy and who therefore sometimes tended to regard the written word with mystical reverence. On the day of his village tour and during many of his rallies, Sukhbir told people that he knew things about the MNREGA scheme that even the BDO did not know because he had carefully studied all the official documents relating to it. When I went to his house, he showed me a large pile of papers and books and told me that he had memorized everything they contained. When I went to his office, he sought to impress by me showing me a signed document that nominated him as the head of the union for the whole Punjab. The document was allegedly written and signed by a Delhi-based SC leader named Archna Singh, whom Sukhbir described as being like Mayawati's little sister in terms of power, but on closer inspection I realized that it had probably been produced by Sukhbir himself. The text was written in Punjabi, was full of grammatical errors, and turned out to have been signed by Sukhbir and his female collaborator, Desa Rani.

Sukhbir frequently used documents to hoodwink people into believing in his influence and ability to sort things out for them. One person from his village claimed that in his attempt to obtain followers, Sukhbir had given a widowed SC woman a sealed envelope with a document that he claimed entitled her to a five-*marla* plot of land and told her to keep it safe and sealed in the envelope. The illiterate widow believed Sukhbir, and it was only when someone decided to open the envelope and look at its contents that she realized she had been fooled: the document was a handwritten note, probably written by Sukhbir himself. This may have been a malicious fabrication to discredit Sukhbir, but even if it were, it did highlight something central to his way of operating. During the speech quoted earlier, Sukhbir showed people a "signed" document that entitled people to five years' worth of unemployment benefits for all the time that the Punjab government had failed to run the MNREGA scheme. When someone in the crowd asked to see it, he handed it over, but seconds later asked the person to return it because he wanted everyone to pay attention to what he was about to say. Suspecting some trick, my assistant managed to get hold of the document while Sukhbir was distracted and saw that it was a random document that had nothing to do with MNREGA unemployment benefits.

To impress followers and gain their allegiance, Sukhbir also boasted improbable contacts at the highest levels of national government. However, he rarely claimed high-level contacts in the Punjab government, perhaps because he thought that national leaders sounded more impressive to his followers, but also perhaps because locals were keenly aware of who had connections with which politicians and could have more easily verified whether his claims were true than with high-level politicians in distant Delhi. As in his speech, Sukhbir frequently claimed to know Rahul Gandhi and to even be on friendly terms with him. To drive the point home, he often referred to him intimately as "Rahul Ji." Likewise, he claimed to know Sonia Gandhi and during speeches even suggested that he was on terms of friendly banter with Manmohan Singh. Once, when he was organizing a rally in Delhi, he asked his followers, in a humorous tone, not to spend their time in Delhi getting drunk, smoking bidis, and eating *kulchas* (veggie burgers) on the street. He claimed that during their previous Delhi rally he had gone to see "Manmohan Ji," who had allegedly agreed to raise MNREGA wages to Rs. 500 a day and to compensate people for all the time when the scheme had not been implemented. Sukhbir then claimed that as he was preparing to leave, Manmohan Ji tapped him on the shoulder and said that there was one more thing he needed to say. He explained that he believed Sukhbir when he said that there was poverty in the Punjab, but he had seen his followers eating *kulchas* and smoking cigarettes on the street, and people might easily be led to believe that Punjabi SCs were not in fact poor. Manmohan Ji concluded that if Sukhbir wanted people to take his demands seriously, he should tell his followers to abstain from alcohol, bidis, and *kulchas*.

Sukhbir almost certainly never met Manmohan Singh and, as one of his ex-associates told me, just popped into a hotel to have some food and then returned claiming to have spent an hour with him. The point of his story was to impress followers into believing that he was powerful because he had high-ranking contacts and he was therefore in a position to help them, to amuse them with a funny anecdote, but also to ensure that they were on their best behavior since they would be lodging at the main Delhi Gurudwara, a place where they could eat and sleep for free but where smoking and drinking were strictly forbidden.

I did not have the chance to join Sukhbir and his followers on one of these Delhi excursions, and I never quite managed to figure out whether these rallies achieved anything. Sukhbir and his associates told me that they used the occasions to press their demands before Parliament and that Sukhbir also used them to meet the Congress leadership and high-ranking SC leaders. He showed me pictures of him in Delhi with an SC leader, Archna Singh—the one who was a slightly less powerful version of Mayawati—but an Internet search produced no significant entries under her name.

Given the highly unrealistic nature of Sukhbir Singh's demands, it is unsurprising that Sukhbir Singh's rallies and "meetings" in Delhi never achieved their stated objectives. It was, for example, highly improbable that the government would pay all his followers Rs. 100,000 in unemployment benefits for all the years that the MNREGA scheme had not operated; would raise MNREGA payments from Rs. 184 to Rs. 500 daily; would provide MNREGA work year-round; would provide everyone with five-*bigha* plots; and would give everyone government jobs with pensions worth Rs. 20,000 per month.

It is unclear to me what these rallies achieved and why they actually took place. One of Sukhbir's many detractors claimed that they were an excuse for Sukhbir and his associates to travel and have some fun but that it was also a moneymaking scam. The allegation was that Sukhbir took a Rs. 20 commission for every passenger who went to

Delhi. With an average of four hundred passengers on each of these trips, Sukhbir therefore made some Rs. 8,000. Sukhbir, with his usual hyperbole, claimed that "one or two hundred" buses left Tehsil X for Delhi on these occasions.

Although Sukhbir usually boasted high-level connections in Delhi, he did occasionally claim connections with some local leaders and officials. A picture of him with the main local gangster (Gurbachan) adorned one of the walls in his office, and he claimed to know the local SHO and the BDO, and that these two even feared him. They feared him because "they knew" he commanded a vast army of followers who could paralyze all of Punjab if they did not concede to his demands or if they were abusive toward any poor person.

Sukhbir sometimes tried to take credit for protests that he had done nothing to organize. In his speech, for example, he claimed credit for unrest in a village that lay on the main highway to Delhi and encouraged people to take a look at the newspapers if they needed evidence. He perhaps knew that no one would bother looking for these old newspapers. Anyone who did would indeed have found evidence of unrest in that particular village but would not have found any mention of Sukhbir Singh and his Ambedkar union. Villagers claimed that the root of that particular incident of unrest had been that two drunken police officers had randomly abused and beaten two Bazigar-caste youths who had done nothing wrong;[13] they were simply making their way home from work on a construction site one evening. The police admitted to having made a mistake but claimed to have beaten the young men because the Crime Investigation Department (CID) had informed them that some dacoits armed with weapons were traveling around the area on a motorcycle. They had mistaken the young Bazigars for these dacoits because they were carrying long steel rods that the police thought were weapons but were in fact construction materials. Subsequently, when village Bazigars heard that the police were beating up members of their community, they stormed the police station located in the village, captured the offending police officers, locked them up in a room, and protested against police presence in their village by blocking the main road from Tehsil X to Delhi.

The Bazigars in question told me that they had always been opposed to the police presence in their village, but this event had been the last straw. They were angry because the police had transformed their community *dharamsala* (religious rest house) into a police station against their wishes, and from the time of their arrival the police officers had been abusive toward members of their community and had demanded free milk and *lassi* from them on a daily basis. The Bazigars were also angry with the Jats who dominated the *panchayat* because they had handed over the Bazigar *dharamsala* over to the police and not their own *dharamsala*, which they managed to keep for themselves. That day, after locking up the offending police officers and blocking the main highway to Delhi, the Bazigars not only demanded that charges be filed against the officers but also that the police station be removed from their village.

According to Sukhbir, however, the protest had erupted under his command. That day I happened to visit the union's headquarters as the roadblock was already under way and the police officers were locked up in the *dharamsala*. Sukhbir told me that his workers had blocked the highway, and he had called "one of his workers" in the village and ordered him not take any further action until he received orders from him. Sukhbir did this in front of roughly twenty union members and myself. After that he pretended to phone the deputy inspector general of police (DIG) in Patiala and spoke to him on intimate terms, using his first name; Sukhbir told him that he would try to keep the protests under control, but he wanted assurances that the police officers would be charged for their offenses and that the police station would be removed from the village. While he was doing this, I noticed one of his closest associates winking and smiling at another. Sukhbir subsequently turned to the assembled members and told them that if the police lifted a single finger against one of his followers, fifty thousand protesters would start throwing stones at them.

When I subsequently joined Sukhbir to witness the unrest firsthand, I quickly realized that he had played absolutely no part in the protests. Neither the protesters nor the police even took note of him, and he quickly disappeared into the crowd. When he reappeared and took me back to town on his motorcycle, he asked me whether I had noticed how much people respected him and, without waiting for an answer, went on to say that I had finally seen what Sukhbir Singh was capable of. A couple of days later, when he gave the speech quoted earlier, he claimed that the SHO, the ASI, and the DSP had all been waiting for him where the protests had erupted and had subsequently accompanied him to his office, where they had sat begging him to release the officers. Sukhbir claimed that he had consented to release the policemen only once the senior officers had agreed to place charges against them and to immediately remove the police station from the village. A month later, when I went to make further investigations, people told me that no charges had been placed against the officers, and the police station was still in the village.

Finally, just as Sukhbir sought to impress his power and influence on his SC followers, he likewise sought to pressure bureaucrats and impress political leaders with the number of his followers. This not only allowed him to press demands on bureaucrats but also to obtain money from politicians for the delivery of a block of votes during elections. As previously indicated, the demands articulated during these rallies were frequently unrealistic, but they did gain him publicity and attention from politicians and officials. When, for example, Sukhbir Singh and three hundred of his supporters blocked the main highway to Delhi to protest against the BDO for allegedly failing to enroll some people onto the MNREGA scheme and for not paying some who were enrolled, Sukhbir managed to get the local BDO and the *tehsildar* (revenue officer) to come and discuss things with him and had the entire event published in the local Punjabi-language newspapers. The fact that the BDO and the *tehsildar* had to come and meet him was an achievement and a show of power on its own, since ordinary people normally have to stand in line to meet such notables.

After they turned up, Sukhbir negotiated with them for about half an hour and then returned to his assembled followers and victoriously declared that they had conceded to his demands. As usual, he was exaggerating, and many people never received their MNREGA money, but he did manage to get the BDO to enroll a number of people in the scheme. When I later asked some local politicians about why officials who knew about Sukhbir's antics conceded to some of his demands, they told me that they were worried about negative publicity. The BDO, for example, did not want Sukhbir Singh's accusations against him published in newspapers. During the roadblock, Sukhbir accused him of stealing people's MNREGA money and then got his followers to repeatedly chant "Death to the BDO; long live the MNREGA union; long live Sukhbir Singh" (*BDO murdabad; MNREGA Union Zindabad; Sukhbir Singh Zindabad*).

I later learned that the BDO would have had good reason to be nervous about these public accusations because he was involved in a scam that eventually cost him his job. When I first met him and asked him about Sukhbir Singh, he told me that people "like him" were troublemakers and blackmailers. He then went on to tell me that he was implementing the MNREGA scheme and that the minister of rural development had made him spend all of the MNREGA money on labor and none on materials. He said that the SAD was doing this to employ as many people as possible to maximize its chances in the forthcoming 2014 national elections. Later, shortly after I left the field, newspapers reported that he had been suspended as a result of investigations that confirmed that he had submitted fake invoices for MNREGA materials that were never used. It is worth noting that prior to this, the *sarpanch* in Sukhbir's home village had told me that he had reason to believe that Sukhbir was in fact putting pressure on the BDO to get a share of the MNREGA money he was stealing. However, the *sarpanch* never told me what evidence he had for his claim and merely told me that he had his sources. If true, however, it might explain why the BDO referred to Sukhbir as a blackmailer.

Sukhbir's frequent rallies and the publicity they generated also managed to bring him to the attention of political party leaders. As his earlier speech indicates, Sukhbir was very keen to distance himself from political parties in front of his supporters because his SC audience took it for granted that political parties were corrupt and rarely fulfilled their promises. However, only two weeks later Sukhbir was urging his followers to vote for the Congress Party, and he held a rally for ex-Congress leader Captain Amarinder's son in front of his office. So how did Sukhbir justify this to his followers after all he had said in his speeches? Before Captain Amarinder's son arrived that day, Sukhbir told the crowd of roughly two hundred people that he did not support either the Congress Party or the SAD, but voting for the Congress Party would be voting for the lesser evil. Both parties, he said, were equally rotten, but at least the Congress Party occasionally did something for the poor. A Congress Party leader from Sukhbir's village subsequently claimed that the real reason why Sukhbir had decided to mobilize the Congress vote was that he had been offered Rs. 600,000 for his bloc of votes, which Sukhbir claimed to consist of several thousand people. People claimed that Sukhbir had initially tried to get the attention of local SAD leaders, including Gurbachan, but they had not thought it worth their while to invest in him.

It is unlikely that Sukhbir Singh managed to garner more than five hundred votes. The Punjab Congress Party leadership was probably aware of this, but, as I was told, every vote counts. Moreover, as the same Congress leader told me, it was better to keep very vocal people like Sukhbir Singh on your side because they could create a great deal of negative propaganda if they were against you.

Sukhbir told me that he had contested the provincial elections in 2012, and admitted in an off-guard moment during which he was inadvertently frank, having received no more than about five hundred votes. As is the case with other bosses described in this chapter, the point was not to win elections but to demonstrate his control and ability to deliver a certain number of votes and to establish his personal sovereignty by gaining publicity. I was unable to obtain a clear account of what exactly had taken place in 2012, but it seems plausible to assume that his five hundred or so votes caught the attention of at least some local politicians and subsequently contributed to allowing him to trade his votes for money in 2014. It also arguably gave him a public platform with which to gain an audience among the general public.

Sukhbir's case illustrates an ethos according to which bosses need to wield and project their authority if they are to be credible players.

Lacking substantial economic means, political contacts, and followers, Sukhbir greatly exaggerated the extent of his personal sovereignty. Thus, he was able to convince at least some people that he was worth following and to convince local- and state-level power brokers that he was a force to be reckoned with, or at the very least a political force that could not be completely ignored. However, his authority was extremely tenuous because it was constructed on a fragile edifice of half-truths and bluffs. By 2014, it was far from clear whether Sukhbir was ever going to gain more authority. Sukhbir had detractors who felt that he was corrupt and led people astray, and he had lost a number of followers as a result of his break with Khushwant. Nevertheless, he was resourceful and skilled at improvising and kept moving on to find new supporters. After the breakup, he even moved on to do *seva* in villages near the border with Haryana.

Sukhbir was clearly aware of the limits of his capacity to boss and was in fact cautious when dealing with the authorities. Unlike most of the other bosses described in this book and others in Tehsil X where I did my fieldwork, Sukhbir had not committed murder or any other significant act of violence. The case of Gurbachan, the main *goonda* in Tehsil X, indicates that only those with clear political support in high places could exert violence with impunity. Despite his running gambling dens, capturing disputed properties, randomly beating up people in the streets because he did not like how they had looked at him, and even murdering a debtor, lawyers in Tehsil X claimed that Gurbachan did not have a single police case against him. They claimed that in exchange for his services, the head of the constituency had effectively granted him impunity from the police.

Sukhbir had no such impunity and therefore merely boasted a capacity for violence. He claimed that if the police raised a single finger against one of his followers, fifty thousand people would immediately start pelting the local police station with stones. However, he had no more than five hundred followers, and none of them ever threw stones at anything. During the roadblock, Sukhbir had told his followers not to let anyone through and to beat anyone who attempted to do so. However, when a number of motorcyclists did try to get through, he let them pass without any hassle. This is not to say that Sukhbir did not get into any trouble with the authorities: his roadblock did after all land him a First Information Report (FIR). Nevertheless, he did know that he could not afford to engage in excessive violence because he did not have the protection necessary to escape police action or harassment.

In fact it is also arguably the case that his unrealistic claims and demands were a way for him not to appear too threatening. To most local politicians and bureaucrats, Sukhbir Singh was a somewhat comical figure they did not take too seriously and whom they did not feel posed a significant threat to their interests. In addition to being unrealistic, his demands were largely limited to issues surrounding the implementation of the MNREGA scheme. He did not, for example, address the broader structural issues of caste and class dominance keeping SCs politically and economically subordinated. Other than obliquely, Sukhbir Singh did not question elite dominance over village *panchayats*, and he never raised the issue of the capture of the village commons by prosperous farmer businessmen.[14] Had he addressed these issues, it is far more likely that that the latter would have taken some form of action to stop him by, for example, having the police file fake police charges against him. In two villages that I visited, SCs who sought to assert themselves in *panchayats* were threatened with the possibility of fake police charges and subsequently desisted from trying to assert themselves. Sukhbir avoided this fate by posing as a somewhat comical figure and by keeping the scope of his demands narrow.[15] This indicates that he had no intention of overturning the system, what he sought was to become a part of it and to get a share of "the pie." In other words, although he drew on the language of social justice and the fight against the rich and powerful—like the other characters described in this book—and he did bring some benefits to his followers, he was also a political entrepreneur seeking to join the ranks of the very same people he decried.

CHAPTER 4

THE HENCHMAN

David Picherit

THREE DAYS to get an administrative document—a basic map of electoral wards—is not unusual. On my way back from the Mandal Parishad Development Office, I meet Kondappa proudly driving his bike. Hardly surprised by my lack of bureaucratic experience, he accompanies me back to the office. He stays outside and pushes me back to the main desk where three men sit looking down their noses at everyone who walks in. No one pays any attention to me. I finally ask a question and the employee replies rudely. Kondappa, who was waiting in the corridor, furiously enters the office. He rushes in, shouts, and smacks the three men's necks, "Get up! Give a seat." Surprised and panicking, the three men start to compete to give us a chair, addressing Kondappa as "sir." Kondappa turns with his most furious glance to the public officer and orders him to give me the papers. His reply only exacerbates Kondappa's fury, who shouts the name of his boss and threatens to beat him up. The employee stands up again, but Kondappa hits the desk and orders him to sit down: "I am an elected Dalit leader; I know where you live. I am coming back in two hours. This is democracy! He is here to get public information. Useless bastards; I will make you do your work."

The room falls silent. Nobody knows where to look and tries to avoid eye contact by looking at the rotating fan. Kondappa addresses another officer, a smartly dressed woman, about the lack of initiative. She simply replies, "I am the daughter of S. Reddy." Kondappa immediately changes his tone and speaks kindly to her, "Madam, I know your father; he is a very gentle man. My name is Kondappa. Madam, please give him my greetings." He glances over at the employee and we leave. "You should not come here alone. Next time you ask me first; I'll call and they'll come to us. In their offices they behave like kings." Two hours later, the paperwork was ready. Over the coming weeks, I felt compelled to acknowledge his power in front of his friends. "I have to be rude; otherwise nobody will do the work. This is a democracy, but you have to use violence to get any document. You're lucky I am a boss. Dalits usually have to struggle to get a small piece of paper," explains Kondappa. He did, however, omit a crucial point: he knew that everybody knew he was the henchman of a famous local faction boss, G. M. Reddy (GMR). Three-time losing candidate in the last MLA (Member of the Legislative Assembly) elections, GMR is a major industrialist in the town and son of a Naxalite (Maoist guerrilla) and a faction leader. Well known for dedicating his life to the Dalits' cause, Kondappa is also respected for his long-term loyalty to GMR: his authority and confidence derive from this relationship.

Using (the threat of) violence in the name of both democracy and the Dalits' struggle points at the specificities of being a Dalit henchman in the factionalized politics of South India. What does it mean to be a henchman and an aspiring boss in Andhra Pradesh today? What is Kondappa's sphere of power, and how does it relate to his boss's power? Central to bossism systems of governance and their extortive nature is the role of the henchmen. However, the role of these figures and, more crucially, their relation with their bosses are often neglected and unproblematized by overestimating the obedience and loyalty of the henchmen. This contrasts with the dynamic and contested positions, roles, representations, and practices of henchmen across spaces and times in Indian history and also within the everyday life of local power relations. The terms of the relations between henchmen and bosses are never fixed but rather are fluid and shift according to power relations shaped by caste, kinship, class, political party, and/or religious affiliations, as well as to the uncertain aspirations and opportunities of the henchmen themselves. As is "boss," "henchman" is a loose category whose practices and representations are continuously reformulated and contested within specific sociocultural and historical contexts. Therefore, Kondappa might embody only few of the multiple facets of henchmen across South Asia. He juggles his roles as a loyal henchman to an upper-caste boss and as a local Dalit boss; he builds his own agenda and personal sovereignty within the contested limits of his affiliation to this upper-caste boss. It is precisely this "juggling" that is at the core of the story I am about to tell: a story that will allow us to further explore the "art of bossing" across South Asia in all its contingent, insecure, and opportunistic dimensions.

Rayalaseema, a four-district region of South Andhra Pradesh, provides a fascinating case study of violent local faction politics turning into a mafia system of economic and political accumulation through licensed and unlicensed violence. In Rayalaseema, faction bosses historically rule over particular territories. The colonial delegation of administrative, juridical, and political power helped the formation of bosses-cum-landlords. In the second half of the twentieth century, Reddys and Kammas—landowner castes—have benefited from the green revolution to take the lead in business activities and form political factions to establish their dominance over the democratic system. While the Congress Party has historically been controlled by Reddys, many Kammas established themselves in the Communist Party in the 1960s. Other Kammas engaged with the Naxalite movement to counter faction leaders and establish their own factions.[1] In the 1980s, the rise of a Kamma political party, the Telugu Desam Party (TDP), reinforced violent fights between political factions that continue today. This factionalism strongly shapes the local imagination and legitimization of contemporary bossism. Political and economic factions are also a key ingredient of the fictionalized fantasies of power sustained by Telugu cinema. In such narratives factionalism has long been presented as a traditional culture of violence and power embedded in the local sociocultural milieu, sometimes as an exceptional zone in Indian democracy and capitalism.

However, the contemporary modes of governance signal that in reality today's factionalism has had to adjust to agrarian changes, neoliberal policies, and economic globalization. The new economic opportunities, the rise of lower castes, and the decline of old forms of patronage have fostered the emergence of new bosses through economic and political violence and reformulated political clientelism between them, their henchmen, and the population. In this process, the Reddy and Kamma bosses of Rayalaseema have continued to honor their reputation as powerful leaders: Between 1982 and 2014 (when united Andhra Pradesh was separated from Telangana), eight of the twelve chief ministers of Andhra Pradesh were from this region, but the accumulation of economic and political power by "modern" faction bosses nowadays arises from investments offered by land speculation and estate development, mining contracting, construction industries, granite quarries, and wood trafficking. Those businesses are grounded in internal and intimate relations with the state and politics.

The perpetuation of the Reddy and Kamma stronghold did not mean the social reproduction of dynasties of faction leaders. A large number of new bosses emerged from small peasant families of Reddy and Kamma castes in the 1990s. An iconic boss from Chittoor district is C. K. Babu, known as the "Tiger of Chittoor." Babu (a Reddy) was elected five times as MLA in Chittoor. He built his authority and political career on allegations of murder, kidnapping, and racketeering. Rumors of his violent style consolidated his reputation as a boss who had control over the state, the police, and the judges and hence gave him impunity. He is believed to kidnap civil servants who do not follow his rules; be involved in major land grabbing; take a percentage on every factory and shop; and inspire fear among police (unable to enforce warrants against him). In 2003, to defend the honor of his nephew, who was insulted in a bar, he rushed to the place and burnt the young son of his TDP opponents alive (he was acquitted in 2005). Bosses like Babu showed that violence could be effectively used to marginalize the old faction-type leaders. His fearless and unconventional "political" methods were admired by the local Dalit population. He is known for never bowing to ministers and other politicians.

Other figures have clawed their way to the top, such as Adikesavulu Naidu, "the liquor baron," who started as a worker in a sugar factory (a factory he bought years later) and later built a huge industrial empire in South India. A Chittoor Member of Parliament (MP representing TDP, then Congress in 2008), he also became head of the Tirumala Tirupathi Devasthanam (TTD)—one of the world's wealthiest temples—and developed his empire, including private hospitals and colleges as well as real estate in Bangalore. More famous is the well-documented story of the Reddy brothers, sons of a police constable in Chittoor, who became the most famous mafia mining dons of India in the 2000s and politicians in the neighboring state of Karnataka.[2]

Such figures who made fortunes and reached power in a short time through violence and money have deeply shaped the imagination of power and local politics. But it was not only this style of bossism that challenged faction politics; in the same period, as in Uttar Pradesh,[3] the rise of low castes has considerably changed the political landscape. Since the 1980s, Dalits have organized through unions, movements, networks, and nongovernmental organizations (NGOs) in South India.[4] In Chittoor, Dalit mobilization has been intense,[5] and it is against this wider background that we should look at the rise of Dalit henchmen like Kondappa. These movements responded partly to caste atrocities perpetrated by Kammas and Reddys but also to their marginalization within political parties and movements like the Naxalites. Dalit organizations had diverse ideological, financial, and organizational perspectives on how to shape and promote the Dalit agenda. Using violence and/or elections, promoting caste and/or class perspective, restricting leadership to Dalits or to others were widely debated issues. It hardly resolved the divisions between Malas and Madigas (the main castes among Dalits), who finally launched their own caste-based movements in the 1990s. This process did not translate into a Dalit or caste-based political party like the Bahujan Samaj Party (BSP) in North India: Madigas and Malas followed leading political parties without accessing leading positions. Whatever the failures, Dalit organizations have fostered the self-confidence of Dalits and the emergence of leaders.[6] Long caricatured as brutal followers only vertically incorporated into political factions, Dalits have contested this dominant perception of factionalism to promote social ties among Dalits and to legitimize violence against Brahmins and dominant castes. Some articulated juridical tools based on rights and atrocities;[7] others strongly advocated for using the same (violent) weapons as the Reddys and Kammas. In the 2000s, the decline of the Dalit organizations led to disenchantment among Dalits: Caste relations had not been radically challenged; a lack of capital had hampered the rise of Dalits; legal rulings had not kept their promises; the financial cost of entry into politics was still too high. The overwhelming desire for power in the here and now, combined with the confidence and skills gained through Dalit organizations, pushed some Dalits to emerge as henchmen and bosses in local neighborhoods. Those who were in the Naxalite movement—once influential but nowadays weak in Rayalaseema—could also gain respect as specialists of violence.

In this process, bossism tends to appear to many as the quickest way to achieve power, especially perhaps for Dalits, whose main asset as henchmen is the ability to control certain categories of population in specific neighborhoods, albeit for their own individual ambition and money. However, what is clear is that they have remained related to a Kamma or Reddy boss; Dalit henchmen have become instrumental in extracting political and economic resources for their bosses. Thus, they are crucial figures in the workings of Mafia Raj systems, but the relation between Dalit henchmen and bosses is not a straightforward one of obedience. On the one hand, henchmen have their own pragmatic and personal agendas, have made loyalties temporary, and have monetized relations with bosses. On the other, the agency of henchmen hardly crosses the limits (more or less loosely) defined by the boss, who has to contend with the volatility of loyalties. In other words, to link up with a boss appears to be the way to pursue a loose Dalit agenda, to achieve personal power and respect, and to get money. But to be loyal to the boss and to work for the Dalit cause often imply conflicting positions that are only partly resolved through violence and threats of violence. The relation to the boss cannot be reduced to an instrumental and monetary dimension: as with Kondappa, the boss can be admired, protect, and provide self-respect and power. These ambiguous relations signal ongoing processes of social reproduction as much as social changes through bossism.[8]

KONDAPPA IN KOTHAPALLE

Kondappa operates in Kothapalle, a growing town in the Chittoor district, located between India's two southernmost major cities, Bangalore and Chennai, and Chittoor, the district headquarters. Urban and rural economies are now interconnected through the capital investments of leaders in land grabbing, forestry, the granite business, transport, agriculture, and construction and through the circulation of laborers working in the urban construction sector. More than the politico-financial activities, the major change in the town has resulted from the scale of such businesses and the quick shift from one to another activity. For example, granite is transported by trucks and shipped from the port of Chennai to Italy. Such a trajectory involves the illegal acquisition of legal documents and authorizations, as well as the participation of different bosses controlling and managing different stages of the journey. Construction and land grabbing are two well-known sources of profit crucial to financing the electoral democracy. The smuggling of red sandalwood in the district, an endangered wood highly in demand on the international market, also requires close coordination among local bosses, (allegedly) ex-chief ministers' family members, and global criminals located in Dubai and other South Asian countries. This transnational criminal enterprise is said to be led by a boss named the "Junior Veerappan," in reference to the most famous and mythical of the Indian sandalwood and ivory smugglers, "Veerappan," a.k.a. "the jungle cat." Smuggling sandalwood is a particularly violent business before and after electoral seasons, with regular "encounters" or mass killings led by police against woodcutters (mainly poor labor migrants from Tamil Nadu called "smugglers" by police). The struggles between bosses for the control of the business were particularly obvious around the 2014 elections when the new chief minister reorganized a task force that killed twenty woodcutters in the forest in April 2015.

However, this violence cannot hide the fact that today Kothapalle presents a strong fragmentation of power, as confirmed by the large number of candidates for the 2014 legislative elections and a decline in political violence (compared to that at the end of 1990s and in other places in Rayalaseema). I like to stress that periods of conflicts between bosses are alternated with *pax mafiosa*, peaceful times when power relations are reconfigured. This fragmentation of power, despite increased competition, temporarily leads to a period of status quo, observation, and new alliances. The context of the research is also worth mentioning. As one of the main local politicians explained, businesses are increasingly insecure and fluctuate according to global demands and regional political uncertainties. First, impunity was questioned with the imprisonment of Y. S. Jaganmohan Reddy,[9] the main figure in Rayalaseema politics. Second, Telangana agitation for a state separate from Andhra Pradesh reduced the business perspectives in Hyderabad, the capital, where many bosses have invested. Third, the announcement in 2013 of the official separation (carried out in 2014) led speculating in new directions. Conflicts and violence without clear perspectives are too costly to bear, and the major concern is to be able to invest and shift business: when the granite business slows down, bosses must transfer their activities to another; when the land market slowed down in Telangana in the 2010s, they had to move to Bangalore. Only big players can adjust and move forward and only if they have the right networks and support on a regional and national scale.

This was the broad context in which I met Kondappa. The first interaction I had with him was on the phone. I was on my way to meet him in Kothapalle town, but my bike broke down on a small stone path in one of the surrounding hills. I asked a farmer who happened to be there for help. As I called Kondappa to let him know about my delay, he asked me to pass the phone to the farmer. I watched the farmer respond to Kondappa with a series of "Yes, sirs!" Then we pushed the bike up to the main road and found an auto rickshaw to transport the bike to a mechanic. Both the auto driver and the mechanic had to talk with Kondappa, who kept on calling every ten minutes. It was like magic. I was served first. Kondappa told the mechanic to send a boy with me to help me find my way to his residence, but only a drunk was available. I ended up reaching Kondappa with the poor guy sleeping on my back, and on arrival he promptly asked for whisky. "See how powerful I am!" was Kondappa's welcome. After a presentation of his NGO work, I must say I was convinced by his show. The day after—he quickly understood that I had no link with funding agencies—he told me that he had delegated the NGO work to his wife to become a local politician.

Chinnappa, Kondappa's brother-in-law and head of a Dalit NGO, is quite the opposite: quiet, well educated, well mannered, and polite to everybody. Kondappa has a loud voice, shouts at people in the street, walks proudly, and never bows in front of anyone except his boss. Kondappa and Chinnappa behave like an old couple. The show is on every morning when he prepares to go out of his house. The first time I visited in the morning, Kondappa was about to finish his breakfast. Undressed, he lay down on a chair, his feet on a small table. He suddenly farted loudly, "Do politicians do that in your country? This is a Dalit fart, stronger than Brahmin ones!" he laughed, proud of his joke. Chinnappa then made a political remark: "Dalits make a lot of noise, but it vanishes into thin air." This joking signals the boundary between the imagined proper behavior of the boss in the public sphere and his behavior in private. As soon as he leaves the house, Kondappa is onstage and the show starts. He gets on his bike, which has a sticker saying "PSR," the name of his NGO, instead of a license plate. He then drives around, greets everyone, and carefully repeats "Namaste" three times to not give people time to ask for services (as he explained to me). He stops to drink tea in public places; he talks loudly on phones; but he never works: "You've met politicians. Does anyone ever work?" Working is not an option.[10] Well known in the locality, Kondappa has a status to cultivate and maintain: he introduces himself as a Dalit leader and/or as the right hand of GMR.

His main pride comes from being a man with a name. As Kondappa says, "Those bastards [referring to upper castes, non-Dalit state officials, and landlords] used to call my father by making a noise like 'tss tss.' They now call me by my name, 'Oh PSR Kondappa, how are you?'" Having a name is critical for authority and establishing self-made bosses' careers, as shown for all the bosses in this book. Beyond a political title like "Tiger of Chittoor" for C. K. Babu, it is clear revenge for the fate of the Dalits, a clear assertion of dignity for a son of debt-bonded laborers who has climbed the social and political ladder. Making a name is particularly important for Dalits, who cannot rely on a political lineage. "PSR Kondappa" built his name through a combination of violence, loyalty, and social service to Dalits. Proudly marked in capital letters on his motorbike, Kondappa's name is paraded all over town.

His parents used to work as laborers for a Reddy landlord. This past is a notch in his personal social ascension and also an important asset in Dalit politics. His caste and class biography provide him with the legitimacy to speak on behalf of Dalit laborers and the downtrodden. His "Dalitness" has been further reinforced by a political wedding. Kondappa is a Mala, and he married a Madiga woman. For him this intercaste marriage is a vivid example of his commitment to changing local caste hierarchies among Dalits: "We encourage intercaste marriages between Malas and Madigas; this is important to show that we break hierarchies among Dalits to build the movement."

Like many Dalits in South India, Kondappa is a Christian, educated in Catholic schools.[11] He entered the College of Kothapalle in the 1980s (not so common for a Dalit at that time). As most local politicians studied at this college, it is central to the inclusion of Kondappa in political and business networks through classmate friendship bonds in the area, and through the students' union Kondappa started to be interested in politics. Since his twenties, he has been an affiliate of Ganga Mohan Reddy (GMR), who led a faction of the Congress Party. Son of a famous faction leader (ex-Naxalite), GMR is a major industrialist and landowner in Kothapalle. He had a reputation of helping labor unions secure better working conditions. As he told me, he had no choice but to buy industries for the good of workers! Importantly, he is known for commanding strongmen able to threaten and use violence when required.

In the early stages of his career Kondappa focused on rural Dalit NGO work and developed links with foreign agencies. In the early 1990s, he was a founder of one of the first Dalit networks in Chittoor district. Kondappa maintained close links with GMR and was regularly involved in violent acts to grab land or resolve issues. He never killed for GMR and has no criminal cases pending (unlike many politicians in this area who consider themselves too clever to be embarrassed by justice). Nevertheless, he directed gangs in electoral fights and collecting money; participated in collective beatings for land grabbing; made fake administrative papers and electoral lists of all kinds; embezzled funds from public schemes; used muscle and threats against political opponents, state, and police agents; took part in conflicts against labor unionists; and extracted money from contractors, companies, and *maistris* (labor contractors). He turned to politics and reinforced his position in the GMR faction of the Congress Party in Kothapalle. In 2005, he was elected ward member of the municipality. He claimed to be a "real political boss" and delegated the NGO to his wife. This ward became his territory where he could pretend to command. He helped Chinnappa develop his own Dalit NGO, while another brother-in-law, Janumala, is the head of Mala Mahanadu (a caste-based movement). This turn toward politics points to using disenchantment with the NGO sector as a way of challenging caste and class relations.

The existing galaxy of unions, networks, movements, caste associations, and political parties reflects a political fragmentation of the Dalit movements. These organizations are closely associated with and financially dependent on local faction leaders. In Kothapalle, Mala Mahanadu unofficially follows the Yuvajana Shramika Rythu Congress Party (YSR-CP, led by Jaganmohan Reddy); Dandora (Madiga Reservation Porata Samithi, a Madiga movement) follows the TDP; and Bharat Ambedkar Sena (a new movement that arose from a scission with Dandora) is supported by the Congress Party. Such divisions certainly highlight the generalized will to power of many Dalit leaders—and their imagination of leadership sustained by faction leaders. Yet the lack of capital makes those small leaders unable to sustain an influential movement. While Reddys and Kammas have invested in new economic opportunities, Dalits have remained economically marginalized (even in 2014). Politics is used as a platform to gain power and financial success, but this is achieved only by becoming dependent on local political bosses with capital. In such a context, the position of Kondappa—and his role as henchman—is deeply contested by Dalits, including Chinnappa, his close friend and family member. Chinnappa is concerned with education and services for people rather than the use of violence as ways of being respected. He rejects violence but always preserves his future: He completely cut ties with his past as henchman for a BJP leader in his youth to become involved in development, but he remains connected to politicians to advance his NGO agenda.[12]

THE HENCHMAN AND THE BOSS

Kondappa's career as henchman and local small boss is intertwined with the career of GMR, and his profile shares similarities with that of Sukhbir Singh (see Chapter 3), but a key difference is Kondappa's relation to a powerful boss. Their relation is based on long-term loyalty. The foundation of the relation between a henchman and his boss is often events that had the capacity to create intimate and asymmetrical bonds. According to Kondappa, GMR was the first person who gave him respect and support: "He trusted me immediately and when I was nobody." A long time ago, GMR appeared in his life, financed his education, and allowed him to develop his career and acquire (self-) respect. "He changed my life, I could have been a day laborer, but I became a very powerful politician," he often mentions. GMR not only provided him with an education and material support, but he also gave Kondappa a sense of dignity: "He is very good at judging character; he knows if someone is good, and if he thinks so, he gives you a chance. But if you mess up with him, you're finished."

GMR relies on a large network of henchmen across the constituency—one of the largest in India—that could potentially be useful for elections, business, and state control. Kondappa was one of them. His NGO had many advantages for GMR: located in remote places, it is self-financed, potentially brings in votes, and provides information and contacts. Contrary to Kondappa's affectations, he is not the "elected" henchman of GMR but only one of his numerous "right hands." According to Kondappa, GMR is gentle but strong, rich, and powerful. Everybody knows about his villa, his swimming pool, and his Mercedes; such luxury goods signal a VIP political culture and the importance of wealth and prestige in politics. These symbols need to be visible to produce fascination, veneration, and respect. GMR is believed to command eight thousand people who are ready to follow him, as he is a man able to make the right decision and stick with it.

Kondappa considers himself *vishwaasamu* (loyal) to GMR, to whom he has dedicated his life. Kondappa knows that he has no chance to compete with him. He fights with everyone, everywhere, argues with upper castes when needed, but he always submits to GMR. Kondappa expects his social mobility to be correlated to his boss's economic and political success—and eventually his electoral victory. This topic always excites him a lot. When he talks about it, he usually stands up and asserts that GMR, once elected, will give him a very powerful political position: he will climb the political ladder, he will be surrounded by people, and he will go onstage to deliver public speeches. More important, he will have two bodyguards and a car with flashing lights—an important symbolic and material sign of power in India. These dreams of power signal that his personal ambitions are strongly interwoven with his boss's life. Whatever democracy cannot provide, his boss will deliver. The dignity he has acquired is shown by Kondappa's public attitude. His biggest achievement is the right to claim himself GMR's "right hand." He considers himself a part of the boss's body. Above all, Kondappa wants to be respected for that: "I've done many things in politics, but trust is important. I've been loyal and I always will be."

This claim of loyalty is nevertheless often used by Kondappa to play the boss himself. Kondappa's power is encapsulated in his boss's sphere of power, but this does not make him a fool or blind follower. Kondappa has his own agenda, somewhere between being a henchman and a Dalit leader. Bosses usually give latitude to henchmen, allowing them to conduct their own affairs in specific neighborhoods and to establish their local muscular and financial stronghold. A number of bosses, for example, delegate the management of particular public schemes to their local henchman, and this has become one of the critical elements discussed between henchmen in their assessment of bosses.[13]

Far from being fixed, relations between henchmen and bosses are rather uncertain, fluid, and temporary, with ever-growing uncertainty. A Dalit boss in a specific neighborhood or territory can also be the henchman of a bigger boss (but not all henchmen are bosses in local neighborhoods) and may cherish a dream of replacing him—even if this is an unlikely scenario. This impacts the ways bosses watch over their henchmen: "Money has become important; it doesn't guarantee loyalty, but it does help keeping people around. I still have people following me whatever I do; I'm like a part of their family. But now people also want money," explains GMR. Henchmen know all too well how successful elections can change their everyday lives: you become respected; people come to you for support; you feel powerful. From drivers to henchmen, they increasingly follow the winner of elections. This requires the boss to juggle with rising uncertainties of loyalty: he must be able to attract schemes and deliver funds and must win elections to keep followers. Only major bosses can live without electoral politics and, nowadays, mainly for only short periods. While henchmen might change bosses for better opportunities, bosses are in a constant state of competition and fear losing power and money. All these changes force the boss to act as a powerful and fearless leader, yet Dalits have often remained encapsulated in the sphere of power of upper-caste bosses for whom they ensure the process of extraction of economic and political resources. Kondappa acknowledges this, but he perceives it as the main asset to act for Dalits (because NGOs, according to him, have no power).

POWER AND DEMOCRACY

Kondappa might expect the democratic game—through GMR's electoral success—to change his life, and he strongly supports bossism. Whatever the failures of GMR, Kondappa considers him to be a boss who is far above the turpitudes of democracy. GMR's authority is not based on electoral politics but on his capacity to rule despite an official title. This contrasts with Kondappa's perception of elected leaders. The Congress Party is strongly divided into two factions locally with both competing for the ticket to contest MLA elections. Despite being a reputed and rich industrialist and landlord, GMR never got the ticket. His rival (now ex-MLA) is caricatured as a puppet in the hands of Delhi's gentle-bourgeois politics and is described by Kondappa as a weak man without followers.

"He had the ticket through Sonia Gandhi [an insult in local politics], but he has no power. Without his job [meaning without being elected], he is nothing," says Kondappa. This clear distinction between elected leaders performing a job and powerful bosses ruling over a territory is very widespread among Dalits in Rayalaseema. Such a distinction reveals an ambiguous relation between real politics and democracy. Kondappa's dignity is based on a social-mobility trajectory that saw him escaping from hard manual work (his family were laborers) and becoming a politician who does not have to work. The term "job" has pejorative connotations. This ex-MLA has based his reputation on always being available to work for the poor and to be at hand when required. This quality made him popular (as it does for many politicians like him across the country) but is not a sign of power. The local MLA is often criticized for lacking power and for acting and posturing in a way not fitting for a local politician. He is believed (by Kondappa) to have his position thanks to his maneuvers within the political party: "He talks nicely to the Delhi people; he knows how to deal with powerful people. That's all. He has nothing, and nobody respects him. People have been showing respect to the MLA for five years, but not to him." Contrary to bosses who are respected for being fearless and able to "talk in the eyes of powerful people"—a common saying locally—the ex-MLA relies on his political party to impose his will. He does not have substantial money—he owns a transport company—but Kondappa accuses him of being where he is now as a result of quota politics. This ex-MLA is suspected of building his career on the electoral calculations of the party. The party selects and imposes him as the local candidate, but this does not mean he has real power among the population.

The expression "Delhi politics" refers to an almost emasculated and amoral form of politics. It is considered to be the domain of tricks, money, treason, smiling, seduction, and compromises, while bossism is the domain of leaders who command people through respect, muscle, and fearlessness.[14] The boundaries may be blurred in everyday practices (including those of Kondappa), but there is still a deep fascination with leaders, who should not depend on compromise and negotiation alone; bosses are expected to establish their authority over people. According to Kondappa, GMR is one of them: "Elected or not, people follow him. He can command more than ten thousand people [this number varies from day to day] in the blink of an eye. He's here to serve the people, not to make money. He's already rich. And he is able to speak straight, to look ministers in the eye."

The establishment of long-term loyalty with followers appears to carry more weight than everyday electoral politics. Kondappa distinguishes between the corruption of ideals through endless and unavoidable compromises and power based on long-lasting relations and the capacity to command people, have muscle, and be respected. This distinction also shapes his understanding of political titles of electoral democracy. Titles remain temporary and uncertain and fluctuate with the contingencies of political life, while bosses' power remains over time. GMR's name evokes power and fear. This reputation is often contrasted with a temporary title derived from electoral games: "You can buy elections, but what then?" At the heart of this distinction are bossism's moral codes that see personal relations as vital. "Delhi" is imagined as the place and the symbol of the dispossession of this power. Ultimately, local issues should remain local. Indeed, what Kondappa suggests is less an opposition between democracy and power than a critique of the interference of external Delhi politics in the local economy of power that promotes, through political titles cyclically distributed by electoral politics, leaders without power and therefore unable to get things done. It reflects the contradictions and the tensions among Dalits between fighting against faction leaders and supporting one who has enough power to act for Dalits. Indeed, there is a general distrust of politicians among Dalits. As mentioned by Gorringe,[15] Dalit leadership is relational and has been shaped partly through Ambedkar's ideals. When Dalit leaders become entangled in regional or national politics, they lose their legitimacy at the local level: they are often accused of being corrupted and bowing to the upper castes to finance their election at the expense of the ideals of pure politics.

Bosses can no longer—if they ever did—ignore elections. To survive as a boss, they need elected positions because they provide protection and opportunities to do business. Electoral positions provide impunity from justice, control over the police, and direct access to the state resources up for grabs. Without a ticket from the Congress, GMR ran in the 2014 elections under the auspices of a different political party (a smaller one). Elections are not necessarily to be won—running for office ensures being known, prestige, and a place on the local political map; it shows followers you have the money to run and signals to rivals that you are on the scene. Bosses know very well that wheels will be set into motion, and they all know someone who has disappeared from the local map of power. To navigate the violent competition for economic and political resources, bosses need to pay attention to electoral positions and to the building of compromises and alliances.

DAILY UNCERTAINTIES AND UNCONTROLLED CHANCE

While the production of insecurity and scarcity is crucial to the art of bossing and to bossism as a system of governance, the very same economic and political uncertainties contribute to shaping illusions of power and the *extraordinary* character attributed to bosses. Bosses are people in control; however, being in control in uncertain political economies is a real challenge. Bosses with different degrees of power all have to deal with the illusion of control, which makes improvisation, the capacity to be able to take decisions quickly, and, more important, luck central and indispensable qualities. Those qualities are vital to shaping ideas of what a powerful and extraordinary man is and to creating a world in which there are endless possibilities for changing the rules of the game, and this is also true for henchmen. In short, they reinforce the theatrics of power by dramatizing bosses' lives and in turn become a source of entertainment and discussion around town. We see these "dramatizations" and the crucial role of figurations in the art of bossing throughout this book.

This is clearly why people like Kondappa love politics. Despite his moral critique of politicking, he is at his best when planning, tricking, taking risks, and showing off. For him, and he is not alone, it is a very entertaining and addictive game. Kondappa spends a great deal of time polishing his boss style; his macho posture and voice; and the way he sits, walks, and greets people. Such physical, language, and social transformations engender critics who stress the ongoing tension between Dalit leaders working in NGOs at the service of the poor Dalits in the past and a contemporary world of muscle and money politics. Chinnappa always finds Kondappa's show pathetic: "You should stop shouting like that and show some respect." Kondappa replied, "Hey, who are you to talk like that? I am a leader [in English]; this is how it works, hey, ho do this, do that." Chinnappa, usually quiet, replies, "What kind of politician are you? You just go and eat, telling everyone I'll be this or that in the future. But the future is now, and you are just a poor Kondappa fucked by GMR; you're a Dalit, that's all."

A normal day for Kondappa starts with receiving a few people at home and then meeting close friends at the tea shop around 8:00 a.m., punctuated with a number of phone calls. His official life starts around 10:00 a.m., when he goes out on his bike. When it is quiet, the most pressing problem is where to have lunch for free, such as weddings and official ceremonies or parties hosted in other leaders' houses. Lunches with meat and alcohol are preferred and are followed by a nap. Busy periods make him run here and there, meet GMR or other leaders, and deal with Dalit issues or fights. But lunches are never missed. He then goes back into public around 4:30 p.m., having tea in public places, looking for a party in the evening. He often takes the initiative to bring people together in a "lodge,"[16] where he shares food and drinks in a room.

Most days, however, there is something that breaks this daily routine. A friend in need, a fight to break up, an issue with government officials cr other party members—such events require improvisation and action and usually give Kondappa an adrenaline rush. One lazy day we were having tea when he received a phone call: a Dalit leader had had a bike accident and was being moved to the local hospital. Kondappa suddenly woke up. He said he had to go because the doctor would not cure his friend properly: "The state works against Dalits," he said pompously. This comment on a political issue promised that there would be an altercation. We jumped on his bike, and Kondappa drove along the busy road, shouting, boasting, threatening people loudly but still issuing polite greetings here and there. His arrival was the usual show: he parked his bike at the entrance to the public hospital, the watchman argued, and Kondappa proclaimed his powerful status loudly for all to hear. He slowly swaggered through the door. Kondappa never waits in line. He started to ask the nurses and doctors questions. Things became serious when he saw other Dalit leaders from two other organizations arrive. The competition started. He ordered a nurse to treat his friend and then went along the corridor, followed by a nurse carrying useless bandages. He publicly stated to his friend that he should feel at home and that he would talk to the doctor—"a friend." The Dalit friend was assured that he would be cured. Kondappa managed to instill silence and a tense atmosphere in the corridor. He then called the doctor; people replied obsequiously. "The doctor is busy," said a nurse. Kondappa asked again. Two young Dalits, who had come with other less powerful leaders, obeyed Kondappa and rushed off to find the doctor, who took his time to come see what was happening. Kondappa greeted him politely: "He is my very good friend. You should take good care of him; he is an important Dalit leader." The doctor reminded him that this was indeed what he always did. "Then why do so many people die in the hospital? I want the best room. With AC," ordered Kondappa. Surprised, the doctor left. Kondappa was able to leave too and ordered his men to deal with the details (such as paying for the room).

Respect and power are never taken for granted by people like Kondappa. They know all too well the fragility of their position and the weakness of muscular power: it has to be continuously maintained through presence, friendship, and the threat of violence. Kondappa has no henchmen; he does not have the financial means. Yet he commands many people through fear, promises, friendship, and threats. Shouting, rushing, boasting, threatening, and showing muscle fill up his days. When nothing happens, Kondappa can improvise. "In politics, you never know when the worm could turn. Even if you have control, you cannot rely on it. You have to maintain control."

Even major bosses, with established wealth who can command respect, cannot rely on the status quo. Bossism requires the personal intervention of henchmen who make domination visible at all times. The dynamics of power require being permanently alert. The fragmentation of power has increased the precariousness of this career, but the shaky foundations of power also give aspiring leaders the chance to bet on uncertainties of such political life to climb the rungs of power. Nothing is permanent in politics, and someday, somehow, things can change. Henchmen like Kondappa do not only adjust to uncertainties; they sustain and create them with a deep belief in social change or at least in the possibilities of changing situations that seem fixed and condemned to be reproduced. They continuously search for, identify, and attempt to penetrate the interstices of state and politics; they spot weaknesses, anxieties, and mistakes of state agents and minor politicians to take advantage of situations; they spread rumors, false information, data, or ideas to modify the contours of their social world; they use strength and muscle; they show off and boast to impose their views: henchmen are powerful actors who reject the routine of social reproduction.

But this is not enough. Plans and subterfuge can help, but ultimately they need chance, opportunity, and luck. Small bosses have to do their best to be ready to seize opportunities. Believing in chance is something Kondappa has deeply interiorized, and the best he can do is to be prepared, provoke chances, and help luck on its way. Proclaiming his ambitions is his best tactic. "I will be municipal chairman," he announced the first time we met. One year later, his ambitions had changed: "I will be a member of the government SC/ST [Scheduled Castes / Scheduled Tribes] commissions. GMR has good relations;

he will support me. I have asked him; this is what I want. This is a very important position, one with red beacons and bodyguards. Two, I think. You live in Hyderabad, and then you command many people."

Boasting and showing off have a performative dimension. These performances help build personal confidence as much as inspire respect and fear. Becoming a boss requires, according to Kondappa, letting everyone know about your personal ambitions: "You have to stand up and say I will be someone. People look at you with respect and think, 'Oh, if he becomes that, he will help us.'" Followers are created on the basis of ambitions projected into the future. "I have to announce what I want; then people will think, 'Ooh, he might be the next chairman'; so when there's an opportunity, I will get a chance." It is all in the attitude rather than the desire. Kondappa behaves like a future boss. As explained previously, playing with the illusory nature of power is crucial to cultivating authority. Chinnappa might make fun of him, but Kondappa inspires respect for his determination. His ambition is supported by a detailed narrative that outlines how he will get the position and support. He says again and again that he will have power in the future and he could be helpful to his supporters.

Kondappa lives on the promise of a better position in the SC/ST commission, a dream that is silently sustained by his boss, Ganga Mohan Reddy. In reality, GMR hardly ever promised him anything concrete. He lets people like Kondappa dream bigger and bigger. He never discourages expectations. Chinnappa strongly criticizes GMR for such a trick: "GMR will never give Kondappa anything. He is a Reddy, so everything goes to his family and friends. Kondappa is a loser; he gets nothing from his leader. He can just move around proclaiming he will become something. He will only become a beggar and a drunkard."

INTOXICATING ILLUSIONS OF POWER

One can hardly fail to notice the impressive volume of alcohol drunk by ambitious henchmen. This is very obvious during informal meetings in the rooms of small local lodges. The same scene repeats itself almost every evening. Annoyed by the bell being repeatedly rung by Kondappa, the waiter enters the room and explains that a single ring is enough. A loud voice reverberates, "Hey! Who are you to talk this way? It's dirty in here; I want the room cleaned right now; we are VIP guests. Go and clean." As the waiter tries to reply, Kondappa shouts, "I am PSR Kondappa; ask your boss. I am a municipal councilor [ten years ago]. Go." Kondappa rings the bell again. The waiter comes back and acquiesces to Kondappa: "We want three R.C. whiskies, one Kingfisher lager. *Cooling*. Glasses."

"Yes."

"Yes, sir!!! You go in, give my name, get the drinks, and come back." As he is about to leave, Kondappa shouts, "Repeat the order." He does and leaves again. Kondappa rings the bell. "Cigarettes. Gold Flake. King size. Two packets. Wait, I'll call them." He phones the restaurant, gives his name. And concludes, "He will give us the best food."

The waiter comes back ten minutes later and opens the bottles with his teeth. Kondappa asks, "Where is your village?"

"Neeraguttapalle."

"I know it very well. Where in the village?"

"SC wada."

"I know it. Do you know R. Reddy? He's my friend. And the *sarpanch* [elected village council head]? My close friend. I am a Dalit leader; I know all the Dalit people there. Okay, go."

The first order is delivered and Kondappa leads the group. The waiter plays the role of the subaltern and is humiliated in front of everyone for the sake of Kondappa and indeed himself; after all, he expects a good tip. Far from being intimidated by the display of social relations and Kondappa's claim to be a leader, the waiter knows how to behave, how to show respect and submission. Indeed, both understand the rules of this "social game" played almost every evening.

We are in a double room of a small lodge, and Kondappa has invited people from various castes, classes, and parties to the party: a tailor and *karekarthudu* (party worker) from the Kamma-caste TDP; Gopal Reddy, a government employee at the district *panchayat* office and affiliated with the Congress Party; the former head of the tomato market, M. Khan; and Gorappa, who was recently elected as village *panchayat* leader. This is his first time in the lodge. Indeed, his wife was the one actually elected, but nobody mentions it. No women are allowed to come to the party.

After a few drinks, the meeting becomes a bit messy. Gopal Reddy starts to narrate his first sexual experience when he was sixteen with an old lady in a field. He cries. The Kamma tailor sings loudly, and the head of the tomato market laughs at his own jokes. Kondappa keeps repeating that the whisky is excellent, while Gopal Reddy starts a new story. Apparently he cured his son of cancer by taking him to Mumbai's best hospital. He also incidentally mentions that he is up to his ears in debt. He cries again; everybody keeps silent. Kondappa is also about to cry but prefers to ask for another round of drinks. Meanwhile, M. Khan looks in the mirror ten times and laughs. Gopal Reddy tries to stand up but quickly reconsiders the situation: "Too dangerous!" Everybody laughs. On the way back to their bikes, Kondappa wakes everyone up by shouting at the poor, skinny hotel guard who mentioned in front of everyone that they had been at the same school; the guard has ruined Kondappa's efforts to act as if he were a boss all night.

These informal meetings are a central part of local politics and reflect the great pleasure of being together, conversing, drinking, and having fun away from the constraints of domestic life. This is often a main incentive, with political maneuvering used as a pretext to get together. It further deeply contrasts with the political analysis of factions focused on major violent events that neglects the spaces of discussions and compromises maintained between different castes, political parties, and factions. Those unofficial meetings play their roles in building the *pax mafiosa*.

The meeting that I just described preceded elections, and everybody was trying to guess alliances and personal plans. Who is doing what and for whom? In addition, M. Khan had just changed his political party to join YSR-CP's local leader and was then appointed manager of a branch of a state bank. This is a reason for Gorappa's presence; as the elected *sarpanch*, he is deeply indebted after spending Rs. 70,000 on the elections against a Rs. 10,000 to 15,000 monthly wage. And that is when the nightmare started for Gorappa: "Everybody promised me that money would come from government and that I could pay the loans back. But now no money has come. People are coming to me for water and other problems. So I have to take out loans to repair everything and pay interest on them. When I call a politician, he never answers."

Kondappa mentions to Gorappa the help he could get from M. Khan, who has recently been appointed as a government bank manager. This is the plan: get money through M. Khan.

Panchayat elections are fiercely contested, as they represent the most accessible way to obtain power and prestige at the local level. However, in some localities, the cost of elections is clearly on the rise, and some upper castes consider that elections imply spending more money that they will recuperate: they would rather support people from lower castes by lending them money and maintaining indirect control on the area without supporting the cost of democracy. Many of the candidates are from poor and low-caste backgrounds (through quotas). They dream of a well-to-do life and a name for their families, yet Kondappa claims his life has changed after being elected, despite the debts: "I now have a name, and my children will benefit in the coming years. I also can enter those places and meet those people."

These nocturnal meetings show the contemporary proliferation of centers of power that crisscross caste, community, and class.[17] These events have the capacity to foster fantasies of power. Who is invited? Who is close to the town's powerful people? What happens during these meetings? The organizer of such events needs to be careful to invite people who can get along despite caste hierarchies: the kind of food (meat, such as beef) and the quality of drinks (brand of whisky) and cigarettes are carefully discussed, and everyone tries to determine what should be ordered or not. A room in a lodge has the advantage of being more caste neutral than Kondappa's house (no upper caste would go to see him in his house). However, it should also be noted that most lodges are clearly linked to a caste and owned by faction leaders.

FRIENDSHIP

These environments offer spaces for negotiating, providing services, constructing alliances, spreading rumors, plotting, and so on. Planning, discussing, developing tactics, or making deals is the basis of these meetings. Kondappa tactically uses these meetings to establish bonds of friendship for the future. "We have to use our brain; that's all Dalits need. We don't have money to bribe people, we don't have guns to kill *nayakullu* [leaders], so we need to use our brains." "Using brains" refers to the necessary skills needed to deal with the state and bureaucrats. According to Kondappa, power is located in politics despite a lack of capital: bribery is the last step of negotiation. Dalits cannot compete with Reddys and Kammas in regard to money; they need to focus on what money cannot buy, which is obligation and dependence. In regard to vote buying, bribery is expensive and uncertain, so Kondappa focuses on social relations instead. This does not bring more certainty; the multiple loyalties henchmen engage in often end up in clashes. Caste, kinship and political affiliations, debt relations, and personal ambitions create multiple forms of dependence, leading to endless stories of betrayals and lack of loyalties, within the family, the caste, and the faction followers. Reinforcing ties across castes, classes, and political parties appears central to Dalit politics in times of political uncertainties. Networks of influence are slowly built on a long-term perspective. The changing forms of loyalty and the need to survive in politics lead many to maintain good relations with one another. Some of the people in the room have changed political party and boss during their careers. Everyone considers politics as unstable and flexible nowadays. The everyday work of minor politicians and henchmen consists of juggling personal relations and eating and drinking together to maintain their social life. The evening meetings help Kondappa know the character of a person, to explore how he could support Dalits, and, above all, if he is in need of support. Any and all information is useful: a businessman expecting help, a *maistri* wanting a contract. For example, from the meeting Kondappa now knows that Gopal Reddy is in debt, which means that Gopal Reddy could be open to corruption. As Kondappa mentioned, "No one will support Dalits. But at some point, they have issues or problems, and we could help them."

During the meeting, people share a lot in terms of fun, jokes, intimacy, and emotions. This is very welcome, as it provides a place to relax from political violence, betrayals, and failed expectations. The Kamma tailor insisted on friendship: "We all know each other from childhood, we're all in different parties, and it will remain like this. Friendship is more important than politics." As detailed by Schneider and Schneider about the working of mafia,[18] the language of friendship plays on reciprocities and hierarchies. "Once you need help, you've lost," repeats Kondappa. Reciprocity should be based on friendship sustained by many invitations to weddings and other ceremonies. Meetings at the lodge also allow leaders like Kondappa to have government employees from different castes sit down at the same table. Learning the subtle art of networking and influencing is not only related to their low caste and class position but also to their conceptions of a state as a social relation. One has to personalize every relation; one has to build ties on a long-term basis and spend time, energy, and money to create obligations and dependence. Those exclusively all-male drinking meetings—which happen in most of the fieldsites examined in this book—reveal the complexity of social relations in which henchmen engage. In these spaces, vertical and horizontal relations are continually undermined, distorted, and asserted in subtle ways. The rules of ordinary daytime interaction are put on hold to let friendship and hedonistic pleasure coexist with masculine prowess, status claims, and vulnerability. Contrary to public spaces where alcohol consumption takes place (like bars), I have never seen the lack of self-control fueled by alcohol erupt into fights between the guests; rather, the extraordinary time and space of these meeting (nighttime, discretion, lodge) reinforce a release of tensions of the protagonists expressed through male friendship and concrete experiences of fun and pleasure.

Having power over bureaucrats—who always fear politicians and their power to transfer state employees—is a key element of the struggles of Dalits. This relates to the local history of domination by the state reconsidered through everyday stories of humiliation in government offices. The tactics used to avoid government offices combine personal narratives of social mobility and power with larger narratives of the state: the state must come to the Dalits. Avoiding state offices has become a key element of power. "Nobody goes to their office; that's for the poor to do. I call them and they come. I tell them what work to do in the evening and that's it," claims Kondappa, who considers going to any government office a sign of low status. He has a network of bureaucrats he can call and meet in the evening in any lodge; they must come to him. In addition, only a few consider the state a powerful institution. Everyone jokes about bureaucrats fearing *goondas* (criminals) or the district collector officer fearing the MLA and the faction leaders. Bringing state employees "home" reveals much about the everyday workings of the state outside the walls of the offices. Going to the office means facing a state employee who will ask for "formalities" (in English). This is considered to be a very humiliating situation, and the aim is to reverse the position of the actors. The formalities might remain in place but will be negotiated as a service given by the state employee to them. Kondappa will, for example, consider the employee in terms of friendship or alliance ("He is with us") and give him a subaltern position in the micro-hierarchies: "I am a powerful leader; he will do the work."

This politics of negotiation suggests a shift from violent caste conflicts around issues of annihilation of caste toward a form of voluntary participation in the extraction of economic and political resources. Violence is not forsaken but is encapsulated in the spheres of power of bosses: anti-caste activism has been subsumed by boss politics. The tension among local Dalit leaders regarding the use of politicking skills and violence still persists. Dalits refer to the weapons of the strong where the word "strong" refers to a nebulous mix of upper castes, landowners, politicians, and faction leaders. Upper castes are thought to rule through violence and money, and Dalits have to show their muscle by using the same methods as Reddy and Kamma bosses. Nevertheless, this is shaky ground. As Chinnappa mentions, the police are controlled by MLA, and Dalits do not have impunity unless they work for a boss. Kondappa is perfectly aware of the limits of his sphere of action and the selective enforcement of the law. He certainly deals with Dalit issues using his own name and is always under pressure from Dalits to maintain his leadership and act like a Dalit boss. During an evening meeting with Dalits, two Malas tell a story about a land and housing issue with a Reddy. The main point is to establish the Reddy's political relation, status, and influence in his neighborhood. The Malas ask for immediate and direct action. Kondappa brags and claims they will teach him a lesson. Different plans of attack are presented, but he decides to postpone the action and reconsider the plan. Later on, the issue is settled through the intervention of GMR. Kondappa has to deal with social pressure for action: between the imperatives of appearing to be a strong leader and the realities of justice. Venkatesh is a Kamma owner of granite quarries who is locally known for his political violence while he was a BJP MLA candidate. His opinion highlights the tensions around Dalit bossism: "They don't have the guts. They are hungry but not hungry enough to take power." According to Venkatesh, people like GMR do have an appetite for power and are ready to use all means possible to take and keep it. "GMR is from a powerful family. He knows what it takes to command people." This is not surprising to hear from a Kamma about power as a personal quality inherited by birth rather than a process of reproduction of inequalities. This argument of inheritance of bossism is now strongly contested but nevertheless remains present. As Kondappa declares solemnly in front of his friend about GMR, "You have to be rich, but money does not make you a leader."

LOYALTIES AND SUCCESS

What is currently emerging from these transformations is a status quo. Henchmen and minor politicians are avoiding violent struggles during this uncertain period, preferring to cultivate networks for potential future alliances. Insecure periods are more peaceful because people use them to observe and prepare themselves for the next battle. Nonetheless, what is clear is that most of the people surrounding bosses and politicians have worked for different leaders in their careers. The fragmentation of power, the new opportunities, and the desire to "make it" quickly, here and now, pushed Kondappa's friends to encourage him to change bosses before the 2014 MLA campaign, but he remained loyal, which brought him both respect and made him a subject of mockery. They all admired his relation to GMR but also considered it to be a waste of effort. The imagination of a past made of loyalty, trust, and violence against contemporary monetized relations between bosses and henchmen is a recurrent discourse. Henchmen refuse to "lay down their life" for a leader. Trust and loyalty might have been considered a lifetime, often inherited, relation to a boss. Now the attachment to a leader must bring some immediate and regular rewards. "He has no money, nothing, and GMR does not provide him with anything. His daughters are studying medicine, but he can't pay the fees anymore. He just goes here and there to tell how GMR is great, how he is his close friend. I am his right hand, bla bla bla. . . . That's not the way it is. He needs money and GMR will lose the elections again. Stupid!" asserts Chinnappa. To the contrary, most of the YSR-CP followers have something to show to explain their attachment: a house built thanks to a YSR scheme; a scar on the body as evidence of the free surgery the individual was able to get in private clinics thanks to health and antipoverty schemes. But this should not lead us to believe a different trajectory: this political party—as do TDP and Congress—relies heavily on muscular politics.

The interpretation of the success and failures of Kondappa reflects the ongoing changing relations between bosses and henchmen. Kondappa is credited for his capacity to negotiate with everyone. His loyalty makes him someone who can be trusted. This reputation gives him the power and confidence to move around in town, shout and order people around, beat up his adversaries (when he was young), and run and deal with bureaucrats. Being a henchman and an aspiring boss carries various meanings and shapes across South Asia and in the very local context of the town. Kondappa could draw the shape of his role in relation to the local political economy of power, but this role is constantly debated, adjusted, and contested: it is never fixed or taken for granted nor defined only by the boss.

Kondappa makes a living, but his position is tenuous, which is the economic reality of Dalit henchmen. Most do not make a profit from their activities. For many, it consists of nothing more than begging all day in front of leaders. As another henchman, Madiga Subash, explains,

> Everyone claims he will arrange this and that, that they know the minister and other influential people. But I need to spend days in leaders' houses, waiting, doing nothing just to get enough to eat and drink. How can I pay my kids' education? Look at Kondappa! He will go begging to GMR. We Dalits have to bow all the time to get whisky and so on. Whoever got the job promised by leaders?

Indeed, none of the Dalits have managed to procure a powerful position: there is a class of minor politicians that can only pretend to be someone. Any attention from a leader is overinterpreted as a sign of influence: for example, phone calls, words, and photos with leaders kept in pride of place.

Kondappa has definitely made a name, and he is very much respected. His violence, his fearless attitude, his body, and his general behavior have helped him build a large network with bureaucrats, politicians, and development agents from different castes, a network that can extend up to the ex–chief minister (who lives twenty-five kilometers away). Thus, he can consider himself successful if he compares himself to other Dalits. What is striking is that the failures and the disillusion with a Dalit agenda of annihilation of caste pursued through Dalit movements, unions, and NGOs in the 1990s brought a sense of disempowerment that leads many to consider bossism as the best way to combine personal ambitions and struggles for Dalits. But in this scenario, Dalits are more often reduced to a vote bank brought by henchmen to the boss. In addition, there is the control and violence they can exercise over Dalits, which makes them important in the eyes of the boss. GMR would rather send Dalit henchmen to clear up a situation within a Dalit neighborhood: the condition of social mobility for Dalit henchmen relies on their ability to crush other Dalits.

But Kondappa remains without capital. His limited funds have vanished. Behaving like a politician takes money. His extravagant spending on his friends is well known, as Chinnappa mentions: "He was elected as ward councilor, and he got loads of contracts for roads, water, and so on. He made huge money from that, and then he started behaving like a king, you know. 'Hey, I am PSR Kondappa, ward councilor; bring me this and that.' But he spent a lot to get respect. I told him, but he could only reply, 'Ooh, these are important people, not like your HIV or orphans; none of them vote.'"

CHAPTER 5

THE ADJUDICATORS

Paul Rollier

"MY LIFE WAS all about guns, real estate, and fights. I was in it for fun. You just looked at me the wrong way, and I'd have taken my gun out! I was a real *badmash* [criminal] then." Kalashaan never became the underworld boss he had hoped to be. He sits outside his shop, a tiny room overlooking a narrow alley leading to Hira Mandi, Lahore's so-called red-light district. Day and night, people come to make phone calls from one of his landlines, to upload credit onto their mobile phones, or to rent one of his rickety motorbikes. Kalashaan—"Kalashnikov," as he is known locally—is a sturdy man in his early thirties. He lives in a three-bedroom apartment farther down the alley, together with his wife, his newborn son, four brothers, and elderly parents. I spend some of my afternoons with him behind the counter, chatting with his friends and neighbors as they come and go, sip a cold drink, and help themselves to mobile recharge coupons. Nowadays Kalashaan worries about his younger brother, Amir, who runs a decrepit *paan* (betel chewing) stall in the adjacent alley. When I first met Amir, years ago, he sold *paan*, soft drinks, and opium and was forced to move his stall every month because of pressure from rival vendors and policemen. Now and then, after work, the two brothers gather with friends to play cards, drink, and smoke through the night, and on Sundays they fly racing pigeons from a friend's rooftop.

As is the common pattern in Lahore's criminal milieu, Kalashaan was part of a group of five associates involved in property disputes and the illegal acquisition of land. He also spent a few months in jail for intentional and attempted murder, but he managed to strike a deal with the victims' families to get out rapidly. "Only five percent of the murders that are committed here are actually warranted [*jaiz*]—those concerned with honor, daughters, and wives—and mine wasn't," Kalashaan commented on one occasion, "but I'm not into crime [*badmashi*] anymore. And anyway, it's not the same thing nowadays. Real *badmashs* were powerful people; now they're all catamites [*gandus*]!" Kalashaan captures a widely held view, according to which a figure once stood at the apex of the so-called underworld in the region: the dignified criminal, a strongman who stood up for the destitute in his neighborhood and who behaved like a gentleman. Whenever he used force, he did so reluctantly, out of compulsion to reclaim his honor or to dispense justice. But people contend, nostalgically perhaps, that altruism has given way to self-advancement and vanity and that this Punjabi Robin Hood has now lost his manliness and has become self-indulgent, trigger-happy, and licentious.

For a while, Kalashaan and Amir imagined that a life of crime would grant them upward social mobility and perhaps make them part of Lahore's "top-ten" bosses: these men of substance known for their family feuds, their kingly demeanor, and their extensive contacts to the highest echelons of power. Following in his elder brother's footsteps, Amir committed murder soon after he turned eighteen. Over the next few years, his family tried to get him out of jail, first by bribing a judge and then by paying blood money to the aggrieved party. They eventually succeeded, but Amir came out dejected, afraid of reprisal, and ashamed that his family had contracted so many debts to secure his release. Kalashaan was able to benefit from his run-ins with the law. He is often seen on familiar terms with the police constables who stroll the alleys, shaking hands and offering them cigarettes and bottles of Coca-Cola in the summer. People in the neighborhood often call on him for help whenever a son or a brother is arrested, as is commonly the case for such local strongmen with a degree of influence.

> I talk to the SHO [station house officer] to get the guy released. I still have a few contacts within the police, which I made while I was in detention. When you spend weeks in custody, you start talking to the officers there. And when you're out again, you sometimes run into them on the street, so you invite them to have a cold drink. That's how it works. Now I can go in the police station and ask the officer what the accused did. Then I negotiate the amount to get the guy out.

As in much of South Asia, mediating between residents and the local police in cases of arrest is the most recurrent form of service that neighborhood bosses in Lahore seek to perform to establish their local authority. Among the urban poor in Pakistan, the police are often said to be "the other face of Satan," the corrupt and arbitrary arm of the law that one should avoid as much as possible. In many ways, for the working-class Lahoris among whom I work, the state is not necessarily imagined as more lawful than the bosses that I document, and the available avenues to seek justice often involve resorting to individuals who have embraced a life of crime at some point in their lives. While Kalashaan and Amir have both been convicted and incarcerated for murder, they failed to capitalize on this experience to become real adjudicating bosses. Yet their itinerary foregrounds paradigmatic aspects of the local forms of bossism in urban Punjab that I explore, such as the nostalgic appeal of the redeeming gentleman-criminal, the contingency of homicides leading to a reversal of fortunes, and an understanding of the licit and the permissible that upsets the conventional dichotomy between the legal and illegal domains.

This chapter offers an ethnographic view of Lahore's criminal milieu. A number of analysts have highlighted how, over the course of the last decades, Pakistan's military establishment has used Islamist militancy as a tool to further its strategic ambitions.[1] Criminal underworlds in South Asia are not simply the underside of democratization and neoliberal governance but are often integral to the functioning of national economies and to the domain of legitimate political power. In neighboring India and Bangladesh, for instance, *goondas* (criminals) and *mastans* (thugs) have gained considerable prominence as political brokers and aspiring politicians in recent decades. Interpreted as a direct consequence of corruption symptomatic of an unbridled neoliberal regime,[2] or of the rise in power of the lower castes in the political sphere,[3] the presence of criminal figures in political life is steadily progressing and takes forms that disrupt the conventional distinction between legality and crime. However, most recent studies are concerned with the public and visible interventions of these shadowy figures in South Asian politics, in particular in the context of electoral contests and communal riots. While in Mumbai and other Indian metropolises criminal milieus tend to be perceived as a pervasive realm enmeshed in political power—"the underworld is the overworld"[4]—in Pakistan criminal life remains to a large extent distinct from electoral politics. However, drawing on the intuition that banditry, gang rivalries, and the genesis of state order are part of a same continuum,[5] I suggest that criminal bossism in Pakistan supports the production of a social order, the materialization of the law, and the "fiction" of the sovereignty of the state, at least as much as it undermines them.

Lahore's political economy of crime is distinct from that of other major urban centers in the country. Partly because of its relatively homogeneous ethnic and linguistic composition, the capital of Punjab does not display the level of routine violence and terrorist attacks experienced in Karachi or Peshawar, where organized crime, armed warfare, and party politics occasionally intersect in particularly violent ways. Unlike Karachi, for instance, where intense competition for resources and means of coercion has led to a fragmentation of state authority and a "palimpsest of sovereignties,"[6] Lahore seemingly presents a more familiar situation. In Punjab, the country's largest province, the political patronage of criminal formations does occasionally give rise to entities that command discretionary powers in their respective locality, especially in rural areas. But, however spectacular their ability to punish and kill with impunity, these "de facto sovereigns"[7]—whether militant Islamist groups, despotic landlords, or members of so-called criminal mafias—never seem to jeopardize established political hierarchies and the supremacy of the military in the province. The Pakistan Muslim League-Nawaz (PML-N), headed by the former three-time prime minister Nawaz Sharif and his brother, the former chief minister of Punjab, Shahbaz Sharif, has now been able to dispense with specialists in violence and thuggish tactics. Of course, influential bosses and their families honor their respective political connections to retain a degree of criminal impunity, but the PML-N does not (or does no longer) appear to exercise overt patronage over them.

In a country grappling with Islamist militancy and where the purpose of social research is often conflated with active spying, investigating Lahore's underworld poses certain methodological challenges. This has been particularly true since the event that took place in Lahore in 2011, when an American undercover operative, Raymond Davis, gunned down two alleged agents of the ISI, the largest of Pakistan's intelligence services. A CIA car rushed to whisk him off, killed a pedestrian on the way, and Davis eventually fell in the hands of the local police. The case quickly led to a diplomatic standoff, with public opinion insisting that Davis should be tried in Pakistan, and Islamist organizations threatening to take violent action if the American spy was exfiltrated to the United States. Davis was eventually freed and repatriated after the payment of blood money [*diyat*], whereby the relatives of the victims agreed to pardon Davis (or were coerced into doing so) in exchange for hefty compensation and help to immigrate to the United States.[8] Several Pakistani dailies highlighted the irony that the American government resorted to an Islamic provision present in Pakistan law to release an agent spying on organizations that seek to implement sharia law. But there was also much disappointment among Pakistanis with regard to the country's pliable judicial system, the extent of CIA operations in the country, and the impunity with which a foreign murderer could get away with it.

This disappointment echoes the concerns frequently voiced by my interlocutors concerning juridical iniquity, the moral basis of violence, a supposedly effete national sovereignty, and the obsessive fear of (sometimes imaginary) spies. Compounded by the wide currency of conspiracy reasoning in the public sphere, this apprehension stems from Pakistan's political history,[9] as well as from a popular belief according to which (Pakistani or foreign) intelligence services are the true manipulators of the state, omnipresent but elusive, and serving the private interests of a particular social class, an ethnic community, or an enemy country.[10] Already suspect in the context of the "war on terror" in the region, since the Davis affair many hold the epistemological and political distinction between intelligence gathering and the production of ethnographic knowledge as fictive, thus resulting in a conflation between spies and researchers.[11]

Trying to get acquainted with the Lahori criminal milieu and neighborhood bosses predictably raised suspicion. Having undertaken fieldwork in Lahore's low-income neighborhoods in the past, I relied on friends' contacts with what local English-language newspapers refer to as "proclaimed absconders" and "anti-social elements,"[12] men who were often trying to evade police arrest and their foes. Most of them welcomed me with cordiality, and I sometimes met them over a dozen times in the course of that year. Yet some conceded that the Davis episode obliged them to be more cautious with outsiders. At the same time, my interest in their lives was also an opportunity for them to narrate a fantasized version of it, in which they came out as more heroic, upright, or brutal than they actually were. I treat these accounts as commentaries that provide a textured sense of the Punjabi criminal milieu, but also as self-legitimizing narrative devices that are central to the "art of bossing" and to the production of criminal biographies in Pakistan.[13] Thus, the quasi-mythical tone that my interlocutors adopted was not simply the product of my curiosity; it also emerged in their everyday interactions in their respective neighborhoods and in the way ordinary residents talked about local criminal figures. This particular register of bossism reverses the conventional polarity between the legal and the criminal: it foregrounds the stories of honest men, who one day reluctantly take the law into their own hands to dispense justice among the vulnerable or to defend their own honor in the face of adversity. While police reports and journalists refer to them as "*goonda* elements," "miscreants," and *badmash*, the protagonists of this chapter prefer the term *pehlwan* (lit., "wrestler"), which suggests charisma, physical strength, and righteousness.[14] Alternatively, they sometimes call themselves *dere-dar*, a concept that expresses the idea of prestige and courtly authority and denotes the fact of running a *dera*, a place halfway between a living room and an underground den.

YASEER'S *DERA*

I spend many long afternoons behind Amir's stall, trying to keep abreast of the local gossip and befriend his customers who return here at regular intervals to consume his addictive *paan*. This is where I frequently catch up with Yaqub, a thin man in his late twenties. Recently married and the father of a baby girl, he makes plastic jewelry at home with his wife, struggles to make ends meet, and is now contemplating selling hashish, like one of his uncles, a weaver who lives in the neighborhood. But his goal, he once said, is to become a private gunman for some rich Lahori industrialist. Yaqub is certainly drawn to the apparently glamorous lifestyle of gangsters and sometimes shows me some of his friends' Facebook profiles: young Lahoris who go by the names Killer Gujjar, Boxer Butt, or Silver Tiger, posing nonchalantly on rooftops with sunglasses and toting a Kalashnikov. For him, as for many others in the neighborhood, the archetype of the boss has a name: Gogi Butt, a.k.a. Big B., a feared, influential, but supposedly righteous and trustworthy strongman of Lahore. As he has never met Big B., Yaqub often brags about his access to another influential boss of the local underworld, Yaseer, a reclusive actor-turned-gangster, who supposedly maintains regular contact with Big B.

One day, in the sweltering summer heat, Yaqub and I are standing in an alley in the Old City, waiting for his friends to take us to Yaseer's *dera*. I am warned that Yaseer has many enemies, so it took much effort to convince him to let me come. Suddenly three young men emerge on gleaming mopeds. We shake hands and I ask one of them about his unusual license-plate number: 302. "*Qatl-e-amd* [intentional murder] is section 302 of the Penal Code. It suits me! My phone number also ends with 302." As I sit behind one of them, I can feel a gun beneath his *shalwar-kameez* (traditional dress) pressing against my thigh, but Yaqub nods reassuringly. We exit the narrow lanes and drive past the city's main Sufi shrine, zigzagging our way through the late afternoon traffic. We finally dismount next to a dilapidated building, and one of Yaseer's colleagues instructs me to speak in English from now on: "Otherwise, he'll think you work for the police."

A large steel door opens, leading to a narrow staircase and into a living room where a dozen men greet us, most of them in their late twenties and thirties. As we shake hands, I see a number of pistols lying around the sofa, and with a wondering smile Yaqub gestures toward a monitor displaying live footage of the street below. The *dera*, adorned with framed pictures and cinema posters on the walls, is rather austere. Historically *deras* are men's guesthouses in the countryside where villagers, but also drug addicts, dacoits, and thieves, would find shelter and protection. In rural areas they belong to landlord families, who use them as open reception rooms where villagers gather and socialize. The owner, the *dere-dar* (boss or kingpin), is typically resourceful and well connected with bureaucrats and dignitaries; hence villagers often seek his help for a variety of day-to-day problems. Research conducted in rural Punjab indicates that local *dere-dars* cultivate their influence and prestige by employing *goondas* (criminals) to act as bodyguards and threaten rivals and, in return, offer these *goondas* a degree of protection from the police.[15] In contrast to the traditional rural *dera*, its urban form, as found in Lahore and other metropolises of the Punjab, is not as accessible to the public and is not predicated on caste dynamics, political patronage, or the possession of agricultural land. In the working-class areas of Lahore where I conducted fieldwork, these are usually plain brick lodges attached to a house or a rooftop, where the owner entertains his guests and supplicants, hangs out with his friends, and organizes drinking sessions. In most cases, these are semiclandestine places, wherein illegal activities are carried out, conferring an air of secrecy on them, and which can only be visited on invitation or recommendation. Aside from alcohol consumption, adjudications (*faisla*) and gambling tend to be the mainstay of urban *deras*, the latter being an extremely lucrative enterprise in the country, although considered un-Islamic and punishable by imprisonment. Despite this disreputable feature, the institution of the *dera* and the figure of the *dere-dar* continue to evoke prestige, influence, profuseness, and magnanimity; hence, running a *dera* is not necessarily driven by profit and is generally not seen to be.[16]

As we sit, one of the younger men on the sofa declares that he is Yaseer and that I should talk to him only. A thin man with long hair in a white *shalwar-kameez*, he displays self-confidence despite his boyish features. While sharing a bottle of soda, I explain my attempt to document the lives of outlaws in Lahore and persuade him to let me record our conversation.

> You want to know how I entered the underworld? Well, to tell you the truth, it all started with firecrackers when I was about fourteen! Yes, firecrackers! I just loved the *maachis* [match stick] bomb: I loved the loud bang it made! I just grew a taste for it [*shauq*]. Then it got banned, but still, one day I got hold of some in the bazaar, but on my way home the police caught me. I begged them to let me go, but they beat me up badly and lodged an FIR [First Information Report] against me. Three days later, I was released. After that I started to get interested in firearms. I grew up in this neighborhood, next to the old city. My father was a property dealer, so he didn't look after me much. Whenever I went to school, I'd always carry a weapon, and me and my friends just played around with it, for fun. But one day I got into a brawl, and that was like Judgment Day for me: time was suspended. I fired. I shot the guy. He died! I was sixteen then. Ended up spending seven years in a juvenile prison; that's where I discovered the world. When I came out, I had hair on my chin; I'd become a man. But outside things got ugly. I would spend all my time with former detainees like me. And one day I just got into another fight. Bullets whizzing from all sides, but nobody injured, and someone eventually managed to reconcile both parties [*sulah karwana*]. Then five years ago, in Anarkali bazaar, a friend of mine squabbled with a shopkeeper; I took part in the ensuing gunfight: one dead and five injured. After that, people in my neighborhood got the jitters; upon seeing me they'd say, "Here's the boss [*bhai aa gaya*]!" So I thought, if that's what people call me, why don't I show them what I'm really made of? That was five years ago, and since then I've enjoyed their respect.

Two other men in the room chime in, detailing their partnership in running a clandestine gambling house and match fixing. I inquire about the security camera overlooking the entrance outside and their panoply of weapons in the room. Where is danger coming from, I ask, from the police or from rivals? "From North Waziristan!" laughs Yaseer, in reference to a stronghold of Islamist militants. "I'm kidding. Lahore's Old City can be quite dangerous. There's a new 'culture': people want to have guns and to come across as tough. Conflicts here start with a joke, for fun, but a trifle easily builds into personal rivalry and a feud [*dushmandari*]. You get arrogant, you start being disrespectful. and before you know it. you get into fights and murders. And then, it's a cycle of revenge. My younger brother got killed like that. If you're a *goonda-badmash* [criminal] and kill someone, people condemn you. But if you have self-respect [*gairatmand*], you might win their admiration." His friend next to him reflects: "Our aim is just to get money, because that's how you get respect [*izzat*] nowadays. If you have money, people give you 'protocol.'"

The eldest man in the room, sitting at the back, had remained silent until now. He turns to me with a smile: "Don't listen to him," he says; "this guy is a murderer, but he's a gentle devil [*sharif shaitan*]; his devil only comes out when he drinks." The others burst out laughing. Their deferential attitude toward him and his polite circumspection toward me arouse my suspicion. He continues:

> These guys think they can't enjoy this work without a drink. Drinking brings out the devil in you: You're not a "gentleman" anymore; you just feel like annoying people around you. . . . Now, maybe you wonder what triggers these fights. Typically, in Lahore, you'd squabble with a constable, and as you talk, you just start a verbal duel [*barhak*]; you shout "oooye!" provocatively. It's our "culture"! If you don't insult your loved ones, it means you don't love them: sisterfucker means I love you. [He pauses.] Now, I am Yaseer, the guy who was fibbing to you is my surviving son, Mudassir. The other one was murdered: that's his picture on the wall. And this bastard here is my nephew, and that's his partner. The people you see in this room are all well mannered! We're not disrespectful, and we don't tease women. But getting into brawls is just part of our "culture." You won't find any *don-shon* in Lahore, no *dabangs* here [these two terms are directly borrowed from Bollywood cinema]. What

> you've got are *pehlwans* or *dere-dars* when the guy is honorable, and *badmashs* when they are not. And we're not *badmashs*: we're "gentlemen"! But when difficulties arise, we stand up. The vendetta we fell into following the murder of my son leaves us no choice. If we fight, we may survive, but if we don't, we'll die.

While screening me, Yaseer had let his son Mudassir speak for him. Although the first was fictional, these contrasting accounts capture two dominant narratives of bossism prevalent in the region. The first, espoused by the younger generation, foregrounds the glamour and fun associated with the life of a gangster, a life in which guns, motorbikes, and alcohol authenticate one's assertive masculinity and willingness to transgress established rules. Mudassir's fantasized experience in jail, however, is a typical locus of actual criminal biographies; the vast majority of my informants, such as Kalashaan and Amir, do regular stints in prison and often compare detention to an educational institution where aspirant bosses can graduate with a "double MA" in crime. The father, Yaseer, on the other hand, expresses the supposedly distinctive Punjabi ideal of the "dignified criminal" (*sharif badmash*, gentleman *badmash*), a man who reluctantly crosses the law on ethical grounds. This view, consubstantial to the notion of *dere-dari* and bossism in the region, represents the boss as a paragon of probity, chivalrous and charitable toward people from the neighborhood yet fearless and uncompromising toward his enemies. The dignified criminal is said to be affable toward kind people but brutal with malicious ones. He is therefore not represented as intrinsically violent; his brutality is only a riposte to an iniquitous society. Conversely, the vulgar criminal (*badmash*, lit., "a person of bad profession") is conceived as someone who cannot "control his tongue" and who lacks discernment. Driven by greed and his own pleasure, he is said to be ignorant of good manners, too loud and indifferent to moral rules, especially those concerning women. The effort that all my informants put into affirming this ethical stance in the course of their daily lives suggests that it is precisely the sine qua non for outlaws seeking social respectability. Likewise, their frequent allusions to honor (*izzat*, *gairat*) in the context of acts of violence underscore the extent to which conflicts, if they comply with certain rules such as those of the vendetta (*dushmandari*), can contribute to the symbolic affirmation of their prestige and valor within a specific social class.[17]

In his youth, Yaseer had worked as an actor for Lollywood, the city's now defunct cinema industry, known for its connections to the underworld since the 1970s.[18] But his career eventually came to end in the early 2000s as a result of the murders and periods of incarceration that ensued from his long-standing family feud. He nostalgically recalls the beautiful actresses with whom he had starred and his frequent appearances on Karachi's film sets. In contrast to Karachi's senseless world of violence, which he attributes to the "Indian" duplicity inherent to its *muhajir* population (Urdu-speaking partition immigrants), Lahore's criminal milieu, he claims, derives from its distinctive "culture" of good-humored coarseness. While in Pakistan, Punjabi identity is often stereotyped as unsophisticated and boorish, for him and many in his milieu, Punjabis' crude conviviality and impulsiveness are endearing, though these traits may easily degenerate into brawls. But Yaseer's notion of "culture" (in English) also conjures a disappearing order in which the rural outlaw is imagined as a "social bandit" protecting the downtrodden. The ruthless hero fighting social injustice first emerged as a local figure in pre-partition Urdu literature and later in Punjabi cinema from the 1970s onward and confers a distinct moral contour to local narratives of crime and its protagonists, a feature that is supposedly lacking outside the province.

After a pause, Yaseer's son, leaning back on the sofa and tapping the butt of a gun with his finger, says, "This is a local pistol made by Pathans. This one, there, is a *traisat* [Stoner 63] with a thirty-round cartridge, and that's a SIG, made in China." But his father cuts in, "For peace to prevail in Pakistan, we need an Islamic system [*islami nizam*]. Consider Saudi Arabia; there is no crime at all there because they have strict Islamic punishments, while here money and power allow you to get away with anything. If I commit a murder, I can avoid punishment [by paying blood money]. It's the law of the jungle here [*jungli qanun*]; walking down the street, you could die anytime in a bomb blast. I've spent three years in jail. Why? Because to keep your 'balance' in this society, you need to do a bit of 'crime,' even if you don't want to. Given the kind of problems we've had to face, there's no other way around it."

Rather than a desire for a Taliban-style Islamic system, ubiquitous references to Saudi Arabia and the United Arab Emirates (UAE) as the embodiment of Islamic rule, even on behalf of not-so-pious Pakistani Muslims, are reflective of a widespread longing for judicial accountability. These are consistent with widespread popular mistrust toward state-based courts, perceived as dysfunctional and held captive to the vested interests of a corrupt elite, in particular among less privileged social groups.[19] Further, the last two decades have seen a vast "privatisation of penal justice," a direct consequence of the incorporation of elements of sharia law in Pakistani law.[20] Yaseer briefly alludes to it when he mentions the possibility of paying blood money, which allowed the CIA agent to avoid trial. Since the introduction of the retaliation and blood money laws in 1997, homicides are increasingly treated as private offenses against the heirs of the victim rather than as crimes against the state and society. The aggrieved party can suspend legal proceedings and pardon the accused in exchange for financial reparation.[21] This privatization of murder cases exacerbates a sense of cynicism among the population with regard to the courts and to the apparent impunity enjoyed by the most powerful. Conversely, this process allows men like Yaseer to present themselves as pacifying bosses capable of dispensing redress and justice to individuals disillusioned with official legal avenues or who cannot access them. Yaseer thus offers his services of mediation and arbitration in matters of blood money, real estate disputes, family feuds, or disagreements between shopkeepers. There are, however, other actors capable of proposing these services, such as local politicians, neighborhood mullahs, or traders' associations. The decision to solicit an outlaw rather than another type of mediator hinges on a number of factors, including one's financial resources, social capital, ideological sensibility, and contacts in the neighborhood.[22]

Whether related to a family feud (*khandani dushmandari*) with the obligation to take revenge to restore the honor compromised by an earlier murder, or simply to the material conditions of existence that become favorable to illegal ventures, these men frequently talk about "picking up the gun" as a duty that behooves them, as something to be accomplished reluctantly and with utmost civility. In short, one of the essential prerequisites for being a respected boss is to portray one's entry into illegality as a compulsion. This resonates with the way murders are talked about; one would say that "a murder happened by me" (*mujhse qatl hua*) rather than "I committed a murder" (*me ne qatl kiya*). On a different occasion I ask Yaseer why he thinks people prefer the passive voice for such transitive acts. "Someone like me couldn't commit a murder unless the order came from God. I mean, as a Muslim, I fear God. So we Muslims don't mistreat anyone; otherwise God would bring about all sorts of problems on us. So saying 'A murder was committed by me" [*mujhse*], rather than 'I committed a murder' implies compulsion [*majburi*]. Only a contract killer could say, 'I committed a murder.'"

I did meet Yaseer again during one of his drinking-cum-gambling sessions at his *dera*. But a few months later, as I tried to set up another visit through Yaqub, I was informed that he had been arrested.

QABZA AND THE LURE OF RESPECTABILITY

While Amir, Kalashaan, and Yaqub can only hope to become brokers and small-time bosses in working-class neighborhoods, Yaseer and other *dere-dars* of his caliber aspire to attain the dignity of white-collar dons (*safed-posh don*), as one of them once put it. The key to this transition consists in getting involved in real estate. Because of poor urban planning, increased migration to cities, and decreasing returns in the industrial sector, speculation in property and land has become one of the most profitable ventures in the last decade in Pakistan. Those who specialize in the illegal appropriation of land and properties are known as "land mafias" and "*qabza* groups." *Qabza* (lit., "possession, clutch"), or land grabbing, is a common form of illegal land transaction that entails acquiring public and private land, or a property, by seizing it illegally and laying claim to it on the basis of physical occupation. The process usually involves intimidating and bribing government officials.

A number of scholars have recently documented the elaborate squatting tactics and administrative maneuvering involved in regularizing illegal possessions, as well the complex ties between *qabza* specialists, religious groups, and Islamist militant organizations in urban Punjab.[23]

The polysemic concept of "*qabza* groups" emerged in the 1990s.[24] Such groups can be well-off families who collectively draw on their personal connections and resources to carry out the illegal construction of a residential neighborhood, for instance,[25] or powerful organized developers who systematically identify, illegally take over (sometimes violently), and then sell land for a profit in urban centers. These transactions involve a host of actors, including contractors, real estate developers, property agents, and *goondas*, but also police officers, bureaucrats, and elected politicians who facilitate land grabs in some areas while protecting properties from being grabbed in others.[26] Many police officers whom I met stressed the difficulty faced when dismantling these groups, precisely because of the personal stakes of government officials in these activities. These joint ventures constitute what people in Pakistan have come to term "mafias," a term now omnipresent in the press: the country is riddled with "fake degree mafias," "begging mafias," "gas mafias," so much so that even butchers are said to have their own mafia. Even the Punjab chief minister, though often accused of being a mafioso himself, often promises to take action against "mafia lords,"[27] and the Punjab governor recently resigned on the grounds that "land grabbers and mafias here are stronger than the office of governor."[28] In short, the concept lends coherence to what are in fact loose and shifting criminal formations and networks of patronage.

As far as *qabza* is concerned, the most visible part of these formations is usually the so-called property dealer, an essential figure in the neighborhoods where I worked, which designates someone involved in shady land or property transactions. *Dere-dars* often deal with such property dealers, usually to provide manpower to squat in a particular property. With the surge in terrorist activities over the last decade, renting a flat has become increasingly difficult, especially for single males from outside the locality. The police force often entrusts these property dealers with the task of passing on information about prospective tenants.[29] Thus, one can be part of a land mafia while simultaneously carrying out antiterrorism surveillance, a fact that illustrates how the working of the state directly participates in blurring the steadfast lawful/criminal dichotomy otherwise asserted, albeit rhetorically, by its elected representatives and enforcement agencies.

Property disputes and acts of *qabza* are the bread and butter of Yaseer and the other *dere-dars* of his stature. Oftentimes these disputes occur within families. For instance, two brothers inherit a house, but only one of them wants to sell it. He contacts a *dere-dar* who will buy his share of the property and regularize the purchase. Associates of the *dere-dar* can now squat some of the rooms. "Once we have a foot in the house, we try to buy the rest," one of them explained. This entails gradually putting pressure on the reluctant brother, cornering him, so to speak, until he accepts to sell his share. Likewise, if a *qabza* group seeks to take over a building, they may initially approach the widows residing therein, offer them a good deal for their portion, and then pressure the other owners with a view to acquiring the entire building.

THE ADJUDICATING BUTTS

In popular imagination, three men have dominated the Lahori underworld in recent decades: Tipu, Gogi, and Teefi. The first is Arif Ameer Butt, also known as Tipu Truckonwala—the "truck owner." His father, the owner of a sizable fleet of trucks, was shot dead in 1994, like his grandfather a few years earlier. Father and son ran a goods transport company from their base next to Lahore's Old City. According to one version, one of Tipu's cousins was keen to become an actor, so Tipu paid a filmmaker, Hanifa, to produce a film starring his cousin as the hero: Hanifa never produced the film, Tipu demanded his money back, so Hanifa and his accomplice Baba shot Tipu's father.[30] Another account holds that Hanifa and Baba, who were brothers employed by Tipu as gunmen, killed a resident of the Old City. A case was registered against them and Tipu. But the two brothers suspected that Tipu's father was pressuring the police to incriminate them and spare his son. Hanifa and Baba therefore tried to kill Tipu, failed, but two days later succeeded in killing his father.[31] This assassination marks the beginning of a twenty-year rivalry between the two groups.

Hanifa and Baba then formed a gang with a group of renowned criminals and in 1995 went on to attack Tipu's maternal uncle. In those days, Hanifa and Baba allegedly specialized in extorting money from Punjab's rich businessmen, traders, and industrialists.[32] By then, both Tipu's group and his rivals had developed influential contacts with the police hierarchy, which they used to evade arrest but also to register cases against each other. Filing an FIR against your enemy meant that person had to leave town for a few months, thereby giving you the upper hand over your rivals. Tipu also enjoyed the support of PML-N leaders, to whom he sometimes lent his lion during election campaigns.[33]

A few years later, Tipu discovered that his nemeses were now close to the powerful Butt cousins, Teefi and Gogi, who henceforth became his enemies. In the decade that followed, these groups engaged in a number of spectacular attacks against each other. Armed with Kalashnikovs and riding motorbikes, the shooters targeted their victims outside courts and hospitals or at their respective *deras*. Increasingly, the group leaders also had their rivals killed in staged police encounters (*muqabla*) through the intercession of corrupt inspectors. Following each attempted murder, the aggrieved party would take legal action against its aggressor. This led to the trend of intimidating and killing witnesses brought to testify in court, a strategy relatively common since then.[34]

Many of these rivalries came to an end in 2010 after Tipu's return from a trip to Dubai, where he had sent his family. He was shot outside Lahore's airport and died in the hospital two days later, surrounded by his armed men and local politicians. According to Tipu's relatives, Teefi and Gogi Butt were among the masterminds of the attack. By 2012, two key witnesses in Tipu's murder case were assassinated, and Gogi was acquitted of murder charges for lack of evidence. Tipu is survived by his son, who has faced a number of assassination charges in the recent past.[35]

The other so-called underworld don of Lahore, Khwaja Aqeel Butt, also known as Gogi Butt or Big B., is the son of a gas station owner from Gowalmandi, one of Lahore's oldest neighborhoods and home to a prosperous Kashmiri community. Like Nawaz Sharif's family, Gogi's came to this neighborhood from Amritsar following partition. Aside from running his gas station, Gogi's father, a respected figure in the neighborhood, served as an informal mediator in local disputes. Gogi and his cousin Teefi inherited the mantle and shifted their interest to real estate and resolution of property disputes; they therefore form what many would call a land mafia or *qabza* group. Their ties to influential politicians, police officials, bureaucrats, and army men are well documented and have been key to their successful venture.

In the late 1980s, the family and the rest of the neighborhood supported the Pakistan People Party (PPP) rather than their fellow Kashmiri neighbor Nawaz Sharif. They were eventually convinced to support him in the next elections. Following the 1999 coup and the exile of the Sharifs, General Musharraf sought their support and in return offered them key positions in the management of a lucrative local project involving a street of restaurants—"Food Street"—located in Butt's neighborhood. After their return from exile, feeling betrayed, the Sharif brothers shut it down. A few years later, an agreement was reached; the Butts resumed supporting the PML-N and were made chairmen of Food Street again. Their ability to switch political sides (PPP, PML-N, PML-Q, and back to PML-N) while maintaining cordial relations with all parties and institutions, including the army, is remarkable. It is this maneuvering that allowed them to maintain influential contacts in the police. In fact, most of their rivals were killed in staged police encounters, allegedly on the instruction of the Butts. Surges in extrajudicial killings of renowned criminals in Lahore over the last two decades coincided with Shahbaz Sharif's terms in office as chief minister (especially 1997–99). A senior journalist recounted that when Gogi Butt was arrested during that period, his mother went to talk to Shamim Akhtar, mother of Nawaz and Shahbaz Sharif, to sort things out. By the late 2000s, most of Lahore's "top-ten" criminals had been killed or were in exile. The rest, mostly powerful families and *biradris* (clans) caught in intergenerational feuds, were encouraged to make peace with each other. These reconciliations, facilitated by influential *dere-dars*, usually took place in Lahore's main mosques in the presence of senior politicians, notables, and hundreds of witnesses.

After months of failed attempts through Amir and Kalashaan's contacts, I am finally able to gain access to Gogi Butt's *dera*, where I meet one of his close relatives and associates, Kabir Butt (not his real name). I arrive in the alley at night. Above the entrance, perched on a balcony, a guard armed with a shotgun screens me and lets me in. Several men are sitting in the hallway, smoking cigarettes with their Kalashnikovs on their laps. Kabir, a well-mannered, stout, bearded man in starched *shalwar-kameez*, greets me in a spacious living room adorned with framed verses from the Quran on the walls.

While sharing his dish of grilled fish with me, he enumerates the personalities that came to this *dera* seeking his family's support for elections or to enjoy the festivities of *Basant* (kite festival) on their rooftop: Nawaz Sharif, Benazir Bhutto,[36] and the American consul among others. Supporting a political party, he explains, simply entails putting up a few posters displaying the Butts' portrait next to that of a politician: "People understand that we side with him, and they vote accordingly; we don't need to shout slogans." Kabir did get involved in local politics for a few years but soon realized that it would jeopardize his integrity. Likewise, his relatives never entered the political fray, which they regard as demeaning, holding that their role as mediators was a more efficient way of serving people. So he returned to his occupation as an informal adjudicator and businessman: the steel and rice businesses in Dubai and Saudi Arabia, poultry and real estate in Lahore.

"Being a *dere-dar* and arbitrating [*faisla karna*] takes up too much of my time," he laments. As a result he sees only people who come with a recommendation. Just like the institution of the *dera*, the process of adjudication practiced in urban Punjab draws on local traditions now associated with rural areas and is hence sometimes referred to as a *panchayati faisla*. Here is an example of a typical adjudication process leading to arbitration.

A family accuses another of having murdered their son. Both are brought to the local police station, and each party brings dozens of people along with them to impress. The station house officer [SHO] carries out his investigation, but the case is simultaneously brought before an adjudicator, the choice of whom must satisfy both parties involved. The adjudicator carefully listens to each representative to ascertain the truth of the matter. If he cannot tell which of the two is lying, he demands that each party bring along nine individuals to testify. Each of them is asked to swear [*qasam*] that the party representative who brought them along is telling the truth, thereby exculpating him [*safai*]. The deponents must themselves be of good reputation and standing [*sharif*], but if the rival party deems that they are not impartial [*khair-janibdar*], the adjudicator asks the concerned party to bring new ones. This formal adjudication takes place in a mosque, and the deponents put their hand on the Quran while giving the oath. Ideally the final verdict and its binding sentence, which can be written down and taken to the investigating SHO, bring about a reconciliation [*sulah*, "patch-up"] between the contending parties. Aside from the compensation awarded to the aggrieved party [e.g., land, property, money], the adjudicator expects a form of remuneration for his services, euphemistically referred to as "sweets" [*mithai*].

In most cases, however, the process is more straightforward, and neither deponents nor oath is deemed necessary. As one outlaw adjudicator explained, "If I ask someone to swear, and he lies and I find out, then I'll have no choice but to be rough with him. I'll have to shoot him down. That's why I don't ask them to swear on the Quran." Furthermore, within this milieu the verdicts are viewed as binding since the adjudicators tend to have killed in the past or to have had people executed on their orders. Referring to Gogi Butt and his relatives, the same adjudicator added, "You respect them, because they've killed so many people; it's your duty to respect them. They can get anyone killed anytime; they don't need to step out of their homes; a phone call is sufficient. It's like in the movies [*filmi kaam*]."

As exemplified in these descriptions, the urban *dera* is not an alternative site of justice per se, since those seeking the assistance of an adjudicating outlaw may simultaneously turn to lawyers and to the police for justice. Further, these arbitrations are sometimes perceived as iniquitous, because they are subject to relations of power and influence between the opposing sides and the conciliator. But there is a distinctive appeal to these quotidian forms of adjudication. Aside from the fact that the police and judiciary are perceived to be excessively slow and highly corruptible—and they are—in reaching a decision the adjudicator takes into consideration factors that do not receive much attention within formal judicial hearings: the relative power of the contending parties, their reputation, and the need to reach a consensus and avoid embarrassing the loser.

Kabir compares this work to that of a diplomat. "The verdicts that I give often involve crores of rupees, so I take my time. I listen to what each party has to say. Even if someone is lying, I have to listen to his arguments. Of course, I sometimes have to raise my voice if someone doesn't comply, but they usually do. . . . It is my belief in Allah that guides my decisions. Knowing what is right and what is wrong. Because I'll be accountable on Judgment Day!" Aside from arbitrations, the other task expected of a *dere-dar*, Kabir says, is what he and all his fellow adjudicators call "social work"—the display of one's altruistic commitment to the neighborhood: paying for the weddings and dowries of destitute people, helping out orphans, providing recommendations, and occasionally finding jobs for those who have rendered services. One such *dere-dar* specialized in gambling, for instance, and is known to facilitate the work of a local nongovernmental organization (NGO) working in the field of LGBT rights.

Although not made explicit by Kabir, it is the decade-long feud that pits his family against that of Tipu, and now against other criminal groups, which enabled him and his relatives to gain so much influence in the first place and to walk the fine line between legality and crime with such lordly nonchalance. Inflicting death in the context of a family feud is the legitimizing principle par excellence for would-be dons. For those concerned, these feuds entail limited interaction on the streets and heavy protection at all times, a lifestyle that many aspirant bosses, such as Yaqub, Amir, and Kalashaan, repeatedly emphasize when accounting for their fascination with the underworld. A family feud, Kabir told me, "It's like riding a tiger: when you sit on it, you go extremely fast, but as soon as you get off it, you have to run for your life." He and his Butt relatives cannot make peace with his archenemies, he explains, since the countless murders and retaliations on each side have exhausted the trust necessary for a possible reconciliation.

It would be wrong to assume that the bosses that I document here undermine the state and established political hierarchies. A number of senior police officials that I interviewed argue that their priority has always been to maintain peace and order in the city rather than eliminate petty crime. Facilitating a balance of power between the main groups, such as the Butts and Tipus, is key to this endeavor. Just like the influential traders' unions in town who often form "peace groups" (*aman* groups) in their markets, these criminal formations are essential in assisting the police to prevent petty crime and arrest offenders. This pacifying role presumably gives these groups leverage in their negotiations with police officials, politicians, and bureaucrats. This quasi-institutionalized role was evident when, shortly after his coup, General Musharraf attempted to impose a general sales tax on traders, only to provoke nationwide protest and rallies: Gogi Butt is said to have played a major role as a negotiator between police authorities and the leading traders' association (the Qaumi Tajar Ittehad), headed by none other than his own cousin. Kabir did not elaborate on his family's relations with the police but simply explained that he had to deal with them on a daily basis and would sometimes reward cooperating officers, for instance, by facilitating their transfer to a different police station in the city or in the province.

Amir, Kalashaan, Yaqub, Yaseer, and Kabir represent different nuances and career paths of Lahore's so-called underworld. While the younger generation tends to emphasize the glamour of transgression associated with the life of an outlaw, the more established and senior *dere-dars* that I have met espouse the trope of the gentleman criminal, a charitable boss considerate toward the weaker members of society yet capable of meting out violence to assert his honor and right to rule. In this respect, there is a remarkable degree of rhetorical adherence within this section of the underworld to this moral grammar of crime, according to which homicides are deemed legitimate only insofar as they are grounded in ethical considerations. This narrative of the respectable gangster/boss, I suggest, is central to the production of criminal biographies in the region. But of course this self-legitimizing repertoire, designed to justify their activities, cannot be taken at face value nor abstracted from the practical conditions of fieldwork, where access to actual transactions, negotiations, and acts of violence remains largely unavailable.

Within the broader landscape of South Asian bossism, Pakistan's urban Punjab is characterized by a relative compartmentalization between crime and politics. Successful bosses may assist elected politicians in matters of *qabza* in exchange for some degree of legal impunity, but by and large my interlocutors do not seek to enter electoral politics, an oligarchic domain out of reach for those who do not possess a prohibitive amount of social and landed capital and in which the demand for party loyalty can easily hamper other activities in case of regime change. However, the incapacity of the state to guarantee security and access to a fair justice system for all facilitates the outsourcing of some state responsibilities to individuals like Kabir and his Butt relatives. This partial divestment of the state, sustained by relations of connivance between political, state, and criminal actors, implies a form of co-supervision of the urban poor and the territories they inhabit. Located between competing registers of sovereignty, my interlocutors and their *dera*, therefore, support the sociopolitical structure in which they operate more than they undermine it, and this despite their claims to the contrary. The legend of the "gentleman criminal" and the promise of social justice that sustains it cannot conceal the constitutive interdependence between the formal sovereignty of the state and these men who claim autonomy from it.

CHAPTER 6

LADY DABANG

Lucia Michelutti

IN NOVEMBER 2012, when crossing the Yamuna bridge on my way into town, I saw a man throwing a pistol in the river. A bit puzzled, I asked the driver, "Did you see that?" "Yes, I did," he answered; "the short man dressed in the blue shirt just threw a gun into the river." The driver did not seem at all surprised by what we just witnessed. "Is that normal?" I asked, and he answered, "Madam, we live in the Mafia Raj! Forget about the gun. That's my advice. *Goondagardi* [criminal work] is the city pastime." A few months later when I arrived in town, this time by train, there was a dead body lying outside the station. The man had just been found with a bullet in his head. The *rickshawalla* who took me to the guesthouse was completely unperturbed by the event: "*Goondagardi* is the town business. . . . Criminals are protected. . . . They are able to operate and flourish—the party at the government protects them, and they get revenues from them—it is all about '*goonda tax*.'" I asked him, "Do you pay protection money?" He smiled and said, "Of course, everybody does," and added, "don't look at the body; otherwise your day will be marred by bad luck."

After a few months of research I established that protection and extortion are attractive avenues to power and wealth in this provincial town in western Uttar Pradesh. In this part of the world, extortion is an easy way to make money rapidly, and it is quite low risk. The extraction of the *goonda tax*—locally known as *chauth vasuli*, which refers to the Maratha practice of collecting 25 percent of the profit/production for protection—is the backbone of many of the careers of local elected bosses, popularly referred in this part of India as *dabang* and integral part of local "arts" of bossing.

This term entered the popular lexicon following the release of two films by that name—*Dabang* (2010) and *Dabang 2* (2012)—and is now commonly used to refer to gangster-politicians and, more generally, enforcers. *Dabangs*, unlike mere *goondas* (thugs), are people who can instill fear and respect. They are the local de facto sovereigns who can kill and punish with relative impunity and, more increasingly, with democratic legitimacy. It is important to highlight that the *dabangs* I met over the course of my fieldwork represent a qualitative shift from the traditional figures of the *bhai* or *dada* (strongman) in any North Indian provincial town until about two decades ago. The traditional town and neighborhood bosses used to establish their sovereignty through protection rackets, moneylending, and adjudicating disputes.[1] These old-style protectors–cum–social bandits boasted an exceptional muscular physique and reputed fighting techniques—usually acquired through wrestling. They employed their force to establish domination in the *mohalla* (neighborhood) and to acquire "violent" credibility with their patrons (who were often the local politicians). However, today in the words of an aspiring *dabang*, "You just need a pistol, courage, and to get involved in the *bhumi* [land] mafia." By moving into land development and joining forces with developers in the lucrative construction industry, the small-town bosses and their associates have transmogrified into well-financed interstate criminal networks whose criminal capital is used to build up political turfs. In short, traditional specialists of violence stopped supplying their services to the big leaders: they stopped acting as mercenaries for their landlords and patrons and instead began to use their muscular skills to stage a better life for themselves and their families and create their political mafia-esque clans.

Thus, a *dabang* is a person who combines a professional criminal career with a professional legitimate political and business career. One needs only to live for a few weeks in a provincial town in Uttar Pradesh to start to recognize the local bosses. In this corner of South Asia the art of bossing has a powerful aesthetic power. A typical *dabang* uses and crucially shows off his own "crew" as bodyguards; travels in a white 4×4 with flashing lights and party flags; flaunts his or her wealth and power with weapons and ostentatious gold jewelry; and often owns a large farmhouse on the outskirts of town. These strongmen have a recognizable behavioral and figurative style that requires visible violence and/or the threat of violence, as well as visible wealth. Weapons and a large entourage of men are crucial to the *dabang*'s credibility. And not just any weapons will do. German-imported Mausers seem to be a must. The cost of a secondhand Mauser on the black market is about US$15,000—certainly not cheap. The new *dabangs* are not only different from the old wrestler-enforcer-muscleman, but they are also substantially distinct from contemporary professional thugs. *Dabangs'* violent appropriations are often visible because they can operate with relative impunity. *Dabangs* do not care if their spectacular kidnappings or assaults are caught on camera. They actually thrive on the attention. These violent shows publicly advertise their tough and fearless reputation and, most important, their capacity for breaking the law with impunity. Making their criminal activities visible distinguishes them from other types of professional criminals, such as thieves or terrorists or mere corrupt politicians, who tend to keep a low profile because they do not want to be caught by the police.[2] *Dabangs* collaborate with the authorities and aspire to become part of the authorities through elections to acquire extra power and impunity. What is kept obscured and untraceable rather than secret is the organization of their economic activities. Often through land deals and misappropriation of public funds, the new *dabangs* amass an unprecedented amount of capital, which they invest in legal businesses such as cement industries, construction companies, hotel chains, and restaurants. These businesses and properties are often registered under "borrowed names," those of relatives, drivers, or bodyguards.[3] Thus, on the one hand, *dabangs* invest a great deal of energy in enacting a violent reputation and sometimes a Robin Hood and saintly boss image, and, on the other, they take great care to conceal the existence of the organizational structure of their mafia-like enterprises and the names of their associates.

However, contrary to the Lahore bosses we encountered in this book who operate in the criminal underworld, what I describe is a criminal overworld. The protagonist of this story is a fascinating and fearless, violent businesswoman who has risen to power and wealth in an extremely violent and male-dominated corner of North India. Locals often refer to her as "Lady Dabang" (the gangster lady).[4] She is a remarkable woman. She arrived in the district when she was a teenager—escaping an abusive father from the nearby state of Madhya Pradesh. She was forced to marry a man thirty-eight years older than she and gave birth to her first child at the age of fourteen. She started her *dabang* career by allegedly cutting the throat (so she is popularly known to have done) of a doctor and by allegedly killing a policeman. According to folklore they both tried to rape her. Locals say she was a prostitute. She said she was a health-care assistant. From working in the local hospital she moved on to act as a criminal broker and informer for the police and local big men; then she moved to land grabbing and joined forces with local property developers and the construction industry in the late 1990s. Simultaneously, she started her political career. Allegedly through powerful "boyfriend-protectors," she entered into local politics and subsequently moved on to contest state and national elections. She is now a multimillionaire thanks to land speculation and alleged appropriations of public funding.

Her story not only challenges both the underworld and standard society ethical code but, more crucially, exemplifies a mini-revolution in the local political economy gangsterism and politics in this part of the world. Western Uttar Pradesh has undergone tremendous economic and social transformations over the past two decades. Today more than two hundred million people live in the state, a fifth of whom are Muslim. The rest are mostly Hindu and divided broadly between three mutually antagonistic caste groups: the upper-caste Brahmins and Thakurs; the lower-caste Dalits; and the "other backward classes" such as the Yadavs.

This region of Uttar Pradesh has been increasingly perceived in the popular national perception as the Sicily of North India. Western Uttar

Pradesh is widely known for its endemic violence; for being culturally shaped by the macho ethos of its dominant castes like Jats, Yadavs, Gujars, and Rajputs; for being marred by communalism and caste-based conflicts; and for poverty and underdevelopment. Available statistics and sociological studies have defined this area as the cradle of a "subculture of violence" and the home of "institutionalized riot systems."[5] However, what it is perhaps deeply misleading is the portrayal of this region as a poor provincial backwater. On the contrary, "money," as informants again and again emphasize, "is not an issue here."

In 2014 a provincial town in the studied region was the place in India where the largest number of luxury packet holidays were sold.[6] This is a land where fortunes have been made in one generation, where the divide between rich and poor is widening, and where upward mobility and entrepreneurship are fully entrenched in the imaginations and fantasies of the younger generations. It is one of the *mofussil* (provincial) and rural areas of the country where a twenty-first-century Indian version of the American El Dorado is taking place. The economy of this region has been changed by the commercialization of agricultural land. Real estate prices are skyrocketing as a result of quicker access to Delhi, thanks to the construction of the Yamuna Expressway and to its proximity to the industrial and residential hubs of Noida and Faridabad. Demand from investors from Delhi, Haryana, Gujarat, and West Bengal, as well as global speculators, have intensified since the late 1990s. These developments have given rise to an intense scramble for valuable economic assets and opened up a space for *dabangs* and their flexible organized companies to regulate and control the production and distribution of particular illegal commodities or services related to urban development and infrastructure expansion. From Delhi to Agra on the national highway, shopping malls, gated townships, education complexes, flyovers, and religious temples and new ashrams run by international gurus are mushrooming. The area from Delhi to Agra includes Braj (the mythical Land of Krishna), which has been actively promoted by the government and private projects as a profitable religious and tourist hub. It is in this local booming economy that *dabangs* and their power syndicates pursue violent forms of capital accumulation through increasingly cartelized "land mafias," "sand mafias," "construction mafias," "oil mafias," or "water mafias" and "temple rackets." The power syndicates involved in the area are many: they are also flexible, volatile, fragmented, and in constant flux. To complicate their mapping, the sociocultural and economic area in which they operate overlaps with four states: Rajasthan, Haryana, Delhi, and Madhya Pradesh. Most local mafia networks are hence interstate criminal groups, which makes them difficult to police.[7] Unfortunately, there is a complete lack of coordination between central and state police bodies. India does not have a national-level agency to coordinate the efforts of the state police forces and central enforcement agencies to fight organized crime. "There is no agency to collect, collate, analyze, document, and function as a central exchange of information relating to international and interstate gangs operating in India and abroad."[8] It follows that by simply crossing the border into Rajasthan, a *dabang* who commits a murder in Uttar Pradesh can easily avoid being investigated, caught, and prosecuted. So, this area enjoys an extra layer of relative impunity due to its interstate geographical character.

High levels of crime live in symbiosis with routinized forms of social and political violence and conflicts. This is one of the regions of India where over the past two decades lower castes have politically challenged the domination of upper castes and where communal tensions have been at their highest. More specifically, over the past twenty years, Uttar Pradesh politics has been characterized by the struggles and shifting strategies of two major political groups: the Yadavs and Dalits and the two political parties with which each is respectively associated, the Samajwadi Party (SP) and the Bahujan Samaj Party (BSP).[9] Both Yadavs and Dalits have benefited a great deal from affirmative action policies, rising up to be the key protagonists of both India's "second democratic upsurge" and its rising "patronage democracy."[10] Hence, the careers of contemporary *dabangs* have not only been shaped by economic liberalization or by their criminal skills or personal charisma but also by the opportunities created by a lively multiparty competition paired with a high level of communal and caste-based conflict in the areas where they rule.[11]

Democratic competition, as Wilkinson argues, produces a heightened scramble for monetary and political resources and turns money and muscle power into prerequisites for electoral success.[12] Moreover, the need for muscle power is at its peak in areas with deep community divides where voters desire forceful representatives whom they perceive can protect their group-based interests most credibly.[13] It has been established that political parties select criminal candidates in those areas where social divisions are the most contested,[14] and this was precisely the setting for Lady Dabang to be approached by several political parties to contest municipal (*nagar palika*), state, and national elections from the late 1990s.

It was from this period that Uttar Pradesh started to witness the political rise of iconic bosses like D. P. Yadav in Aligarh, Raja Bhaia in Kunda, Ramkant Yadav in Azamgarh, the Ansari brothers in Varanasi, Mr. Tiwari in Gorakhpur, and, along with them, an increase in aspiring *dabangs* and enforcers across the state.[15] It follows that by 2002 almost 50 percent of political candidates in Uttar Pradesh had criminal charges registered against them or were under investigation. Criminal candidates won 206 of 403 seats, an absolute majority of 51.1 percent, and earned for the SP, which governed the state between 2002 and 2007, the title of "Goonda Raj." The 2007 election to the Uttar Pradesh State Assembly marked the end of the SP's rule and the rise to power of the rival BSP. Counter to what many had hoped for, this election was no less criminalized. Indeed, in 2007, the number of criminal candidates from both parties increased, and the winning BSP fielded the highest proportion of criminal candidates (34 percent). The SP returned to power in 2012. Despite a vocal anticriminalization campaign launched by the Election Commission and several civil society groups (including the Anna Hazare movement), a total of 189 legislators, or 47 percent, of the 2012–2017 elected State Assembly had criminal charges pending against them (according to the affidavits they were now required to file by law).[16]

Lady Dabang is a Category A "history-sheeter."[17] In 2012, she had nineteen criminal cases, two for murder and four for extortion, pending against her; this list does not include the numerous civil court cases she is currently involved in, mainly white-collar crimes to do with property disputes and land fraud. By 2012, Lady Dabang had established a powerful (criminal) political enterprise. Ordinary people use the terms "company," "lobby," "firm," or "mafia racket/cartel" (in Hindi English) and *parivar* (family) to refer to these criminal enterprises and political clans. To protect both their illegal and legal activities, the companies need to be active in the political, judicial, and security systems of the state with money and violence. Companies have internal "concentric circles" of power.[18] The boss is often surrounded by a circle of about twenty or thirty young people who are often derogatively known as *chamchas* (sycophants). These young men (and seldom women) need to show courage, reliability, and devotion to their boss. Bosses are then surrounded by a trusted inner circle, which is formed mainly by family and kin. A further circle is composed mainly of local goons and their crews, gunmen, moneylenders, and businessmen and government administrators who know they are dealing with a *dabang*'s company but do not know how the company works internally. Another important figure in this circle is the lawyer. Finally, there is a further protective circle at the level of the territory that the boss is actually de facto governing or aspiring to control. The reputation and operations of *dabangs* are territorialized. The boss relies on the complicity, collaboration, and silence of the local population.

Lady Dabang and her crew are specialized in land grabs and illicit land speculation. When she was a municipality councilor, she was accused of grabbing municipal land and properties and of making high profits by selling them to estate developers from Delhi and Mumbai. However, according to the town residents the police have taken very little action against members of her firm. In 2010, when the SP was no longer in power, Lady Dabang shifted alliance and moved in with the BSP to obtain the necessary political protection that keeps her out of jail and her political criminal business going. She has been very successful in this game, and her career shows that she had relevant and effective contacts in Lucknow that are helping her and her sons slow down court proceedings and get prestigious political parties' tickets from two of the most powerful state political parties, the BSP and SP. In her own words,

> During my tenure many big leaders filed cases against me. They used to complain about me in Lucknow [i.e., to the chief minister]. They would try to involve me in false cases and send me to prison. They used to audit and reaudit my work again and again. So I got smart; I tackled them very cleverly. I hired ten of the best lawyers available. I followed their advice. They have not been able to trap me yet. . . . I am winning.

I met Lady Dabang in 1999 when she was not yet a proper *dabang*. At that time, she was not hanging around with renowned lawyers from the capital, and she was not yet entangled in state and national political scams related to the construction of the Yamuna Express. By then, however, she was already implicated in a murder. By then, she had also already run in the State Assembly elections.[19] I met her at a political party meeting being held to discuss the forthcoming 1999 national election campaign. The event was organized at the home of V. Kumar, an emerging figure in the political landscape at the time. Lady Dabang was in the company of another woman, an MLA (Member of Legislative Assembly) who was visiting from Mumbai. I was quite surprised to see two women at a party gathering in the *mohalla*, as such parties were usually strictly men-only events. Women were not part of the political life of the neighborhood, and most lived in *parda*.[20] Houses were divided (and still mostly are) into female and male quarters. Women rarely mixed with male guests, and if they did, it was only with close family friends. Therefore, every event that I attended was really two events: the men gathered in one part of the house and the women in another. On most of these occasions, my research interests led me to spend time in men's company, although in the case of public events, I did not have the choice of whether to spend time with men or with women. Women were (and still are) peripheral to the public political culture of the neighborhood and town. I clearly remember being impressed by Lady Dabang's confidence, directness, and the way she looked straight into the eyes of her male interlocutors. Her body language was very different from the body language of the women I had met in the neighborhood. She was not conventionally beautiful, yet her self-confidence made her quite attractive. V. Kumar introduced her to me as "the local Phulan Devi." Phulan Devi, popularly known as the Bandit Queen, was a criminal politician from a lower caste, operating in the nearby Chambal River area. In 1996, Phulan Devi won elections with an SP ticket from the nearby Mirzapur constituency. She lost her seat in the 1998 election but was reelected in the 1999 election and was a sitting member of Parliament when she was assassinated in 2001. Over the past ten years, Phulan Devi has become a myth and achieved heroic international status.[21] Today, her figurality is an integral part of the aesthetic power of Mafia Raj in North India and beyond. Lady Dabang and I sat in a corner talking about Phulan Devi. Then she went to fetch some tea and offered me hot samosas. When I left, Rajiv (a twenty-two-year old party worker) followed me and advised me not to be seen with her. "She doesn't have a good reputation . . . she's a *randi* [prostitute] . . . she's after power and is in a relation with A. P. Yadav [a powerful local party boss]." I still remember being very surprised by this remark. Very rarely did people talk openly about extramarital affairs, and almost never when local figures of authority like A. P. Yadav were involved. I thought Ravi was exaggerating and did not make much of it. The following day I inquired about the affair, but nobody seemed to want to talk about it. I forgot all about it until a few months later when A. P. Yadav was publicly criticized for keeping part of the campaign budget for himself and his alleged "mistress."

It is popularly known that party leaders gave large sums of money to the election candidates to organize their campaigns. Locally this money was seen as community money that needed to be shared. Allegedly A. P. Yadav received a large sum to distribute for the election campaign in 1999 but kept it for himself, or so people suspected. The neighborhood coordinated a spectacular protest. One morning, the residents woke up and found the streets covered with hundreds of leaflets. The text was written in powerful satirical language and portrayed the local politician as a eunuch. It described how the local politician had completely lost control of his manhood and had become the puppet of his mistress. The party leadership soon learned about the episode and

A. P. Yadav was suspended. Indeed, the political fortunes of the local leader ended then, whereas his alleged mistress became a very successful multimillionaire and powerful *dabang*.

In March 2012, I returned to follow up on the Uttar Pradesh state elections, and I bumped into Lady Dabang while reading an election complaint that I collected at the local town Election Commission office. The complaint was accusing a certain Mrs. X of hiding a large sum of money to be used to buy votes in the upcoming elections:

> Mrs. X has procured a huge amount of money, approximately eight crore rupees [eighty million] for use in the elections. This money is hidden in an *almirah* [cabinet] and bed at her residence located at XXX. Apart from this there is information about a substantial amount of money kept at the flats of her sons . . . and at a farmhouse on highway [addresses given]. Please organize a raid tonight. No information about this action should be given to local police of town X. For any assistance you may contact S. C., advocate, on [telephone number given]. . . . This lady has a long criminal history.[22]

When I came across this complaint, I was sitting in the Election Committee control room drinking *chai* (tea) and having a conversation with the local officers. In the room there were four low-level officers and a couple of visitors: two party workers and a local journalist. I asked who Mrs. X was; my question received smiles and a sudden silence. The men looked at each other; then Ravinder Kumar said, “She is a goon, a proper *dabang*: she is a bad woman.” Another officer added, “She used to be a prostitute; now she is a *crorepatri* [billionaire] . . . *bhumi mafia* [land mafia] deals. . . . She is dangerous, very dangerous.” Another man mumbled a joke and made sure I could not properly understand it by using the local Brajbhasi dialect—everybody in the room started laughing. On the way out, I asked the friend who was accompanying to translate the joke. Slightly embarrassed, he explained, “He said that people in town can still remember what kind of sex services they could get from her for forty rupees and seventy rupees.” And that is how I was reintroduced to Lady Dabang fifteen years after our first meeting in a nearby town. Needless to say, I was intrigued and impressed by her career progress: How did she make it? How did she become a boss?

At first, I did not realize that I had already met her. It was only when I started to make inquiries in the neighborhood that I remembered. My long-term informant Pavan reminded me, "She's not good; don't mix with her. She had many boyfriends; she is a *goonda*, a proper *goonda*. . . . She used to be with Mulayam; now she's shifted to Mayawati. Behenji seems to like her. . . . They have something in common." I asked him what they had in common. He looked at me cheekily: "An affair in this neighborhood!!! Don't you know that Mayawati used to make *chapatis* [bread] for Mahendraji and go to have a bath in the Yamnunaji, at the neighborhood *ghat*?"[23] He was referring to Kumari Mayawati, the current leader of the BSP and former Uttar Pradesh chief minister who, according to *mohalla* rumors, had a long and important affair with a local political leader in the late 1980s. Over the past fifteen years, many people have confirmed this story, and it has become part of the folklore of the district.

It is also true that Mayawati seems to have a soft spot for this area and openly patronized and protected this region with a Rs. 250 crore package during her tenure as chief minister between 2007 and 2012. The so-called dream project linked up with the construction of the six-lane superhighway connecting Delhi to Agra was a cash cow. Many local politicians, including Lady Dabang, were implicated in huge scams. Court cases are still pending while her wealth increases.

Mayawati is another remarkable woman from humble origins who has risen to power and wealth in an area mainly dominated by men. She is known to be a strong authoritarian leader with a masculine, aggressive outlook. Her style subverts upper-caste notions of femininity and ladylike behavior associated with meekness, mildness, subservience, docility, and hierarchical forms of address.[24] Lady Dabang has a photograph of Mayawati hung above her bed. It is the only photograph in her expensively furnished bedroom. I was invited into this private room a couple of times when she did not want party workers listening in on our conversations. Bodyguards and party workers were not allowed to enter this space.

Both her farmhouse and townhouse are decorated in a very eclectic style. Spartan office furniture and corporate black leather sofas are mixed with girly pink flowery upholstery, blue velvet armchairs, and diffuse red lighting that would not be out of place in a Mumbai nightclub. The room in her townhouse where she usually meets her visitors features a flamboyant red armchair surrounded by executive chairs. The walls and ceiling are decorated with panels featuring birds and pink and yellow flowers. Painted birds and blooms in luscious bright colors alternate with large mirror panels. The sidelights are red, and an opulent chandelier completes the decor of this board-cum-*darbar* room.[25]

Her office has a conference table with a light brown top. This very modern table is accompanied by flowery paneled walls and a cacophony of decorative pieces featuring pots, dolls, stuffed animals, gods, and herons. Painted herons, heron statues, and pots decorated with herons seem to be almost an obsessive pattern. I could not help thinking about the wonderful book by Raheja and Gold that describes that herons, in North India's oral traditions, are viewed as duplicitous and conniving and that these traditions view women dangerously split between virtuosity shaped by obligations to families and husband and an alternative moral perspective shaped by themselves. In this world, the heron's words spoken through local epics and songs become a critique of women's subordinate position.[26] Lady Dabang certainly incarnates many alternative moral perspectives: lying on the conference table are the *Bhagavad Gita*, the Indian Penal Code, the BSP manifesto, and a picture of her grandchildren. I think this stylistic hybridity and symbolism fully reflect her personality and her being simultaneously a boss, a businesswoman, a mother, and a grandmother.

During her political public appearances, she dresses in impeccable *kurta pyjama* and actively cultivates a very clean, sober, professional, and masculine look. A few years ago, she asked (and pretended) to be addressed as "Netaji"—an honorific term usually used for male political leaders. In this particular area of Uttar Pradesh, when people talk about Netaji, they are generally referring to Mulayam Singh Yadav (the former leader of the SP). According to Lady Dabang, "He may be the Netaji of Uttar Pradesh, but he is not the Netaji of western Uttar Pradesh. I am!" she told me, smiling, when I inquired about her title.

By the same token, she is quite proud of being known as a strong boss, and more important, she does not hesitate to behave "like a *dabang*" in public. On these occasions the masculine *kurta pyjama* is substituted with long folk skirts matched with T-shirts, high-heeled silver sandals, hair down and curled up, and red lipstick. This attire is not very conventional for a middle-aged woman, mother, and grandmother. This is the region where recently a *khap panchayat* (village extralegal court) prohibited girls from wearing jeans and where wearing Western clothes is considered highly provocative, inappropriate, and ultimately dangerous, as it can "provoke rape."

By dressing in this way, Lady Dabang sends an important message: I am powerful and I can act however I want to, which includes living without her husband and not apologizing for her many alleged boyfriends. As a musclewoman with a very unconventional pedigree and ambiguous origins, she needed to be a hundred times more fearless and violent than her male competitors. To be a woman and a boss in which she graciously calls "a patriarchal society" is not a joke. She does not get much respect through honor, so she needs to instill fear. Wealth is also used as the material proof of her success.

In the *Mahabharata*, she said, the power of *danda* (force) derives from the fear it inspires, and that fear pervades every aspect of human society, from the top to the very bottom of the scale. Most of the world lives in constant fear. "People are scared of the police, the *khap panchayats*, the mafia, the criminals, their husbands, and their fathers. They are also scared of failure and of being humiliated. People's lives are defined by insecurity in this country. But if one overcomes fear, they can become someone like me who does not know how much money I have anymore." She also added that people are easily intimidated by simply a person with no fear and that they violence and confidence can bring freedom. "It is all written in the *Gita*, to be fearless and act violently to follow your own dharma. . . . It is through fear and by breeding uncertainty around you that one maintains power."[27]

Lady Dabang actively cultivates her fearless image and mystique by being elusive and secretive. She carefully stages her figural power. Contrary to the practice of many of her male strongmen colleagues, she does not hold open-door *darbars*. If you want to meet her, you must make an appointment. To add to her mystique, her assistant changes her mobile number on a weekly basis for security reasons. She is scared of having her phone tapped by her enemies. As a rule she never answers her mobile phone, not even if one of her sons is calling her. In public, she is vigilant, not very talkative, and says only what she thinks is necessary.

It is not easy to meet her; however, whenever I was granted an appointment, I was able to have private conversations with her for long stretches of time. In what follows, I paraphrase portions of some of our conversations over the past two years and let her words illustrate her life. Lady Dabang never shied away from talking about the violent crimes she had committed. On the contrary, she bragged about them. As a matter of fact, I never had to ask her to talk about her criminal career; she spontaneously offered detailed descriptions about the court cases in which she is currently involved. In one of our meetings, she commented that one should never judge a man by his action before knowing his motives. So what were her motives? Lady Dabang justifies her violent outbursts as acts of self-defense or even more forcefully as acts necessary to make a better life for herself and her family. Her involvement in the *bhumi mafia* was described as an opportunity offered by "the poor" (*garib log*) of Chandra *mohalla* and by the gods. According to her, poor people in Chandra *mohalla* gave her full access to local common land, which she then sold to property developers. The profit was her "Uncle Scrooge's Number One Dime." She realized that she could make a fortune through land speculation and became a violent land aggregator. However, the people of Chandra *mohalla* that I talked to accused her of land grabbing and of being dishonest, conniving, and ruthless.

Duplicity is indeed inherent to herons I thought, while scanning the room and looking at the decor before she arrived. Netaji, a.k.a. Lady Dabang, arrived in a convoy of three cars; two were occupied by bodyguards ("my boys" as she referred to them later). I counted ten men, and all of them were carrying weapons. Before the boss was allowed to get out of the car, they inspected the house thoroughly. After five minutes, they gave the okay and Netaji was allowed in. For once I had the feeling that the bodyguards were not showing off but were actually doing their job. They seemed genuinely concerned about security. I must confess that I felt a bit uneasy. I stepped into the house and was struck by the expensive furniture and decorations. The manicured backyard was the size of a cricket ground. One of her men told me that the previous year she had the Sri Lanka cricket team playing in this garden during a weekend-long party.

When Lady Dabang joined me, she looked relaxed and ready for a chat. I made a comment about the bodyguards' "careful inspection," and she quickly remarked,

> I have lots of enemies . . . but don't worry, we're very well looked after. . . . My boys are well trained and loyal. What do you want to ask to me today? I was very young when I came to this town with my mother. Did I tell you this before? I used to stay in a temple in a very small room. I had no father. My mother was very poor. I had one younger brother. My mother is an illiterate woman from a backward village. She was married to my father, who instead came from a good family and was well educated. He never accepted this arranged marriage and went for a second marriage. He threw my mother and us out of the house. My mother did not know where to go. We started to move here and there and finally arrived in this town. We used to break coal in exchange for *chapatis*. It was difficult to survive. . . . The second wife of my father is very beautiful. My mother is not beautiful; she is short and has dark skin.
>
> People exploited us a lot. . . . I sat for hours and hours at the door of big men asking for help. It was then that I realized that I had to transform myself from prey into a hunter. I started to help our local big man and the police. I have become an expert in helping people to get bail. . . . I was brave and used all the extra money I earned to buy books and get an education. . . . I soon realized that that one should not be poor in this world. If you are poor, you need to take your destiny in your own hand; one needs to get out of poverty before being able to do something good in this world. However, even if a woman is well educated, ultimately she has to become a housewife in our society. Males dominate women [*purush pradhan ka joota hota hain*]. . . . It does

not matter if you are educated or not. When a girl is born, she is in the parents' clutches [*shekanje*]. When she grows up, she is in the brothers' and parents' clutches. After marriage she goes to the in-laws, and she became their slave. A woman is always in prison. . . . Of course, parents also love boys more than girls. . . . Girls need permission for everything, but boys don't need any permission. Now, yes there are some changes. I like girls a lot. I am very happy to see girls as pilots, doctors, lawyers . . . but even with this progress women are still suffering. . . . They often have to deal with worthless husbands. . . .

I was forced to get married with a man much older than me. He is very old. I am paying people to look after him now. When we got married, he earned one hundred fifty rupees per month. He was very naïve. I had to look after myself and my sons and my daughter. What can you do with one hundred fifty rupees per month? We didn't have any family. People used to humiliate [*pratadhit/yatna*] us continuously. When I walked in the streets, people teased and bullied me. They spread rumors that I was going to the hotels at night to make money [*Hotel Jaa rahi hain, raat ko paise kama kar layi hai*] and verbally abused me.

They used to make fun of me because my husband was so old. . . . However, having said that . . . if a woman decides to do something, then no one can stop her; I'm a living example of it. In order to be free in this country if you are not born rich and with status, the only way to get ahead is through muscle and politics.

She never told me explicitly that she had been a prostitute. By the same token, locals never forgot to remind me of her humble, rough, and alleged amoral beginnings. Equally, many questioned her caste: "Come on . . . look at her features. . . . She doesn't look like a high-caste lady," they often said.

After working as a servant, a nice police officer managed to get me a job as a nurse. In the hospital I got harassed a lot . . . sexually harassed, but I would react and beat people up. . . . People started to get scared of me. . . . Most women were sexually exploited in the hospital, and I started to speak out for them and for poor people. I had good contacts with the police. I also worked as a police informant and got good money. I developed contacts, and people soon came to learn that if someone misbehaved with me, I would be doubly bad back! Some police officers used to abuse me and misbehave [*gaali dete thee aur battimize karte the*], but I taught them a lesson.

It is this *chavi* [reputation] that helped me and my sons to win elections. . . . My younger son is the town *block pramukh*. . . . We got ninety-six votes from BDC [Block Development Committee] members. I coerced ninety-six members to vote for him and won the elections unopposed. This is a big election. It's an important post. Mayawati gave my family the ticket to contest this election. Behenji called me and told me to let my youngest son run in the elections. This election was won by pure "muscle." Pure *goondagardi*! People in town got scared. They thought that I was moving my influence from town X to the whole district. . . . They were correct. That was what I was going to do, and I did it. To be a *block pramukh* is a big thing. It is almost equivalent to being an MLA. The status is almost the same.

At first we tried to peacefully convince the BDC members to vote for us, but they wouldn't. In January 2010, on a very chilly winter night, I got twenty cars and picked up eighty BDC members from their houses while they were sleeping. I picked them from their homes at night because I would never have got them in the daytime. They were scared. I got a guesthouse in X and locked all BDC members in. I locked them inside the guesthouse for one month . . . basically till the election date . . . so they couldn't be influenced, intimidated, or bought by other political leaders and by my enemies. . . . Without money and muscle nobody supports you nowadays. *Block pramuk* elections (but also *zila parishad* [district council]) are based only on money and power. I locked the BDC members in the guesthouse for a month. They were fully catered to three times a day. I gave them the best; they got the five-star hotel treatment, but I didn't allow them to use their mobiles. They were under house arrest. I called all the BDC members' families to join their relatives in the guesthouse, as they couldn't get out of the guesthouse. I made quite tight arrangements and made sure that they couldn't escape. I told the BDCs' family members that if they wanted to file an FIR [First Information Report] against me, they could do that. But in the end, they were very happy and even wanted to stay longer in the guesthouse. They didn't want to leave. They had a great time. Ask them! After one month [after the election], they left the guesthouse, crying. BDC members are illiterate, so they do not know what and whom to vote

> for. At the very last minute, a person decided to contest elections against my son. My men followed him and made him understand that it was better for him to accept money and leave the election field. He withdrew his candidacy. There was no opposition left for that election; this is a sign of power.

This is Lady Dabang's version of her "kidnapping." The whole town knows about it—including the police—but nobody lifted a finger. When I questioned a local police officer about it, he said that there were no complaints from the BDC members or their families, so there was no reason for the police to intervene. This level of visible impunity is how bosses rule in everyday life.

Lady Dabang does not have a monopoly over illegal activities in the district by any means. She faces strong competition from other companies whose strongmen have the backing of the SP's patrons, as well as emerging patrons in the Bharatiya Janata Party (BJP) camp. One of the dynamics at the heart of the present Uttar Pradesh Mafia Raj is its instability due to the availability of multiple and often competing centers of protection within the ruling party. Overall competition for power at the center and a lack of information create a great deal of insecurity and lack of trust among the members of the public, who do not know where to go for protection. As has been argued in the mafia literature, a lack of trust in a context where the state is unable to provide basic security generates the popular demand for mafia protection enterprises.[28] In this competitive environment the area under study has witnessed a proliferation of self-made political bosses.

The *dabangs* I met over the last two years all expressed their concerns about the difficulties they encounter in instilling fear and maintaining credibility in this highly competitive democratic world. Their musings suggest that bosses find it difficult to inculcate fear when they enter into politics because they need to become hypervisible and accessible to ordinary people. Fear, as the anthropologist Taussig famously stated, is always stronger in the absence of the thing that causes it than in its presence.[29] Fear is better created by remaining invisible and far from the gaze of the crowd. One of the most compelling dynamics of democracy, however, is that it privileges representation and visibility. These traits are not conducive to preserving and cultivating the mystique of a strongman reputation, and even less so if the strongman is a woman who is considered an "amoral" character without shame and honor. Perhaps it is not a coincidence that both Mayawati and Lady Dabang have adopted a reclusive style, appear in public only when strictly necessary, and cultivate local folklore about their fearlessness and capacity to command.

Cultivating this image is definitely the remit of Lady Dabang's entourage. For example, at one of our meetings when I was waiting for her at her farmhouse, her personal assistant told me, "You're lucky, she seems to be in quite a good mood today . . . and she seems to like you!" Being short-tempered, frenetic, and unafraid of using violence are crucial ingredients to cultivating the reputation as a boss. The *dabangs* I have met all have an air of self-assurance and command, which I think is their best asset. Their presence is in itself intimidating, and even though it is very hard to describe these characteristics, they are obvious to the observer.[30] One ever-present element during public *darbars* is the *dabangs* raising their voices and shouting (most of the time at their assistants and peons) for not handling the crowd properly, for not having let some people in before others, or for having interrupted them unnecessarily. At times, the shouting is accompanied by the brandishing of a stick or, as recently reported, by slapping or kicking some unfortunate individual. These violent exchanges are increasingly being caught on camera.

Cruelty and unpredictability are also cultivated in the popular narratives that mystify the fearlessness of the boss. A couple of months after Akhilesh Yadav became chief minister, people started to be concerned about his lack of authority and incapacity to instill order through fear and respect. A story begun to circulate in the region: Akhilesh was having an animated discussion with his party men in his office in Etawah during a meeting about party issues. Akhilesh became very animated, and one of the party workers put a hand on his shoulder and gently said, "*Bhai*, calm down." Akhilesh kept on talking as if nothing had happened. The day after the party the man was found decapitated;

his head was delivered to the chief minister. People were telling this story with a mixture of horror and pleasure. Some felt almost reassured by it. In a way it showed them that their chief minister was not as weak as the press and media kept portraying him. In short, he was not just a puppet in the hands of his father and uncles.

This example is just one of many I recorded during my fieldwork. For example, the iconic Uttar Pradesh gangster politician Raja Bhaia is known for feeding his enemies to the crocodiles in the pond on his farm. In the local *mohalla* Rajiv Kumar is known for his short temper and for shooting people who do not let him jump the line to enter a temple during a festival. Similarly, Lady Dabang is known for not taking any prisoners. I personally witnessed one of her violent outbursts in the making when I decided to have a chat with her about the coming parliamentary elections. After a number of phone calls and having talked with her personal assistant and one of her sons, finally I received a call and was directed to go to her house in town. When I arrived, I could sense that the atmosphere was tense. Her men in the courtyard were engaged in a lively discussion; they were visibly angry and agitated. I was made to wait in the room just outside her office: "Something came up; Netaji is in a middle of a meeting. I can't disturb her now." I said I had plenty of time and that I could wait. I was offered the usual tea and biscuits. I sat there with my research assistant marveling at the heron decorations and flowery tablecloth. I quickly realized that just a paneled wall (yes, with painted herons) separated the two rooms and that what was being discussed in the office could be heard clearly. The man with whom she was conversing was telling her about some disturbing developments: one of the men of her "firm" had been caught being disloyal and was known to be collaborating with a BJP local leader who was also known to be one of Lady Dabang's historical enemies. She started to swear and scream, "Sale benchod chuttiya [sister fucker] . . . Motherfucker, don't they know who I am? Don't they know they can't play around with me? Do they know what my name is? I am [and she said her real name].[31] No one should dare to betray me! Do they know what I can do?" Her henchman was silent. I think he was scared of saying the wrong thing. As "the bearer of bad news," he was likely already in a bit of trouble. I must say that I was intimidated too. I did not know whether to leave or stay. My research assistant was also looking at me with incredulous eyes. But the real surprise came when Lady Dabang stormed out of the room. It was then that our eyes almost popped out! She was wearing a very tight purple T-shirt and a long folk skirt. Her hair was down and curled. She was wearing heavy makeup and very bright red lipstick. She looked furious, like someone from the set of a Bollywood movie impersonating a Bandit Queen. I was speechless and a bit unnerved. I did not say anything, just stared and tried to think what to do next. She stopped swearing when she saw me and said in a calm, neutral business-like tone, “Sorry, but I have something to take care of now. Urgently. It’s not a good day today; come back another time.” I said, “No problem,” while thinking it was a good time to leave. She ordered her men to prepare the car to go sort things out. They collected their guns and off they went.

Many of these violent exchanges occurred in the month leading up to the national elections. Generally, a boss’s survival depends on several factors, such as the internal cohesion and loyalty of his or her groups, the existence of dispute settlement mechanisms among groups, or exogenous factors, such as law enforcement and policing or, in this case, elections.[32] Elections are crucially important because a change of power means a change of political protection. The event I just discussed happened in March 2014 when Narendra Modi’s victory was pretty much a foregone conclusion. It was with this in mind that local bosses had to start to strategize how to manipulate the electoral process; how to reposition themselves, how to change sides, and perhaps, more important, how to keep themselves protected and in profit. In the words of another local boss, “There are two types of candidates in any election. The ones who run to win and the ones who run to make profit. In this constituency *dabangs* run to make a profit and help ‘clean’ candidates win by selling them votes. You keep the money allocated for the election campaign, and you make more money by selling votes from your protected areas to the two main contending candidates. This is a business strategy. Since last August, after the riots, it was clear that BJP was taking over Uttar Pradesh.”[33]

Lady Dabang never insisted much on fashioning her doings as *sewa* (social work), as some of her bosses' colleagues did. She certainly brought it up and said that she never forgets her origins and what it means to be poor, but she was equally clear that her interest lies in building up her own political and economic turf rather than benevolently patronizing supporters. The interests of her "political firm" come before the interests of the community as a whole, as she proved during her tenure as municipality councillor. Ultimately, she clearly focuses on profit. In so doing, she crystallizes the figure of the personal sovereign who made for herself and her family a life of security and a path to something better.[34] She actually incarnates a fantasy that is shared widely by the society in which she operates, where violence is often viewed as a way to a better life.

CHAPTER 7

THE GODFATHER

Arild E. Ruud

WE WERE LED into a largish room with dingy concrete walls, peeling gray-green paint, and brightly lit by fluorescent tube lights. There were perhaps 100 to 120 people in the room around the one table there. Seated at the simple wooden table was Fakhrul Khan. Member of Parliament. Local party supremo. Godfather of Nawabganj.[1] As we entered the room, he got up to greet us, chairs were vacated, and he motioned us to sit. "Please, give me ten minutes," he said with a polite smile as he waved his hand to indicate that he would need some time to deal with all the requests.

So he turned his attention back to the young men sitting in front of him. They had been in the middle of discussing an upcoming event, and without missing a beat, he continued to instruct them. They were probably from the student wing—the decisive activist organization in town.[2] He gave strict, detailed instructions: the kind of people to invite up onstage, the banners and decorations, the seating arrangements, the order of invited guests. His voice deep and powerful, they listened attentively, all looking straight at him, hardly blinking, occasionally nodding, uttering a short, weak "Yes, sir."

When he had finished, he waved his hand and dismissed them. He lit another cigarette. Then suddenly, he called them back. "Security. You make sure there's security." More detailed instructions amid hints of a threat from the Islamists. The ten or fifteen of them stood still in rapt attention. "Yes, sir." They nodded again, and as he waved his hand once again, they left. He turned to the others. "And? *Kichu bolba?* What do you want to tell me?" His manner of speech was rustic, colloquial, blunt. He was tall and stooped, in his fifties, growing fat, dressed in a large, white starched *kurta* that did not sit well on him. His skin was dark, his movements were heavy yet quick and impatient, and he was the only one in the room smoking.

A man came up to the table. A humble greeting. "Sir . . ." A small request, a matter quickly dealt with. Then the next. Sometimes he listened a little, but often he seemed to have known about the matter beforehand. A thin man who had brought his young boy only managed half a sentence of his plea before Fakhrul Khan blurted out, "What? He still hasn't done it?" He quickly turned to party activists next to him. "Give him twenty-four hours. If he hasn't done it by then, kick him out of the party. We don't need those sort of people in our party. Twenty-four hours." He was clearly the man in command. Making decisions. Knowing matters in detail. The thin man thanked him profusely and dragged his boy away hurriedly.

Fakhrul Khan offered me cigarettes. Now there were two of us smoking in a room of a hundred, in a country where every second man smokes. "Ten more minutes? Just ten more minutes?" he said again with an apologetic smile. But before I could answer, he had turned his attention to the supplicants. There were more matters to be dealt with, one after the other. He dealt with them quickly. It was a daily routine for him, this *darbar* (court), as it is for politicians throughout the subcontinent. Occasionally, he picked up his phone and called someone, talked in the same loud voice, and made us all privy to the conversation. At other times, he sought advice from his party activists. Some supplicants were just dismissed. "*Pore. Pore.*" Later. Later.

Fakhrul Khan is popularly known as "the Godfather" of the town and district of Nawabganj. The English term is used, and the reference is to mafia bosses of American popular culture. But the Bangladeshi godfather is more than a mere criminal lord; he is first and foremost a politician. Fakhrul Khan is the elected Member of Parliament (MP) for one of the constituencies of Nawabganj district, and he has a long record of party work with the currently ruling Awami League. At the same time, he has a reputation for using brutality and extortion to bolster his position and to intimidate opponents and for his unsavory associates. Hence the epithet "godfather." He has used this combination of the licit and the illicit with great success for many years, to the extent that he is the unquestioned lord of the five hundred thousand inhabitants of his provincial hometown.

There are many political leaders in Bangladesh who have successfully combined legitimate political engagement with brutality and violence as a modus operandi and who have been called godfather.[3] The most famous of all is perhaps Ershad Sikdar, who ruled the provincial town of Khulna for many years and was associated with whatever party was ruling the country. He was arrested in 1999, accused of thirty crimes, and rumored to have killed sixty people. He had at some point been council member of the city corporation, but he was not really a politician. He was a thug who amassed fabulous amounts of money, which he used to buy political position, influence, and associates. It worked up to a point, but in the end his brutality overwhelmed his strategic thinking and he murdered a young activist of the then ruling party. He was convicted of the murder and hanged in 2004.

A more typical godfather was Joynal Hazari, three times MP from Feni, in the southeast of the country. All throughout his career Hazari was closely associated with the Awami League and never shifted his allegiance the way Ershad Sikder had done. Joynal Hazari was a political leader first and exploited violence and organized crime in his locality for political purposes rather than for just financial gain. Hazari's particular method had been to establish a network of committees at different levels throughout the district, committees that he filled with school dropouts, laborers, the unemployed, rickshaw pullers, and others willing to take an active part in muscular forms of politics. They engaged in extortion and corruption, often claiming up to 30 percent of government contracts. And they did so with considerable brutality. In Hazari's last period as MP, according to one report, more than 120 political activists were killed in Feni. When his party lost the 2001 election, Hazari fled to India—allegedly in a convoy of ten cars filled with associates, valuables, and weapons.

Contemporary godfathers include the MP elected from Lalbagh in Dhaka in 2014, Haji Selim. For many his rise from humble origins embodies the very essence of Lalbagh, a name often associated with prostitution, drugs, guns, and violence. Another famous contemporary godfather is Kader Siddique in Tangail, a rural district north of Dhaka. He had his own armed force during the 1971 Liberation War and never entirely surrendered arms afterward. More than four decades later, he is still the strongman of the district. He set up his own political party and repeatedly tried to be more closely associated with the Awami League. He also supported his brother, Latif, who was elected MP four times and has held three different cabinet portfolios. Then there are Sheikh Selim in Gopalganj and Abu Abdullah Hasnat in Barisal, both undisputed leaders in their districts and both commonly referred to as godfathers. An added twist to the tale is that they are also both cousins of the prime minister. Yet another local strongman and known godfather is the former body builder, mayor, district secretary, MP, and for one period Parliament whip, Mujibur Rahman Sarwar. For years he was the supremo of the town of Barisal, and his personal history is allegedly a sinister mixture of murder and extortion. Last but not least is Shamim Osman, the MP and supremo of Narayanganj and perhaps the first name to come to mind when Bangladeshis say "godfather." He is the most well-known member of a family of great political influence (one of his brothers was an MP, and both their father and grandfather had been MPs) and economic clout. He also has a reputation for muscularity, even violence.

The list could be much longer. Godfathers are a particular kind of politician in Bangladesh, and many, possibly most, leading politicians are not godfathers. However, godfathers can be found in all the major political parties, often holding positions of substantial influence.[4] There are traits of the same methods among other politicians as well, but individuals such as Fakhrul Khan are more purebred. The pure godfathers hold or have held elected office, and most are senior in the sense of having been politically active for a long time. Some took part in the Liberation War, although quite a few are leaders who cut their political teeth and established themselves during the unsettled decades that followed the war. They established their authority while fighting other political movements, while fighting the police and the government, and often while fighting rivals within their own movement. In the political culture that developed over those years, an expanding range of sources of influence was mobilized—party activists, money, family connections, and armed gangs. The forms of political action varied from street processions and rallies to covert shoot-outs, coercion, or even kidnapping, depending on occasion. Their "art of bossing" lies in their ability to master these forms.

This was the formation of a political culture that allowed or even encouraged clusters of heterogeneous groups to form around individual leaders. Such individual leaders, bosses, some of whom would rise to be known as godfathers, are basically idiosyncratic CEOs of informal, multipronged enterprises. The man in the middle has personal qualities that hold the operation together. He relates to very different kinds of people, people who each render services that help the enterprise and its CEO and who are in turn helped by him. The enterprise employs mobilization politics, it greases, it intimidates, and it awards contracts—all by using different people. A well-established enterprise, such as the ones run by godfathers, will consist of activists and thugs, trade union leaders, contractors, and businessmen, in some cases even cultural activists and a few journalists, and of course police officers and civil servants. The formation of such heterogeneous networks was made possible by the decades of political rivalry before democracy was reintroduced and by the intense "toxic" rivalry of the democratic era.[5]

The godfathers of Bangladeshi politics do not belong to a subculture of criminals who have somehow gained access to elected offices. In this way they are different from the godfathers of American popular culture or Italian Mafia, and they are different from the bosses discussed elsewhere in this book. Bangladeshi godfathers are politicians first, but they are politicians who also make use of the ways of the underground. They represent a combination of the licit and illicit, but they come mostly from the side of the licit. They operate in an uncharted political space, a space that accommodates heavy-handed coercion alongside legitimate mobilization. This space is the outcome of years of historical development rather than of malicious intent. Godfathers also often have special personal qualities that allow them to be different personae in different contexts, to be both godfathers in the ominous sense and popular and legitimate parliamentarians, that allow them to be nimble and flexible in strategic choices and to maintain a wide network of contacts in very different social classes.

This chapter investigates the making of one such godfather, Fakhrul Khan.[6] It focuses on the historical context that made his rise and the rise of other godfathers possible, and it investigates the particular blend of violence, activist politics, and networking that he and they represent.

THE MEMBER OF PARLIAMENT

When I interviewed Fakhrul Khan a little later, after the *darbar*, his commanding style had disappeared. Instead, he was charming, generous, and talkative. A bit into the conversation he received a telephone call, and again he changed; he became alert, listening intently, obligingly. The change of style was revealing of the tremendous nimbleness of his character. After a brief conversation on the phone he immediately made some more calls. He then explained that a RAB officer had had a heart attack and was being taken in a helicopter to a hospital in Dhaka.[7] The officer's in-laws, who had called, were locals from Nawabganj. They had asked him if he could help, as their MP. He could. He had phoned the director general (DG) of RAB and told him what had happened. He had asked the DG to look into the matter: "If anything can be done . . . his family is very worried." Fakhrul Khan had a good relationship with the head of RAB. The DG would oblige. Fakhrul maintained a good relationship with as many as he could in RAB. And in the administration. And in the police. Heart attack? Problems with your neighbor? Fakhrul Khan will help. You just ask. He provided small services, or big services, not only to the little men and his activists who appeared at his *darbar* but also to the established, the powerful, always depending on and creating a wide web of debts.

We have highlighted earlier that Mattison Mines's intervention on the South Asian "big man" was a useful corrective to the Dumontian perspective.[8] The logic of power and authority invested in an individual is an important one in the South Asian context and can arguably be seen as creating personal sovereignties. Fakhrul Khan had created his own realm where he was the sovereign, and he had used violence and intimidation to get there. However, this perspective should not overshadow the fact that class and family are clearly also crucial in the making of modern political godfathers in Bangladesh. Primordial forms of kinship such as clans and caste do not play a major role in Bangladeshi society or politics, but the networks formed from class or family or networks at particular junctures in the lives of budding politicians, during college in particular, constitute crucial elements in the making of both licit careers and opportunities on the darker side of political life.

Bangladeshi godfathers are entrepreneurs in politics and business who often enforce their will to rule by using threat, intimidation, and pure violence, but who also secure public goods that are distributed through the networks they control. John Sidel's study from the Philippines portrays bosses that seek monopolistic control in similar ways.[9] But in this book we show that control is not monopolistic. In particular there are significant challenges facing a political boss in a highly competitive democracy such as Bangladesh. The control that bosses exercise is monopolistic only at opportune moments, and instead their command needs to be constantly maintained and defended. The power that resides in the formal institutions of the state is substantial and much coveted as security. But even when the heights of command have been conquered, there is a range of alternative sources of power with which the leader may be challenged, either by people from within the same party or from outside. A fair number of leaders in both the two main Bangladeshi political parties have, for instance, reputations for being "clean" and for relying on their image as social workers or political workers rather than on criminal links. This indicates the substantial appeal "clean" has on voters. Leaders who do *shamajik sheba* (social service) and use arguments, rules, and persuasion rather than muscle or intimidation attract admiration.[10] For Fakhrul Khan this strategy (if indeed that is what it is) is, above all, incarnated in his bête noir and rival, city party leader Shamsul Islam. The latter's reputation for social service is one that Fakhrul dismisses with a grunt but that no doubt has helped build his opponent a solid public image as one of the foremost socially engaged politicians in the country. To a very substantial portion of the voting public, Shamsul Islam is what Fakhrul Khan is not, and vice versa. Nonetheless, Fakhrul Khan himself does engage in similar activities, as do probably most politicians in South Asia, and the time and effort he puts into the *darbar* are an indication of this. The recent history of Bangladesh, with its highly contested elections, makes it imperative to woo the electorate. The constant attention from the media, expectations from organizations such as trade unions or nongovernmental organizations, and challenges from the legal system all militate against the efforts by political bosses to attain and maintain monopolistic positions of power. And sometimes the challenges can be successful.

First, however, we investigate the historical context that opened opportunities for the ambitious with access to arms. This is the history of modern Bangladesh, and it is Fakhrul's history. And in spite of particularities, is also the history of many of the other godfathers of the country and their rise to prominence and positions of power.

ARMS AND THE NEW NATION

Fakhrul Khan's career began at Fulbari College in Nawabganj in the late 1970s. This was the only college in town. It had five to six thousand students at the time and was the hub of student life and activism. "Before he became a student leader he used to move around the city on his small bicycle. Many would make fun of him. Don't tell him I told you this. He wasn't influential back then, even if he was from a political family." The sight of Fakhrul Khan as a young man on a bicycle appeared funny years later because that unostentatious vehicle contrasted even then with his stated ambition and with the fact that he belonged to the most prominent political family in town. The family was very much an Awami League family; in fact, to a considerable extent the family *was* the Awami League in town. The party had not been in power for some years when Fakhrul entered college, but it still had substantial local clout and a powerful organization. Fakhrul's father, Salauddin Khan, was well known as a former MP elected first in the 1970 election and then again in 1973.[11] He was the foremost party leader in town. Moreover, Fakhrul's paternal grandfather had also been an influential political leader in the provincial town back in the 1950s. Both grandfather and father had been prominent in the establishment of the Awami League in town in the heady years before independence. The family's prominence in Nawabganj's political history before and in the years immediately after independence is undoubted.

It was in the years that followed the war of independence that links were forged between party politics and armed or muscular enforcement. This is a less explored aspect of the early history of independent Bangladesh's political culture, but it is evident enough in contemporary accounts. The links between organized politics and muscular politics were propelled by the unusual circumstances of the war and had developed to such an extent that by the time Fakhrul was old enough for college, violence had become part of the country's political culture. It is within this history that his rise took place.

Fakhrul decided to run for the post of vice president of the college student union not long after he joined the student organization. The decision was perhaps not unnatural for the son of the former MP, but he was also a novice activist, and more senior student leaders resented his presumptions. In the end, cheating secured him the election. By then he already had a group of followers who were not college students but restless young men from Arambagh, the neighborhood where the family lived. The family's position was strong in Arambagh, and the restless young men were enlisted as party activists. On the day of the vote these activists came to the college grounds. Fakhrul's rival at that election explained how it worked:

> I was the candidate with the most support. I had been working in Chhatra League for many years, and Fakhrul Khan was just one of the new activists. We were all leftist. He was too. In the leftist wing of the Awami League. Fakhrul decided to be a candidate too, and on the day of the voting some ac-

> tivists came on campus. They told us, "The voting is over. You can go home." They were Fakhrul's men. We knew them. "The voting is over." So we went home. There was nothing we could do.

Quite the innocent affair. But the losing candidate is now an associate of Fakhrul Khan and an establishment figure himself with no desire to rock the boat. Leftists who were engaged in student politics at that time but today are no longer members of the town's establishment told a very different story: "They created mayhem. There were clashes during [that] college student union election. One student was killed. They used sticks and guns. The police did not come to help us."

The audacity of rigging a college union election is surprising coming as it did at a time when the country was ruled by an autocrat president, Ziaur Rahman. Not only was he opposed to the Awami League, but his claim to fame at the time was steering the country away from the disorder the Awami League government had created a few years earlier.[12] He established the Bangladesh Nationalist Party (BNP) to counter the broad influence of the Awami League. In Nawabganj, however, the local Awami League power holders were so influential that the new government chose to tread carefully. Awami League activists and leaders had an organization and considerable popular support, and they had muscular power in the form of both *mastans* (thugs) and arms.

The easy connection of Awami League and muscular politics had developed since immediately after independence, if not before. During the war, defectors from the regular prewar Pakistani army and ragtag guerrilla groups of volunteers were slowly organized into the Mukti Bahini, the armed wing of the independent government-in-exile. The Mukti Bahini was armed by the Indians but never completely coalesced into a coherent and disciplined army. Large parts of it remained basically a guerrilla force. In addition, there were other groups, including the famous band of independent strongman Kader Siddique and various leftist groups.

The effort to disarm these groups after the war was only partially successful. Within the first year of independence, law and order became a major political issue. The country was famished and in upheaval, and armed gangs engaged in robberies and large-scale smuggling across the border to India. There were even armed attacks on police stations at a rate that reached "alarming proportions."[13] The government called in the army on several occasions to quell smuggling and mayhem, but these efforts were often frustrated because many criminals had political protection.[14]

In this situation several additional forces were set up and armed. The first was the Rakkhi Bahini, an official force of many thousand officers but few directives. Soon after the so-called village defense forces were set up by the ruling party in different districts, then the Voluntary Force (Shecchasebok Bahini) and the Red Force (Lal Bahini) were set up by individual Awami League leaders and responded to them. Last, the Bangladesh Rifles was established—an armed border guard that in practice answered to party leaders in the different border districts. All these groups depended on their loyalty to the ruling party and often to individual Awami League leaders.

The many forces constituted mechanisms through which rivalry over resources turned violent. Clashes between the various armed groups "were common."[15] Unrest was widespread throughout the country and in the countryside in particular. The village defense force in reality "meant the suppression of political opposition" according to contemporary reports.[16] No fewer than five MPs were assassinated in the first three years of independent Bangladesh, as well as three thousand party activists.[17]

In addition to the government-supported militias, there were armed leftist insurgents such as the Shorbohara movement and armed groups of criminals—*mastans* and dacoits. The dire law-and-order situation was part of the rationale for the declaration of emergency in late 1973 and the constitutional changes that in 1974 led to the establishment of a one-party state.

THE POLITICAL FAMILY

As mentioned previously, Fakhrul's family was influential in both the town and district of Nawabganj. It was a prominent political family. Nevertheless, it had to cope with rivalries. A former associate, Sarwar, became a serious opponent not long after independence and launched himself as a candidate for the municipal election in 1973, against the official party candidate supported by Fakhrul's father. The rival won and the town was split in two, Fakhrul's father and his rival Sarwar each holding sway over their own geographical halves of the town, each organizing their activists.

After the assassination of President Sheikh Mujibur Rahman in August 1975 and a series of coups and countercoups, the one-party state was replaced by a new army-based government. The new government pledged to introduce rule-based governance and to end the violent and erratic self-service of its predecessor. In spite of his promises, general-turned-president Ziaur Rahman used similar styles of armed vigilantes to establish his government's political presence in the different parts of the country. A youth organization called the Jubo Complex was introduced, supposedly to promote economic and social development. "In practice the 93,990 members spread throughout the land were essentially groups of young toughs and thugs kept on leash for use in elections, demonstrations, referenda or simply to smash the opposition whenever Zia or the BNP required it."[18]

In Nawabganj, the military takeover in 1975 weakened the Khan family's position. They lost their various businesses, Salauddin himself was arrested, and the eldest son had to flee. The family fortunes were at rock bottom for a while.

The link between crime and politics was strengthened during this period because of the need of new political constellations of matching the organized and armed presence of the Awami League and its leaders. President Zia was murdered in 1981, and after a brief interlude another general took power, H. M. Ershad. Again there was a need for some form of legitimacy, and a new political party was established, the Jatiyo Party. This was even more a motley crew of the ruthlessly ambitious and disgruntled than the BNP established some years earlier. Support from local power holders was generously greased with licenses and government support. Corruption reached new heights, violence against opponents was increasingly common, and armed gangs became integral to everyday politics.

Locally, the Khan family was invited into this new setup. Fakhrul Khan's elder brother, Aminul, joined the regime and the Jatiyo Party. The crossing over to another political party by the eldest son of the oldest Awami League family in town was viewed by some as an act of disloyalty, but the distance between the Awami League and the Jatiyo Party was never very great, at least in some important respects. It was even less great in Nawabganj precisely because of the Khans—the town's most influential political family to be found with a foot strongly planted in both camps.

THE MAKING OF THE GODFATHER

With his brother establishing links to the *régime du jour*, Fakhrul was engaged in the Awami League–affiliated student organization and hence formally in the opposition. He was busy establishing himself as a local leader, increasingly influential on his own terms. His rise showed his hybrid authority from the beginning: part street smart, part violent, part political activist. His small gang of *mastans* from Arambagh had helped him gain a political platform as a student union leader. All along but increasing in scope, the gang also intimidated local businessmen for money, in particular beyond the neighborhood where they lived, the family turf.

This original racket was straightforward: a protection for cash business. His men would go to a businessman or a contractor in the process of constructing a building and ask for money. They would politely engage in a conversation and at some point say something along the lines of "I am Fakhrul's man. Perhaps you would like to contribute to our cause." If this request did not produce the desired result, they would harass him. Threats first, but violence if necessary. "At the early stage, in Nawabganj, their arms were cut rifles, machetes, and *lathis* [heavy long wooden sticks]. Hockey sticks were also very popular. Nowadays they are using more updated weapons, such as pistols. Not in those days." Yet those were not innocent days. It is very easy for instance to destroy any machinery or equipment left on a construction site or to scare workers to prevent them from coming to work. Their reputation for brutality was soon well established. They were dangerous men. To avoid unpleasant situations, most businessmen quickly formed a working relationship with them and, in the case of more influential businessmen, directly with Fakhrul Khan himself.

> Fakhrul's men would go to a businessman or someone wanting to construct a building and ask for a toll. The style was simple. If the businessman was not very influential, he would pay; if he was influential, they might exchange heated words, threats, and counterthreats. But if the businessman already had a good relation with Fakhrul Khan, then he would call him, and Fakhrul would talk to his cadre and scold him, "Hey, I know him; he's my man; leave him alone."

Such extortion is the common pattern for local *mastans* and their political masters. It pays reasonably well and secures an income. The downside is that the income is relatively inflexible, slow, unpopular, and only substantial with much effort. On the plus side, it enables the local politician to maintain a gang of enforcers at little cost.

The gang of *mastan*-activists ruled the streets of Arambagh and the surrounding areas, intimidated opponents, and put pressure on local businessmen to donate money to the party. The *mastan*-activists were also involved in the political movements of the day, in particular in the movement against Ershad's government later in the 1980s. This was a student-driven movement consisting of a series of protracted street processions, *hartals* (strikes), and blockades. Fakhrul as student leader was in the forefront of the protests in Nawabganj and as a consequence rose to local political prominence. His Arambagh *mastan*-activists worked alongside the large number of regular student activists. He was becoming the most visible and well-known activist leader in town. His charisma was coupled with organizational skills that made him very successful. At the height of the movement there were demonstrations every day.

It is alleged that Fakhrul's *mastan*-activists also took part in the counterdemonstrations in the afternoon. These demonstrations were in favor of the government, that is, in support of Fakhrul's elder brother, the Jatiyo Party MP.

Money and extortion, some racketeering, and the political game, playing both sides and maintaining influence while tipping the scales, made up Fakhrul Khan's formative years as political *neta* (leader) in Nawabganj. In addition, there was a certain amount of violence and brutality. Several murders had already been attributed to the family; all were their opponents. In the first half of the 1970s, the murders of Rokon, a student leader; a little later the murder of Almas Rahman, who was an Awami League leader; and a double murder in 1988 were all attributed to the Khan family.

In spite of this, Fakhrul Khan was close to many of the sons of the local cultural elite; they were all engaged in the fight against the Ershad government, and they felt like comrades-in-arms—living a thrilling life and sharing in danger. Many of them later distanced themselves from him but still feel like equal members of the class of educated Bengalis who hold the rights and status of fully entitled citizens. "We were friends then. We, the cultural activists, and him. He was dangerous, yes, perhaps, but we fought for the same cause. Against the autocrat. Besides, we knew him from college." And Fakhrul knew how to appreciate this link, his friendship with activists who perhaps were more engaged for idealistic reasons than for power. To illustrate this, one activist told me that at one point Fakhrul had walked up to him on the college grounds and warned him that there was going to be violence. "I will leave campus in five minutes. I don't know what will happen to you after that." Then they shared a quiet cigarette and left at the same time. A kind of friendship and mutual understanding could live on in spite of the violence.

In the end the Ershad government fell, and open elections were held in 1991. At this point, Fakhrul Khan was well established as the main party leader for the Awami League in Nawabganj. Many of the first generation of Awami League leaders had passed away by then, and positions within the party were open to the ambitious. But he was not allowed to run for Parliament in 1991, possibly because his reputation at that point was already considered too unsavory for the electorate. This was a strategic choice shaped by the self-image of the Awami League and its senior leaders. The first-generation leaders were professionals—lawyers, schoolteachers, university lecturers—who had been decisive in the mobilization of the 1960s and who were now fielded as the party's pride and honor. But their ability to mobilize was no longer what it had been, and the party lost both in Nawabganj and at the national level.

Five years later the party wanted to win and consciously chose candidates with a proven capacity to mobilize. Fakhrul Khan was fielded in Nawabganj and won. The Awami League government stayed for its full five-year period, and Fakhrul Khan was the MP. It was during those years that he established himself as a dominant player, not just in the party but in the town, securing for himself control over vast resources. Once he was in power, his methods were also more varied and often subtle. A businessman who had a smallish operation in Nawabganj said, "You had to pay [if they asked you to]. *Dite-i hobe*. Everybody knows this. If you didn't, something would happen. We didn't know what."

However, with Fakhrul Khan as the MP, the game changed. What had been a protection-cum-extortion racket became a game involving deals with government resources, at least as far as the bigger players were concerned. "No tender bids were dropped in Nawabganj without their knowledge." Whereas he had previously had to intimidate individual government officers, such as police officers, or he had to make individual and cumbersome deals with them, he was now in a position from which he could command them—and if that was not sufficient, transfer them. To avoid such setbacks to their career prospects, many officials simply bowed with the wind and offered forthcoming support. "There isn't much we can do. He is the MP," was the excuse. In his position he influenced the distribution of business opportunities and government contracts. "He can talk to anyone in the district administration, and they will do as he says. Anyone. Of course! The MP is king." By being personally involved in many deals, he made sure willingness was rewarded. A win-win situation all around. Protection from police interference was particularly useful when dealing with unions or government regulations in the rapidly expanding textile industry.

The distinctive feature of godfathers is their links to the underworld and the usefulness of violent enforcers to influence formal, administrative processes. This tool remains useful even for an MP. Control over enforcers helps influence decisions through intimidating individual decision makers such as bureaucrats or businessmen. Even when not actually used, enforcers help maintain a reputation, the fear of potential violence. At the same time, such gangs are expensive and need to be paid, which underlines the need for godfathers to be intimately involved in the underworld economy. How to get money is a constant issue, because the amount of money needed to pay gangs is considerable and difficult to raise in a legitimate fashion. It is much easier, then, to allow the gangs to earn their own keep. But this depends on the godfather's ability to secure them an area of activity protected from the police or the interference of the administration. Smuggling is one such area that is popular with godfathers, in particular in border districts such as Feni or Sylhet, but also in other towns. Most of Bangladesh is less than four to five hours by car from the border.

The main product smuggled into or through Nawabganj is Phensedyl, a cough syrup popular as an intoxicant, and yaba, a mixture of methamphetamine and caffeine tablets. Much of the meth is smuggled in from Burma (Myanmar) or Thailand and mixed with local products. The abusers are mostly local. Another source of illegal money is gasoline and diesel for buses and trucks. Nawabganj is at a crossroads, and the number of passing trucks is considerable. Siphoning off a little of the diesel is a lucrative business, and the diesel business is a source of substantial money for certain gangs. Increasingly, this particular line of business was under the control of one Tutulbhai—an infamous local crime lord. Tutulbhai was also rumored to control what was left of the red-light district and some of the smuggling of Phensedyl. However, these traditional lines of mafia-like business have been eclipsed by a much richer source, slowly growing in the unreported shadow of the new economy.

Nawabganj is one of the hubs of the textile industry in the country. One of the main organizations in the Nawabganj textile industry is the local chamber of commerce, with Fakhrul Khan's brother as the chairman. The association represents several thousand local companies and in 2014 was a major player in the country's annual US$19 billion textile industry. One opening for criminals came in the form of the piles of leftover waste called *jhut* that accumulated outside factory walls. The term *jhut* refers to all sorts of waste material from the trimming and cutting stages of the production process, or discarded cloth. Much of the *jhut* consists of high-quality material. For the last few years the export of *jhut* has been subjected to government regulations and export fees. In the early days, however, it was just waste. Individual rag pickers and others collected it and sold it as stuffing for dolls or pillows or for the production of rags. The profit from collecting, cleaning, and sorting it was small, but as the textile industry grew and waste became substantial, a decent line of business could be sustained. It was also soon controlled by local *mastans*, who collected directly from inside the factories. Over the years it became established practice that the *jhut* is sold to the local *neta* and his *mastans*. The going rate in the market in 2015 was 500 takas for forty kilograms, but factory owners are leaned on by local politicians to sell the *jhut* at 50 takas for forty kilograms. The profit is divided between the *neta* and the *mastans*. Occasionally, there will be disputes over control of the operation, and occasionally this rivalry may lead to clashes or shoot-outs.[19] Naturally, the local *netas* have close ties to more influential politicians who can provide cover.

One of the main figures in the *jhut* business in Nawabganj was the same Tutulbhai who was also in the diesel business and various other lines. He was originally a bus driver and leader of local *mastans* associated with the Jatiyo Party when it was in power and later the BNP when it was in power. A little after the Awami League came to power in 1996, he again switched loyalty and was soon made a trade union leader—by Fakhrul Khan. Later still, he gained a position as elected member of the city corporation with the support of Fakhrul Khan.

In the end, accusations against this associate came to threaten Fakhrul Khan's own position and career, but before we investigate the circumstances of this threat, we take a detour through the many personalities of Nawabganj's godfather to investigate how he could build his conglomerate of a corporation and how he could create and sustain mutually beneficial relationships with people from very different walks of life.

THE MASTER

Fakhrul Khan is known for his knack for adapting to any individual or situation. People who know him intimately portray him as a man capable in the whole register of Bengali or Bangladeshi personality styles, complete with the different sets of mannerisms and speech patterns. We may unravel at least six different styles that he commands and that are integral part of his art of bossing.[20]

In that room where we first met him, at his *darbar*, Fakhrul Khan showed himself to be bossy and commanding, the man in control. He gave orders and did not expect his orders to be questioned or contradicted. He was the boss with a boss style, almost insensitive to the feeling of others. He was king. At the same time he was a just king. He was generous in that he saw as many people as he could and gave them his attention. He assisted shopkeepers, truck drivers, clerks—ordinary people with ordinary, everyday problems. His commanding style was appreciated by his supplicants because he exhibited energy, and that energy was what they sought. Small acts to him, but important to the individual concerned. His *darbar* was a display of magnanimity and ability. He acted in line with the kingly model, albeit in a contemporary and democratic polity.[21] This democratic king was the friend of the ordinary man, *shadharon manush*, the standard reference point of Bangladeshi politics and equivalent of North India's *aam admi*.

At other times, however, such as with the foreigner, he could be the perfect *bhadralok*, the Bengali gentleman, educated, well versed in culture and literature.[22] He can do so convincingly because he is from a well-established and educated family and belongs by heritage and education firmly in the cultured classes of society. He is *bhadro*, refined, knowledgeable, and sensitive. True to form, he will, when necessary, be respectful. He will be restrained and attentive with seniors, he will hide his cigarettes from them, he will speak courteously to women, and he will display full loyalty to the traditional norms of the social order. These days he insists on being a Muslim *bhadralok*, liberally sprinkling his conversation with Islamic expressions and references to the Quran—"I was saved that day, by the grace of Allah." Fakhrul has a solid record of anti-Islamist actions and a strong, secular reputation.

At the same time he portrays himself as a God-fearing Muslim in the manner befitting a leader in this Muslim-majority nation. This attitude earns him respect, particularly in lower-middle-class neighborhoods, and the sophistication of his manners also allows him to be accepted by members of the cultural elite—officials, important businessmen, old educated families. These aspects of his political public image help people disregard other aspects of him. "I don't know anything about that," smiled the tea seller when we chatted about Fakhrul Khan's sinister reputation.[23]

There are more sides to him. When he speaks to a large audience, he is not the calculated cerebral speaker but the fiery activist. Public speech is "a highly valued form of oral literacy" in Bangladesh.[24] Political activists will generally adopt the speech style made famous by Mujibur himself—a loud powerful voice, appealing to emotions; conscious intonation; clipped and slogan-style sentences; voice rising to express shrill anger, a crescendo, often high pitched throughout but occasionally modulated, brought down to convey reason, intimacy.[25] This style frames most political speeches at mass meetings in Bangladesh, in particular if the speaker belongs to the Awami League family of organizations, as does Fakhrul. In this particular kind of performance, Fakhrul Khan is known as very capable, a man in control of his audience with his rich, deep, full voice, and much appreciated by party activists who recognize that a capacity to speak in public is a mark of political conviction.

However, it is not the mass appeal that secures Fakhrul Khan his influence and power. It is the backroom deals and the unspoken understandings. The source of this power is his charm and powers of persuasion. For all his average looks, he is known as a charming man. He is an intimate reader of people. He will be your pal, that intimate friend you can rely on and who relies on you. His particular brand of charm involves a range of friendly and disarming gestures: he smiles, belittles himself, even ridicules himself: "Uff, I'm so fat!" A former friend said, "He speaks so well. He was always good at convincing people." The friend is now scared of him but acknowledges his ability to inspire confidence in people. "Fakhrul can be very persuasive." When Fakhrul

Khan so wishes, this friend said, "You will feel he is not dangerous. Not to you. He's your friend. You were in college together. Just help him." Even people who do not know him intimately will agree that he can be very charming. Another of his former friends and a longtime party colleague, an activist from the left wing of the party, held similar views. We met on several occasions, mostly in back alleys, in quiet tea shops, or in some back office, but when talking about Fakhrul, he always looked around a little furtively, over his shoulder, peeking around the corner. Every time we met, he would say, "Don't mention my name. I am afraid of him." But he acknowledged that part of Fakhrul's influence was due to his persuasive powers.

Then, Fakhrul has a reputation for being impulsive and for having problems restraining himself. He will suffer no opposition. Many consider this is an important aspect of him, perhaps the most crucial one. He is the furious fighter, the leader who does not back down, who will use all weapons available to reach his goal. That is perhaps what the many who came to see him at his *darbar* saw in him. Fakhrul is not just someone who gives time or offers advice but someone with a reputation for action, a fierce doer. "Give him twenty-four hours!" he ordered at the *darbar.* A famous incident that helped form his reputation took place in 2011, at a meeting at the district commissioner's office. Fakhrul Khan would have physically attacked his rival, Shamsul Islam, had he not been restrained. Shamsul Islam is a party colleague, leader of the city unit of the party, and mayor. They are also bitter rivals. Fakhrul shouted at him and threatened to murder him. There are other such incidents in which he threatens violence and is restrained.

Last, if fury and fighting spirit are part of his reputation, so is his reputation for brutality and unsavory associates: "I know Fakhrul Khan well, and he likes me. But you know, brother, he is crazy. He can do anything. When he wants to be charming, he can be very charming. But he can be so crazy. So angry. He has people killed. You know that. He can't control himself." For many these incidents do not ruin his reputation but bolster it, as a man of great will. This is a common feature of many of the protagonists of this book. The stories are told and retold. They cement the image of a fierce and powerful man. His association with criminals and violence stems back to the company he kept when he started off as a student activist and budding political leader. He engaged first and foremost with the activists of the neighborhood where he lived and grew up. It was with the youngsters there that he formed a small gang. Some called them activists; others called them *mastans*.

> At that time Fakhrul had a gang that he used. There was one Sukkur, who later succumbed to drug abuse. Then there was Sweet, who was later killed in crossfire [a common euphemism for "shot by the police"]. And Johnny and Lal, who later died of brain hemorrhage. And Maksud, who was also killed in crossfire. There were more. They were very dangerous. They unleashed a reign of terror in the town. People were very scared of them. They began by establishing their control mainly over Arambagh [and then moved into other neighborhoods]. No one could submit bids for tender without their blessing. No one could start any building work without their nod.

The crux of Fakhrul Khan, however, is that his brutal associates are but one set of tools in a toolkit that is much more varied. It also contains his cunning, his ability to use the opportunities available to him, his ability to outwit rivals. A well-known example of this is the takeover of Tutpara.

Tutpara was a rundown *bustee* (poor neighborhood) of bus depots, truck garages, small workshops, prostitutes, and beggars. It was a fairly large area centrally located in Nawabganj. As MP, Fakhrul Khan declared in 1999 that the city should be rid of this eyesore and initiated a highly controversial process to evict the inhabitants. But there was much opposition. Local rights organizations lodged complaints with the courts, the matter was raised in Parliament, and the police had to be brought in to move the work forward. The controversy reached such a height that the prime minister had to publicly defend the eviction and the MP. In the end, however, the eviction drive was successful.

In addition to Tutpara being an eyesore, there was another story behind the takeover, one that was well known at the time and still is but that people still now fifteen years later are wary of talking about. Tutpara was prime real estate land, centrally located in the rapidly growing city. It was a very valuable piece of land, and the successful takeover represented a massive business opportunity. Today it houses a shopping complex, a school, and apartment buildings. Fakhrul Khan's friends and allies own businesses there. All those who own businesses there are friends and allies of Fakhrul Khan.

Behind this explanation again there is yet another, which tells the story of Fakhrul Khan as the smart operator, the one who could outwit opponents. One informant I met at a quiet tea shop in a back alley put it simply, as he smiled and looked around, "Fakhrul took over Tutpara in order to cut off Abdur Rajjak's source of money. Nothing else." Abdur Rajjak was the son of the owner of most of the workshops in Tutpara and an activist with the opposition student front, the Chhatra Dal. He was also a well-known killer. The Tutpara eviction was a blow to the opposition BNP in town, a serious setback that weakened its local influence for years. And the Awami League, under the leadership of its MP, came to dominate the city.

Fakhrul Khan had used all his powers and cunning to achieve the takeover. The municipal administration was involved, including the planning department; the police were called in; he used his *mastans*; he fought the case in court; and he fought in the newspapers and even in Parliament. He mobilized his friends and allies in different places, and he contracted debts with individuals whom he would later have to compensate for their trouble. But in the end he won. Abdur Rajjak's brutality could not stand up against the advantages Fakhrul had. "Fakhrul was a politician and educated; [but] Abdur Rajjak was a real thug." Another informant who was politically active at the time recalled that "Abdur Rajjak could kill anyone, at any time. And he killed many." But his problem was that brutality and some money did not add up to the kind of advantages that his opponent had. "Abdur Rajjak wasn't like Fakhrul, even if he wanted to be. He never went to school. Fakhrul is a politician who can use his intelligence, or his *mastans*, or the administration to get things done." Fakhrul knew how to build connections, borrow favors, and use a variety of tools.

Wit, intelligence, the power of persuasion, and the ability to weave a web of reciprocity are personal qualities that helped build his position and his extended multipronged network. He has loyal journalists working for him and a local newspaper; he has businessmen small and large among his contacts and union leaders, school owners, and doctors in private hospitals; and he keeps his activists happy and engaged. And he has his *mastans*. He has a reputation for being strongly antifundamentalist and has kept Nawabganj largely free from Islamists. His loyalty to the Awami League is unquestioned.

He is an all-rounder with a credible political track record. But he also has the track record of someone who associates with unsavory characters and does not hesitate to use their services. It entangles him in dangerous webs because of the need to protect himself by protecting those close to him. That is the situation he has been facing for the last few years, when some of his associates have been accused of gruesome murders, and he has been dragged in as the master of them all.

VIOLENCE AND THE TURNING OF THE TIDE

Sometime after the 2008 election victory, Fakhrul Khan was allegedly involved in an ugly incident that made national news headlines for days on end. It is difficult to ascertain how much he knew beforehand and how much he has been implicated by association. But the incident added to his reputation and figural power as godfather and centered the national media limelight on his family and its position in Nawabganj.

One morning three bodies were found in a back alley in a corner of Nawabganj. They were the bodies of a local city corporation member and his lawyer and a driver. Over the next few days allegations of Fakhrul's involvement were substantiated with various kinds of evidence, including a taped telephone conversation he had had with Tutulbhai—the former *mastan* leader he had brought into the party and made city commissioner. Tutulbhai and the murdered man had had a long-standing rivalry. Tutulbhai immediately vanished. A few days later accusations emerged that a RAB commander had taken money to murder the three men. Tutulbhai was later arrested, and in the end he, the RAB commander, and twenty more individuals have been charged and convicted. Several of them have admitted guilt.

People are murdered all the time in Nawabganj and elsewhere in Bangladesh for all sorts of reasons, including political, and many cases are never solved. What was perhaps special in this case was that the lawyer belonged to the city elite. An upset public seized the opportunity to vent the frustration that many had long harbored, in Nawabganj but more visibly beyond. The murders allowed the media limelight to focus on Fakhrul Khan—a man long suspected of involvement in criminal and violent affairs but never proven. These murders came on top of a series of allegations that involved him, and these allegations received increased traction. He was accused of masterminding the murders, or of at least protecting the murderers, and of creating an environment of fear in Nawabganj. An additional factor was that there was a credible alternative to him in the city in the form of Shamsul Islam, the mayor with the squeaky-clean image. The accusations against Fakhrul reached such a level that in the end the prime minister herself had to be mobilized and publicly give him her support. She took much flak for that, and it cost her in terms of political capital. When Fakhrul Khan, in spite of the accusations against him, was made the party's candidate for the January 2014 Parliament election,[26] many even within the party expressed dismay. He is the current MP for Nawabganj, but it is rumored that he is losing the prime minister's favor. Much implicit goodwill still lingered before the murders and had been sufficient for years for many to be involved with him. "In reality, he is a good man; but there are some bad people using him for their own ends," one of his associates held. But after the murders, particularly for members of the elite, it was becoming increasingly problematic to be associated with him.

THE GODFATHER'S ENTANGLEMENT

The Tutpara story underlines the importance of intelligence, cunning strategies, and a wide web of contacts in a variety of locations. It highlights the need for the power of persuasion, the usefulness of education, and the command of *mastans*. Fakhrul Khan's story is not the story of brutality alone. It is the story where both violence and legitimate forms of politics have a role. In the part that is legitimate his activist story figures prominently, along with his education, his family background, and his personal qualities as a mobilizer and party organizer. Individual political leaders often rely on family connections. As we have seen, Fakhrul Khan's story is about family in the narrow sense of brothers and family inheritance; it is about who he was before he became a godfather. The family's political standing and the activists of Arambagh were part of his starting capital. He also had the crucial personal qualities.

But Fakhrul Khan's formation as godfather is also about engagements and entanglements beyond family in the narrow sense. His particular and unique willingness to associate also with people of other classes—trade union leaders, neighborhood activists, small-time businessmen, small-time criminals—helped build his standing as a political leader in a self-consciously democratic society. His willingness to use coercion and violence in pursuit of the ultimate aim, power, gave him influence and political success. It was not an uncommon strategy, although he employed it more enthusiastically than many others. The power it brought also brought him influence in a political culture willing to accommodate. Fakhrul Khan's political career is the South Asian story of a political establishment that accommodates innovative strategies.

Throughout his career his engagement with the underworld has been both a useful tool and a liability. His bad reputation probably lost him the candidacy in 1991. The prime minister spent valuable political capital defending him on several occasions. The murders in 2008 have dragged him down and cost him dearly in his rivalry with the city mayor, Shamsul Islam.

The struggle to build and maintain power depends to some extent on the ability to sustain an aura of moral superiority. Social service and the *darbar* that all South Asian politicians engage in; the struggle against the Islamists and personal courage in defense of party colors and values more particular to Bangladesh and Awami League but not unknown elsewhere; and the constant battle with newspapers and civil society accusations, with rivals in both party and Parliament, as well as the severalty of police cases and court proceedings, amount to a quicksand milieu in which entanglements may quickly transform from tool to liability.

CHAPTER 8

THE LEGEND

Clarinda Still

Paritala Ravi was arguably the most feared individual ever in the history of the blood-ridden faction politics of South India. He was a prime accused in innumerable murder cases and also survived numerous assassination attempts, the most brutal of which happened on a quiet Friday afternoon in November 1997 when a road near Rama Naidu Studio in Hyderabad was turned into a death field by a bomb which killed 26 people but failed to get its intended target Ravi. . . . How Ravi, a soft-spoken shy guy under a force of certain circumstances retreated into the jungles, became a rebel and how he mounted a volcano of violence to avenge his father's and brother's deaths and how in time he became a folklore legend and eventually a minister in N. T. Ramarao's Cabinet reads more grippingly than any fiction writer anywhere in the world can ever imagine. Ravi's name sent shivers up the spines of not only his rivals but even the law enforcement agencies. He was a rebel, a feudal lord, a Robin Hood, a killer of hundreds and savior of thousands till the day he was gunned down by a death squad allegedly put together by his arch rival Suri who wanted to avenge his father's and brother's deaths, in a bizarre déjà vu. . . . This is the story of a man's phenomenal rise to power and a story of the most intense blood curdling conflict ever heard of between two individuals and it is also the ultimate statement on the oft heard disastrous consequences of a fatal mixture of caste, crime, family feuds and politics.[1]

Inevitably full of filmmakers' hyperbole, there are aspects of Ram Gopal Varma's description of his biopic film about Paritala Ravi that are noteworthy. Paritala Ravi's violence, brutality, and vengeance have a predictable attraction for cinema-goers, but in the same breath we are told that he is also a "government minister," "a soft-spoken shy guy," "a folklore legend," "a rebel," "a feudal lord," and "a Robin Hood." In seeking popular attention for his film, Varma highlights what he thinks will captivate the fans, and in doing so he provides an account of Paritala Ravi's popular appeal. Ravi is not a one-off subject; "boss" figures like him appear frequently in Telugu film, reflecting a widespread desire to see strong leaders in action on the screen, especially among young men who are, for the most part, the consumers of this film genre. On screen, bosses are not just featured in connection with politics, and their characteristics vary; but they are all invariably depicted as powerful, and more often than not, their power is linked to violence. The emotional appeal of violent characters is rooted in the images such as those conjured by Varma; thus, his description tells us something about how and why such politicians have acquired legitimacy in South India. Given the size and success of Andhra Pradesh's film industry, it is no exaggeration to say that the fantasy of the boss pervades Telugu popular culture. Such films not only reflect a thirst for stories of violent political intrigue; they also help produce a certain type of politics in Andhra Pradesh. As K. Srinivasulu suggests, they feed the desire to see political violence represented and also "strengthen the culture of benevolence for followers" and glorify its ruthlessness.[2]

This chapter reconstructs the life story of Paritala Ravi to understand how underworld bosses become political heroes. It shows the making of a party icon and illustrates the contours of a powerful fantasy that is shaping bossism in South Asia at large. Thus, the chapter highlights the economic basis of the bosses' political power; the everyday cultural values that underpin their reputation; and the importance of film and media in the creation of "the art of bossing."

We asserted earlier that this form of muscular politics can be linked to the changing shape of the economy that gives rise to mafia-owned democracies. Ravi's story epitomizes the postliberalization formation of mafia-like structures in Andhra Pradesh: mushrooming black economies and the fusion of old statecraft tropes with newer forms of capitalism.[3] In this chapter we see how the political/criminal careers of Ravi and his adversaries are enmeshed with economic activities such as land acquisition, procuring stakes in industry, mining, media, and other businesses that enable them to accumulate wealth on the scale necessary to uphold their political status, establish territorial domains, and defend their position from would-be encroachers. As earlier chapters in this book show, the state and the judiciary are integral to these processes that propel such men to power.

Springing out of this particular political and economic context, Paritala Ravi's art of bossing is shaped by very common, familiar, and old values such as honor and male prestige, which appear to be especially pronounced in the region.[4] This is not always the case; some bosses advance by subverting traditional values rather than endorsing them. Ravi, however, exploited and exaggerated them. Popular representations of Ravi combine power with morality: we see how Ravi built his reputation not just on violence but on social service, development, mass marriages, and other forms of public benevolence and patronage. Moreover, his violence is morally justified by drawing on a monarchical paradigm of order, control, and authority in the name of defense, protection, and the restoration of honor. On a more personal level, Ravi's actions are explained and exonerated by revenge: he was seeking justice for the murder of his father and brother, and he wanted to reinstate family and caste pride. Muscular power, leadership, and honor are constitutive parts of "macho" politics in Andhra Pradesh.

It is no coincidence that these are the very values so often embodied by the heroes of Telugu film. The worlds of such mafia bosses are built on aspects of what Baudrillard called "hyperreality," the blending of reality and fiction and the creation of myth.[5] Hyperreality need not have any concrete referent in the real world but forms its own reality through images, gossip, conversations, assertions, counterassertions, allegations of crime, and protests of innocence. The representations of protagonists (in film, television, Facebook, blogs and anonymous posts, street gossip, phone communications, political posters) take on a life of their own. These form what we call "fictional realities" in popular imagination. The death of such figures (one might use Y. S. Rajasekhara Reddy [YSR] and Ravi as examples) tends to transform and exalt existing representations while adding the dimension of martyrdom, sacrifice, and purification. As much as the facts themselves, the manner of reporting and remembering animates the myth surrounding Ravi and his larger-than-life enemies. Through a range of media, we see how ordinary people are, in a sense, creating what we describe in this book as fictional reality.

Leaders themselves are often the most active agents in cultivating their figurality by constructing and disseminating images of themselves that tap into men's (and women's) desires and projections of strong, violent leaders. Film and reality become dialogically related: in film, men like Ravi display qualities of the cine heroes, while filmmakers like Varma take events from real life to produce dramas. The bosses of Mafia Raj understand the influence of media: Ravi made a film about his father (and was bombed while filming it), and he became the subject of two films subsequently. One of those accused of conspiring in his murder (the current leader of the opposition, Jagan Mohan Reddy), has arguably used technology and media more than any other leader before him. Since 2009, he has run his own media house, television channel, and online broadcasting network. These leaders are not entirely products of their own creation (however much they may seek to be), but neither are they simply abstractions of a popular fantasy.

BACKGROUND: KAMMAS, REDDYS, AND TELUGU POLITICS

My interest in Paritala Ravi came about after his assassination in January 2005. At the time, I was conducting fieldwork in rural Andhra Pradesh, some distance from the site of his assassination. But even in a village far away from Ravi's constituency, his death had an impact. There were protests in the local towns and unrest across the state. In the nearby town of Guntur, buses were set alight by his supporters; activists attacked Congress offices, and fights broke out between party affiliates. Shops, offices, and businesses were shut in the following days.

In the village where I was living, people stayed at home and suspended their business in town until the trouble passed. There was much discussion about his assassination and disagreement about who was to blame. More widely, his death prompted a debate about the criminalization of politics and caste-based factionalism.

These concerns tally with statistics that seemingly show a rise in the number of politicians with criminal records and an increase in the candidates' wealth, although these figures are to be treated with caution. According to National Election watch statistics, in Andhra Pradesh, 16 percent of the candidates in the 2014 elections had declared criminal cases against them, 9 percent of which were serious. This is only slightly less than Uttar Pradesh, which has 19 percent and 9 percent, respectively. Rayalaseema in the south of Andhra Pradesh seems to have a reputation for a particularly violent style of factional politics. A report in *Frontline* in 2005 estimated that 670 congressmen and 560 Telugu Desam Party (TDP) politicians had lost their lives to factional rivalries between 1990 and 2005. A police officer commented, "The 'only ideology' in these testosterone faction-ridden villages is violence."[6] While Rayalaseema has the worst record, its political culture is little different from that of the rest of South India. Figures like Ravi, with a string of criminal charges against them, clearly have an appeal for sections of the voting public.

Paritala Ravi was from the Kamma caste, and his rivals were Reddys. In the early twentieth century, these two s*udra* peasant castes combined to form the Justice Party, and later the *kisan* (farmer) movement. Under pressure from the *kisan* movement and the increasingly vocal landless poor, postcolonial governments passed a raft of land reforms.[7] The main beneficiaries were the former tenants and cultivators, the Kammas and Reddys. These newly landed castes benefited from high food prices and cash crops in the 1950s and the Green Revolution in the 1970s.[8] Newly affluent landowners educated their children and expanded into business, commerce, construction, transport, and industry.[9] Kammas and Reddys thereby broke the Brahmin dominance of the state and have competed with each other for political, economic, and social dominance ever since.

Land and economic power went hand in hand with politics for the Kammas and Reddys, who respectively make up 5 percent and 7 percent of the state's population. Kammas are predominant in coastal Andhra Pradesh, while the Reddys are more influential in Telangana and Rayalaseema. Kammas and Reddys vied for political supremacy initially in the Congress Party before the Kammas took over the Communist Party.[10] But it was the TDP that gave the Kammas their political vehicle. Subsequently, the Reddys largely dominated Congress, while Kammas dominated the TDP.[11]

This caste-party link was entrenched further by YSR, a charismatic Reddy Congress politician who was chief minister from 2004 until his death in 2009. His story is linked to our protagonist because his son, Jagan, is alleged to have been behind Ravi's murder.[12] The two families belonged to rival factions in Anantapur.

YSR was from Rayalaseema, the reputed heartland of factional politics and the setting of this chapter. In 1998, YSR's father was killed by a bomb planted by eleven TDP activists (now serving life sentences) in what would later become YSR's own constituency, Pulivendula. One of the accused was killed in retaliation, and four of the accused died during the trial.[13] From the very start YSR was mired in political violence.

YSR was an ambitious strongman politician who made use of liberalization's opportunities for state-capital alliances in the same way his TDP predecessor had done, but with renewed vigor. Where the TDP had failed to amend laws to gain access to environmental resources, YSR succeeded.[14] He set up mutually advantageous alliances such as the Brahmani Steels land acquisition in Cuddapah, and the Andhra Pradesh Mineral Development Corporation coalition with private companies for mining in Araku.[15] His government worked with private companies to mine bauxite, laterite, calcite, limestone, mica, and clay in the tribal region in the north of the state, riding roughshod over legislation to protect forests and tribal rights.[16] "The success of this formula of combining a neo-liberal primitive accumulation agenda with populism to amass unprecedented levels of wealth is now visible not just in Araku but also across coastal Andhra and Rayalaseema," comment Prasad and colleagues.[17] Despite YSR's obvious accumulation, his pro-poor schemes (for housing, health insurance, free electric power to farmers) made him popular nevertheless, and his untimely death in a helicopter crash in 2009 transformed him into revered political figure.

Jagan Reddy expected to take the reins after his father's death. However, Congress at the national level chose not to appoint him. Angered by this snub, Jagan broke away from the Congress and set up his own party, the Yuvajana Shramika Rythu Congress Party (YSR-CP), commonly known as the YSR Congress. He took with him staunch YSR supporters across the state and the majority of Rayalaseema Reddys. This severely diminished the strength of Congress in Andhra Pradesh and effectively split those caste-party loyalties that had been more clear-cut.[18]

The emergence of new parties, coupled with the powerful Telangana movement, had radically altered the electoral scene by the 2014 elections.[19] New players came to the fore, and established parties collapsed. Even before the election results, it was clear that Congress had been demolished, in part due to the YSR-CP but also due to Congress's role in splitting the state. Several leading Congress politicians defected to the TDP and Bharatiya Janata Party (BJP). With the specter of the new state on the horizon, voters were persuaded to opt for the person they thought would make a success of building a new capital in Andhra Pradesh: the former chief minister, Chandra Babu Naidu. In this situation (and helped by Narendra Modi's BJP), the TDP won by a clear majority.

How does this relate to bossism and Paritala Ravi? At this point we need to turn back to Jagan, a hugely wealthy, maverick leader whose popularity defies his tarnished reputation.[20] Jagan is suspected of having used state funds for private gain, and in 2012 he was imprisoned for sixteen months under the Prevention of Corruption Act for disproportionate assets and providing "quid pro quo favors" for water, land, and other resources.[21] He was also accused of money laundering and tax avoidance. The YSR Congress claims the accusations are false and that this is a case of political vendetta.[22]

More significantly here, Jagan has been accused of orchestrating the murder of Ravi. The Central Bureau of Investigation (CBI) investigated Jagan but did so under his father's instruction during his rule as chief minster. Unsurprisingly, Jagan was cleared. But with Chandra Babu Naidu now chief minister, the TDP has reopened the case. However, before we get to the murder, let us consider Ravi in more detail.[23]

PARITALA RAVI

Paritala Ravi was born in 1957 in Anantapur district in Rayalaseema. His father, a Kamma landlord called Sriramulu (1935–75), was influenced by the Communist movement in his youth. Sriramulu became a Naxalite leader close to Kondapalli Seetharamaiah, the man who later founded the People's War Group, an underground Communist revolutionary organization.

Sriramulu allegedly gave away much of his inherited three hundred–acre estate and led low-caste workers against powerful local landlords. Two of these landowners were Gangula Narayana Reddy and Sane Chenna Reddy. The feud that eventually killed Ravi was initiated when Sriramulu and his followers occupied their land. They hired men who killed Sriramulu in May 1975.

After Sriramulu's death, Ravi's younger brother, Hari (1960–82), stepped into his father's shoes. At the age of nineteen, he joined the Naxalite movement and continued to forcibly seize farmlands in the area. In 1982, he was killed in a so-called police encounter. According to the website of a pro-TDP Kamma youth organization (KYSS), he was arrested at his house in Venkatapuram, taken to a village nearby, and shot dead by a police inspector in plain view of the villagers. Gangula Narayana Reddy and Sane Chenna Reddy are also thought to be behind the assassination of Hari.

After his father and brother were killed, Ravi was next in the firing line. He fled and took refuge in the house of a maternal uncle. He worked on the family farm, and he married his uncle's daughter, Sunita, in 1986. He is believed to have worked as a full-time party member in the Naxalites for several years.[24] On June 1, 1983, Gangula Narayana Reddy was killed by People's War Group members in a lodge in Anantapur. It is widely believed that Ravi ordered the murder. Next Ravi set his sights on Gangula Narayana Reddy's son, Suri (see Table 8.1).[25]

TABLE 8.1 *Ravi–Suri Incidents*

1975	Ravi's father, Sriramulu, killed by Suri's father, Gangula Narayana Reddy, and Sane Chenna Reddy
1983	Gangula Narayana Reddy killed by Ravi in retaliation
1991	Sane Chenna Reddy killed in retaliation
1993	TV bomb blast by Ravi kills four of Suri's family (mother, brother, brother-in-law, sister) and a maid
1996	Suri's colleague and Sane Chenna Reddy's son, Obul Reddy, murdered
1997	Suri's revenge on Ravi with a car bomb attack in Jubilee Hills kills twenty-six people
1999	Suri's colleague and Sane Chenna Reddy's second son, Ramana Reddy, murdered
2005	Ravi shot dead in Anantapur
2011	Suri killed in Hyderabad

Sane Chenna Reddy became MLA of Penukonda in 1989. He and his two sons, Ramana and Obul, joined forces with Suri (the son of Gangula Naryana Reddy). This faction is said to have enjoyed an impunity that enabled them to get rid of several of their adversaries. Two anonymous reports and other blogs claim that Suri and his associates unleashed a "reign of terror," keeping this area in a state of fear by committing "atrocities," including, allegedly, sexual attacks on women.[26] This period of violence is a crucial one in Ravi's career. In 1991, Sane Chenna Reddy was shot. His son, Ramana, took over as MLA in the election that followed (see Table 8.2). Ramana was also later killed in 1999. Ravi was linked by the Anantapur police to both deaths.

Ravi broke away from the Naxalites in 1992 to join the TDP,[27] and it was through the TDP that Ravi expanded and consolidated his power. From 1994 until his death ten years later, Ravi was the TDP MLA for Penukonda constituency.[28] To achieve this position required armed support, so Ravi exploited his Naxalite links. In 1992, the People's War Group in this area split into two groups.[29] The Reorganization Committee (ROC) was allegedly the "pocket organization" of Ravi, which functioned as his underground wing, armed with automatic weapons and land mines.[30] The other group, Redstar, was at the service of the Reddys.[31] Effectively, the Reddy faction and Ravi's

TABLE 8.2 *MLAs in Penukonda Constituency, Anantapur District, Rayalaseema, Andhra Pradesh (1989–present)*

1989	Sane Chenna Reddy (Congress) (killed in 1991)
1991	Sane Ramana Reddy (Congress) (killed in 1999)
1994	Paritala Ravi (TDP)
1999	Paritala Ravi (TDP)
2004	Paritala Ravi (TDP) (killed in 2005)
2005	Paritala Sunitha (TDP, wife of Ravi, now in the Andhra Pradesh cabinet)
2009	Parthasarathi (TDP)
2014	Parthasarathi (TDP)

Source: Adapted from Wikipedia, "Penukonda," last edited December 15, 2017, https://en.wikipedia.org/wiki/Penukonda.

Kamma faction had an armed force at their disposal. In the position of MLA and with both the ROC and popular support behind him, Ravi's power was at its height. His sights were fixed on Suri, the leader of the Reddy faction.

In October 1993, Ravi sent a portable television set loaded with explosives to Suri's house while he was away.[32] When unsuspecting members of Suri's family switched on the television, the bomb exploded, killing five people, including his mother, brother, sister, brother-in-law, and a maid. Along with his father's death ten years earlier, now most of Suri's family had been killed. Suri fled to Karnataka to plot his revenge.

Later, in November 1997, Suri triggered a remote-controlled bomb hidden in a car parked near Rama Naidu Film Studio in Jubilee Hills, Hyderabad. Ravi was producing a film about his father called *Sriramulaiah*. The car bomb killed twenty-six people, including six members of a television crew. But the bomb missed its target, and Ravi was left unscathed. Suri and six others were found guilty and sentenced to life imprisonment.

Ravi appeared invincible until the 2004 general elections. Suri was still in jail, but Suri's wife, Bhanumathi, ran against Ravi on the Congress ticket. Ravi was warned not to campaign for the elections after a tip-off about a plot to kill him.[33] Ravi's wife, Sunita, campaigned on his behalf. Two of Ravi's henchmen, Suresh and Chaman, were arrested.[34] On the polling day, Ravi and his men were taken into "preventive custody," charged with kidnapping and shooting a Congress polling station agent. The results showed that Ravi had won by a clear majority of twenty-four thousand votes in his constituency. But Congress came to power both in the state and at the national level. With YSR now the chief minister, a Rayalaseema Reddy whose family and party was in direct opposition to Ravi's, the situation was about to change.

Soon after YSR won, Ravi's security was allegedly reduced from ten to two men. Ravi requested the restoration of adequate security but was denied it. He sought redress through the High Court, which directed the government to restore his security of "5+5 men." Ravi gave an interview saying that he believed that YSR, Jagan, Bhanumathi, Suri, and Diwakar Reddy had conspired with the police to kill him.[35]

On January 24, 2005, when Ravi was leaving a TDP party meeting in the TDP office in Anantapur, he was shot. His bodyguard and another follower were also killed. Ravi's death provoked widespread unrest. On the same day, the *Hindu* reported protests in all district headquarters. TDP activists went on a rampage, forcing shops to shut, damaging party offices, and pelting government property with stones. In Vijayawada (near my own fieldsite), twelve state buses were burned and local TDP activists called off meetings and stood on the road to block traffic. They held YSR's government responsible and demanded his resignation, the arrest of Jagan, and a CBI investigation.

Soon after the assassination, one of the accused, M. Rekhamaiah, surrendered to the police. Within a week, eight of the alleged conspirators had surrendered. Eventually, of the sixteen men accused in the case, one became an informer, three were killed, eight were sentenced to life imprisonment by the Anantapur District Court, and four were acquitted.[36] Moddu Sreenu, alias Julakanti Srinivas, the prime accused in the Ravi murder case and a close associate of Suri, was killed in Anantapur jail in November 2008.[37] Chandra Babu Naidu alleged that YSR's government had an interest in eliminating Moddu Sreenu to cover up evidence, a charge that YSR denied. Suri himself was shot dead in a separate incident by his former aide, Bhanu Kiran, in Hyderabad in 2011 after a dispute related to money from the illegal settlement of land disputes.[38]

POLITICAL MURDER

The setting of Ravi and Suri's rivalry is close to YSR's hometown, Pulivendula. Together, these families dominate the political theater of Anantapur. Whether or not YSR's family was involved in the murder of Ravi was a matter of intense discussion, both in villages and the corridors of power. A month after the assassination, for example, when a TDP MLA suggested YSR was involved in Ravi's murder, it sparked an acrimonious four-hour Assembly debate during which an enraged Congress MLA threw a microphone at the opposition bench that injured one of his colleagues.[39]

At the very least, we know that Ravi was killed soon after YSR came to power and that YSR was responsible for reducing Ravi's bodyguards. Ravi had his own private protection, but YSR is thought to have deliberately exposed him to attack. More serious are the allegations that Suri and Jagan set up their own private army, the Jana Rakshana Samiti (People's Protection Force) to counter Ravi's ROC.[40] Jagan strongly denies this.[41] A document by a CBI investigator, leaked to the media in 2005, apparently exposes the nexus between Jagan and Suri.[42] The document discusses a man called Dantuluri Krishna, who was the "neighbor and frontman of Y. S. Jagan Mohan Reddy." It says that "Suri struck a bargain through Krishna to eliminate Paritala Ravindra." Krishna was sentenced to five years in prison for conspiring to kill Ravi. Since Krishna had been Jagan's close aide, suspicions were raised about Jagan too.[43] CBI investigators questioned YSR, Jagan, and (J. C.) Diwakar Reddy, but their names were deleted from the charge sheet after the CBI failed to prove their complicity in the murder.[44]

To his staunch supporters, Ravi's murder was a politically motivated assassination at the highest level. The anonymous author of the Telugu Desam essay "A Factionist Becomes Chief Minister" claims that the murder of Ravi "is the best example of nefarious game of YSR in eliminating his political rivals."[45] The author argues, "There is no doubt that the murder of Paritala Ravindra . . . was not only premeditated and calculated, but also sponsored, endorsed, supported and executed by the State government, with the active role of the Chief Minister, his son, certain ministers, several Congress leaders with long history of criminal background and also with the clear connivance of certain senior police officials, executed through hired professional killers."[46] Moreover, the author claims that within nine months of YSR coming to power, forty-four other TDP functionaries had also been murdered and that police did little about it, apparently co-opted by the Congress under YSR.

Ravi's wife, Paritala Sunita, took her husband's place as the MLA for Penukonda in 2005.[47] When the TDP came back to power in May 2014, she was invited to join the cabinet. The first thing she did was to put Jagan "on notice," declaring that her husband's murder case would be reopened with the permission of the chief minister and that this time "no culprit would escape."[48] She alleged that Jagan had hatched a conspiracy with Suri and supplied bulletproof jackets to the shooters, Moddu Seenu and his gang, to eliminate her husband.[49] Sunita's father, Kondaiah, has filed an FIR (First Information Report) accusing Jagan, Suri, Gangula Bhanumathi, Konda Reddy, J. C. Diwakar Reddy, and a senior police official of conspiring in the murder.[50]

An odd twist to this story is that one of the men named in the FIR for conspiring to murder is now Sunita's colleague, J. C. Diwakar Reddy. He switched from the Congress Party to the TDP in March 2014. Chandra Babu Naidu subsequently promoted him to a position alongside Sunita. To make Sunita share a dais with a man she believes to have helped kill her husband is a questionable move (indeed, she threatened to leave the TDP when Diwakar Reddy joined). Perhaps Chandra Babu Naidu was seeking to consolidate TDP influence in Anantapur or even seeking to reduce factional rivalry. Sunita has stayed in the cabinet so far.[51]

Jagan claims he is being unfairly targeted by both the Congress and the TDP, and the BJP (who support Jagan) has claimed that the charges against him are a political vendetta.[52] Jagan is a powerful figure in Rayalaseema in particular, and he has ambitious plans in the newly divided state. Building on his father's popularity, he has substantial support and a property, media, and mining empire. The TDP seeks to diminish his popularity and drive him out of politics.

DEATH: TRANSFORMATION AND PURIFICATION

Ravi's death transformed him from a powerful local boss to a statewide icon of the TDP. Thousands attended his funeral. Chandra Babu Naidu (then TDP president) and senior party leaders traveled from Hyderabad to Venkatapuram to attend.[53] Videos show the cavalcade of white 4×4s on the road, the crowds gathered at his funeral, the mass weeping, and showers of petals at his funeral.[54] The theatrical and public way in which he was assassinated, and the widespread and graphic media coverage it received, meant that his death was visually imprinted onto television viewers across the state. Until then, Ravi was notorious for factional murders and the television bomb in Anantapur. But after his death, his image was purified, evoking sympathy for him and his family. But it also raised suspicions because he was shot so soon after YSR came to power.

Ravi's family, which, like YSR's is a political machine of its own, capitalized on popular sympathy and molded Ravi's image further. They have, for example, set up organizations such as the Paritala Ravi Memorial Trust and the Paritala Ravi Smaraka Seva Samithi that work to construct a sanctified memory of Ravi.[55] Media-attended commemorative events are held annually on the anniversary of his death.[56] One loyal fan made a lifelike wax statue of him (Fig. 8.1), which has been placed on the swing bench on his veranda in Venkatapuram.[57]

Supporters in the TDP's Non Resident Indian network took part in the celebrations in London on the sixth anniversary of his death.[58] On his birthday, Sunita was presented with a shawl woven with Paritala's photo. His tomb was garlanded, and relatives brought plates of food and a birthday cake. A library was opened in Nasanakota, the village where Ravi's brother was shot.[59] Following tradition, another set of mass marriages was conducted by Sunita in 2010, photos of which can be seen on Paritala Ravi's website.[60] Through the Paritala Ravi Memorial Trust, Sunita and her son, Paritala Sriram (who is now being groomed to enter politics), run social service programs, blood donation

FIGURE 8.1. *Wax statue of Paritala Ravi next to his mausoleum. Photo courtesy of the official Paritala Ravi website, http://www.paritalaravi.com/photo-gallery .html.*

camps, and educational schemes.[61] Statues of Ravi have been erected all over Andhra Pradesh but particularly in Anantapur. All of these events, rituals, services, and institutions ensure that Ravi is remembered not as a violent vengeful "factionist" but as a benevolent, caring, powerful leader: an honorable family man and now a deified ancestor.

Ravi's death also gave the TDP an opportunity to elevate him to the level of an icon. As a political figure he has been exalted to legendary status. A decade after his death, his image appeared on TDP campaign posters across the state in the 2014 elections, alongside the founding father of the TDP, the movie star–turned–politician, N. T. Ramarao. Figures 8.2 and 8.3 cast them as salt-of-the-earth leaders, with Ramarao

FIGURE 8.2. *TDP legends: N. T. Ramarao and Paritala Ravi. Source: "Paritala Ravi Story," https://www.youtube.com/results?search_query=paritala+ravi+story.*

FIGURE 8.3. *TDP campaign poster for 2014 elections with Paritala Ravi* (left) *and N. T. Ramarao* (right). *Photograph by author, Vijaywada, January 2015.*

styled as a peasant farmer. If we compare this with a very similar process of posthumous deification of another of Andhra's popular leaders, YSR, we begin to appreciate how powerful (and useful) death can be in both enhancing and transforming a leader's status.

MAKING A LEGEND

We know that Ravi enjoyed enormous popularity, but was his support due to intimidation or genuine loyalty? Fear was certainly a key element of his rule in the area. A report by the Andhra Pradesh Civil Liberties Committee in 1998 pronounced, "The entire district kneels down before him. Everyone is afraid of him." Ravi had against him "54 serious criminal cases—16 of them murder—and a few dozen more in which he was prime suspect, but not charge-sheeted."[62] A senior police officer said, "He was never convicted in any case, naturally, since witnesses would invariably turn hostile in court, refuse to testify, or simply vanish."[63] Fear was also instrumental in enabling Ravi to gain control of resources.

It is true that it may have been difficult or dangerous for villagers in Anantapur to show anything but support for Ravi. But the relationship between Ravi and his followers is not, I suggest, based on fear alone. Rather, Telugu posts about Ravi often invoke *abhimanam* (affection or esteem). This word suggests neither a detached alignment of values nor a fear of reprisal but rather a positive emotional attachment to a superior. A relationship of *abhimanam* involves feelings akin to the devotion one might display toward a god or a highly esteemed father figure. Fear can be part of *abhimanam*: you may be frightened of displeasing or angering your god/leader/father because your survival depends on him, but you may give him love for providing, protecting, and caring for you as well.[64]

Abhimanam is not just evident in the number of votes he received (presumably not all of which were coerced) but also in the way people talk about him. Ravi's Facebook page ("liked" by 19,253 people) gives a sense of the reasons for his adulation: "The Real Lion of Rayalaseema"; "AP King"; "Anantapur Don"; "real hero"; "King Ravi, elder brother"; "there is no one else in the world like you"; "legend"; and so on. Indeed, using words like "Don" (as in mafia don) and "lion" give the impression that he was admired because of his violent reputation, not despite it. Many posts refer to his common touch. YouTube videos contain a multitude of comments such as, "Paritala Ravindra the real hero of the poor people. Really 'salute' to you sir," and "I really value him, he worked for common man not for political or business fellows."

The devotion that people had for Ravi rests principally on two aspects of his reputation: he was an awe-inspiring "man of the people" who took care of the poor and vulnerable, but he was also presented as a "man's man," a "man of honor" who could protect and provide for others and master a violent world.

Honor and Masculine Prowess

A key element of Ravi's status is honor. This is a highly gendered form of power, the substantial moral achievement of masculine prowess. This macho aspect is observable in the emphasis on strength, power, and quite literally the ability to win fights. Indeed, as a heroic defender, he embodied some of the key characteristics of the heroes in Telugu film: swift to act and masterful, able to defeat his assailants and defend his territory against the odds. A good example of this is his fans' celebration of his almost supernatural ability to escape death, such as the bomb planted by Suri on the film set in Jubilee Hills. Here we can also compare him to mythical heroes such as Veerappan, who heroically, even magically, seem to evade the clutches of the state. The evasion of death is a sign of almost paranormal power.

Ravi is hailed as a protector of the people who hit back against the Reddys' alleged reign of terror in the 1980s.[65] He was not a wordy intellectual or a privileged cosmopolitan but a man of action: a rough-and-ready product of the violent politics of Anantapur, whose circumstances toughened him enough to counter fierce opposition. He matched fire with fire, so it is said. The man who now occupies Ravi's former position, B. K. Parthasarathi, the current MLA of Penugonda, commented, "He was a man without fear. He was a person who stood by his word, no matter what happens. He had financial resources. He was a strong man. So that's why people sought his support and why he got the support of the people. He stood up for people. . . . He was a man who stood by his word. If he assured you something, he would do it, whatever the consequences. That was his greatness."[66]

There is one particular incident that is often related as an illustration. Allegedly, when Sane Chenna Reddy was the Congress MLA, he campaigned to be reelected in the 1989 elections. He toured villages to gather support. (Chenna Reddy was at the helm during the alleged "reign of terror.") Ravi procured guns and gathered supporters in the villages in the area. The story goes that when Chenna Reddy came to the village to campaign, Ravi and his supporters blocked the road and prevented him from entering. As an MLA, Chenna Reddy had a police escort with him. Ravi and his followers apparently shot guns in the air and stated that while they had no quarrel with the police, they would not allow Chenna Reddy to enter. Chenna Reddy retreated. This incident apparently strongly contributed to Ravi's reputation as a man unafraid to stand up to even the most ruthless of opponents. Later, after Chenna Reddy won the election, these villagers were attacked in retribution.[67] But when Ravi won a large majority in 1994, their loyalty was rewarded.

Ravi is widely believed to have blood on his hands, but his supporters claim violence is only ever perpetrated against those who "deserved it." For example, according to one account, in 1996, while Ravi was MLA, the ROC killed Obul Reddy, the alleged "sadist" and serial rapist. A pro-Ravi blog states, "Obul Reddy along with his three henchmen, was in a lodge in Hyderabad with a prostitute when he was attacked by ROC. He was taking a bath. That prostitute was sent away from the room and the henchmen were hacked down. Then they brought Obul Reddy outside from bathroom. His throat was slit almost completely, and his genitals were cut down brutally. They escaped from there immediately. Paritala Ravi was the prime accused."[68] It is notable that this account is used to glorify Ravi: We are told of how gruesomely Obul Reddy was tortured and murdered, but it is presented as a fair response given the nature of Obul Reddy's crimes. Cutting off his genitals, for example, is presented as appropriate punishment for his multiple rapes. In other words, this is payback, showing Ravi as a leader who can deliver justice.

Ravi's violence is always described as measured and rule bound. He did not act irrationally or out of mindless brutality in the way that his enemies apparently did. On the contrary, he is depicted as a restrained and even reluctant fighter. For instance, KYSS claims, "He only killed those he needed to; he never killed women and children."[69] One Ravi Yadav on a YouTube video asserts, "He killed many culprits and criminals because people of those mentality have no right to live in a society. There are many criminals in Anantapur district who are illegally encouraging all crimes and committing rapes, extortion, and murders. . . . So he entered into this violence and is punishing all the culprits."[70] Unlike his "immoral" adversaries, he is thought never to have perpetrated violence gratuitously or for enjoyment. As one of our young male informants in coastal Andhra Pradesh commented, "Although he may have done some bullying, he took good care of the people. People are not particular about whether he was a rowdy or not. They only remember whether he helped us or not. That is how he is remembered."[71]

Above all, the driving force behind his ruthlessness had one important legitimizing factor: to avenge the death of his brother and father. This compulsion to act to restore the family name and to punish those who had committed crimes against him exonerates him. Indeed, it is through the violence that he accumulates honor for himself, his family, his party, and his caste group, and he proves to others his masculine prowess. In other words, Ravi's is a legitimate, "good" kind of violence, which affirmed his masculinity and restored his family name and caste honor and thus enhanced his political reputation. In this respect, we can link Ravi to revenge politics in Pakistan.

Paritala Ravi as Robin Hood? Service to the Poor

But a large part of Ravi's reputation is also for his development work and social service. For example, the pro-TDP Telugu daily, *Eenadu*, reports on January 25, 2005, "His family provided wheat and barley to villagers in nearly nine villages, which are 'entirely dependent [on him],'" and continues: "He organized and paid for nearly 300 weddings of poor peasants who could not pay expenses or dowries, in a district in which droughts are recurrent. He rebuilt the temple of Venkateswara in a village [in the area] and community halls for the poor. He built roads in two villages with his own money. He spent nearly 4 crore [Rs. 40 million] on that."[72] The bio-data on Paritala Ravi's Facebook page also claims that the villagers of Anantapur were wholly dependent on him.[73]

One of Ravi's most notable contributions was mass marriages. In 2003, he married two thousand couples.[74] After this, mass marriages were inaugurated as a TDP event by Chief Minister Chandra Babu Naidu.[75] This is a customary means for leaders to position themselves as benevolent patrons, providing for their followers in an act of fatherly generosity. In Andhra Pradesh, landlords used to (and in some places still do) fund their servants' weddings, including gifting the *tali* (wedding necklace).[76] Ravi took on this role not for one couple but for hundreds, and it shows that the couples, their families, and those attending accepted him. It is an effective method of cementing leadership on a mass scale in an especially personal way.

Mass marriages are repeatedly noted on Ravi fan forums. He gifted the gold *tali* and silk clothes to each couple and fed hundreds of thousands of people.[77] These events would have left a lifelong impression on the couples and no doubt contributed to Ravi's adulation as a real-life hero.[78] Moreover, the auspiciousness and excitement of multiple marriages transmutes into gratitude and adoration for a great benefactor.

This sort of altruistic work for the poor is used to put a positive twist on Ravi's involvement with what many mainstream politicians call an underground guerrilla movement, the Naxalites. Ravi's personal "army," the ROC, was forged before Ravi's time with the Naxalites, yet the violent element of the Naxalite connection is played down. Instead, Ravi's Naxalite links are used to portray him as a Robin Hood figure, stealing from the rich to give to the poor. The Naxalite image is brought up in reference to his father giving away his land and seizing the lands of "greedy" Reddy landlords to distribute among the poor. Ravi's Naxalite link is thus depoliticized: it is no longer connected to communism, socialism, or factionalist or caste-based politics in Anantapur, but rather it is used to conjure his likeness to a more generic mythical figure: a man who champions the rights of the poor by undermining the exploitative feudal rich.

LIBERALIZATION, ECONOMIC INTERESTS, AND DISPLAYS OF LARGESSE

But these displays require wealth, of course, which raises the question of his own estate, but it is hard to find any details about economic activities. One can find information about the political violence in which he was involved, but information about his business matters is scant. We do know that the control of resources is key to his influence. The current TDP MLA, B. K. Parthasarathi, gave a sense of this when he told us, "Once you grow in politics, it is natural that you would get more opportunities for making money. You will have the support of important people. So there is some advantage that comes with political power."[79]

Ravi was apparently active in land settlements in Anantapur, Bangalore, and Hyderabad during the real estate boom and the construction of Hitec city.[80] The KYSS website also notes his involvement in the "government contract business." But in Kadapa and Anantapur the principal economy is minerals. Ravi owned a granite quarry, and he mined limestone for cement. Balagopal gives some insight into how Ravi operated in the area:

> Larsen & Toubro had a bad time with the cement factory it set up near Tadipatri in Anantapur district a couple of years ago. It almost decided to give up and go away, unable to cope with the heavy handed demands made on it for allotment of civil works, not to mention plain extortion. Gangs led or supported by local factionists (as the leaders of these armed gangs have been known since British times) would drive up to the local manager's office in jeeps or tractors and demand, on pain of having the office wrecked, that the work of laying a road connecting the factory with the nearest high way, or a link railway track connecting it to the Chennai-Mumbai main line, or even the work of building a compound wall, should be allotted to them at the price

> acceptable to them, and no talk of quality control, if you please! L & T must be familiar with the urban mafias of Mumbai and Gujarat, but it appears to have found the unpredictability of the numerous rural gangs of Anantapur a bit too much. As the factory is located at the limestone-rich trijunction of the three main Rayalaseema districts of Anantapur, Kurnool and Cuddapah, the rulers of the state were understandably apprehensive that the travails of L & T would hit the development prospects of that mineral-rich region hard. A good enough reason for a law to control organized crime syndicates? But who or which were the main gangs that gave a rough time to Larsen & Toubro at Tadipatri? The major tormentor and the main beneficiary of the arm-twisting methods of making quick money at L & T's expense was Paritala Ravindra, a Telugu Desam Party (TDP) legislator from Penukonda in Anantapur district.[81]

As Balagopal shows, political success is achieved on the back of the control of economic resources. Land, money, control of services, and government resources allow leaders to acquire, protect, and reward political dependents and display largesse to their people. Political power also offers protection against legal action and enables leaders to use intimidation to further his business interests. Fear and intimidation are central to this modus operandi. In 2001, Balagopal said this of him: "Paritala Ravindra is, without doubt, the most feared person in Anantapur district. You have only to walk up to any business place in the district and mention his name and demand money, and you will get it 99 times out of 100."[82]

But Ravi's fortune was dwarfed by YSR and the Reddys in Congress, who made their name in mining. YSR and Jagan are alleged to have links with Karnataka mining barons, the Gali brothers, one of whom, Gali Janardhana Reddy, is presently the tourism minister for Karnataka. Gali and Jagan are currently being investigated by the CBI for illegal operations. (As chief minister, YSR is alleged to have undersold 10,670 acres of government land to the Gali brothers for mining.) YSR is accused of pulling the strings behind the Gali brothers' operations.[83] The way in which YSR operated, then, appears to be quite similar to that of Paritala Ravi. The anonymous author claims that YSR's position in Congress allowed him to take advantage of nationalization, which in turn allowed him to bully his way onto protected land and attempt a land grab. He thereby acquired assets that would start a process of accumulation for the consolidation of power.[84]

Parthasarathi's study of violence in the town of Vijayawada is instructive for us here. In the 1980s, Vijayawada was also characterized by a political and economic battle between the Kammas and Reddys, as well as the Kapus in this case. The period Parthasarathi studied culminated in intense gang violence peaking at the death of Vijayawada's own Paritala Ravi, a man called Vanga Veeti Mohan Ranga. Parthasarathi says,

> The economy, dominated by the Kamma entrepreneurs, is typical of a provincial economy; instead of manufacturing industries, the emphasis is on a variety of legal and illegal economic activities which ensure quick profits. The maintenance of a large scale illegal economic sector is facilitated by the patronage of gangs by most entrepreneurs. This further generates collective violence. Violence, legitimized by the dominant group, has thus come to present a normative aspect of the city. It is no longer regarded as deviant behavior, but is perceived as a legitimate form of expression. . . . It is a product of the political system."

It is rational and targeted, he claims, and constitutes the only viable "effective means of entering or remaining in political life."[85] According to Balagopal, a similar pattern had become entrenched in Anantapur: "[Armed factions have] invaded electoral politics, development works contracts, real estate and finance deals. All these issues symbolizing modernity, development and democracy are mediated by the armed might of these village factions grown into quite modern mafias, whose style of operation still has a rural ambience, an earthy smell."[86]

In the face of inadequate public services in places like Anantapur, politicians like Ravi rely on money from business and industry to provide for "their" people. If a politician can successfully fulfill his voters' needs and provide protection for them, they reelect him. Once in power, access to state-owned resources and contracts becomes easier, allowing such a leader to unevenly and arbitrarily provide for his political allies and followers, offering favors at his whim. It was Ravi's accumulation of resources that allowed him to distribute goods and services, conduct mass marriages, physically and militarily protect his people, defend his territory, and subdue his enemies. The provisions and protection that followers receive appear not as the products of plunder but as the munificence of a strong leader, emanating from his singular generosity and power.

The control of economic resources is crucial to political success and power. Both the TDP Kammas and the Congress Reddys had wealth, assets, and land at their disposal. In turn, political power gave these politicians both the opportunity and the legal impunity to increase their wealth, which they used to enhance their political status. In this sense, the modus operandi of both Ravi and YSR may be compared to that of Anton Blok's mafia: "entrepreneurs who use private, formally unlicensed violence as a means of social control and economic accumulation."[87]

As Sidel says of similar Robin Hood–like gangster politicians in the Philippines, "The myths propagated by and about local politicians in provinces like Cavite work to claim that power is not simply reducible to money and state office."[88] Discussing the development works and weddings that Filipino politicians (very similar to Ravi) sponsored, he says, "These various mechanisms thus represent claims that the 'big man' is essentially irreplaceable and indispensable. Moreover, legitimation along these lines obscures the *derivative nature of power, its origin in the predatory state, and its role in the process of capital accumulation*. Through Nardong Putik's Robin Hood escapades, Governor Remulla's funeral donations, and Senator Revilla's public works projects, power is equated with personal benevolence even as its source in the state apparatus and the cash economy remains conveniently hidden."[89]

In this sense, the strongman politician is not so much stealing from the rich to give to the poor but rather stealing from the state and local competitors to give to the poor. He does this more strategically than ideologically to enhance his power and consolidate his position while ostensibly appearing to act always and only in the interests of the people. The romance of Robin Hood is closely echoed in Ravi's image as a man of the people, with Naxalite roots and the son of a man who gave away lands to the poor for his Communist ideals. Yet his actual operations are far less fairy tale. The same can be said for YSR but on a larger scale.

Higher-level leaders can benefit from these operations, yet the higher they rise, the more important it becomes to distance themselves from the operations. As Balagopal argues of Chandra Babu Naidu, "Chandra Babu Naidu benefits politically from having such fearsome leaders and legislators in his party, notwithstanding, the anguished noises he periodically makes about organized crime and its deleterious effect on development. . . . The TDP and the Congress, therefore, have no intention of cutting off their links with these 'organized crime syndicates,' which has the consequence that the police are loath to touch these gangs. And then of course the leaders and the police can get together and blame the criminal justice system for being too lax."[90] The often-neglected economic operations of the "Anantapur Don" require more scrutiny if we are to understand how he achieved and sustained his political status.

To the filmmaker, the story of Paritala Ravi has all the elements for an action-packed drama with a powerful boss at the center. But the case of Ravi can also tell us about the way in which violent individuals acquire authority in the eyes of their supporters and the importance of social service and support to the poor, as well as displays of generosity and protection and the role of revenge and honor in creating a very masculine sort of appeal. It also gives a glimpse into the world of revered boss politicians (on both sides of the conflict) and the relationship between personal wealth, the exploitation of resources, state power, party politics, and criminality in a liberalized economy. We should note that this story of organized crime, political killings, Naxalism, caste conflict, capital accumulation, party politics, and conspiracy is present in the networks of elite politicians in the distant capital as much as the dusty villages and ramshackle towns of Rayalaseema. Mafia Raj works across regional, national, and global networks, yet the foundation of values that bosses draw on can be found in ordinary villages.

CONCLUSION

THE ART OF BOSSING

BARKER, HARMS, AND LINDQUIST argued that "we live in a world populated not just by individuals but by figures—people who loom larger than life. . . . Such figures are important because they serve as anchors for local, national and transnational discourses about contemporary social life and its future."[1] Adopting this approach, we suggest that the figure of the boss is an important prism through which both contemporary reality and the anthropological analysis of power can be reconfigured. Analytically this tool has proved to be a productive way for retrieving the experiential dimension of bossism and its lived ethnographic dimensions. Journalists, fiction writers, and academics tend to focus on spectacular large-scale international organized criminal traffic or on famous charismatic criminal bosses, such as Al Capone, Pablo Escobar, or Dawood Ibrahim and his D-Company in South Asia. In contrast, our work concentrates on small-scale, provincial bosses or aspirant bosses and their criminal political and economic enterprises. Such characters may not share Dawood Ibrahim's exemplary fame or the clout of Roberto Saviano's Neapolitan Camorra bosses or Mexican narcotraffickers, but in their localities they possess their own figural power. Their mafia-like activities and personal mastery have transformed them into figures of bossism. Thus, they stand out in their villages, neighborhoods, or towns and regions. They distinguish themselves because they are *dabangs*, *mastans*, *badmashs*, or godfathers. And as figures "they represent and give voice to something larger than themselves,"[2] offering an insight into the nature of criminal-political formations in postcolonial South Asia.

As noted previously, there is a general lack of studies on the workings of Mafia Raj. We do not have systematic knowledge (either historical or anthropological) of what happened to the well-studied colonial criminal tribe, the dacoit, the social bandit, or the Robin Hood noble criminal as they encountered new market forces, ongoing processes of privatization, and violent processes of dispossession and modern democracy. The life trajectories of the protagonists of this book reflect on such transformations and highlight how forms of crony capitalism and politics are embedded in social relations through the language of revenge, honor, masculinity, protection, reciprocity, and vernacularized understandings of democracy. Importantly, their lives highlight how definitions and concepts such as "big men," "mafiosi," "social bandits," "informal state actors," "gangsters," and "warlords" are rendered useless. They show that there are many ways of being a strongman and of embodying, performing, and embracing the figure of the boss. Our portrayals capture the range of contradictory practices and values behind the making of bosses' sovereignty.[3] Crucially, they render everyday bossing a *tangible* object of ethnographic study and make legible and visible the unstable character of bosses' charismatic forms of authority and the quotidian painstaking work that is necessary to create, cultivate, and maintain such forms of power. Charisma is well known to be a slippery descriptive and analytical concept.[4] In particular, the process of "arousing charisma," of becoming a Weberian "supernatural, superhuman" individual "set apart from ordinary men" is rarely an object of study.[5]

Thus, the figure of the boss has allowed us to study *empirically* the making of personal sovereignty and production and management of awe. Next, and equally important, it has also allowed to bring together *analytically* fields of research that have mainly been kept apart in anthropology, and in the social sciences more generally, and in so doing helped us conceptualize the art of bossing. Democracy, the state, entrepreneurialism, mafia, strongmen/big men, and personality politics and charisma are classically approached and theorized separately. Work on crime, violence, businessmen, and politics is often compartmentalized. Such separation, we argue, obscures the workings of concrete forms of power that are rooted simultaneously in force, crime, money, fantasies of power, mythologies, and democracy. It conceals how some people rule (or boss) today, how plundering, extraction, and territorial control coupled with democracy are shaping the nature of authority across the world. It obscures how methods of enforcement, coercion, and desire to rule effected through business acumen, violent dispossession, and political work are part of similar repertoires of personal sovereignty to be found in many parts of the contemporary world, such as Italy, Mexico, Brazil, Russia, Colombia, Argentina, Jamaica, Turkey, Indonesia, Thailand, and the Philippines.

Thus, we argue that the figure of the boss has allowed us to capture an ethos of (criminal) power and styles of personal sovereignty that belong to the current age. The ethnography of bosses' quotidian experiences challenges cultural relativist and monistic positions. The logics of enforcement and extortion are techniques of sovereignty that are recognized cross-culturally and should not be studied as exotic local practices that belong to underdeveloped localities or as a particular expression of governance belonging exclusively to postcolonial countries. What we are witnessing are not throwbacks to the past. On the contrary, this is more likely to be the future.[6] The success of strongmen leaders in contemporary world politics may reflect a global appreciation for individuals who cultivate a bosslike attitude. Business acumen and cinematographic figurality increasingly provide a template for building a charismatic authoritative style of leadership. We live in a world where celebrity and adoration can be systematically managed and marketed.[7] As Murthy and De la Fuente pointed out, this is the age of "aesthetic capitalism." The supply side of this kind of capitalism is never only material and physical but is above all about the supply of *fascinatio*n and *seduction* and the creation of affect.[8] Despite this global convergence, the ways in which the bosses of this book function, as well as their figural aesthetic power, are unmistakably South Asian. In the region, bosses' styles of governance contribute to creating pockets of mafia-owned democracy (Mafia Raj, Goonda Raj, and Mastanocracy), which are distinctively shaped by the South Asian cultures and a unique passion for the political, as well as some of the highest rates of electoral participation and contestation in the world.

Our intimate portrayal of the art of bossing allows for a focus on the cultural and historical particularities of South Asian Mafia Raj without trapping us in these particularities. More specifically, we conceptualize such an art form as the performance of personal sovereignty. Bosses are ultimately individuals who "make themselves respected."[9] Such personal mastery requires the creative mixing of an array of skills, qualities, and resources. It requires moral flexibility and a capacity for making credible threats. It requires deal-making skills and business acumen. It requires careful daily staging, framing, and scripting. It requires a quasi-dramaturgical capacity to improvise. But above all it requires making prompt tactical and strategic decisions every day. Here Certeau's opposition between strategy and tactic, and between "who plans and governs" and "who improvises and poaches in the street," is not tenable. [10] South Asian bosses are often simultaneously lawmakers and law breakers; they are adjudicators and criminals, frauds and legitimate businessmen, social bandits and gangsters. Thus, binary opposition between illegal and legal violence and/or legitimate and illegitimate authority, personal and popular sovereignty, fiction and reality becomes redundant. We argue that the artistry behind bossing lies precisely in juggling these multiple identities, registers, activities, and imaginaries through acts of give and take and mythologies both outside and within the rules.

In her book *Purity and Danger*, Mary Douglas describes how entities that defy the rigid categories that humans construct are often viewed as dangerous and powerful.[11] Bosses, by demonstrating that they have the guts to deal with, manage, and run dangerous, opaque, and volatile worlds, perform their personal mastery and stand out from mundane everyday life. In the process, they are often renamed with artistic nicknames branding their uniqueness. Like nonmechanical reproducible objects of art, these are individuals who at times come to possess auratic qualities.[12] But it should be noted that the cultivation of an aura can be understood only against the canvas that animates it. Our canvases are the local Mafia Raj, with their own histories, political economies, criminal-political types, and figural power.[13] As Barker, Harms, and Lindquist pointed out, the study of figures "does not depend on drawing an artificial line between scholarly discourse and the form of discourse we encounter among our interlocutors in the field"; rather, it "involves participating in a kind of folk sociology, where social imaginaries are populated by certain recognizable social types. And it is against the backdrop of these types [and criminal political economies] that particular figures acquire their significance and their force."[14]

It follows that the art of bossing provides a window into the ways power is concentrated, embodied, and wielded by individuals and simultaneously coproduced by multiple actors, performances, representations, and mythologies. Bosses' power is not dispersed and subjectless; it has individual authors. At the same time bossing relies on the cinematographic charisma of Mafia Raj, which is saturated by seductive social types such as the social bandit/Robin Hood, the wrestler, the genteel gangster/mafioso, and the gangster-politician. Importantly, the figure of the boss also encapsulates the fantasy of the self-made entrepreneurial man/woman in the new Indian, Pakistani, and Bangladeshi neoliberal economies, and with it notions of self-assertion and rebellion, as well as of self-control. These multiple tropes are acted and performed in a variety of spaces: bazaars, *deras* (dens)/wrestling arenas, prisons, parliaments, courts, university campuses, hotels, lodges and nightclubs, workplaces, religious festivals, commemoration ceremonies, sport and political events; in several aesthetic sites such as movies, videos, fiction, TV, the Internet, party manifestos and propaganda, local newspapers; as well as in regional epics and religious heroic traditions. In the following sections, we illustrate how figurations as performances in the ethnographic present and figurations as mythical narratives are central to the alchemy of the art of bossing and the coproduction of authority.

MIXING LORDLY AND MAFIA STYLES

> Them folks who think they can get by justice, with laws that are equal to everybody, with hard work, dignity, clean streets, with women the same as men, it's only a world of fags who think it's okay to make fools [*sic*] of themselves. And everybody around them. All that crap about a better world leave it to them idiots. To the rich idiots who can afford such luxuries. The luxury of believing in a better world, a just world. Rich people with guilty consciences, or with something to hide. Whoever rules just does it, and that's that. Sure he can say he rules for the good, for justice and liberty and all. But that's sissy stuff; leave all that to the fools. Who rules, rules. Period.[15]

This quotation is from a popular "nonfiction novel" on bosses and the cocaine trade by Roberto Saviano, a globally known Italian author who became famous for reporting on Neapolitan organized crime. His best-selling book was then turned into a blockbuster movie and TV series, *Gomorra*. The quotation is from a DEA telephone tapping. The speaker is an Italian mafioso boss who, using "a bastard Italian, some dialect thrown in, mixed with English and Spanish," is addressing an audience of representatives from Latin American and Albanian criminal organizations. The event is described as resembling a university seminar for "aspiring bosses." The boss, Saviano points out, is teaching not only how to be a mafioso but "how to rule" to a new generation of Mexican and Latin American representatives of drug cartels. "That training lesson about how to be in the world wasn't only for mafia affiliates but for everybody who decided they want to rule on this Earth."[16] Here the Mafia boss represents the prototypical modern independent authoritative figure à la Sennett. [17] We have discussed how such a figure of "modernity" does not need to express (or pretend to express) love or care for others to rule. But what do the bosses of this book actually do? How do they rule: with love or without love? Do they follow Saviano's boss's teachings or not? Throughout the book our portrayals show a tension between paternalistic and autonomous styles of personal sovereignty. We show how seizing opportunities with the help of violence and criminality is at the heart of what makes a simple fixer become a powerful autonomous boss. Bosses are often macho action men and ambitious independent individuals who are mainly interested in maximizing profit for themselves and their families. However, from our stories we also find that bosses who use criminal and violent entrepreneurship as a form of social mobility and self-enrichment often seem to still feel the need to legitimize their positions in the long run by using lordly–cum–Robin Hood idioms, particularly when they enter into formal politics.[18] The idea of building a just society by using the rhetoric of "social work" (*seva/sheba/khidmat*) for the poor or for "common people" (*aam/admi/awam*) or religious imaginaries is not considered by the bosses of this book as morally opposed to their violent way of operating. On the contrary, in our settings bosses' acts of giving and taking range from the benevolent exchanges of services, favors, and gifts couched in the rhetorical language of social work to semilegal and illegal and violent economic activities popularly referred to as "criminal work" (*goondagardi/durniti*).[19] Examples of this complex mix of "carrots and sticks" are present in a variety of degrees in all our stories and are an integral part of the art of bossing.

Across South Asia, generosity or self-sacrifice is often expressed in the language of kinship. The idea of a protector as parent (or relative) is a strong cultural construct. Traditionally, patron-gods and kings have been referred to as parents: *maa-i-baap* (mother and father) in Hindi. Kinship terms such as *bapuji* (honorable father), *bhai* and *dada* (brother), and *behenji* (sister) are used by Hindi speakers to refer to politicians or local leaders who are seen as treating their supporters with love, self-sacrifice, and devotion. Terms such as *bhai* and *dada* are also used to refer to local violent protectors and bosses, a term derived from Middle Dutch. Speakers of Telugu, Bangla, or other South Asian languages use parallel terms. It should be emphasized that the language of kinship and parenthood is widely used both in politics and in the criminal world.[20] This is not specifically a South Asian phenomenon, as the usage of terms such as "godfather"/*padrino* clearly indicates. Such language metaphorically suggests nurturing and care for the others. It is embedded deeply in strong paternalistic/lordly styles of authority that are used to justify the legitimacy of power by showing interest in others and in the public good.

We show that altruistic acts of giving performed by bosses (as kinsmen) are often public and spectacular. When bosses enter politics, their speeches are punctuated by claims such as "I do not work for my own family, as "the Bluffer" stated." Others like Ravi ("the Legend") do social work and "development" for the poor and appear to act like a classical social bandit. The godfather builds his muscular strength in opposition to his rival, who instead does *shamajik sheba* (social service), and uses arguments, rules, and persuasion rather than muscle or intimidation to build his power. Similar to "the Godfather," "Lady Dabang" is not very interested in showing herself doing *sewa*: "Before doing *sewa* for the poor, one needs to become rich," she commented in a conversation. It follows that our portrayals show how bosses deal with the moralities of *sewa*, virtuousness, and individualism, in different ways. Their lives reflect the varieties of ethics on the ground.[21] However, what all our stories indicate is that bosses' selfless acts of giving are often arbitrary, episodic, and symbolic, and most definitely unpredictable. Bosses do not provide for everyone who comes to ask for their help, but the knowledge that some people are occasionally helped is enough to give rise to the hope that the petitioner may be helped too. Such arbitrariness contributes to spreading Robin Hood mythologies that are simultaneously kept alive by a variety of media. In this case, the magic of chance not only contributes to creating uncertainty but also creates hope. In principle, these discretionary acts of giving "do not bind recipients, yet are imbued with the potential of a relation."[22] As in the case study of the 'Ndrangheta in Calabria, Italy, episodic acts of *sewa* "[do] not immediately initiate a relation, but creat[e] a dormant potentiality" that is a core ingredient of effective forms of bossing.[23] It should also be noted that when bosses are elected, their struggle to build and maintain power depends to some extent on their ability to present an aura of moral authority. When they become official public authorities, they often have to deal with accusations in the newspapers, in the media, and from civil society and political rivals, as well as in police cases and court proceedings. Mafia Raj are indeed highly competitive and often polarized environments; these are worlds where the illegality/legality of the art of bossing may quickly transform from an effective and seductive tool into a liability, as "the Godfather's" story shows.

NEW MASCULINITIES: SHOOTING RATHER THAN WRESTLING

Bossism is undoubtedly a muscular, testosterone-charged style of authority.[24] Indeed, the gender dimension of this way of doing power should be noted. Most obviously, the bosses are largely men. There are exceptions to this, such as "Lady Dabang," but on the whole we are dealing with male leaders with an entourage of mainly male advisers, supporters, henchmen, and bodyguards. The bosses occupy largely male spaces in their day-to-day work, and the people with whom they most frequently interact are predominantly men. In short, this is a man's world and self-consciously constructed as such. But more important, it is a *macho* world, where stylized versions of masculinity and of criminality have to be perfected to achieve success. These men are often acutely aware of their public image because it is imperative that they are seen as strong, virile, and dominant individuals.

In the region, the ideal of a strong, wild, and dangerous boss has historically shaped bossism cultures. An old repertoire of tropes of honor, kingly leadership, and heroism valorizes criminal heroes and feeds into the value placed on toughness and physical strength. For example, certain politically successful caste groups (such as the Yadavs in North India) capitalize on ideas of community honor and divine kinship to legitimize the use of brute force.[25] This finds expression in the widespread idioms of fearlessness and virility that surround political life and the popular imagery that advertises politicians' heroic (*bahadur*) capacity to protect, as men who can "get things done."[26] It is, however, the figure of the *pehlwan* (wrestler) that traditionally has been of paramount importance in evoking the idea of muscular masculinity, good health, and social charisma across South Asia. More than a sport, *pehlwani* is a way of life and a moral tradition, "a meeting of muscles and morals."[27] These echoes of kingly and ascetic virtuous violence give a sense of history and rootedness to bosses' new type of muscularity.[28]

Today, wrestlers with well-fed and strong bodies are said to have been replaced with a physically weaker but more ruthless, profit-oriented, and less-dignified caliber of actors.

The phenomenon of "shooters" is said to epitomize the breakdown of wrestling cultures and of the respectable genteel criminal (the *sharif badmash* or bandit king). The shooter is represented as a mere contract killer sitting on the back of a motorbike who shoots and runs. In Pakistan, poverty and greed, together with the influence of Bollywood movies, are said to have made everyone into a potential criminal. Similarly, the Bangladeshi figure of the *mastan*—an ascetic figure who fought his inner urges to resist the material, carnal temptations of the world and help the oppressed—has an altogether different meaning today. The contemporary *mastan* no longer yearns for an elevated place in the next world but desires it in the here and now. He is no longer detached from the aspirations of material life but is very much an advocate for this life. He dresses well. He eats well. His leisurely pursuits are exclusive; his tastes, opulent. Such a lifestyle requires money, and lots of it. For this reason, all new *mastans* possess a burning desire to generate wealth. In popular cinema, the *mastan* is portrayed as a working-class upstart: young, armed, and striving for his class interests.[29] The *mastan*, like the Pakistani *badmash* (or the Indian *goonda*), is violent, angry, and seized by a sense of injustice. He represents the frustrations of young people in a dysfunctional state, taking the law into his own hands, and championing an ideology of selfhood.

Therefore, the bosses of this book are not simply avatars of the saintly wrestlers or lordly figures with whom we are already familiar. On the contrary, the fusion of muscle power with capitalism and democracy represents a break with the past. Today's violent protectors are nurtured in different spaces and have diverse sociological backgrounds. The personality of the boss becomes particularly important precisely because the power of the boss is often detached from hereditary status and caste/community sovereignties. Thus, what becomes a source of conversation and admiration is not always heritage: instead, what is often celebrated are personal individual achievements. A number of bosses in our stories have checkered histories and come from a life of hardship ("Lady Dabang"), some are from lower castes (Sukhbir and Kondappa), and others come from more privileged backgrounds and the traditional "martial" dominant caste and communities (Jamal and Ravi). Mostly, their origins are not so predictable: some are literally fighting their way to the top. Importantly, their stories suggest that in present conditions even people from a privileged background need to assert themselves by force, at least in the early stages of their career. They need to prove that they are not "ordinary." This is not to say that caste, ethnic identity, and class are not important. Two key conditions to becoming a boss are intergeneration and inherited feuds. In this context one often does not become a boss out of his or her own volition. In other sites, bosses' capacity to dominate particular territories is also linked to caste and community forms of territorial governance, but not in as straightforward a manner as might be first thought. Control over territories by bosses who belong to the so-called dominant caste is strategically used to run markets, extract resources, and win elections. Kinship bonds and marriage alliances are important ingredients for bossing. We have shown how the networks formed from class, family, or networks developed at particular junctures in the lives of bosses, college in particular, also constitute crucial elements in the making of their careers.

Finally, we show how local structures of caste dominance in India often have important electoral affinities with bosses' electoral successes. "Territorial" forms of democracy, as Witsoe conceptualized them, go hand to hand with mafia-esque bosses. In such systems

> electoral outcomes are influenced by relations of dominance and subordination within specific territorial spaces, and conversely, the ways in which electoral practice reinforces, and can even produce, territorial [mafia-like] dominance. This relationship between territorial dominance and electoral practice explains the violence that accompanies the electoral process in India, and also explains why, in stark contrast to the experience in many democracies, local elections tend to be more intensely contested, and usually involve more violence, than national elections.[30]

As Varese pointed out, Machiavelli has long ago "taught us that Prince has to reside among his people."[31] It should be stressed that when bosses operate outside their home territories, they act in a more peaceful and covert manner because their position is weaker. Outside their territories, bosses cannot take advantage of their local reputations and be protected by local connections; therefore, they tend to operate not through rackets and extortion but through subtler ways, such as by infiltrating legal economic sectors. For example, a number of Kothapalle henchmen-cum-bosses operate as estate agents in Bangalore. They present themselves as businessmen: they wear suits and have elegant business offices. When back in their place of origin, they switch to their muscular attire and more visible violent businesses.

Where Do Women Stand?

What role do women play in developing such figures and Mafia Raj modes of governance? What is their role in the art of bossing? It should be noted that in terms of gender, bosses' stance is often hypermasculine and traditionally patriarchal. Gangster-politicians, whether from working-class and low-caste backgrounds or from the higher castes and middle classes, all offer a reassuring vision of a conservative, male-dominated world. This is not to say that women are missing from this world. On the contrary, they are critical to creating and maintaining the status and reputation of strong male leaders. In cases where the family forms the bedrock of the strongman-politician's political machine, faithful wives and "good" daughters are of paramount importance. A common quip is that a man who cannot control his own household has little hope of controlling a region. The family and household are his jurisdiction in microcosm, and their state of order or disorder is indicative of his ability to rule. In this respect, controlling women's sexuality and display of respect, deference, and modesty is often a crucial element of the strongman's political reputation. This requires women's constant participation in the production of "macho power"; what looks like unthinking obedience may in fact be a consciously and continuously manufactured contribution to the family's reputation.

This active and calculated involvement of the bosses' wives, mothers, sisters and/or daughters becomes especially evident when the leader himself is forced out of action (due to illness, injury, and imprisonment or in the case of death, for example) with no obvious replacement. It may well be the women of the family who take over the day-to-day operations, step in and run the family business, and even take on the leadership, all in the name of upholding the family reputation. That they are doing this on behalf of their husband/son/brother rather than to fulfill their own ambition helps the women's own image and the man to whom such loyalty and devotion are shown.

Moreover, wives and mothers often do the underrecognized, indeed often invisible, work of organizing and facilitating marriage alliances, forging and maintaining kinship alliances with important families, networking with other bosses' wives, and providing food and hospitality at social gatherings. Their private influence over their husbands may be strong, but they have to be careful not to appear to be pulling the strings, even if behind the scenes the reality is quite different. Outside the home, other women play important roles in the rise (or fall) of aspiring mafia dons. Fieldwork in several of the sites revealed the key role of mistresses and prostitutes in the lives of the strongmen leaders. There is the predictable use and abuse of women of course; women may be treated as objects of pleasure and entertainment to be controlled, used, mistreated, and exploited at the boss's whim. Leaving aside the debasement of the women involved, these women are used as a medium through which men can communicate to other men their supposed heterosexual potency, virility, and ability to dehumanize and dominate. However, we also see other aspects of gangster masculinity at work: the importance not just of showing dominance over women but the desire to be sexually attractive to women and have the ability to attract and acquire women. This is not quite the same as simply buying women: they seek to compete in the sphere of sexual relations too, if only to boast about another game they have mastered.

In such a male-dominated world the phenomenon of the female boss is an intriguing figure. In a sense, "Lady Dabang" is little different from her male counterparts; she may be a woman, but she must play the same macho game to compete. Indeed, she may have to exaggerate her "masculine" capacities to compensate for what she may be perceived as lacking. Yet she is, of course, fundamentally different and must manipulate the rules with her difference in mind. She is essentially a woman who has transgressed the norms and limits usually imposed on her gender. She is someone who has made a career for herself not only outside the home in the public domain but often in a violent and aggressive world of extortion, exploitation, and political domination.

In this masculine environment, she strays a long way from what is expected of her as a female family member and contradicts fundamental ideas of what it is to be a woman in South Asia. If womanliness is centrally associated with fertility and maternity in South Asia, then violent, destructive, and politically powerful female leaders may be perceived as dangerous, if not pathological. In Hindu mythology, this kind of power is exemplified by the goddess Kali, who demonstrates the havoc female power can unleash when not constrained by patriarchal structure.[32] In these circumstances, how do women leaders acquire the respect, love, and cultural legitimacy that powerful leaders so often seek from their supporters? Do they simply rule by brute force and fear, without any regard for how they are seen by others or any concern for adhering to convention? We know that influential women in South Asia often gain power through their family connections or lineage or by taking the place of a martyred husband.[33] Once in position, their power is often maintained on condition that their sexuality is contained and purified by marriage and motherhood or effaced altogether through renunciation and celibacy (e.g., BJP [Bharatiya Janata Party] Hindu political activists, such as Sadhvi Rithambara and Uma Bharati).[34]

Women in politics also have a special place in Bangladesh and Pakistan. The most prominent are almost always wives or daughters of successful male politicians who have either been assassinated, kidnapped, or met an otherwise unfortunate end. Female successors are seen as the natural replacement for their male kin when there are no men available and a continuation of the political legacy. Both in Bangladesh and Pakistan, women serve as extensions of or substitutes for male politicians. However, in all of these cases, the female leaders' sexuality has to be a very carefully managed affair if they are to attain enduring respect and authority. Problematic aspects of femininity need to be managed so that blood and kinship will override them as women secure positions of power in South Asia.[35] However, this is certainly not the route taken by "Lady Dabang." She is quite the opposite. Her case brings into focus the limitations and prospects for women in systems of Mafia Raj, as leaders and followers as well as subjects and victims. Equally, it highlights the highly gendered nature of this particular form of governance.[36]

Transgressing the Law: The Power of Murder

Transgressing the law is an important ingredient in the art of bossing. It is crucial to remember that bosses are often objectified by the law as criminals, and they use this reputation to establish their authority. It is not in spite of criminal accusations that they are popular but because of such charges and/or allegations. We suggest that it is often the transgression of official laws rather than social codes of behavior that helps produce accretions of charisma and fantasies of power. Being suspected of murder is an accolade for bosses, not a stigma. As Gambetta said of the Italian mafiosi, "Being suspected of a serious criminal offence has a particular by-product: it provides hard-to-fake evidence that one is 'bad,' and it spreads knowledge of this trait."[37] And indeed murders or attempted murders (real or pretended) are at the center of local folklore and self-mythologies of the protagonists in this book. The Legend is implicated in a series of murders and vendettas and was eventually murdered by the enemy faction. The Godfather and his clan associates were allegedly engaged in seven murders. The authority that "Lady Dabang" wields springs from the alleged murders of a doctor and a policeman who had allegedly tried to rape her. "The Rookie" was charged with attempted murder and also spent time in jail. The Adjudicators are all, in one way or another, implicated in feuds and murders and have been imprisoned. Revenge is at the heart of their killings or attempted killings and morally justifies such acts. The Henchman regularly takes part in beatings, land grabbing, extortion, and rackets and uses his muscle and name to intimidate opponents and voters during elections.

The other featured low-caste boss, "the Bluffer," is the only character in the book who does not have a violent criminal curriculum vitae, although he is a former police officer and has been trained to use force.

Brute strength is often used explicitly (or passively) to achieve authority and to be recognized as someone capable of killing and commanding. Reputations are built by ensuring that there are witnesses to the violence being meted out. The possession and spectacle of expensive and powerful weapons are also an integral part of bosses' authoritative shows. In many of our case studies, when a violent authoritative reputation is established, bosses then switch to more sophisticated activities where authority is the means and no longer the goal. In short, bosses start to command and rule. Intimidation is enough. As Volkov points out, "[The capacity to kill] becomes similar to a commercial reputation"[38]—people come to you of their own accord to enforce services or settle disputes or to offer a ticket to contest elections. A local strongman in a neighborhood in western Uttar Pradesh explained in an interview: "After all it is not what you do and how capable of doing violence you are. What counts is what people believe you are capable of doing. It is the people who make you a *dabang*! Not the other way around. . . . If people see you as powerful, then you are." Many of the bosses in our stories manipulate this very Machiavellian take on power. Authority is also explained as an illusion that needs to be constantly crafted and nourished. A number of bosses say they were surprised when in the early days of their careers they discovered that people were drawn to them and followed what they said. In the words of Jamal, "I can't really explain why [I am authoritative]. . . . People were intimidated by my temperament, but I didn't realize that at the time. If I go to Maulvi Bazaar now, I could summon twenty boys immediately." The ability to improvise, to think ahead and calculate risks, and to convert physical force into a profitable entrepreneurial activity and solid power is central to the art of bossing.

Being "Smart" and Codes of Behavior

Being smart and clever are qualities often attached to the bosses we encountered in this book. Strength is certainly important, but without a brain and respect for social conventions, it is useless. A distinction that people often make across our sites is between criminals, who use violence without thinking and without rules, and bosses, who are muscular and clever and use violence only when necessary. Such a distinction is often reinstated by using both the language of honor and the language of education or by explicitly evoking indigenous statecraft manuals like the *Arthashastra* or the *Mahabharata*. For example, Chinna, a Dalit young man and aspiring boss involved in racketeering in rural Andhra, commented during a conversation, "There are some uneducated people around here. They will recklessly go and beat someone up. They don't give it a second thought. But if they have studied, they know how to plan it out; they think beforehand and afterward what to do. An educated guy will strike in a planned way."

In contrast to the brainless thuggishness of the uneducated, who lash out indiscriminately, educated men use violence in a controlled manner, dominating street culture by outsmarting others. They have rules. Too much violence can be counterproductive and come back to haunt you, as in the case of "the Godfather." One of "the Adjudicators" explains this danger by using a metaphor: "It is like riding a tiger [*sher*]: when you sit on it, you go extremely fast, but as soon as you get off it, you must run for your life." The art of bossing needs to be cultivated. In western Uttar Pradesh, one of the most cunning and resilient political bosses was nicknamed "Chanakya," which is how the famous Indian political philosopher Kautilya and writer of the *Arthashatra* is often popularly referred to across South Asia.[39] One of the bosses Michelutti met in the field was writing a PhD thesis on Chanakya. Guddu Bhai (fifty-five years old, presently a BJP party man, accused of murder and kidnapping, now an "estate developer"), while discussing his dissertation topic, said, "It is about the art of ruling as lined up in the *Mahabharata*. . . . I am not sure if you know it, but Chanakya was about no nonsense. He was purely concerned with matter-of-fact politics."

In his writing Chanakya put a lot of effort into describing what force is, how (and when) it should be used to expand influence and maintain control over territories and populations. Guddu Bhai concords with Chanakya and said that before "killing" (his words), "peaceful negotiations and forms of collaboration should be preferred." Such tactics include "weakening the enemy" by using bribery and blackmail and by causing internal fights among the rival factions. In such an endeavor being able to acquire information is crucial. Bosses depend heavily on local knowledge and an extensive network of friends and accomplices, many in the political and criminal justice systems, who must be cultivated face-to-face on a daily basis, as "the Henchman's" transgressive drinking parties in the lodge well exemplify. Good intelligence helps strategize, diffuse strategic rumors, and spread uncertainty. Uncertainty, if well staged, has the capacity to spread paranoia and enhance the magnitude of bosses. A key weapon of control and plundering (through extortion) is thus not actual violence but the threat of violence: intimidation. Coercion and trading favors are pillars of bossism.

Spectacle and Entertainment

All of the bosses we encountered in this book are in constant dialogue with authoritative fictional cultural exemplars that exalt social bandits or men of honor à la Hobsbawm. In short, the massive popular repertoire on the outlaw icon not only influences the ways bosses are locally viewed and legitimized but is actually an integral part of the ways that Mafia Raj are created and reproduced. In these worlds the mythical Robin Hood outlaw (the protector) and the real brutal self-serving mafia boss (the aggressor) coexist without contradiction. Our characters do not act most of the time as saintly bosses; nevertheless, the persistent figuralities of the *pehlwan* or the old bandit king do the heroic job for them through a variety of mediums.

For a start, cinematographic footage depicting the gangster as the savior of the people and portraying bosses as rebels and revolutionaries are an integral part of bosses' figuralities. Regional action movies made by Lollywood, which created the Punjabi hero;[40] or Telugu, Tamil, and Malayalam cinema in South India; Bangla movies in Bangladesh; and Bollywood are at the heart of bossism and its contingent legitimacy. The relation between mafia, bosses, and art is an old one indeed. It should be remembered that the term "mafia" is said to have its origins in fiction, apparently coined in a play, *I Mafiusi della Vicaria*, performed in Palermo in 1863. As Gambetta explains in the local dialect, the word *mafiusu* means "arrogant, cocky, and bold."[41] The play is about "a group of prisoners in Palermo jail who command particular respect: although individualistic and quarrelsome, they are members of an association which defines behavioral rules, including an initiation ritual and hierarchical structure, that claims it can influence the political and administrative system of the island."[42] The production was a tremendous success and helped popularize the term "mafia." Today, this term has entered languages across the globe. "Fiction reality" criminal literature and movies are feeding into the making of bosses' mythologies and cultivating fascination for such figures by an international public and by bosses themselves. Recently El Chapo, the notorious Mexican drug cartel leader, while absconding, was caught by the police because he was making contact with movie producers.[43] In his hideaway, he was reading Saviano's book *Zero Zero Zero* on the cocaine trade. In Mumbai, which for many years has been described as the mafia capital of South Asia, the first gangs to emerge in the 1960s and 1970s immediately made links with Bollywood. Producers are said to habitually accept donations from godfathers, who in this way manage to recycle black money and make huge profits. Some movie scripts are even rewritten by the godfathers themselves, who also decide whom to cast in the movies.[44]

Therefore, it is not coincidental that two of the bosses we research in this book have acted in criminal dramas. The story of "the Rookie" (the boss Jamal) shows that the figure of the modern *mastan* was consolidated in popular imagination through the character of "Baker Bhai" in a television drama series in the early 1990s. Baker Bhai was a Robin Hood figure, a gangster who lived in a deprived part of the big city and protected the poor. The boss Jamal himself played the part of the *mastan* in a number of television serials largely produced by Channel S and a *Londoni*-financed private television channel based in Maulvi Bazaar. Jamal's talent in the arts—a writer, actor, and musician—provided him with figurality that helped him stand out and launch his career with a political party. Similarly, Lahore's bosses' figuralities feed on both regional (Bollywood) and local histories and traditions and ideas of what being Punjabi means. One of the bosses, Yaseer, was himself an actor-turned-gangster. In his youth, Yaseer worked as an actor for Lollywood, Lahore's now-defunct cinema industry known for its connections to the underworld since the 1970s. By the same token, the very term *dabang* was made popular in the region by the Bollywood blockbuster movies *Dabang* (2010) and *Dabang 2* (2012); and the myth of Phoolan Devi, epitomized in the movie *The Bandit Queen*, is an integral part of the local figurality of "Lady Dabang." Given the size and success of Andhra Pradesh's movie industry, it is no exaggeration to say that the fantasy of the boss pervades Telugu popular culture. Major political leaders like N. T. Ram Rao, founder of TDP (Telugu Desam Party), and Pawan Kalyan began their careers as actors. Film and reality become dialogically related: in movies, men like "the Legend" display qualities of the cine heroes, while moviemakers, such as the director Varma, take events from real life to produce dramas.

But it is not only through the cinema industry that mafia-esque fictional realities are produced. Consider, for example, the case recorded by the High Court in Allahabad in the state of Uttar Pradesh. In 2005, the court commissioned a report to define what and who can be termed "mafia" or "mafioso." The word "mafia" has increasingly been used in a number of Indian government orders and circulars since the early 1990s, but it has yet to be legally defined. The High Court nominated Shri G. B. Pattanaik, the principal secretary of the state government, to prepare a report to define what "mafia" means in the state of Uttar Pradesh. The report was submitted on April 26, 2006. The final court recommendations are a fascinating seventy thousand–word document. Mario Puzo's novel *The Godfather* is used as source to illustrate "mafia in Indian context." The book is said to have "immortalized the structure of 'Mafia': though it is a fiction but is near to truth."[45]

> As discussed hereinabove leader [*sic*] of organized gang or "Mafia" always tends to perpetuate their organization from one generation to other. At initial stage [*sic*] such leaders (Dons) directly indulge into criminal activities

> with the organization but at later stage after developing full infrastructure of the organized crime they used to cover themselves under the mask of gentlemenship to avoid consistence [*sic*] police surveillance and threat of prosecution. Arrangements are being made to join the main stream of society to under [*sic*] cover criminal activities. . . . We can have a glimpse of such actions in one other novel by Mario Puzo namely "Last Don." However, such incidents can be also noticed in our society where hardened criminals and leader [*sic*] of organized gangs after earning plenty of unlawful wealth, money and prosperity joined the political organization and other social organizations for their protection and recognition and achieved a status or high offices to protect themselves.[46]

Besides novels and movies, religious repertoires and heroic idioms contribute to the way in which bosses are imagined. In India, "local protectors" are traditionally often associated with lineages of local rulers, princes, and kings who can be transformed into hero gods.[47] The fact that popular Hinduism makes no categorical distinction between the divine and the human facilitates the production of heroic demigods.[48] Thus, local sociocultural templates and religious traditions play a role in transforming flesh-and-blood bosses into living heroes and, after their death, eventually into godlike figures. Notions of divine kinship create extraordinary bosses and powerful intimate links between strongmen and their caste/communities and kin. This shared divine kinship grants bosses figurality and creates a structure of intimacy between them and the people. Strong cultures of martyrdom and hero making exist also in the Muslim tradition.[49]

New technologies are also enabling homemade movies and videos to be circulated through WhatsApp or YouTube. These recordings and digital footage are an integral part of bossism today. For example, Khan Mubarak, a local emerging mafia don in North India, recently circulated a video filmed with a mobile phone. The video features a terrified businessman with a bottle on his head while the boss is threatening to shoot him.[50] The businessman was being punished for not having paid *goonda tax*. Hours afterward, he was set free but died of a heart attack, reported his brother in an interview. "We didn't file a complaint because we are scared of them," he added. The mafia don was allegedly protected by the current Samajwadi Party government. Bosses' power is represented and reproduced by what has gradually become a constant and instant digital assemblage of elements. Thus the figurality of bosses is a perpetual work in progress and is shaped by a variety of scripts, ranging from court reports and documented trials to rumors, newspaper stories, contested biographies and books, forged documents, political speeches, and movies.[51] For example, Sukhbir produced theatrical performances, speeches, and fraudulent documents. Like others in this book, Sukhbir claims to be a social worker, a quasi-Robin Hood–type figure fighting the corrupt and powerful on behalf of the poor, but it is clear to everyone that he in fact collaborates with the powerful and the state to get things done. He is a bluffer. He is an improviser, a master at the art of *jugad*/bossing. In a context with limited opportunities for social mobility, he has understood that bossism can potentially provide him with a path toward status, respect, and even wealth, and he has improvised himself a niche in politics through the MGNREGA (Mahatma Gandhi National Rural Employment Guarantee Act) scheme. Like others in the book, he needs to convince people that he is a person who can get things done (that he can boss), so he adopts the VIP style of Punjabi bosses as they exist in reality and to some extent in cinema. His followers may occasionally see through his boasting and in some cases may even be aware of the fact that he is corrupt, but this does not prevent them from seeing that he does get some things done. This is a case in which bluffing is a way of producing authority. Faking can actually produce results.[52]

The portrayals we provide show that bosses are often truly entertaining characters, and the public seems to appreciate the nature of their performance and the ability of an individual to create reality rather than just passively commenting on it. For example, performances at court trials and movies are at the heart of the making of the legend. Similarly, the production of biographies and counterbiographies is central to the struggle for power of the godfather in provincial Bangladesh. Thus, the fictional realities we encountered in the field go beyond the impact of movies on politics and society at large, a field that has been well documented in South Asia.[53] The fictional realities we encountered are mundane, fragmented, and uncontrollable. A multiplicity of actors and representations participate to create living figurations and produce tangible atmospheres crucial to instilling fear, love, admiration, and respect for bosses.

Figuration can hence be best analyzed as a form of spectacle with the capacity to create "moods," a "politics of presence,"[54] and "affective atmospheres."[55] Such a genre of spectacle is close to what Rancière calls "theatre without spectator": "that is a performative space where the gap between actors, spectators and the stage is blurred so that spectators become actors in a theatre that can be performed without spectators."[56] Thus, bosses' living figurality is not only "viewed," but it is coproduced and coexperienced and is an integral part of the complicities and opportunistic partnerships that connect bosses with their population. This is one of the reasons that political parties look for candidates who are figures of bossism in their own localities. Such figuration is not only a mere instrument to amaze or placate the electorate or to publicize particular rhetoric or party agendas; it is an intimate mode of power in itself.

Crafting Complicities: I Am Going to Make Him an Offer He Can't Refuse

The relationship between bosses and the populations they command is extremely volatile. It should be emphasized that people live in contexts in which there are overlapping repertoires of authority; bosses are not the only authority in a given context, and people pay their dues to several of them at the same time.[57] The unstable and evanescent relations between bosses and their citizen-subjects distinguish this relationship from patron-client or king-servant relations and their spectacular acts of generosity. Consider, for example, the case of the relation between bosses and the labor force in contemporary South India.[58] Bosses supply squadrons of laborers in the right place at the right time, which undermines the unionization of labor. They also settle disputes and collect debts. Today the exploitative relations between bosses and laborers are temporary, monetized, and opportunistic. Low-caste laborers, from debt-bonded to casual laborers, increasingly alternate between jobs and sectors and move across states. The direct dependence of laborers on landlords in rural South India has vanished. Today, they circulate in search of jobs through multiple and temporary forms of indirect dependence on bosses. Laborers have learned to negotiate multiple modes of domination and authority.

In this regard, Sidel argued that local strongmen are successful mostly because they keep populations in a constant state of scarcity and insecurity, not because they automatically command respect from the people (as Migdal also suggests).[59] Our ethnographies show that the bosses' capacity to rule is not necessarily based on brutality or benevolent charismatic acts à la Robin Hood but rather on opportunistic partnerships, as in the case of the laborers or forms of routinized complicity. It follows that Mafia Raj cannot be painted as a monochrome picture of victims, villains, criminals, or heroes. These are worlds in which it is often difficult to establish who is the victim and who the perpetrator, as individuals may be both at different times and in different spaces. In order to survive, bosses' regimes need to live in perfect "symbiosis with a myriad of protectors, accomplices, debtors of all kinds, informers, and people from all strata of society, who have been paid, bribed, intimidated or blackmailed."[60] This is the terrain where the bosses' power grows and, once established, is often retrospectively accepted by the community. Later still, it may be formally democratically sanctioned.

Complicities are carefully crafted and negotiated in everyday life and embedded in local kinship, caste, communal, kin, and friendship relations. Pockets of mafia-owned democracies engage successfully in a creative game of trust/distrust that allows bosses to rule over a particular sphere of interest by taking advantage of their local community support and caste agonistic relations or factions. In the case of South Asia, it is not so much government distrust (although it is undeniably also there) that provides a "robust pillar for mafia business," as Gambetta has argued for in Italy. [61] In our setting local animosities and conflicts between and within communities provide fertile ground for bossism to prosper (the case of Uttar Pradesh epitomizes such a trend).

Mafia methods such as extortion and protection typify the shady collaborations and social exchanges that bossism requires. Importantly, paying extortion money can also be beneficial for the victim. Unlike a bandit or a thief, the boss must maintain "on-going social relations with his victims, so he presents himself as a protector. But this hardly obscures the fact that he is the menace as well, his capacity for violence being deployed to regularize a protection racket."[62] Protection is often a "shadowy contract" in which violence, personal interests, and fantasies of power intersect.[63] As Tilly famously pointed out, "Which image the word 'protection' brings to mind depends mainly on our assessment of the reality and externality of the threat. Someone who produces both the danger and, at a price, the shield against it is a racketeer. Someone who provides a needed shield but has little control over the danger's appearance qualifies as a legitimate protector, especially if his price is no higher than that of his competitors."[64] Gambetta also argued, "The violence of extortion and the self-interest of the 'victim' tend to merge and to provide an inextricable set of reasons for cooperation: the advantage of being a 'friend' of those who extort one's money and goods is not therefore simply that of avoiding the likely damages that would otherwise ensue, but can extend to assistance in disposing of competitors."[65] Ultimately bosses are both potentially illegal violent protectors and illegal violent aggressors.[66] Appreciating the fine boundaries between protection, understood as the provision of genuinely desired services, and extortion, understood as the extraction of a price for unwanted or bogus services, is crucial to understanding the duplicity and ambiguity that unite citizens and the boss in South Asian Mafia Raj.[67] In this context, consent is always contingent and precarious. Trust and loyalty are difficult to maintain, and the authority of the boss needs to be continuously reasserted.

It follows that the position of boss is perpetually insecure. Indeed, it is not just citizens (or particular businesses) that are vulnerable in this scenario; bosses live in constant fear too. They fear losing their position, their money, and their power. They continuously have to look over their shoulders to guard against ambitious young men and their own henchmen. Cheating and betrayal are the daily bread and butter of bossism "realpolitik," as shown throughout this book. Contrary to the literature, relations between bosses and patrons or between bosses and henchmen are anything but straightforward.[68] As "the Henchman" and "the Godfather" presented in this book illustrate, enforcers are often unpredictable "hot heads" with their own agendas. They are highly individualistic bosses in their own right. In competitive and uncertain environments, emerging bosses often take the opportunity to maximize their personal profits and "career" opportunities by having multiple patrons or creating their own gang and declaring their independence. This allows the henchmen to operate on their own terms, following their own rules to achieve their own ends. Thus, bosses tend to break (and operate outside) patronage structures because their ultimate aim is independence.[69]

Mobilizing Popular Sovereignty

In regard to the role of elections (and democracy) in making and unmaking bosses' capacity to command and control people and resources, we have explored the bond of complicities that bosses developed within their turfs. We have shown that systems of Mafia Raj are "neither hegemonic nor subaltern but a hybrid mix of both."[70] Here we ask, How do elections generate bossism? Why do some bosses contest elections? And why do some prefer instead to stay away from formal politics? Ultimately, what is the role of elections in the art of bossing?

Indisputably, elections are an important part of South Asian bossism. Besides the profit involved in adopting a political career path and the impunity that such a career grants, there is a particular aura of prestige and status that goes hand in hand with political public posts. Such an aura is perhaps hardly comparable with that in other places such as Italy, Nigeria, Jamaica, or Thailand, where bosses tend to operate at the periphery of political life and where "they often leave the politicking to the professionals, to the career politicians."[71] As Karim, an informant told us, in South Asia, "when you are an MP or MLA or city mayor, you are a *raja* [a king]; you are like a god and rich." In India it is said that "those who renounce the lure of power are worshipped, not because their example is capable of emulation, but in sheer awe of their ability to transcend the irresistible."[72] We have described how democracy has been vernacularized and how, since its introduction, it was quickly seen as an effective system of upward mobility. As a matter of fact, the high levels of political participation in South Asia are often highlighted. What is less discussed is that Indian, Bangladeshi, and Pakistani citizens (not only bosses) have also begun to contest elections at astonishing rates. Comparatively, Italian and Russian bosses do not seem to have the same socioeconomic and cultural motivations to enter directly into politics, preferring instead to be king makers rather than kings. But leaving aside the "cultural explanation," as Kondappa, "the Henchman," commented, "Only major bosses can live without electoral politics and, nowadays, mainly for short periods only."

In South Asia bosses increasingly need elections to rule. Bosses often hold (or have held) public office: "The Godfather" is an elected MP; "the Legend" was a former MLA, and his widow is currently a minister; "Lady Dabang" is a former municipal councilor with aspirations to build a political dynasty. Her son has contested both national and state elections in the last three years. "The Henchman" is a former ward representative, and so on. Many of the bosses in this book have also at some point during their careers helped other bosses control vote banks through coercive tactics. Indeed, some are still providing such services, such as Kondappa and Sukhbir Singh. We have explored how different historical trajectories, political economies, and importantly, the organization of party machines shape the ways in which bosses enter (or do not enter) into politics in our settings. We show that the very nature of party organization and its capacity to monopolize violence shape "various types of interaction between political actors and violent entrepreneurs as well as various modes of penetration of organized criminal violence within the political arena."[73]

Besides discussing the structures of local party machines, we also show that direct conversions of crime into politics are more likely in settings where there are high levels of polarization and competitive politics, such as in Uttar Pradesh or Andhra Pradesh. For example, in Uttar Pradesh, multiparty competition correlates with higher levels of communal and caste-based conflict,[74] as well as a higher number of criminal political candidates.[75] Moreover, the need for muscle power is at its peak in areas with deep community divides where voters desire forceful representatives who can credibly protect their group interests. It has been established that political parties select criminal candidates in those areas where social divisions are the most contested.[76] The case study of Uttar Pradesh shows how "Lady Dabang" operates in a highly competitive context. Western Uttar Pradesh presents a violent form of bossism that is triggered by the coexistence of multiple and competitive centers of power, which tend to clash. However, in other settings, such as contemporary Punjab, we find that two-party competition correlates with more muted levels of bossism and with monopolistic forms of Mafia Raj. In Punjab, the SAD leadership controls the bosses.[77] In Pakistan, entering the political stage requires social and landed capital not accessible to many violent entrepreneurs, who are often happy to remain behind the scenes and do not seek election.[78] There are of course exceptions, as shown in work on Karachi by Laurent Gayer.[79]

Thus, while a number of strongmen operate by colluding with the state and/or by backing particular candidates or parties with money and muscle, and others such as Lahori bosses do not wish or desire to enter politics and/or to compromise themselves with politics, there are bosses who instead run in and win elections. Across our fieldsites, elected bosses are not thought of as a separate class of bosses but live on a spectrum that includes a large variety of figures: the henchmen, the party musclemen, the criminalized politician, and the gangster-turned-politician. Thus, within the figure of the boss there are other figures, avatars of the boss figure: the gangster-politician is one such example. In Bangladesh the gangster-politician ("the Godfather") is more a politician than a gangster; his ties to a political party are more important and more enduring. Both bosses and *mastans* are trained in criminal entrepreneurialism as they work and rise in activist politics.

Student politics, in particular, is one of the domains where the crafts of the art of bossing are acquired. In this part of the world the party colors that one has once chosen can be changed only at great risk and in most cases unsuccessfully. In India, bosses from north to south do not seem very concerned about party loyalty: maintaining impunity often requires party swapping. Here the capacity to change party is an essential skill of the art of bossing. Hence, elections are crucial because a change of power means a change of political protection. Bosses need to be involved in electoral politics to gain and/or maintain their impunity.

We have shown how electoral democracy keeps bosses on their toes. From our examples we see that even seemingly untouchable bosses will fall (though sometimes only temporarily) when they lose an election. Bosses' power, as we have emphasized throughout, is precarious and needs to be constantly reinstated and wielded. But it is important to remember that elections are not necessarily to be won, as stated previously: Running for office ensures being known, prestige, and a place on the local political map; it shows followers you have the money to run and signals to rivals that you are on the scene. Bosses know very well that wheels will be set into motion, and they all know someone who has disappeared from the local map of power. To navigate the violent competition for economic and political resources, bosses need to pay attention to electoral positions and to the building of compromises and alliances. In many ways elections and the theaters, spectacle, and media attention that they provide become an integral part of the bosses' figural power.

Despite the importance of elections, bosses' real authority is often thought to be based not on electoral politics but on their capacity to rule (and to make money), even without an elected title. "He had the ticket through Sonia Gandhi [an insult in local politics], but he has no power. Without his job [meaning without being elected], he is nothing," says Kondappa about an elected MLA. Titles gained through electoral wins are considered temporary and uncertain. This clear distinction between elected leaders performing a job versus powerful bosses ruling over a territory is very widespread in many of our sites. Such a distinction reveals an ambiguous relation between real politics and democracy and the state.

Contrary to bosses who are respected for being fearless and able to "talk in the eyes of powerful people," simple politicians (without local preexisting forms of authority) have to rely on their political parties to impose their will. It follows that authority merely based on elections is seen as an emasculating form of politics. G. M. Reddy (GMR), "the Henchman" boss is one of these "real" bosses: "Elected or not, people follow him. He can command more than ten thousand people [this number varies from day to day] in the blink of an eye. He's here to serve the people, not to make money. He's already rich. And he is able to speak straight, to look ministers in the eye." The adjudicators also prefer to stay out of politics and distance themselves from the state to keep their personal sovereignty and capacity to adjudicate.

In short, elections cannot buy bosses' an auratic type of authority. They cannot buy charisma. Official titles may indeed have the opposite effect, by routinizing the power of the bosses. Part of the art of bossing lies precisely in sidestepping what Weber famously called the "bureaucratization of charisma" and, in doing so, maintaining the liminal power of the boss over time.[80] It follows that analyses that illustrate transitions from gangsterism to politics as synonymous with transitions from illegality to legality are often misleading. To stop daring and not engage with Mafia Raj may result in loss of authority and in some cases violent retaliation.[81]

POWER ON THE MOVE

The art of bossing captures the instability and fragility of bosses' authority. Sovereign power as a project is always tentative and unstable.[82] However, given its charismatic features, bosses' authority is particularly unstable. Weber famously argued that "pure" charisma resists capture or domestication, and Hansen and Verkaaik also point to its tentative, *emergent* character as a defining characteristic.[83] Bosses present themselves as in control of their lives. Paradoxically, however, what they spend their lives doing is trying to be in control. Bossism needs regular public recognition and rites of renewal: a violent act, the spectacle of an election, a Robin Hood–style public performance, a highly publicized court trial, a murder, and so on.

While we were writing their stories, the protagonists of this book continued to practice the art of bossing. Their stories since our fieldwork underscore how their personal sovereignties always remain tentative and never fully, definitively formed.[84] “Lady Dabang’s” husband died in in the autumn of 2017. This happened just before an important local election. In town, gossip spread like wildfire: “She killed him to get the sympathy vote.” Even the press reported “the gossip.” Her son was contesting the elections. “Lady Dabang” was not able to get a party ticket because her curriculum vitae was considered too criminal. The “untainted” son contested on her behalf but without much success. He lost badly despite the sympathy vote. “Lady Dabang” is certainly struggling to pass on her legacy and routinize her power. Her son, as locals often point out, “doesn’t have charisma or balls.” Bosses’ authority as a form of personal, tentative, charismatic authority à la Weber is difficult to routinize. Succession for charismatic leaders is often a problem. It is always difficult to create new successors without losing the power of the creator (the boss-cum-artist). Thus, to create a political dynasty is proving problematic for a “gangster-turned-politician.” “Lady Dabang” has decided to run in the next town mayor elections in 2020. She came to the conclusion that her son is not ready yet, but will he ever be? In February 2017, state elections took place in the state of Punjab. The SAD (Shiromani Akali Dal) monopolistic Mafia Raj has been challenged by the Congress victory. It remains to be seen how this change of power will affect “the Bluffer.” Sukhbir Singh has closer ties to Congress than the Akalis. This may now facilitate his political career, but at the same time the Congress might not trust him that much. Bosses’ authority is always fragile, but Sukhbir’s personal sovereignty is particularly tenuous because it is built on a fragile edifice of half-truths and bluffs. His charismatic power relies on his comic entertainment and the capacity of such “entertainment value” to protect him while he is cheating the system. In Andhra Pradesh, Paritala Sunita (the widow of “the Legend”) has become an MLA, and she is currently the minister for SERP (Society for the Elimination of Rural Poverty), women empowerment, child welfare, disabled and senior citizens' welfare in Chandra Babu Naidu's cabinet. Ravi's power has certainly become "dynastical." However, this process is never complete. His wife needs to keep Ravi's aura alive. When Sunita was invited to be part of the cabinet, she immediately sought to reopen her husband's murder case and put Jagan "on notice." Over the past few years, Paritala Ravi has been transformed into a figurehead and martyr of the party, and his image is used in election campaigning. His style of leadership is still admired and emulated (and criticized by some), and social media and the *rakta charitra* movies continue to glorify him as "the boss" of that region. In Pakistan, Amir is still selling *paan* in the Old City in Lahore. Yaseer has been incarcerated for a few months. Gogi Butt's close relative Kabir Butt still adjudicates at the family *dera*. Gogi himself, however, was recently summoned to court as an accused in the murder case of his nemesis, Teepu Traakonwala. When the judge refused to grant him pre-arrest interim bail, he managed to flee the court premises on a motorcycle. The police reportedly "did not bother to apprehend the accused."[85] His escape caught on cameras is another proof of being an extraordinary figure. His figurality is larger than ever. In Bangladesh, "the Rookie," the youngest and emergent boss with whom we started this book, is currently on the run from the authorities. His addiction to Phensedyl morphed into a heavy reliance on yaba—a drug available widely in Southeast Asia that contains methamphetamine and caffeine. After years of domestic abuse, his wife and infant son left him. He married again. Yet the violence continued. Addicted to hard drugs, with no money, prospects, two broken marriages, and two estranged infant children, in May 2017 Jamal attacked an ex-lover with a bespoke machete (*da*) that he used for "enforcement." He fled the village and remains at large.

GLOSSARY

aam admi**:** common man
abhimanam**:** affection
akhara**:** local wrestling gymnasium
apradhi**:** criminal
badmash**:** criminal/rascal
badro**:** refined
bahadur**:** heroic
Bazigars: caste name
basant**:** Kite Festival
behenji**:** sister
bhadralok**:** gentleman, educated Bengali
bhai/bhaia**:** strongman; lit., "brother"
bhumi mafia**:** land mafia
bigha**:** five-eighths acre
biradri**:** lineage/clan
block pramuk**:** chair of the block
boro bhai**:** big brother
Brahman/Brahmin: the highest caste/*varna*
Chamar: a large Scheduled Caste
chamcha**:** sycophant
chavi**:** reputation
Chhatra Dal: student wing of the BNP
company/firm: terms that refer to power syndicates in North India
crore: ten million
crorepatri**:** billionaire
dabang**:** strongman/boss
dada**:** local strongman; lit., "elder brother"
dalal**:** agent/pimp
Dalit: downtrodden, used to refer to former untouchables
danda**:** force
darbar**:** court
dera**:** den
dere-dar**:** boss or kingpin
desi**:** made in South Asia

***diyat*:** compensation
***doyal*:** generous
***durniti*:** criminal work
***dushmandari*:** feud
***faisla*:** adjudication
***gandu*:** catamites
***ghat*:** a segment of river frontage
***goonda*:** criminal
***goondagardi*:** criminal work
***hartal*:** strike
history-sheeter: Indian police term for a criminal with a long record of serious crime
***hoondi*:** money laundry
***jagga/goonda* tax:** extortion money
***jasusi naval/upanyas*:** detective crime novels in Hindi and Urdu
Jat: intermediate-status caste group; dominant peasant caste in North India
***jugad*:** the art of making do
***jungli qanun*:** law of the jungle
Kamma: caste name
***karekarthudu*:** party worker
***kedar*:** cadre
***khap panchayat*:** caste/village extralegal court
***khidmat*:** social service
***komotoshil*:** powerful
***lakh*:** one hundred thousand
***lok sabha*:** lower house of the Indian Parliament
Madiga: caste name
***maistri*:** labor contractor
Mala: caste name
***mastan*:** enforcer/thug
***mohalla*:** neighborhood
***mukti juddha*:** freedom fighter
***murobbi*:** elder
***nagar palika*:** municipality
Naxalite: member of a militant revolutionary group
***nayakullu*:** leader
***neta*:** leader, career politician
***nitishil*:** principled
***noshto*:** corrupt
***paan*:** a quid composed of betel leaves, tobacco, areca nuts, lime, and kattha (a brown paste extracted from the acacia tree)
***panchayat*:** statutory local government body
***parda*:** veil, seclusion, avoidance behavior, especially of married women
***pehlwan*:** wrestler

***qabza*:** land grabbing
***qatl-e-amd*:** intentional murder
***qisas*:** right to retaliate
***rajniti*:** politics
Rajput: an elite caste in North India
***randi*:** prostitute
Reddy: caste name
***salam*:** greeting
***samjik*:** socially adept
***sarpanch*:** elected village council head
Scheduled Caste (SC): bureaucratic term for former untouchables castes
Scheduled Tribe (ST): bureaucratic term for tribal communities
***seva*:** social work
***shadharon manush*:** common man
***shalish*:** tribunal
***shalwar-kameez*:** baggy pants and a long shirt that comes down to the knees, often referred to as the national male dress in Pakistan
***shamajik sheba*:** serving society
***sharif*:** good reputation
***sher*:** lion
***shommani*:** respectable
station house officer (SHO): the police officer in charge of a police station
***sulah*:** reconciliation
Syed: a "caste" of Muslims claiming descent from the Prophet Mohammad
***tali*:** wedding necklace
Tehsil: administrative division
Thakur: a caste name
***thana*:** a police station
***tikadar*:** head contractor
***vishwaasamu*:** loyal
Yadav: a landowning caste, also known as Ahir
***zila parishad*:** district council in India

NOTES

INTRODUCTION

1. On social banditry, see the debate between Hobsbawm (1969); Blok (1972); and Wagner (2007). On criminal heroes, see Kooistra (1989); Rediker (2004). On the Robin Hood principle, see Seal (2009).

2. See Lush, accessed April 11, 2018, https://uk.lush.com/products/smugglers-soul-1.

3. Blok (1974); Sidel (1999a: 71–72); Volkov (2002).

4. The term "boss" derives from the old Dutch and old High German *bass* and *basa* (aunt, uncle, and kinsman). It entered American English in the early nineteenth century and was initially employed to avoid the term "master," which was historically associated with slavery. Thus, originally a term of respect used to address an older relative, it began to be employed to refer to a person in charge who was not a master type but rather a paternalistic father figure. The term was simultaneously adopted to refer to mob-mafia-like bosses and/or party machine bosses.

5. Blok (1974: 38).

6. On the power of liminal/threshold figures, see Turner (1969) and Douglas (1966); on magicians, see Mauss and Hubert (1993: 19); on diviners, see Kapferer (1998); on danger and charisma, see Worsley (1968).

7. S. Ahmed (1992: 289).

8. We are inspired by Hansen and Stepputat (2005, 2006), who advocated an ethnographic *practice* approach to the study of de facto sovereignties, such as informal structures of illegal networks, strongmen, insurgents, and vigilante groups but, importantly, also the tentative forms of authority that are produced by market forces, ongoing processes of privatization, and crony capitalism.

9. We build on recent work by Barker, Harms, and Lindquist (2014: 1–18) on the concept of the figure; and on the work of Pine (2012) on the figure of the personal sovereign in Naples.

10. On the figure of the "bandit king," see Shulman (1986); Kasturi (2013).

11. Brass (2006: 4).

12. Hansen and Stepputat (2006: 304).

13. See also Comaroff and Comaroff on "palimpsest of sovereignties" (2006: 9).

14. The Association for Democratic Reform (ADR) and National Election Watch have created a unique database of affidavits submitted by candidates contesting state and national elections since 2002, illustrating the presence of politicians with criminal records in Indian politics (see "Assembly Elections 2018," ADR, accessed Febru-

ary 12, 2018, http://adrindia.org/). We are not assuming that the rise in proportion of politicians with a criminal record necessarily signifies a rise in the criminalization of politics. The growing number of criminal cases registered against bosses is also indicative of a marked judicialization of conflicts. However, these statistics also often hide much darker realities. In a prototypical Mafia Raj, no one even gets a chance to lodge a First Information Report (FIR) against a boss because of his or her ability to subvert police process and the judiciary. Hence, the most powerful bosses are often not taken into account in these statistics.

15. See, for example, Martin (2009, 2015a).

16. See, for example, BRAC (2006); Ruud (2010).

17. See Centre for the Study of Developing Societies (2008: 31).

18. For explorations of the growing nexus between crime, politics, and the economy in South Asia, see Brass (1997); Hansen (2001, 2005); Jaffrelot (2002); Harriss-White (2003); Manor (2007); Gooptu (2007); Michelutti (2008); Witsoe (2009); Jeffrey (2010); Vaishnav (2011); Berenschot (2011); Gill (2013); Gayer (2014); Ruud (2014); Kumar (2014); Sanchez (2015).

19. Competition in the context of clientelistic politics of shadow states creates conditions for extralegal economic and muscle resources, making the rise of criminal politicians more prevalent where political contestation is highly competitive (Brass 1997; Wilkinson 2004; Lieven 2011; Ruud 2011). On the concept of "the shadow state," see Harriss-White (2003); on the rent-seeking economy, see Bardhan (1984, 1988) and Khan and Jomo (2001).

20. For anthropological insights into crime, bossism, and mafias, see Kane and Parnell (2003); in Africa, see Bayart, Ellis, and Hibou (1999), Standing (2003), Roitman (2004), Smith (2007), Vigh (2006); in Russia, Verdery (1996), Humphrey (1999), Varese (2001), and Volkov (2002); in East and Southeast Asia, Rafael (1999), Sidel (2004), and I. Wilson (2009); in Latin America, Arias (2006, 2016), Auyero (2007), Jones and Rodgers (2009), Goldstein and Arias (2010), and Jaffe (2013); in the Mediterranean, Blok (1974), Gilsenan (1977), Schneider and Schneider (2003), and Pine (2012); and in Japan, Kaplan and Dubro (2003). See also work by Strange (1996) on the political empowerment of criminal actors as a global trend.

21. See Santoro (2011) for a discussion of Mafia becoming a folk concept. The term and concept of "mafia" have been long debated. One interesting approach is to study this criminal phenomenon purely as an economic activity: on mafia as an "enterprise syndicate," see Blok (1974); on "Mafia enterprise," Arlacchi (1993); and on mafia as a protection industry, Gambetta (1988) and Varese (2001). Tilly (1985) has instead highlighted the relation between mafia and political sovereignty by introducing the very interesting notion that organized crime can be compared to both war making and state making (see also Volkov 2002). Varese (2011b) and Armao (2000) pointed out that what distinguishes mafia from other types of organized crime is that the former fundamentally uses politics and the judicial system to make a profit.

22. This folk definition of mafia is close to the analytical definition proposed by Armao (2000), according to whom, when organized crime—conceived as a struc-

tured and permanent group of individuals who use violence to make profit through criminal activities—meets politics, it gives rise to a third type of system called mafia.

23. *Vohra Committee Report* (n.d.).

24. For the Italian original version of the conversation, see Abbate and Lillo (2015: 20). Carmierati is said to have borrowed the term *il mondo di mezzo* (the world in between or Middle Earth) from J. R. R. Tolkien.

25. On this point, see Sen (2007a). Her work on urban gangs/vigilantes is one of the few available studies that explores contemporary criminal gangs in India and is in dialogue with concepts and theories developed in the field of the sociology of mafias. In a recent global atlas of mafias, the subcontinent is completely absent (Maccaglia and Matard-Bonucci 2014).

26. For a recent overview of this literature, see Rao and Dube (2013).

27. The anthropology of the state has produced a proliferation of studies that challenge the view of the state as an organizational category distinct from society. See, for example, Abrams (1988); Mitchell (1991); Fuller and Harriss (2001); Corbridge, Srivastava, and Veron (2005). For postcolonial critique of state/society boundaries, see Chakrabarty (2000); Kaviraj (2000); Chatterjee (2004). Much of the ethnographic work on the state tends to focus on "the effects of state," on discourses and representations about corruption (Gupta 1995); on criminalization (Siegel 1998); on terrorism (Aretxanga 2002); or on how democracy is imagined rather than on realpolitik. Notable exceptions are the works by Wade (1985); Heyman (1999); Harriss-White (2003); Jeffrey (2010), which look at how politicians subvert the state bureaucracy.

28. By "Middle" India, Pakistan, and Bangladesh, we mean South Asian towns with a population between one hundred thousand and one million. See Harriss-White (2015) on the concept of "Middle India" and the general lack of studies on small towns.

29. Ortner (1995: 185).

30. Dahl (1957: 202).

31. Sennett (1980: 190). We draw on notions of authority from Sennett—in particular with regard to his view of authority not being synonymous with legitimacy à la Max Weber and his compelling suggestion that in the modern world people "feel attracted to strong figures we do not believe to be legitimate" (ibid.: 26). However, contrary to Sennett, we conceive personal sovereignty not as a completely autonomous and independent field.

32. On the performance of personal sovereignty as an "art," see Pine (2012). On sovereignty as a principle of political power, see Agamben (1998) and his focus on the body as a site of, and object of, sovereign power. See also Hansen and Stepputat's (2005) compelling interpretation, as well as Buur and Jensen (2004); Das and Poole (2004).

33. Pine (2012: 17). See, in particular, Pine's usage of "contact zone" as a liminal space where "getting by" brushes with organized crime.

34. Over the last few decades, the discussions about power have gravitated around a continuing critical engagement with Marx and Marxism, particularly the Grams-

cian variety, and the work of Foucault (1991) and more recently the work of the Italian philosopher Giorgio Agamben (1998). "The current Foucauldian-Gramscian-Nietzschean obsession with power" produced a tendency for all "culture" to be seen as an effect of power relations and to be "explained" in terms of "domination and resistance" (Gledhill 2009: 9–10). Power had become anthropology's "new functionalism" (Sahlins 2002: 13), an explanation for everything that ended up explaining very little.

35. Sidel (1999a: 4). In his classic work on bossism in the Philippines, Sidel highlights that the literature on strongmen, such as the famous work by Migdal (1988), ignores the role of force and the coercive nature of the police in the making of strongmen's rule. Similarly, the work on clientelism and patronage in South Asia tends to overemphasize how leaders distribute resources rather than their role as violent protectors and enforcers. For a critical discussion of this literature, see Martin and Michelutti (2017).

36. For a sense of the wide interest in these topics, see Brass (1997); Varshney (2001, 2002); Wilkinson (2004); V. Das (2007). On Maoist insurgency, see Shah (2006).

37. On the big man debate, see Sahlins (1963); A. Strathern (1971); Godelier and Strathern (1991).

38. Mines (1996); Mines and Gourishankar (1990). Dumont has argued that the "world renouncer" is the only type of socially valued individual in Hindu culture, but only to the extent that he is an "individual-outside-the-world . . . both exterior to and superior to the society proper" ([1970] 1980: 234).

39. Ryter (2012: 105).

40. Vaishnav (2017).

41. Barker, Harms, and Lindquist (2014: 1). Lindquist sums up: "While the figure is contingent on a specific socio-historical context, the type consciously accentuates particular characteristics in order to form the basis for comparison" (2015: 162). And he shows how Barker, Harms, and Lindquist (2014) clarified this distinction "by comparing Walter Benjamin's '*flaneur*,' considered specifically against the backdrop of the transformations of nineteenth-century Paris (Benjamin 1986), and Georg Simmel's 'stranger,' which consciously accentuates particular characteristics at the expense of historical specificity (Simmel 1971), a form of abstraction comparable to Weber's ideal type (1978)" (Lindquist 2015: 160).

42. However, we conceptualize the figure of the boss "as an ethnographic site that mediates a wide range of processes and structures which are themselves in flux" and ultimately as "a figure of our times." The figure simultaneously grounds in specific historical times and ethnographic places (Barker, Harms, and Lindquist 2014: 1).

43. See Aretxanga (2002, 2003: 400) for a discussion of "fictional realities" and fantasy of power; see also Siegel (1998).

44. See Vidal, Tarabout, and Meyer (2003) on the transformation of senseless violence into meaningful violence.

45. Edberg (2004: 104).

46. See Jaffe (2012) on the iconization of the criminal in Jamaica.

47. On party machine and bossism, see Scott (1969); Migdal (1988); in Italy, Chubb (1996); in East Asia, Sidel (1999a); in Indonesia, I. Wilson (2015); in the United States, Mandelbaum (1965) and Banfield and Wilson (1966); in India, Weiner (1963).

48. Price and Ruud (2010: introduction).

49. Hansen and Stepputat (2006: 296).

50. Sidel (1999a).

51. According to Armao, "The mafia is not an anti-state but a state within the state. It develops on the inside and drives a process of fragmentation into sovereignty clusters that on occasions compete, clash or collude; each has a specific life cycle and a different degree of structure" (2015: 3).

52. Gayer (2014: 39).

53. Armao (2015: 3). For Armao, when organized crime (a structured and permanent group of individuals who use violence to make profit through criminal activities) meets politics, it gives rise to a third type of system called mafia. See also Armao (2000).

54. For a historical review of such processes in India, see Jaffrelot (2002) and Bear (2015); in Bangladesh, Adnan (2013); in Pakistan, Amin-Khan (2012), Mallick (2014), and McCartney (2015).

55. Stiglitz (2002: 58).

56. Chandra (2015: 46).

57. Corbridge (2010: 305).

58. Kochanek (1993: 230); see also Jahan (2015).

59. Civico (2015: 144).

60. See also Chandra's discussion on "patronage democracy" (2004: 6–7). Patronage democracies have been conceived as democracies in which elected political leaders have the power to distribute the vast resources controlled by the state to vote on an individual basis. In a mafia-owned democracy, however, what is crucial is not redistribution but criminal partnerships between the state and private capitalism based on the power of enforcement by force and intimidation.

61. On parallel states, see Jaffe (2013). See also Leeds (1996); Barrow-Giles (2011); Gayer (2014).

62. In the Indian context, Kohli argued that Indira Gandhi's authoritarian rule (especially 1975 to 1977) undermined provincial institutions and led to the replication of the central authoritarian regime at the state level and, consequently, to the development of parochial politics, which became the bedrock of criminal elements in Indian politics. See Bardhan (1984, 1988); Kohli (1991); Corbridge, Harriss, and Jeffrey (2013). Analysts of Pakistani politics have similarly argued that the military alternately restricted and enabled political mobility, thereby promoting the growth of factionalism and political violence, which intensified with the upsurge of the heroin and arms trade in the 1980s. See Rais (1985); Waseem (1994); Jalal (1995); and Martin (2015a). In Bangladesh, the Awami League lost power to a military coup in 1975. This ushered in an era of military dictatorships that lasted until 1990, when democracy

was "restored." This unstable period also coincided with the rise of brute force, which helped create the foundations of the era of "confrontational" politics between the two major political parties and their bonded clients vying for resources and patronage (Lewis 2011; Gardner 2012). "Deinstitutionalization" processes happened at the same time as a devastating combination of natural disasters and human-made disasters, which together created conditions that helped further an unholy alliance of political violence and crime, corruption, and nepotism. Autocracy gave way to democracy in 1990, but the deadly rivalry between the two main political parties is breeding a shadow space where enforcers and their political bosses thrive (Lewis 2011).

63. Nonstrom (2000: 36).

64. For "infrapowers," see Hansen and Stepputat (2006). See Berenschot (2011) for a discussion on musclemen and "mediation"; Berenschot emphasizes that the state's limited capacity to implement these has fueled both the demand for and the supply of fixers. Because the state is too understaffed and underresourced to implement these schemes, fixers take up the job.

65. Harriss-White (2003: 7).

66. Jaffe (2013).

67. Civico (2015: 23).

68. Favarel-Garrigues and Gayer (2016: 29).

69. Sidel (1999a).

70. On this point, see Briquet and Favarel-Garrigues (2010). For example, in southern Italy the Democrazia Cristiana won each election for fifty years. But in the Italian systems of Mafia Raj the boss usually acts behind the scenes. He does not contest elections.

71. Aretxaga (2003: 395); see also Comaroff and Comaroff (2000); and Lund (2006), who sees claims to public authority as largely legitimated through reference to the notion of the state.

72. Quotation in the heading is from Raghu Bhaiya, neighborhood boss from western Uttar Pradesh.

73. See, for example, Mazzarella (2003).

74. See, for example, see the movies *Satyaa* (1998), *Omkara* (1999), and *Sarkar* (2005) in Telugu; *Gabbar Singh* (2012) (an adaptation of the Hindi movie *Dabangg*) and *Gangs of Waseppur* (2012) in Bengali: *Billu Mastan* (Billu the *mastan*, 2002); *Shontrashi Bondhu* (Terrorist friend, 2002); *Rangbaz o Police* (Gangsters and police, 2003); *Kothin Purush* (Strong man, 2004); *Ajker Chandabaj* (Today's extortionist, 2004); *Ek Lutera* (One robber, 2004); *Mastan Number One* (2005); *Shirsho Shontrashi Greftar* (Arrest of the top terrorist, 2006); and *Banglar Don* (Bengal's don, 2007). For novels, see Vikram Chandra's *Sacred Games* (2007) and Sukit Saraf's *The Peacock Throne* (2007).

75. Importantly, he is the younger brother of Chiran Jeevi, the Telugu megastar, ex–central minister of tourism, ex-MLA, and currently an MP.

76. For information on Bangladeshi action movies, see Hoek (2013).

77. Ishtiaq Ahmed, one of the most prolific writers of this popular genre, died in

2017, having written close to a thousand detective novels. See Orsini (2009); Daechsel (2003). On the increasingly sanitized figure of the detective in Urdu crime novels, see Nisar and Masood (2012); Orsini (2004).

78. Ibrahim (2015: 7).

79. Ibid: 8.

80. See, for example, Dwivedi and Lau (2014).

81. Schneider and Schneider (1999: 169).

82. R. Bhushan, I. Joshi, B. Kang, A. S. Panneerselvan, K. S. Narayanan, L. Rattanani, Y. P. Rajesh, and S. Sivanand, "Law Makers or Breakers," *Outlook*, August 14, 1996, http://www.outlookindia.com/magazine/story/law-makers-or-breakers/201907.

83. Rafael (1999: 10).

84. "Personal mastery is rare; it commands respect. But a self-possessed person does more than elicit respect. The one who appears master of himself has a strength which intimidates others" (Sennett 1980: 84).

85. See Pine (2012: 9).

86. Sennett (1980: 27).

87. "The dilemma of authority in our time . . . is that we feel attracted to strong figures we do not believe to be legitimate," figures who will use their hold over people for selfish and destructive ends (ibid.: 26). Sennett shows that in our very efforts to reject paternalistic and autonomous authorities of the modern kind, we end up tied even more closely to, trapped even more tightly by, that which we struggle to negate.

88. See Hansen (2001, 2005); Michelutti (2008). For more recent mafia practices, see Michelutti (2014a, 2014b).

89. Hansen (2001: 72); see also Kakar (1996); Michelutti (2008, 2014a).

90. See Humphrey (2004: 418).

91. For a review of this literature, see Schneider and Schneider (2008).

92. Rodgers (2001: 1). This may also explain why fiction, movies, TV, and so on are often employed instead to provide a sense and illustration of mafias.

93. Robbins (2013). On power as "action," also see Graeber (2009).

94. There are few exceptions. See the comparative ethnography of extramarital sex by Hirsch et al. (2010) or the collaborative ethnography of war and peace in Sri Lanka by Spencer et al. (2014).

95. Watson (1997); Gingrich and Fox (2002).

96. This study is part of a larger research program titled "Democratic Cultures," which envisions new anthropological strategies to study ideas and practices of democracy cross-culturally. The program produces comparative ethnographic studies exploring processes of vernacularization of democracy across the globe. The larger research team is currently investigating questions of leadership and charisma, cultures of elections, and the relation between business cultures and democratic governance across Bangladesh, India, Nepal, and Pakistan. For details about the research team and outputs, see its website, https://www.ucl.ac.uk/democratic-cultures.

97. Michelutti, Picherit, Rollier, Ruud, and Still build on a body of data collected over the course of several years; three members of the team have conducted research

and worked in more than one of the countries under study: Martin and Rollier have both worked extensively in India and Pakistan, while Ruud has worked in India and Bangladesh. Hoque conducted research in Bangladesh and the United Kingdom, while Michelutti has been undertaking comparative research in India and Venezuela for the past ten years. Such experiences greatly facilitated the development of our comparative research questions and data analysis.

98. In this respect the work and advice of Barbara Harriss-White has been extremely important for designing the fieldwork and collecting and analyzing data.

99. Sluka (1990: 124).

100. Traditionally the term *darbar* was used to refer to any formal court gathering where the king/raja/maharaja was present. Today it is often used to refer to the daily open meetings in which the local politicians/bosses meet the public.

101. Osburg (2013: 301).

102. Robben (1996: 72).

103. According to Robben, "Seduction prevents interviewers from probing the discourse of the interviewee and, instead, makes them lose their critical stance toward the manifest discourse" (1996: 72). Robben points out, however, that a desire for seduction is inherent in anthropological research. He states, "Anthropologists want to be seduced because it gives them the desired feeling of gaining access to a hidden world" (ibid.: 97).

104. The extreme case of the Italian writer Roberto Saviano, who for the past eight years has faced constant death threats for exposing the public secrets of the Naples mafia in his book *Gomorra*, epitomizes such danger.

105. On "cultural intimacy," see Herzfeld (1997).

106. On the ambiguity of protection and extortion, see Tilly (1985).

CHAPTER 1

1. *The Departed* is an American crime-thriller movie directed by Martin Scorsese.

2. "South Asia" is a term with undefined boundaries. It also includes Sri Lanka, Nepal, and Bhutan, and sometimes the Maldives and Afghanistan. Here we use it as a shorthand reference to Pakistan, India, and Bangladesh.

3. These are by no means steadfast categories. In the 1990s, for instance, formally democratic India unleashed military and paramilitary repression on recalcitrant regions on an even larger scale than authoritarian Pakistan (Jalal 1995: 199).

4. For an analysis of such trends, see Harper and Amrith (2012).

5. For India, see, for example, Searle (2013, 2014); De Neve (2015).

6. Deleuze and Guattari (1988: 95).

7. Staff Reporter, "The Ten Most Polluted Cities in the World," *International Business Times*, January 23, 2017, http://www.ibtimes.co.uk/world-environment-day-10-most-polluted-cities-world-1504260.

8. For an analysis of this development for India, see, for example, Harriss-White (2003); for Pakistan, see Gayer (2014); for Bangladesh, see Lewis (2011) and Gardner (2012).

9. See *Fragile States Index 2015*, Fund for Peace, 2015, http://fundforpeace.org/fsi/wp-content/uploads/2017/05/Fragile-States-Index-Annual-Report-2015-ver-9.pdf.

10. For a qualitative study of the persistence of poverty in India and a discussion of such trends, see Gooptu and Parry (2014).

11. We updated figures presented by John Harriss (2010). See also Kumar (2002) and Dreze and Sen (2013: chap. 1) for a discussion on India's social development compared to that in the rest of South Asia; and Pritchett (2009) on the Indian "flailing" state.

12. India has a score of 7.5, where 10 would mean nonfunctional.

13. For a critical overview and explorations of the underbelly of the Indian boom, see works by Banerjee and Piketty (2005, 2011); Bandyopadhyay (2011, 2012); Corbridge and Shah (2013) and Bear (2011, 2015).

14. Harriss-White (2010: 152).

15. These figures were also used by the finance minister A. M. A. Muhith in one of his speeches. See Staff Correspondent, "Black Money on the Rise: Muhith," *bdnews24.com*, April 8, 2016, http://bdnews24.com/economy/2014/04/08/black-money-on-the-rise-muhith.

16. According to S. A. Zaidi (2014: 112), Pakistan's underground/black economy is estimated to be more than the real economy (no figure provided). Its size adds to the huge problem of taxation in the country: about 1 percent of the population pays income tax. According to Shahid Zia, a Pakistani economic expert, estimates of the size of the informal economy range between 30 percent and more than 90 percent of GDP. See Nasir Jamal, "Is Informal Economy Shrinking?," *Dawn*, June 2, 2014, http://www.dawn.com/news/1110027.

17. For discussion on the overlaps between different economies, see Roy (1996); Harriss-White (2010).

18. For a recent exploration of the "sand mafia," see Rege (2016).

19. As Hill writes, the "criminalization of goods and services that some politicians or voters deem immoral or harmful but that others consider desirable may be counterproductive"; excluding legal entrepreneurs, it "generates even greater revenues to the criminal world" (2006: 15–16).

20. Besides the informal and sometimes illegal nature of these relations, their opacity poses certain limits to ethnographic inquiry. We therefore acknowledge that many of the transactions and business partnerships that our protagonists engage in may have escaped our attention. We further explore the operations of local mafias in a forthcoming volume edited by Barbara Harriss-White and Michelutti, preliminary titled "The Wild East? Criminal Political Economies across South Asia."

21. More generally, *jugad* is perceived as a resourceful way of getting by, as a virtuous practice or as a corrupted one (Jeffrey, Jeffrey, and Jeffrey 2008b: 5; Jeffrey and Young 2012; and Jauregui 2014). Jeffrey, Jeffrey, and Jeffrey have shown that young unemployed Indian men live in a highly competitive world in which source, force, and the need to improvise become paramount concerns.

22. On the use of *jugad* in politics, see Ruud (2003).

23. Pine (2012: 10), see also Pardo (1996, 2000) on "the art of making do" and legitimacy in Naples.

24. For a discussion on the thresholds between large-scale organized crime, microlevel organized crime, and the informal economy, see also Van Schendel and Abraham (2005).

25. For India, see, for example, Sanchez (2015).

26. The disproportionate size of the military in the country's economy is now well documented. Its profit-making activities are akin to that of a Mafia Raj insofar as it is oriented toward the interests of a particular group (retired and serving army personnel and their civilian clients) at the expense of the general public. In the name of national interest, the armed forces have repeatedly used coercive methods against civilian authorities and owners to acquire resources, such as land, for personal private benefit. Much of these profit-making activities are carried out by the armed forces' "welfare foundations," which are some of the largest conglomerates in the country. Their activities include insurance, banking, educational institutions, gas extraction, cement production, and agro-industries (see Blom 2011: 31–32; Siddiqa 2007: 198–99).

27. Prabhat Sharan, "The New Mafia Raj," *Deccan Herald*, accessed October 3, 2015, http://www.deccanherald.com/content/235260/mafia-raj.html.

28. For an examination of a variety of extractive industries across South Asia, see Harriss-White and Michelutti (forthcoming).

29. Levien (2011); Springer (2013).

30. For the relation between black money and election campaigns, see Vaishnav (2011); Kapur and Vaishnav (2013); and Sukhtankar (2012).

31. Concerning this connection in Bangladesh, see Adnan (2013); in India, Suud (2014); in Pakistan, McCartney (2015).

32. See Schneider and Schneider, who have recently conceptualized "the mafia as a normal facet of capitalism, no more outside its political economy than the other capitalisms to which we add such qualifiers such as 'merchant,' 'industrial,' finance,' 'proto,' or 'crony'" (2011: 3).

33. See Whitehead (2008) for discussion about this phenomenon in Mumbai.

34. Gooptu (2007).

35. Harvey (2005). Harvey famously argued that later forms of capitalism are centered on speculative real estate investments. Today, because of underconsumption, capital is no longer invested in productive assets. In the contemporary world more is produced than what people are ready to consume. It follows that investments in productive assets are no longer profitable, and huge amounts of money are being funneled into real estate. On property relations in the age of neoliberalism, see also Hann (2007).

36. For Mumbai, see, for example, Weinstein (2008); for Karachi, Gayer (2014); for India, Nilsen and Oskarsson (2016). For examples of "mafia capitalism" in Japan, see Hill (2006); in post–Soviet Russia, Varese (2001); and in Hong Kong, Chu (2000).

37. Paoli (2003: 165); on racketeering as a legitimate industry, see also Reuter (1987).

38. Gooptu (2007).

39. Spencer (2003: 3).

40. Varma (2004: 7).

41. Michelutti (2008).

42. On the concept of processes of vernacularization of democracy, see ibid.

43. Ruud (2011: 67).

44. Witsoe (2011a: 73).

45. Piliavsky (2014).

46. Dasgupta (2014: 348).

47. Hansen (2001).

48. This does not apply to the contemporary Pakistan Punjab.

49. On elections as rituals, see Banerjee (2014).

50. Hansen and Stepputat (2005: 4).

51. See especially Kakar (1996), who describes how young men after their first experience in custody swagger proudly as seasoned criminals.

52. On unemployment and illegal economies, see Gooptu (2007).

53. For a comparable argument, see Mosse (2011).

54. Dasgupta (2014: 350).

55. A. R. Rabbi, "Customs Seize Prince Moosa's Land Rover," Dhaka Tribune, March 21, 2017, https://www.dhakatribune.com/bangladesh/crime/2017/03/21/customs-seize-moosa-range/.

56. Such imaginations are similar to those Achille Mbembe (1992) recorded when discussing the African hustler who is the product of a popular culture that is frequently a provincialized imitation of an oligarchic entrepreneurial elite that inflates an aesthetic of success and wealth to often absurd proportions.

57. See, for example, Wilkinson (2004); Manor (2007).

58. Jahan (2005).

59. One lakh equals one hundred thousand; one crore equals ten million.

60. See Akram and Das (2009).

61. Ruud and Islam (2016).

62. Banyan, "Campaign Finance in India: Black Money Power," *The Economist*, May 4, 2014, http://www.economist.com/blogs/banyan/2014/05/campaign-finance-india.

63. Vaishnav (2017).

64. Martin (2015a).

65. Interviews by Arild Ruud, Dhaka (2009–10).

66. Verniers (2014).

67. BRAC (2006).

68. Van Schendel (2009: 252–53); Ruud (2010, 2014).

69. Ruud (2010: 94); Andersen (2013).

70. Jahan and Amundsen (2012).

71. For an account of politics in rural Pakistan Punjab, see Martin (2015a).

72. Briquet and Favarel-Garrigues (2010: 2).

73. Martin and Michelutti (2017) contrast monopolistic Mafia Raj in Punjab with competitive Mafia Raj in Uttar Pradesh.

74. See Gayer (2014).

75. Armao (2015).

76. Gayer (2014: 138).

77. Das and Poole (2004).

78. Agamben (1998).

79. For the case of Pakistan (Karachi), see, for example, Gayer (2014: 49).

80. Khan (2011) notes that during the 1990s Pakistan's Supreme Court was transformed into a power broker between a military-backed executive and a fragile Parliament; prominent politicians claimed violation of their political rights. But it is important not to overemphasize the use of public-interest litigation (PIL) as a political tool in Pakistan in regard to India; Pakistan's PIL jurisprudence has a more conspicuous flavor of political elite struggle than India's; Pakistan's variant of judicial populism is distinctive because of its political overtones (e.g., Benazir Bhutto's constitutional challenge to certain provisions in electoral laws); politicized PIL cases allowed the Supreme Court to create direct inroads into the purely political territory of the legislature and executive.

81. On police rackets in Mumbai, see, for example, Eckert (2003).

82. For comparison, see the case of Indonesia described by Pemberton (1999).

83. Following the enactment of the *qisas* and *diyat* laws in the mid-1990s, the heir of a victim of murder now has three options: exert the right to retaliate (*qisas*), renounce that right, or renounce it in exchange for blood money (see Mehdi 2013: 151–53).

84. Wasti (2009: 263, 280).

85. On *khap panchayats* in India, see Kaur (2010).

CHAPTER 2

1. Smoking in public is an exclusively male pursuit in Bangladesh. Women, therefore, are excluded from this moral economy.

2. A *Londoni* is someone of Bangladeshi origin who resides in England. The overwhelming majority of British-Bangladeshis originate from the province of Sylhet in Bangladesh. The college in question was situated in an area that Gardner refers to as "the 'Londoni' belt" (1995). Extensive migrations from this area in the twentieth century have facilitated the creation of an affluent "Londoni class," which many in the area aspire to and seek patronage from.

3. The Bangladesh Chhatra League (BCL) is the student wing of Bangladesh Awami League, a mainstream center-left political party.

4. Van Schendel (2009: 252–53).

5. Lewis 2011: 89–90.

6. Jamaat-e-Islami (far-right/Islamist political party).

7. Islami Chhatra Shibir (student wing of Jamaat).

8. Prior to founding the BNP, Gen. Ziaur Rahman served as the country's first military administrator, succeeding Sheikh Mujibur Rahman as premier. "Zia" is responsible for the liberalization of the economy and the introduction of Bangladeshi nationalism, thus shifting the political center to the right. The secular constitution was amended to include Islam as the state religion. Islamist parties such as Jamaat-e-Islami were invited back into the political mainstream under his leadership.

9. Bangladesh Independence Day.

10. Jatiotabadi Chhatra Dal (student wing of the BNP).

11. Brass (2003).

12. Secondary School Certificate (Matriculation: the equivalent to General Certificates of Secondary Education in Britain).

13. Brass (2003: 258–61); Ruud (2010).

14. Gardner 2008.

15. Brahmanbaria is a subdistrict bordering Dhaka to its west and Sylhet division to the north. Bordering India to the east, it is also the gateway to Chittagong division to the south of the country, thus making it one of the most strategic and important hubs for smuggling in the country.

CHAPTER 3

1. The Mahatma Gandhi National Rural Employment Guarantee Act offers people one hundred days of guaranteed, government-funded wage labor per year.

2. Balimkis are the Dalit community traditionally engaged in sweeping.

3. On bluff and relation between bluffers and audiences, see Newell (2012).

4. On the charisma of "infrapower," see Hansen and Verkaaik (2009).

5. See Jeffrey, Jeffery, and Jeffery (2008a).

6. Kumar (2007) has argued that the BSP's ideological discourse against issues of purity/pollution has found little resonance in a state where Brahminical values were never particularly dominant. See Jodhka (2004) for a discussion on Sikhism and the relative absence of Brahminical values in Punjab.

7. For a recent exploration of comedic entertainment, see Hall, Goldstein, and Ingram (2016, 73).

8. Ibid.

9. The Chamars of Punjab are frequently called Ravidasias in honor of Guru Ravidas.

10. Unit of area standardized to twenty-five square yards.

11. Gill (2013, 2014).

12. Martin (2015b).

13. Bazigars were traditionally a seminomadic caste whose members traveled around villages performing acrobatic acts. Today they are mostly wage laborers and small farmers.

14. Martin (2015b).

15. On humorous performance being protected from the scrutiny that would be applied in other discursive domains, see Goffman (1959).

CHAPTER 4

1. Prasad (2015).

2. Their political careers and the mining industry were based in Karnataka; money was registered in Rayalaseema where the two brothers were supported by Y. S. R. Reddy, ex–chief minister of Andhra Pradesh (2004–9).

3. Michelutti (2008).

4. Mosse (2011).

5. Picherit (2015).

6. Still (2014a).

7. Carswell and De Neve (2015).

8. The rising circulation of labor allowed Dalits to get rid of old forms of control over agricultural labor only to enter into dependence on new sectors without transforming the socioeconomic position of Dalits.

9. Jagan, as he is known, is the son of Y. S. R. Reddy. Jagan, now leader of the YSR-CP, has been involved in major corruption scams over the last fifteen years.

10. Indeed, politicians do work continuously, but Kondappa conceptualizes "work" in a different way.

11. Mosse (2015).

12. Picherit (2015).

13. Such logic often partly explains the wide disparities across villages and districts about the implementation of schemes.

14. Michelutti (2010).

15. Gorringe (2010).

16. "Lodge" refers to a hotel in South India. In the case detailed, the lodge provides large rooms with a fan and twenty-four-hour room service.

17. Witsoe (2011).

18. Schneider and Schneider (2007).

CHAPTER 5

Parts of this chapter first appeared in *L'homme* 219–220 (2016): 63–91, and are translated and reprinted here with permission.

1. Haqqani (2005).

2. Sanchez (2015).

3. Jaffrelot and Kumar (2009); Witsoe (2011).

4. Mehta (2004: 134).

5. Tilly (1985: 169).

6. Gayer (2014: 49).

7. Hansen and Stepputat (2005: 1–5).

8. "Raymond Davis vs *Qisas* & *Diyat* Laws," *The News*, February 23, 2011, https://www.thenews.com.pk/archive/print/612043; "Raymond Davis Case: Religious Parties Out to Thwart *Diyat* Move," *Dawn*, February 17, 2011, https://www.dawn.com/news/606907; Huma Imtiaz, "Behind the Scenes of Raymond Davis's Release," *FP*, March 16, 2011, http://foreignpolicy.com/2011/03/16/behind-the-scenes-of-raymond-daviss-release/.

9. We are here thinking of the key role that Pakistan played during the anti-Soviet jihad in Afghanistan in the 1980s; the American, Saudi, and Iraqi interferences that followed; and the recovered status of "frontline state" in the context of the fight against terrorism after 2001.

10. Verkaaik (2001).

11. On the links between anthropology, military institutions, and intelligence activities, see D. Price (2008).

12. With respect to criminality, these archaic formulas used by the country's anglophone press come for the most part from the Indian Penal Code of 1860 (Kennedy 1993). This style, which often combines a formal register with sensationalism, also reflects a certain postcolonial continuity in the ways in which the police forces conceive of criminality.

13. Given my methodological choices, the difficulties of access, and the potential risks involved, I was not concerned about the extent to which my interlocutors were "representative" of Lahore's criminal milieu. I therefore exclude vast sections of it (major arms and drug dealers, kidnapping groups, and Islamist militants) while being aware of the consequent limitations.

14. On the athletic and moral tradition of wrestling in South Asia, see the work of Alter (1997). On wrestling in Lahore, see Frembgen and Rollier (2014).

15. Chaudhry (2015: 168); Martin (2015a).

16. On the Punjabi *dera*, see Nelson (2011: 325); Lyon (2002: 70); Chaudhary (1999: 90–91); Eglar (1960: 30); Slocum, Akhtar, and Sahi (1960: 30). The institution of the *dera* in the Pakistani Punjab differs from its contemporary evolution on the Indian side, where the term is used to designate a religious center where a guru lives (see Ram 2007).

17. The notions of honor and respect in the criminal milieu that I describe evidently resonate with their use in the context of gangs and street culture in the United States; see, for instance, Bourgois (1995); and Sanchez-Jankowski (1991: 143). On the notion of *izzat*, see Raheja and Gold (1994: 86–88); and Fischer (1991: 108–11).

18. Bin Rashid and Sher Khan, "Goonda Raj," *Express Tribune*, November 25, 2012, https://tribune.com.pk/story/468607/goonda-raj/.

19. Siddique (2013: 21–22).

20. Cheema (2012: 892–900).

21. Mehdi (2013: 151–53).

22. A number of analysts suggest that sharia-based modes of dispute resolution, dispensed by *ulema* (scholars of Islamic jurisprudence) that are not part of the offi-

cial religious establishment, may be an appealing alternative platform of social justice among the urban middle-class; see Zaidi (2016); and Nelson (2016). However, in the neighborhoods of Lahore where I carried out my research, this was certainly not the case.

23. Moatasim (2015: 159); Siddiqa (2013: 16–17); Hull (2012: 239, 241); N. Khan (2012).

24. Nadeem (2002: 76).

25. Moatasim (2015: 183).

26. Hasan et al. (2013: 47). On the connivance of police officials and elected politicians in land grabbing, see Muhammad Faisal Ali, "'Land Grabber' Held after Encounter," *Dawn*, December 6, 2008, https://www.dawn.com/news/333268.

27. Murtaza Ali Shah, "Shahbaz Sharif Warns Land Mafia of Strict Action," *The News*, October 4, 2012, https://www.thenews.com.pk/print/91049-shahbaz-sharif-warns-land-mafia-of-strict-action.

28. Abdul Manan and Ali Usman, "'Failure to Serve': Punjab Governor Steps Down over 'Differences,'" *Express Tribune*, January 30, 2015, https://tribune.com.pk/story/829965/failure-to-serve-punjab-governor-steps-down-over-differences/.

29. "FIR Reporting Centres to Be Set Up Soon," *The Nation*, May 31, 2011, http://nation.com.pk/31-May-2011/fir-reporting-centres-to-be-set-up-soon.

30. Waqar Gillani, "A Chapter of Enmity Closed," *News on Sunday*, January 31, 2010, https://jang.com.pk/thenews/jan2010-weekly/nos-31-01-2010/she.htm#6.

31. Ali Noshad and Shahnawaz Khan, "Monday Attack Continuation of 9-Year Rivalry," *Daily Times*, May 27, 2003, http://archives.dailytimes.com.pk/Reporter/noshad-ali-and-shahnawaz-khan- [site discontinued].

32. The practice of extortion is termed *jagga tax*, a synonym of *goonda tax*. The term may derive from the legendary Jagga Singh (or Jatt), a Sikh Robin Hood figure who became a symbol of local resistance against the British in early twentieth-century Punjab. Alternatively, the term may derive from Jagga Gujjar, a Lahori who supposedly levied a tax from local butchers on every goat sold on the market in the 1960s. The son of an influential *dere-dar*, he is also remembered as someone who looked after his neighborhood, chasing drug dealers and protecting young women from harassment.

33. The lion (*sher*) is a privileged symbol to evoke force and masculinity in Punjab, a symbol used as a political emblem by the PML-N. Tipu can be seen with his lion in the following video: "Teepu Pehlwan (Late) TruckanWala Lahore with His Lion," uploaded February 21, 2001, https://www.youtube.com/watch?v=vfTgf9_ja0c.

34. "Absence of Witnesses Benefits Criminals," *Dawn*, November 12, 2001, https://www.dawn.com/news/5880.

35. On the feud between Tipu and the Butts, see Shahnawaz Khan, "'Gangland Thugs' Egotistical Rivalry Claims Another Life," *Daily Times*, May 12, 2005; Shahnawaz Khan, "Zafari Nath's Murder at Lakshmi Chowk: Teefi and Gogi Forced Naths to Accuse Me: Bichhu," *Daily Times*, April 24, 2004, https://dailytimes.com.pk/?page=story_24-4-2004_pg7_14 [site discontinued]; Shahnawaz Khan, "Bad Blood

the Cause of Hundreds of Deaths," *Daily Times*, April 26, 2004, http://www.dailytimes.com.pk/default.asp?page=story_26-4-2004_pg7_25 [site discontinued]; Ashraf Javed, "Top 10 Underworld 'Kings' Killed or Went Underground," *Daily Times*, October 16, 2010, http://nation.com.pk/16-Oct-2010/top-10-underworld-kings-killed-or-went-underground; Jam Sajjad Hussain, "Underworld Dons Now on Police List J. S. Hussain," *The Nation*, June 16, 2011, http://nation.com.pk/16-Jun-2011/underworld-dons-now-on-police-list.

36. He claims that while sipping from her flask of whisky, Benazir Bhutto even proposed some work to the Butts on behalf of the CIA.

CHAPTER 6

1. For descriptions of the figure of the *dada/bhai* in provincial North India, see Gooptu (2001); Hansen (2001); Michelutti (2010).

2. See Volkov on the visibility of violent entrepreneurs in post-Soviet Russia: "A robber does not qualify as a violent entrepreneur but a stationary bandit does, since the latter strives to establish permanent tributary relations with inhabitants of his domain and provides certain services to justify his demand to tribute" (2002: 28).

3. This practice is very common in other mafia systems; see, for example, Pine on camorra in Naples: "They use *prestanomi*, or 'borrowed names,' such as names of spouses and kin, on titles of their properties and businesses" (2012: 30).

4. Throughout the text I have changed the names of people and places to ensure their privacy and safety. In addition, I changed some of the characteristics of participants (such as age/occupation) to further conceal identities.

5. See, for example, Dreze and Khera (2000); Oldenburg (1992); Marwah (2014). On riots and communalism, see Brass (1997).

6. Divya Sathyanarayanan, "Booking from Small Cities like Mathura, Muzaffarpur, Ludhiana Driving Luxury Travel Boom," *Economic Times*, May 6, 2014, http://articles.economictimes.indiatimes.com/2014-05-06/news/49661518_1_tui-india-kuoni-india-non-metros.

7. For a further exploration of the local interstate criminal economies, see Harriss-White and Michelutti (forthcoming).

8. On lack of coordination and training of the Indian police force with regard to the control of organized crime, see Sharma (1999: 112).

9. Yadavs are a low to mid-ranking caste of pastoral agriculturalists, and Dalits are former untouchables, in this case mainly from the Chamar leathersmith caste.

10. Yadav (2000); Chandra (2004).

11. Between my writing and the publishing of this chapter, the BJP won and formed a government in Uttar Pradesh in March 2017.

12. Wilkinson (2004).

13. See Michelutti and Heath (2013, 2014) for a study of these dynamics in this area of Uttar Pradesh.

14. Vaishnav (2011); Banerjee and Pande (2007).

15. For a recent documentary on the Dabang of Uttar Pradesh, see *Dabangs of UP*, NewsX, YouTube, February 6, 2012, https://www.youtube.com/watch?v=cr2VK8I5xOY.

16. We do not use these statistics as an indication of a rise in criminal politics. In these particular settings the most "criminal" politicians did not appear under these statistics because nobody dares to file a case against them.

17. "*History-sheeter*" is an Indian police term for a criminal with a long record of serious crime.

18. A similar "concentric" organizational structure is described by Letizia Paoli in the cases of Cosa Nostra and 'Ndrangheta (2003: 106).

19. I am omitting the name of the party to preserve anonymity.

20. *Parda* refers to wearing the veil, seclusion, and avoidance behavior, especially of married women.

21. On the myth of the "Bandit Queen," see, for example, Assayag (2006); Seal (2009).

22. Anonymized extracts from complaint letter, 1190/CEO/DCEO/2012, dated January 23, 2012.

23. *Ghat* is a segment of river frontage.

24. On Mayawati's style and political career, see Narayan (2005: 158–59).

25. Traditionally the term *darbar* was used to refer to any formal court gathering where the king/raja/maharaja was present.

26. Raheja and Gold (1994).

27. Fear and uncertainty as instruments of governance and the legitimization of violence by the Gita are themes that are also recurrent in gangster and Mafia Raj movies and novels; see, for example, *The Story of My Assassins* by Tarun Tejpal. In this novel "Chaaku learned that almost all of the world lived in colossal and constant fear. Afraid of everything. . . . More than hope, people's lives seemed to be defined by fear. . . . A tiny minority managed to cross the line of fear—of the police and courts and failure and censure and priests and cockroaches—and this tiny minority then became the shapers of the world in which the rest lived. . . . It was then that Chaaku understood the lesson from the Gita he always heard bandied about of fearless and action and the legitimacy of violence" (2010: 157, 158).

28. Gambetta (1993).

29. Taussig (1991, 1997).

30. See Gambetta on "the special air of self-assurance and command" of mafia bosses in Sicily. Such features, he writes, "are hard to describe, but easy to perceive once one sees them" (2004: 203).

31. Names and nicknames are important for bosses.

32. For comparative insights on the relation between violence, mafias, and elections in Italy, see Olivieri and Sberna (2014).

33. The informant is referring to the Muzaffarnagar riots, which happened in August 2013; for an analysis of the riots, see Berenschot (2014). The BJP won elections

in the 2014 Lok Sabha national election; for an analysis of the return to power of the BJP, see Heath (2015).

34. On the enactment of personal sovereignty, see Pine (2012: 10).

CHAPTER 7

1. The names of both the MP and the town are fictitious.

2. Student fronts are among the most important activist organizations for both the two major political parties in Bangladesh. Many political leaders first cut their teeth in student politics; see Ruud (2010); Andersen (2013).

3. The term is also used for criminal lords with few or no significant political connections, in particular leaders of local criminal organizations around particular "businesses." The notorious human traffickers Dil Muhammed and Kala Jahangir, for instance, have both been referred to as godfathers. They bought protection from the local police and from local politicians but were not themselves engaged in politics as such. This is not the godfather of this chapter.

4. Most of those mentioned here belong to the Awami League, but the main rival, BNP, has its fair share. The smaller Jatiyo Party has perhaps more than its fair share of shady characters, although many will not quite have the clout and influence to qualify as godfather. Even the Islamist Jamat Islami has leaders that qualify as godfathers.

5. Islam (2013).

6. This chapter is based on interviews with political activists, teachers, journalists, businessmen, and others from the educated classes. Some of the interviews took place in Nawabganj, but most took place in Dhaka. Dhaka is central to politics in all provincial towns and districts of the country. Almost all interviewees know Fakhrul Khan personally, some intimately, and all had been part of or were still part of political life in that city. Many did not hesitate to characterize him as a violent and dangerous politician, a godfather, although many also painted a much more favorable image of him.

7. The Rapid Action Battalion is an elite anticrime and antiterrorism gendarmerie manned by members from both the police and the armed forces. It is well equipped and armed, and much feared.

8. Mines (1996).

9. Sidel (1999a).

10. *Sheba* or *sewa* has an interesting history as a political strategy. See, e.g., Srivatsan (2015).

11. The 1970 election was the last election in united Pakistan, and Fakhrul's father was elected to the provincial assembly, which never met. The 1973 election was the first election in independent Bangladesh.

12. Rashiduzzaman (1978).

13. Jahan (2005: 119).

14. Ahmed (1984); Mascarenhas (1986); Jahan (2005: 169); Tripathy (2014: 229).

15. Jahan (2005: 130).

16. Hartmann and Boyce (2013: 182).

17. Jahan (1976: 364).

18. Mascarenhas (1986: 129).

19. "Clash over *Jhut* Trade Injuries," *Daily Star*, August 14, 2015, http://www.thedailystar.net/clash-over-jhut-trade-injures-7-37237.

20. The German word *Fingerspitzengefühl* (the feeling at the tip of your fingers) captures the ability to adapt style, mannerisms, words, or phrases to individual circumstances. See Ruud (2011: 66).

21. Concerning the kingly model, see P. Price (1989). For similar portraits of how the kingly model plays out in the case of the modern elected representative, see Madsen (2011).

22. The *bhadralok* in Bangladesh is often associated with Hindus so less commonly used for the Muslim "gentleman." However, the term *bhadro* is still widely used as praise, meaning "gentle, polite, educated."

23. "Black money" and other unsavory aspects of politics are often ignored by voters. See Ruud (2011).

24. Wilce (2004: 206).

25. Tripathy (2014: 67–69).

26. The main opposition party, the BNP, boycotted the election. This means Fakhrul Khan's election victory was not a straightforward indicator of popularity.

CHAPTER 8

1. "RGV Signs Vivek Oberoi for Rakta Charitra," *Indian Express*, April 27, 2009, http://indianexpress.com/article/entertainment/entertainment-others/rgv-signs-vivek-oberoi-for-rakta-charitra/99/.

2. Srinivasulu (2009: 10).

3. This account is based on my own fieldwork observations made at the time of his assassination in 2005; information gathered from the Internet (blogs, discussion forums, Paritala Ravi's Facebook page); English and Telugu news sites; one anonymous Telugu Desam report; and secondary academic literature. I have also used interviews conducted ten years later, in January 2015, in my old fieldwork site in Guntur district and one interview conducted by my research associate, Srinivas Dusi, with the current Telugu Desam Party Member of the Legislative Assembly (MLA), B. K. Parthasarathi, a man who now occupies Paritala Ravi's former position. In January 2005, Srinivas Dusi and I made several attempts to interview Paritala Sunita, but she was unavailable.

4. Price (1996, 2006); Still (2014a).

5. Baudrillard ([1981] 1994).

6. Sanjana, "Into the Madding Crown," *Tehelka* magazine 6 (38), September 26, 2009, http://www.tehelka.com/2009/10/into-the-madding-crown/.

7. For a discussion of land reforms and their implementation in Andhra Pradesh, see Suri and Raghavulu (1996); Herring (1983).

8. Harrison (1956: 380); Upadhya (1997).

9. Upadhya (1997).

10. See Suri (2002: 67); Harrison (1960).

11. See Suri (2002: 59–63) for a more detailed discussion of caste in politics in Andhra Pradesh.

12. Jagan strongly denies this charge.

13. Kumar (2014: 64).

14. Suchitra (2012).

15. Balagopal (2007: 3907); Prasad et al. (2012); Reddy et al. (2011).

16. Prasad et al. (2012: 16).

17. Ibid.

18. The emergence of other caste-based parties such the Kapu-dominated Praja Rajyam Party (PRP), led by megastar Chiranjeevi, in the early 2000s further complicated the caste-party link (see Pingle 2011). The PRP took away nearly 12 percent of the TDP vote share, but it failed in the 2009 elections and then merged with the Congress Party in 2011 (ibid.: 19–20). More important, of course, has been the rise to power of the Telangana Rashtra Samiti (TRS), which after decades of campaigning and months of intense agitation has now achieved a separate Telangana state.

19. At the heart of this campaign was the marginalization of Telangana by Rayalaseema and coastal Andhra. As the Sri Krishna Committee report states, "Together the two regions have ruled the state through Congress and TDP political formations. Telangana feels dominated by the upper castes of these regions and its struggle is primarily to shake off their yoke" (SKC Report, cited in ibid.: 20).

20. "The phenomenal growth in his [Jagan's] assets—his declared property in 2004 was Rs 1.74 crore, which rose to Rs. 77 crore in 2009 and 365 crore [37 million pounds / 53 million dollars] in 2011—gives enough room for suspicion," comments T. S. Sudhir in "The Many Equations of Jagan's Arrest," *Tehelka* magazine 9 (23), June 9, 2012, http://www.tehelka.com/2012/06/the-many-equations-of-jagans-arrest-2/.

21. "Y. S. Jaganmohan Reddy," Wikipedia, accessed December 17, 2015, https://en.wikipedia.org/wiki/Y._S._Jaganmohan_Reddy; Sudhir, "The Many Equations of Jagan's Arrest"; Devesh K. Pandey, "Fresh Trouble for Jaganmohan Reddy in Money Laundering Case," *The Hindu*, October 1, 2014, http://www.thehindu.com/news/national/andhra-pradesh/fresh-trouble-for-jaganmohan-reddy-in-money-laundering-case/article6462922.ece.

22. Sudhir, "The Many Equations of Jagan's Arrest."

23. The following information about Paritala Ravi comes from a number of sources, including an account from an anonymous blogger. See "Paritala Ravi: Bio-Data," Kamma Yuva Seva Samithi (KYSS), November 12, 2007, http://kyssonline.blogspot.co.uk/2007/11/paritala-ravi-bio.html. The KYSS is a group for the advancement of the Kamma caste and its young people. It is pro–Paritala Ravi and pro-TDP. Although the biography is biased, it does give the most detailed account of Paritala Ravi's background and the events that led up to his assassination, which I have cross-checked with other sources, including online news sources; Telugu and English newspaper cuttings collected during my doctoral fieldwork in 2004–5; and a detailed

unpublished article by Olivier Herrenschmidt (2009), which gives an account of the background of Paritala Ravi's assassination.

24. Mohiuddin (2007).

25. His full name is Maddelacheruvu Suryanarayana Reddy, but he is widely known as Suri.

26. See "Paritala Ravi: Bio-Data"; the blog *Rakhi-Youthrockz.blogspot.co.uk*, "Ravi's Entry into Factionism," January 8, 2011, http://rakhi-youthrockz.blogspot.co.uk/2011/01/ysr-rajareddy-after-narayana-reddy-was.html; and "If a Factionist Becomes a Chief Minister?," accessed December 10, 2015, https://www.scribd.com/document/23120450/factionist-becomes-chief-minister. It is principally about YSR, but one of the chapters describes Paritala Ravi. It is heavily biased toward the TDP, but it refers to cases that are verifiable and provides useful background information.

27. W. Chandrakanth, "Faction Violence Has Its Roots in Medieval History," *The Hindu*, January 26, 2005, http://www.thehindu.com/2005/01/26/stories/2005012605390400.htm.

28. In 1994, Ravi beat the Congress incumbent, Ramana Reddy. According to "Paritala Ravi: Bio-Data," N. T. Rama Rao appointed Paritala Ravi the Labour minister in his government. Paritala Ravi resigned after a few months due to a disagreement on policy but then returned and was reelected in by-elections in 1995.

29. It expelled its leader, Kondapalli Seetha Ramaiah, who was arrested in March 1993. Herrenschmidt (2009) provides more detail.

30. Balagopal (2001: 1285).

31. Herrenschmidt (2009).

32. This is according to police reports summarized by Kumar in *Frontline*. S. Nagesh Kumar, "Murder and Mayhem," *Frontline* 22 (4), February 12–25, 2005, http://www.frontline.in/static/html/fl2204/stories/20050225004803100.htm.

33. "Paritala Ravi: Bio-Data."

34. They were arrested under the Preventive Detention Act, accused of rigging.

35. Telugu Desam Party (2004: 24).

36. Rakesh Reddy, "Paritala Ravi Murder: Life Term for Eight," *The Hindu*, August 26, 2011, http://www.thehindu.com/todays-paper/tp-national/tp-andhrapradesh/paritala-ravi-murder-life-term-for-eight/article2398228.ece. The verdict was given on August 25, 2011, six years after Paritala Ravi's death. The Paritala Ravindra Wikipedia entry states that "the court examined 133 witnesses. . . . The court convicted 8 accused—Hanumantha Reddy, Peddi Reddy, O B Reddy, Vadde Konda, Vadde Srinivasulu, Rekamayya, Narayana Reddy and Ranganayakulu—and the approver was Rammohan Reddy. [Four] accused—G B Reddy, Anand Reddy (Rice Mama), Ramaswamy and Patola Govardhan Reddy—have been acquitted." See "Paritala Ravindra," Wikipedia, accessed May 4, 2018, https://en.wikipedia.org/wiki/Paritala_Ravindra.

37. *The Hindu* reported that "Om Prakash, facing trial for a triple murder and a spate of dacoities, was alleged by police to have bludgeoned Seenu to death with a ce-

ment dumb-bell when the latter was asleep. Seenu (38), second accused in the murder of Paritala Ravi, sustained grievous injuries on the right side of his face and head. He was taken to the Government General Hospital where he was declared brought dead." B. Chandrashekhar, "Moddu Seenu Done to Death in Anantapur Jail," *The Hindu*. November 10, 2008, updated October 9, 2016, http://www.thehindu.com/todays-paper/Moddu-Seenu-done-to-death-in-Anantapur-jail/article15338906.ece.

38. Bhanu Kiran is now in Cherlapally Prison in Anantapur along with Om Prakash (the man who reputedly killed Moddu Seenu). Staff Reporter, "Bhanu Kiran Fears Threat to Life in Prison," *The Hindu* (Hyderabad), May 23, 2012, http://www.thehindu.com/news/national/andhra-pradesh/bhanu-kiran-fears-threat-to-life-in-prison/article3344735.ece. See also Santosh Kumar RB, "Andhra Cops Nab Muddelacheruvu Suri Aide in Bangalore," DNA, January 9, 2011, http://www.dnaindia.com/bangalore/report-andhra-cops-nab-muddelacheruvu-suri-aide-in-bangalore-1492163.

39. Staff Reporter, "Acrimonious Debate over Paritala Killing," *The Hindu*, February 23, 2005, http://www.thehindu.com/2005/02/24/stories/2005022410430400.htm.

40. Mohiuddin (2007: 156).

41. "Jaganmohan Protests Innocence," *The Hindu*, January 26, 2005, http://www.thehindu.com/2005/01/26/stories/2005012605400400.htm.

42. "The CBI document leaked to the media, apparently by anti-Jagan forces within the Congress, relates to the interrogation of Dantuluri Krishna alias Mangali Krishna in the Ravi murder case. According to 'information' gathered by the CBI, Krishna was Jagan's neighbour and 'front man' in his stronghold Pulivendula. This document prepared on April 17, 2005, by CBI's investigating officer V. T. Nandakumar apparently exposes the nexus between Jagan and Ravi's killers." See A. Srinivisa Rao, "CBI Note Links Jaganmohan Reddy to MLA Paritala Ravi's Murder," *India Today*, January 23, 2011, http://indiatoday.intoday.in/story/cbi-note-links-jaganmohan-reddy-in-mla-murder-plot/1/128233.html. See also A. Srinivasa Rao, "Calls Grow for Probe against Jagan after His Close Aide Is Convicted in Attempt to Murder Case," *India Today*, April 25, 2012, http://indiatoday.intoday.in/story/jagan-ysr-congress-party-attempted-murder-tdp-mla/1/186026.html.

43. "All about Paritala Ravi Case," *AP Today*, August 21, 2014, http://www.aptoday.com/newsnpolitics/all-about-paritala-ravi-case/2496/.

44. Hoskote Nagabhushanam, "Twists and Turns in Paritala Case," *Times of India*, August 26, 2011, http://timesofindia.indiatimes.com/city/hyderabad/Twists-turns-in-Paritala-case/articleshow/9739594.cms.

45. This document is biased toward the TDP. See "If a Factionist Becomes Chief Minister?"

46. Telugu Desam Party (2014: 21).

47. She won a by-election on June 2, 2005, defeating the Congress nominee by a margin of more than eighteen thousand votes.

48. Staff Reporter, "Will Reopen Paritala Ravi Murder Case: Paritala Sunitha,"

Times of India (Hyderabad), June 9, 2014, http://timesofindia.indiatimes.com/city/hyderabad/Will-reopen-Paritala-Ravi-murder-case-Paritala-Sunitha/articleshow/36266112.cms. See also "All about Paritala Ravi Case."

49. "Paritala's Widow Says Jagan Was behind Hubby's Killing," *Deccan Herald*, May 30, 2012, http://www.deccanherald.com/content/253354/paritalas-widow-says-jagan-behind.html.

50. Telugu Desam Party (2014: 21).

51. "Paritala Sunita Miffed as Diwakar Reddy Joins TDP," *Indian Express* (Hyderabad), March 24, 2014, http://www.newindianexpress.com/states/andhra_pradesh/Paritala-Sunita-Miffed-as-Diwakar-Reddy-Joins-TDP/2014/03/24/article2127004.ece.

52. "Jaganmohan's Arrest Political Vendetta: BJP," *Times of India*, May 28, 2012, http://timesofindia.indiatimes.com/india/Jaganmohans-arrest-political-vendetta-BJP/articleshow/13607493.cms?referral=PM.

53. "Paritala Murder Case for CBI," *The Hindu*, January 26, 2005, http://www.thehindu.com/2005/01/26/stories/2005012609080100.htm.

54. "Paritala Ravanna Exclusive Video," April 24, 2008, https://www.youtube.com/watch?v=8WHLN-pS-KY.

55. "Paritala Samithi to Conduct Mass Marriages for Poor," *The Hindu*, January 24, 2006, http://www.thehindu.com/todays-paper/tp-national/tp-andhrapradesh/paritala-samithi-to-conduct-mass-marriages-for-poor/article3244146.ece.

56. Footage of some of the events can be seen on YouTube. See, for example, "Paritala Ravindra 10th Anniversary at Paritala Ghat in Venkatapuram Village," January 24, 2015, https://www.youtube.com/watch?v=eO4gMhtJ1S4.

57. "Paritala Ravi's Wax Statue Attracts Fans," January 23, 2012, https://www.youtube.com/watch?v=VmEiwQm8eU4 [site discontinued].

58. "My Edited Video," January 23, 2012, www.youtube.com/watch?v=fH2C2YJN7q4. *See also "6th Anniversary—London," accessed February 29, 2016,* http://www.paritalaravi.com/6th-anniversary-gallery-london.html.

59. "Blood Donations and Libraries to the Remembrance of Paritala Ravi @Anantapur," November 23, 2014, https://www.youtube.com/watch?v=IQrQ_S8vDuQ.

60. "Mass Marriages 2010," accessed February 29, 2016, http://www.paritalaravi.com/mass-marriages-gallery.html.

61. "7th Anniversary," accessed February 29, 2016, http://www.paritalaravi.com/7th-anniversary-gallery.html.

62. P. I. Rajeev, "In Andhra's Samurai Country, Ravi Was Always a Cut Above," *Indian Express*, January 31, 2005, http://archive.indianexpress.com/oldStory/63765/.

63. Ibid.

64. Price (2006: 305).

65. The KYSS website lists a series of rapes, murders, and bombings committed by the Reddy faction (it is a pro-TDP website). Several of the criminal cases against Paritala Ravi also refer to this period. See "Paritala Ravi: Bio-Data."

66. B. K. Parthasarathi, interview with author, March 19, 2015.

67. Mohiuddin (2007).

68. Cited from a Paritala Ravi blog, "He Is Not Dead!!!! He Will Be Back!!!!," October 20, 2007, http://paritalaravi.blogspot.co.uk/2007/10/andhra-tiger.html.

69. "Paritala Ravi Bio-Data."

70. "Paritala Ravanna Exclusive Video."

71. Interview with informant, January 2015.

72. "Development and Social Service in Penukonda," *Eenadu*, cited in Herrenschmidt (2009: 18).

73. "Paritala Ravi: Bio-Data," Facebook, December 26, 2011, https://www.facebook.com/permalink.php?story_fbid=216391985107438&id=101849136561724.

74. "Mass Marriages of 350 Couples on June 2," *The Hindu*, May 31, 2010, http://www.thehindu.com/todays-paper/tp-national/tp-andhrapradesh/mass-marriages-of-350-couples-on-june-2/article776658.ece. Mass marriages have a history in Andhra Pradesh and continue today. They are performed by temples and religious organizations and state departments that deal with provisions for Scheduled Castes, Scheduled Tribes, and/or charities. Some of these may be ideological events (e.g., intercaste mass marriages), others may be to promote religious tradition, and others are about providing to the poor. Most often, particular leaders will be the sponsors of such events or associated with them. For example, the chief minister in conjunction with the Tirumala Tirupathi Devasthanam married sixty-four couples in 2014, and Paritala Sunita and TDP officials conducted a mass marriage event in 2010. See "Mass Marriages 2010."

75. "Mass Marriage Organised," *The Hindu*, June 3, 2010, http://www.thehindu.com/todays-paper/tp-national/tp-andhrapradesh/mass-marriage-organised/article480228.ece.

76. Still (2014a: 53).

77. "Development and Social Service in Penukonda," cited in Herrenschmidt (2009: 18).

78. I am grateful to Srinivas Dusi (pers. comm.).

79. B. K. Parthasarathi, MLA, interview with Srinivas Dusi, the author's research associate, using the author's interview schedule, March 19, 2015. He added, however, that "he was not the kind of person who came into politics to make money."

80. "Top Stories" and "Headlines," *Hyderabad Times*, accessed February 24, 2016, http://thehyderabadtimes.blogspot.co.uk/2010/01/special-story-paritala-ravindra.html.

81. Balagopal (2001: 1285–86).

82. Ibid.: 1286.

83. "Mining Scam: Jagan Reddy Appears before CBI: Party Workers Protest," NDTV, November 4, 2011, http://www.ndtv.com/india-news/mining-scam-jagan-reddy-appears-before-cbi-party-workers-protest-565995.

84. The document by Telugu Desam alleges, "In 1982, the State government nationalized the mining of barite and acquired all *patta* [legally owned] lands of Man-

gampet and handed over to the AP Mineral Development Corporation. Using political clout YSR could take about 2 acres of land on sub-lease. Besides taking of mining in the sub-leased area he also started illicit mining in APMDC area as well and went further to dig up a Geological Monument, which was declared as protected area by archaeological department. By the time the government swung into action and stopped this illegal mining, YSR's baryte company had already dug up the archaeological monument. According to the official estimates (K. V. Natarajan Commission) . . . around 1.5 lakh tons of barite ore, each ton costing Rs. 600, had been illegally excavated. YSR set his eyes on the land of one Mr. Vivekanandam, who had 1.8 acres, and grabbed that land using his political influence and got the sub-lease on his company's name. Aggrieved by this, Vivekanandam moved to the High Court and got stay order but he earned the wrath of YSR subsequently. In revenge, Rajashekhara Reddy's men waylaid and assaulted Rajagopal, uncle of Vivekanandam at a hotel near Abids in Hyderabad. Though Vivekanandam could get back his piece of land finally, YSR's company had already dug up entire barytes ore available in the land, worth Rs. 5 crore (Cr.No.54/92)." See "If a Factionist Becomes Chief Minister."

85. Parthasarathi (1997: 14).

86. Balagopal (2001: 1285).

87. Blok (1974: 6).

88. Sidel (1999a: 93).

89. Sidel (1999b: 93) (emphasis added).

90. Balagopal (2001: 1286).

CONCLUSION

1. Barker, Harms, and Lindquist (2014: 1).

2. Ibid.: 2.

3. Recent anthropological debates had called for "bring[ing] back ambivalent statements, contradictory attitudes, incompatible values, and emotional internal clashes as research objects" (Berliner 2016: 5).

4. See Michelutti (2017).

5. Weber (1978a) presented an image of a strongman who is likely to arouse the feeling of charisma. However, "the process of arousal of charisma is not his concern" (Sennett 1980: 7).

6. On this point, see also Dasgupta (2014).

7. Hariman (1995); West and Orman (2003); Brummett (2008); Lempert and Silverstein (2012); Duffy and Page (2013); Wheeler (2013).

8. De la Fuente and Murthy (2014). On "aesthetic styles" as an integral part of sociality, see Simmel (1968).

9. Blok (1974: 38).

10. Certeau (1984: 37).

11. Douglas (1966). Similarly, Hansen and Verkaaik point out that informal sovereigns, "urban types," are "akin to the traditional healer or diviner who interprets a dangerous and powerful natural world but violates taboos in order to do so. A power-

ful charismatic figure is also allowed to break taboos as long as he/she can perform the key function of interpreting the present and giving a direction amidst an unknowable and ostensibly dangerous environment" (2009: 8).

12. Benjamin ([1927] 2002).

13. See Hansen and Verkaaik (2009) on the charisma and mythologies of the city.

14. Barker, Harms, and Lindquist (2014: 17).

15. Saviano (2015: 10).

16. Ibid.

17. Sennett (1980).

18. For a detailed discussion of "lords," see Price and Ruud (2010: introduction).

19. In South Asia, paternalistic forms of authority are associated with the concept of *seva*, which evokes principles of selflessness and sacrifice that starkly contrast with the image of the power-seeking violent entrepreneur boss (see Ciotti 2012; Piliavsky 2014).

20. These relations are mostly understood and described in a positive light. Although Michelutti (2014a) describes the ambiguities inherent in the practices of protection, they not only run through the Goonda Raj and shape the rule (and the lives) of the dominant and nondominant castes but also, she suggests, are inherent to everyday family life.

21. Jeffrey (2010). On pluralistic moral values, see also Parry (2000); Ruud (2000); Gooptu (2007).

22. Similar patterns of gift giving have been recorded in Calabrian mafia territories by Pipyrou (2014: 412).

23. Ibid.: 423.

24. On South Asian masculinities, see Osella and Osella (2006); see also Sen (2011).

25. Michelutti (2013).

26. See Michelutti (2010: 46); Witsoe (2011); Berenschot (2011).

27. Kakar (1996: 82).

28. Alter (1997); Peabody (2009); Frembgen and Rollier (2014); Rollier (2014).

29. Van Schendel (2009: 252–53).

30. Witsoe (2009: 65–66).

31. Varese (2011b: 81).

32. Babb (1970); Bachetta (1996: 147).

33. On dynastic politics, see Richter (1990); Malhotra (2003); Skoda (2004); French (2011).

34. Bachetta (1996: 150). For more on gender, power, and women in the Hindu Right, see Sarkar and Butalia (1995); Jeffrey and Basu (2012).

35. Jayawardena and de Alwis (1996); Menon and Bhasin (1998); Menon (2010); Lama (2001).

36. On women who use muscle in India, see Sen (2007a, 2007b). On the blurring of femininity and masculinity archetypes, see Ciotti (2017).

37. Gambetta (2009: 34).

38. Volkov (2002: 45).

39. Chanakya is known as the Indian Machiavelli. In *Politics as a Vocation* Weber famously wrote that the true radical realpolitik "is classically expressed in Indian literature in the *Arthashastra* of Kautilya (written long before the birth of Christ, ostensibly in the time of Chandragupta (Maurya)." Weber added, "Compared to it, Machiavelli's *The Prince* is harmless" (Weber 1978b: 220).

40. Lollywood produced a plethora of low-budget action movies intended for a lower-class male audience that presented a particularly vivid articulation of class with Punjabi identity and language. See Rollier (2014).

41. Gambetta (2009: 210).

42. Ibid.

43. See Richard Esposito, "Contact with Hollywood Producer May Have Helped Snare Chapo Guzman," NBC Universal, January 9, 2016, https://www.nbcnews.com/news/us-news/contact-hollywood-producer-may-have-helped-snare-chapo-guzman-n493416.

44. Jaffrelot (2002: 92).

45. See http://elegalix.allahabadhighcourt.in/elegalix/WebShowJudgment.do?judgmentID=52540 (accessed December 1, 2015).

46. Ibid.

47. See Blackburn (1985); Blackburn et al. (1989); Coccari (1989).

48. Fuller (1992: 3).

49. Politicians are never deified in Bangladesh or Pakistan. Their association is temporal, profane, and therefore besmirched by the cynical material world. This is the case even among the Islamists who are motivated by the Prophet's "ideal community" in Medina but concede that it can never be replicated due to the corruptibility of humans. Generally, however, politics is seen as a game for scoundrels, not gods. Successful politicians are not seen as divine agents but competent ones and sometime as heroes.

50. "Uttar Pradesh: Real Life 'Khalnayak' Places Bottle on Victim's Head and Takes Gunshots," YouTube, July 16, 2005, https://www.youtube.com/watch?v=rf7u5Sp7nes.

51. On "myth scripting," see Michelutti and Picherit (2015).

52. See Newell (2012).

53. Srinivas (2013).

54. Hansen (2001) discusses the politics of presence of the Shiv Sena in Mumbai.

55. See Pine (2012: 12–15) on "affective atmosphere" created by the Camorra in Naples.

56. Kaur and Hansen (2016). See also Rancière (1999).

57. Hansen and Stepputat (2005: 4).

58. Picherit (2016).

59. According to Migdal (1988) local strongmen effectively capture parts of their postcolonial states and flourish in societies that host a melange of fairly autonomous social organizations (web societies) and where social control is effectively fragmented.

Local bosses are portrayed as occupying the legitimate role of patrons or responding to patrons who protect them Sidel (1999).

60. Falcone and Padovani (1993: 81).

61. Gambetta (1988: 163–64).

62. Schneider and Schneider (2011: 10).

63. Strathern (2012: 401).

64. Tilly (1985: 170–71).

65. Gambetta (1988: 170).

66. Catanzaro (1992).

67. "This includes relationships that begin with a reciprocal exchange but evolve into something coercive: at first recipients pay up willingly but increasingly they do so because they fear reprisals (even if this fear is not admitted)" (Schneider and Schneider 2011: 12). On extortion/protection, see also Pine (2012).

68. Gayer (2014); Martin and Michelutti (2017).

69. See the discussion about the Bangladesh henchman (bully) in Ruud (2014).

70. Jaffe (2013: 736) makes a similar point discussing donmanship in inner-city Kingston, Jamaica.

71. Vaishnav (2017: 22).

72. Varma (2004: 7).

73. Briquet and Favarel-Garrigues (2010: 2).

74. Wilkinson (2004); see also Heath (2016).

75. Aidt, Golden, and Tiwari (2015).

76. Vaishnav (2017).

77. See Martin and Michelutti (2017).

78. We can also think of many Islamist militant groups in Pakistan that are certainly violent entrepreneurs but do not seek to pursue a political career (TTP, etc.) since they refuse to play the democracy game. Likewise, in India, the Naxalites practice extortion but do not participate in electoral politics. It is the same for the Liberation Tigers of Tamil Eelam (LTTE), apart from a short period during which they contested elections.

79. Gayer (2014: chap. 4).

80. Weber (1978a).

81. See Gayer (2014).

82. Hansen and Stepputat (2005: 3).

83. Weber (1978a); Hansen and Verkaaik (2009).

84. Hoffman and Kirk (2013: 2).

85. See "Tipu Truckanawala Murder Accused Escapes from Court," *International News*, June 22, 2010, https://www.thenews.com.pk/archive/print/244017-tipu-truckanwala-murder-accused-escapes-from-court.

REFERENCES

Abbate, L., and M. Lillo. 2015. *I re di Roma: Destra e sinistra agli ordini di Mafia Capitale.* Rome: Chiarilettere.

Abrams, P. 1988. "Notes on the Difficulty of Studying the State." *Journal of Historical Sociology* 1 (1): 58–89.

Adnan, S. 2013. "Land Grabs and Primitive Accumulation in Deltaic Bangladesh: Interactions between Neoliberal Globalization, State Interventions, Power Relations and Peasant Resistance." *Journal of Peasant Studies* 40 (1): 87–128.

Agamben, G. 1998. *Homo Sacer: Sovereignty and Bare Life.* Stanford, CA: Stanford University Press.

———. 2005. *State of Exception.* Chicago: University of Chicago Press.

Ahmed, M. 1984. *Bangladesh: Era of Sheikh Mujibur Rahman.* Wiesbaden: Franz Steiner Verlag Wiesbaden gmbh.

Ahmed, S. 1992. "The Cinema as Metaphor for Indian Society and Politics." *Modern Asian Studies* 26 (2): 289–320.

Aidt, T., M. Golden, and D. Tiwari. 2015. "Criminality in the National Indian Legislature." Working Paper.

Akram, Shahzada M., and Shadhan Kumar Das. 2009. *Tracking the National Election Process: Executive Summary.* Transparency International Bangladesh, April. www.ti-bangladesh.org/beta3/images/max_file/rp_es_EPT_Final_en.pdf.

Alter, J. S. 1997. *The Wrestler's Body: Identity and Ideology in North India.* Delhi: Munshiram Manoharlal.

Amin-Khan, T. 2012. *The Post-colonial State in the Era of Capitalist Globalization: Historical, Political and Theoretical Approaches to State Formation.* New York: Routledge.

Andersen, M. K. 2013. "The Politics of Politics: Youth Mobilization, Aspirations and the Threat of Violence at Dhaka University." PhD diss., Roskilde University.

Aretxaga, B. 2002. "Terror as Thrill: First Thoughts on the 'War on Terrorism.'" *Anthropological Quarterly* 75 (1): 139–50.

———. 2003. "Maddening States." *Annual Review of Anthropology* 32 (1): 393–410.

Arias, E. D. 2006. "The Dynamics of Criminal Governance: Networks and Social Order in Rio de Janeiro." *Journal of Latin American Studies* 38 (2): 293–310.

———. 2016. *Criminal Enterprises and Governance in Latin America and the Caribbean.* Cambridge: Cambridge University Press.

Arlacchi, P. 1993. *Men of Dishonor: Inside the Sicilian Mafia.* New York: William Morrow.

Armao, F. 2000. *Il sistema Mafia: Dall'economia-mondo al dominio locale.* Torino: Bollati Boringhieri.

———. 2015. "Mafia-Owned Democracies: Italy and Mexico as Patterns of Criminal Neoliberalism." *Revista de Historia Actual* 1:4–21.

Assayag, J. 2006. "'Sur les chasses du temps': Histoire et anthropologie chez Eric J. Hobsbawm." *Revue d'Histoire Moderne et Contemporaine* 53–54:100–113.

Auyero, J. 2007. *Routine Politics and Violence in Argentina: The Grey Zone of State Power.* New York: Cambridge University Press.

Babb, L. 1970. "Marriage and Malevolence: The Uses of Sexual Opposition in a Hindu Pantheon." *Ethnology* 9 (2): 137–48.

Bachetta, P. 1996. "Hindu Nationalist Women as Ideologues: The Sangh, the Samiti and Their Differential Concepts of the Hindu Nation." In *Embodied Violence: Communalizing Women's Sexuality in South Asia*, edited by K. Jayawardena and M. de Alwis, 126–67. New Delhi: Kali for Women.

Balagopal, K. 2001. "A Tough Law for Other People's Crime." *Economic and Political Weekly* 36 (1): 1285–89.

———. 2007. "Land Unrest in Andhra Pradesh-II: Impact of Grants to Industries." *Economic and Political Weekly* 42 (39): 3906–11.

Bandyopadhyay, S. 2011. "Rich States, Poor States: Convergence and Polarisation across Indian States." *Scottish Journal of Political Economy* 57 (3): 414–36.

———. 2012. "Convergence Club Empirics: Evidence from Indian States." *Research in Economic Inequality* 20:175–203.

Banerjee, A., and R. Pande. 2007. "Parochial Politics: Ethnic Preferences and Politician Corruption." KSG Working Paper No. RWP07-031. *SSRN Electronic Journal.* http://ssrn.com/abstract=976548.

Banerjee, A., and T. Piketty. 2005. "Top Indian Incomes, 1922–2000." *World Bank Economic Review* 19:1–20.

———. 2011. *Divided We Stand: Why Inequality Keeps Rising.* Washington, DC: OECD Publishing.

Banerjee, M. 2014. *Why India Votes?* Delhi: Routledge.

Banfield, E., and J. Wilson. 1965. *City Politics.* Cambridge: Cambridge University Press.

Bardhan, P. 1984. *Political Economy of Development in India.* Delhi: Oxford University Press.

———. 1988. "The Dominant Proprietary Classes and India's Democracy." In *India's Democracy: An Analysis of Changing State Society Relations*, edited by A. Kohli, 214–24. Princeton, NJ: Princeton University Press.

Barker, J., E. Harms, and J. Lindquist. 2014. *Figures of Southeast Asian Modernity.* Honolulu: University of Hawaii Press.

Barrow-Giles, C. 2011. "Democracy at Work: A Comparative Study of the Caribbean State." *Round Table* 100 (414): 285–302.

Baudrillard, J. (1981) 1994. *Simulacra and Simulation.* Translated by Sheila Glaser. Reprint, Ann Arbor: University of Michigan Press.

Bayart, J. 2004. "Le crime transnational et la formation de l'état." *Politique Africaine* 93 (2004): 93–104.

Bayart, J., S. Ellis, and B. Hibou. 1999. *The Criminalization of the State in Africa*. London: International African Institute.

Bear, L. 2011. "Speculative State Planning, Informality, and Neoliberal Governance on the Hooghly." *Focaal—Journal of Global and Historical Anthropology* 61:46–60.

———. 2015. *Navigating Austerity. Currents of Debt along the South Asian River*. Stanford, CA: Stanford University Press.

Benjamin, Walter. (1927) 2002. *The Arcades Project*. Reprint, Cambridge, MA: Harvard University Press.

Berenschot, W. 2011. "On the Usefulness of *Goondas* in Indian Politics: 'Moneypower' and 'Musclepower' in a Gujarati Locality." *South Asia: Journal of South Asian Studies* 34 (2): 255–75.

———. 2014. "Muzaffarnagar Riots: Perils of a Patronage Democracy." *Economic and Political Weekly* 49 (12): 15–18.

Berliner, D. 2016. "Anthropology and the Study of Contradictions." *Hau: Journal of Ethnographic Theory* 6 (1): 1–27.

Birtchnell, T. 2011. "*Jugaad* as Systemic Risk and Disruptive Innovation in India." *Contemporary South Asia* 19 (4): 357–72.

Blackburn, S. H. 1985. "Death and Deification: Folk Cults in Hinduism." *History of Religion* 3:255–74.

Blackburn, S. H., P. J. Claus, J. B. Flueckiger, and S. Wadley, eds. 1989. *Oral Epics in India*. Berkeley: University of California Press.

Blok, A. 1972. "The Peasant and the Brigand: Social Banditry Reconsidered." *Comparative Studies in Society and History* 14 (4): 494–510.

———. 1974. *The Mafia of a Sicilian Village, 1860–1960: A Study of Violent Peasant Entrepreneurs*. New York: Harper and Row.

Blom, A. 2011. *Pakistan: Coercion and Capital in an Insecurity State*. Paris Papers, No. 1. Paris: IRSEM. https://www.defense.gouv.fr/content/download/153081/1551240/file/Paris_paper_1.pdf.

Bourgois, P. 1995. *In Search of Respect: Selling Crack in el Barrio*. Cambridge: Cambridge University Press.

BRAC. 2006. *The State of Governance in Bangladesh: Knowledge, Perceptions, Reality*. Centre for Governance Studies. http://dspace.bracu.ac.bd/bitstream/handle/10361/578/?sequence=1.

Brass, P. 1997. *Theft of an Idol: Text and Context in the Representation of Collective Violence*. Princeton, NJ: Princeton University Press.

———. 2003. *The Production of Hindu-Muslim Violence in Contemporary India*. Seattle: University of Washington Press.

———. 2006. "Corruption and Anti-corruption on the Eve of Indian Independence." Paper presented at the Annual Conference on South Asia, University of Wisconsin, Madison, October 19–22. http://www.paulbrass.com/corruption_and_anti_corruption_on_the_eve_of_indian_independence_56373.htm.

———. 2011. *The Politics of Northern India: 1937 to 1987.* Vol. 1, *An Indian Political Life: Charan Singh and Congress Politics, 1937 to 1961.* Delhi: Sage.

Breman, J. 1974. *Patronage and Exploitation: Changing Agrarian Relations in South Gujarat, India.* Berkeley: University of California Press.

———. 2009. "The Great Transformation in the Setting of Asia." Address presented on the 57th anniversary of the International Institute of Social Studies, The Hague, Netherlands, October 29.

Briquet, J., and G. Favarel-Garrigues. 2010. *Organized Crime and States.* New York: Palgrave Macmillan.

Brummett, B. 2008. *A Rhetoric of Style.* Carbondale: Southern Illinois University Press.

Buur, L., and S. Jensen. 2004. "Introduction: Vigilantism and the Policing of Everyday Life in South Africa." *African Studies* 63 (2): 139–52.

Carswell, G., and G. De Neve. 2015. "Litigation against Political Organization? The Politics of Dalit Mobilization in Tamil Nadu, India." *Development and Change* 46 (5): 1106–32.

Catanzaro, R. 1988. *Men of Respect: A Social History of the Sicilian Mafia.* New York: Free Press.

Centre for the Study of Developing Societies (CSDS). 2008. *State of Democracy in South Asia: A Report.* New Delhi: Oxford University Press.

Certeau, M. de. 1984. *The Practice of Everyday Life.* Berkeley: University of California Press.

Chakrabarty, D. 2000. *Provincializing Europe.* Princeton, NJ: Princeton University Press.

Chandra, K. 2004. *Why Ethnic Parties Succeed.* Cambridge: Cambridge University Press.

———. 2015. "The New Indian State: The Relocation of Patronage in the Post-liberalisation Economy." *Economic and Political Weekly* 1 (41): 46–58.

Chatterjee, P. 2004. *The Politics of the Governed: Reflections on Popular Politics in Most of the World."* New York: Columbia University Press.

Chaudhary, M. 1999. *Justice in Practice: Legal Ethnography of a Pakistani Punjabi Village.* Karachi: Oxford University Press.

Chaudhry, A. G. 2015. "Power Structure and Manipulative Strategies in Development Projects: A Case Study of a Punjabi Village of District Sheikhupura." *The Explorer* 1 (5): 165–78.

Cheema, M. H. 2012. "Beyond Beliefs: Deconstructing the Dominant Narratives of the Islamization of Pakistan's Law." *American Journal of Comparative Law* 60 (4): 875–917.

Chu, Y. K. 2000. *The Triads as Business.* London: Routledge.

Chubb, J. 1996. "The Mafia, the Market and the State in Italy and Russia." *Journal of Modern Italian Studies* 1 (2): 273–91.

Ciotti, M. 2012. "Resurrecting *Seva* (Social Service): Dalit and Low-Caste Women

Party Activists as Producers and Consumers of Political Culture and Practice in Urban North India." *Journal of Asian Studies* 71 (1): 149–70.

———, ed. 2017. *Unsettling the Archetypes. Femininities and Masculinities in Indian Politics*. New Delhi: Women Unlimited.

Civico, A. 2015. *The Para-state: An Ethnography of Colombia's Death Squads*. Berkeley: University of California Press.

Coccari, D. 1989. "The Bir Babas of Benares and the Deified Dead." In *Criminal Gods and Demon Devotees: Essays on the Guardians of Popular Hinduism*, edited by A. Hiltebeitel, 251–69. Albany: State University of New York Press.

Comaroff, J., and J. Comaroff. 2000. "Millennial Capitalism: First Thoughts on a Second Coming." *Public Culture* 12 (2): 291–343.

———. 2006. *Law and Disorder in the Postcolony*. Chicago: University of Chicago Press.

Corbridge, S. 2010. "The Political Economy of India since Independence." In The Routledge *Handbook of South Asian Politics*, edited by Paul Brass, 313–36. London: Routledge,

Corbridge, S., J. Harris, and C. Jeffrey, eds. 2013. *India Today: Economy, Politics and Society*. Cambridge: Polity Press.

Corbridge, S., and A. Shah. 2013. "Introduction: The Underbelly of the Indian Boom." *Economy and Society* 42 (3): 335–47.

Corbridge, S., W. Srivastava, and R. Veron. 2005. *Seeing the State: Governance and Governmentality in India*. Cambridge: Cambridge University Press.

Daechsel, M. 2003. "Zalim Daku and the Mystery of the Rubber Sea Monster." *Journal of the Royal Asiatic Society* 13 (1): 21–43.

Dahl, R. 1957. "The Concept of Power." *Systems Research and Behavioural Science* 2:201–5.

Das, S. 1994. "The 'Goondas': Towards a Reconstruction of the Calcutta Underworld through Police Records." *Economic and Political Weekly* 29 (44): 2877–83.

Das, V. 2007. *Life and Words: Violence and the Descent into the Ordinary*. Berkeley: University of California Press.

Das, V., and D. Poole, eds. 2004. *Anthropology in the Margins of the State*. Santa Fe, NM: School of American Research Press.

Dasgupta, R. 2014. *Capital: The Eruption of Delhi*. Delhi: Penguin Press.

Davis, D. 2010. "Irregular Armed Forces, Shifting Patterns of Commitment, and Fragmented Sovereignty in the Developing World." *Theory and Society* 39 (3–4): 397–413.

Davis, J., and A. Blok. 1974. "The Mafia of a Sicilian Village 1860–1960: A Study of Violent Peasant Entrepreneurs." *RAIN* 5:8.

De la Fuente, E. 2000. "Sociology and Aesthetics." *European Journal of Social Theory* 3 (2): 235–48.

De la Fuente, E., and P. Murthy, 2014. *Aesthetic Capitalism*. Leiden, Netherlands: Brill.

De Neve, G. 2015. "Predatory Property: Urban Land Acquisition, Housing and Class Formation in Tiruppur, South India." *Journal of South Asian Development* 10 (3): 345–68.

Deleuze, G., and G. Félix. 1988. *A Thousand Plateaus*. Minneapolis: University of Minnesota Press.

Dickie, J. 2011. *Blood Brotherhoods: The Rise of the Italian Mafias*. London: Sceptre.

Douglas, M. 1966. *Purity and Danger: An Analysis of Concepts of Pollution and Taboo*. London: Routledge.

Dreze, J., and R. Khera. 2000. "Crime, Gender, and Society in India: Insights from Homicide." *Population and Development Review* 26 (2): 335–52.

Dreze, J., and A. Sen. 2013. *An Uncertain Glory: India and Its Contradictions*. Princeton, NJ: Princeton University Press.

Duarte, F. 2006. "A Double-Edged Sword: The 'Jeitinho' as an Ambiguous Concept in the Brazilian Imaginary." *International Journal of Interdisciplinary Social Sciences* 1 (1): 125–31.

Duffy, M. E., and J. T. Page. 2013. "Does Political Humor Matter? You Betcha! Comedy TV'S Performance of the 2008 Vice Presidential Debate." *Journal of Popular Culture* 46 (3): 545–65.

Dumont, L. (1970) 1980. Homo hierarchicus*: The Caste System and Its Implications*. Reprint, Chicago: University of Chicago Press.

Dwivedi, A., and L. Lau. 2014. *Indian Writing in English and the Global Literary Market*. London: Palgrave Macmillan.

Eckert, J. 2003. *The Charisma of Direct Action*. New Delhi: Oxford University Press.

Edberg, M. K. 2004. *El narcotraficante: Narcocorridos and the Construction of a Cultural Persona on the U.S.-Mexican Border*. Austin: University of Texas Press.

Eglar, Z. 1960. *A Punjabi Village in Pakistan*. New York: Columbia University Press.

Elias, N. 1982. *The Civilizing Process*. Vol. 1, *The History of Manners*. Translated by Edmund Jephcott. New York: Pantheon Books.

Elyachar, J. 2005. *Markets of Dispossession*. Durham, NC: Duke University Press.

Evans P., D. Rueschemeyer, and T. Skocpol, eds. 1985. *Bringing the State Back In*. Cambridge: University of Cambridge Press.

Falcone, G., and M. Padovani. 1993. *Men of Honour*. London: Warner.

Favarel-Garrigues, G., and L. Gayer. 2016. "Violer la loi pour maintenir l'ordre: Le vigilantisme en débat." *Politix* 29 (115): 7–33.

Ferguson, J. 2013. "Declarations of Dependence: Labour, Personhood, and Welfare in Southern Africa." *Journal of the Royal Anthropological Institute*, n.s., 19 (2): 223–42.

Fernandes, L. 2004. "The Politics of Forgetting: Class Politics, State Power and the Restructuring of Urban Space in India." *Urban Studies* 41 (12): 2415–30.

———. 2006. *India's New Middle Class: Democratic Politics in an Era of Economic Reform*. Minneapolis: University of Minnesota Press.

Fischer, M. D. 1991. "Marriage and Power: Tradition and Transition in an Urban Punjabi Community." In *Economy and Culture in Pakistan: Migrants and Cities in a*

Muslim Society, edited by H. Donnan and P. Werbner, 97–123. Basingstoke, UK: Macmillan.

Forbess, A., and L. Michelutti. 2013. "From the Mouth of God: Divine Kinship in Contemporary Popular Politics." *Focaal—Journal of Historical and Global Anthropology* 67 (Winter): 3–18.

Foucault, M. 1991. "Governmentality." In *The Foucault Effect: Studies in Governmentality*, edited by G. Burchell, C. Gordon, and P. Mille, 87–104. London: Harvester/Wheatsheaf.

Frembgen, J., and P. Rollier. 2014. *Wrestlers, Pigeon Fanciers, and Kite Flyers: Traditional Sports and Pastimes in Lahore*. Karachi: Oxford University Press.

French, P. 2011. *India: A Portrait*. New Delhi: Penguin.

Fuller, C. 1992. *The Camphor Flame: Popular Hinduism and Society in India*. Princeton, NJ: Princeton University Press.

Fuller, C., and J. Harriss. 2001. "Introduction." In *The Everyday State and Society in Modern India*, edited by C. J. Fuller and V. Bénéï, 1–27. London: Hurst.

Gambetta, D. 1988. "Mafia: The Price of Distrust." In *Trust: Making and Breaking Cooperative Relations*, edited by D. Gambetta, 158–75. Oxford: Basil Blackwell.

———. 1993. *The Sicilian Mafia: The Business of Private Protection*. Cambridge, MA: Harvard University Press.

———. 2009. *Codes of the Underworld: How Criminals Communicate*. Princeton, NJ: Princeton University Press.

Gardner, K. 1995. *Global Migrants, Local Lives: Travel and Transformation in Rural Bangladesh*. Oxford Studies in Social and Cultural Anthropology. Oxford: Clarendon Press.

———. 2012. *Discordant Development: Global Capitalism and the Struggle for Connection in Bangladesh*. London: Pluto Press.

Gayer, L. 2014. *Karachi: Ordered Disorder and the Struggle for the City*. London: Hurst.

Gellner, D. 2008. *Local Democracy in South Asia: Microprocesses of Democratization in Nepal and Its Neighbours*. New Delhi: Sage.

Gill, S. S. 2013. "Gun Culture in Punjab." *Economic and Political Weekly* 48 (8): 16–18.

———. 2014. "Changing Economic Structure, Emergence of New Political Class and Elections in Punjab." Unpublished manuscript.

Gilsenan, M. 1977. "Against Patron-Client Relations." In *Patrons and Clients in Mediterranean Societies*, edited by E. Gellner and J. Waterbury, 167–84. London: Duckworth.

Gingrich, A., and R. Fox, eds. 2002. *Anthropology by Comparison*. London: Routledge.

Gledhill, J. 2000. *Power and Its Disguises*. London: Pluto Press.

———. 2009. "Power in Political Anthropology." *Journal of Power* 2 (1): 9–34.

Godelier, M., and M. Strathern. 1991. *Big Men and Great Men*. Cambridge: Cambridge University Press.

Goffman, E. 1959. *The Presentation of Self in Everyday Life.* Garden City, NY: Doubleday.

Goldstein, D. M., and E. D. Arias, eds. 2010. *Violent Democracies in Latin America.* Durham, NC: Duke University Press.

Gooptu, N. 2001. *The Politics of the Urban Poor in Early Twentieth-Century India.* Cambridge: Cambridge University Press.

———. 2007. "Economic Liberalisation, Work and Democracy: Industrial Decline and Urban Politics in Kolkata." *Economic and Political Weekly* 42 (21): 1922–33.

Gooptu, N., and J. Parry. 2014. *Persistence of Poverty in India*. Delhi: Orient and Black Swan.

Gopinath, R., A. Kumar, R. Trinadha, and O. Springate-Baginski. 2011. "Issues Related to Implementation of the Forest Rights Act in Andhra Pradesh." *Economic and Political Weekly* 46 (18): 73–81.

Gorringe, H. 2010. "The New Caste Headmen? Dalit Movement Leadership in Tamil Nadu." In *Power and Influence in India*, edited by P. Price and A. E. Ruud, 119–42. New Delhi: Routledge India.

Graeber, D. 2009. *Direct Action: An Ethnography*. New York: AK Press.

Guha, R. 1998. *Dominance without Hegemony: History and Power in Colonial India.* Oxford: Oxford University Press.

———. 1999. *Elementary Aspects of Peasant Insurgency in Colonial India*. Durham, NC: Duke University Press.

Guiu, S. 2013. "Constructing Prestige and Elaborating the 'Professional': Elite Residential Complexes in the National Capital Region, India." *Contributions to Indian Sociology* 47 (2): 271–302.

Gupta, A. 1995. "Blurred Boundaries: The Discourse of Corruption, the Culture of Politics, and the Imagined State." *American Ethnologist* 22 (2): 375–402.

———. 2012. *Red Tape: Bureaucracy, Structural Violence, and Poverty in India*. Durham, NC: Duke University Press.

Gupta, A., and A. Sharma. 2006. "Globalization and Postcolonial States." *Current Anthropology* 47 (2): 277–307.

Hagopian, F. 1996. *Traditional Politics and Regime Change in Brazil.* Cambridge: Cambridge University Press.

Hall, K., D. M. Goldstein, and B. M. Ingram. 2016. "The Hands of Donald Trump: Entertainment, Gesture and Spectacle." *Journal of Ethnographic Theory* 6 (2): 71–100.

Hann, C. 1998. "Introduction: The Embeddedness of Property." In *Property Relations: Renewing the Anthropological Tradition*, edited by C. Hann, 1–47. Cambridge: Cambridge University Press.

———. 2007. "A New Double Movement? Anthropological Perspectives on Property in the Age of Neoliberalism." *Socio-Economic Review* 5 (2): 287–318.

Hansen, T. B. 2001. *Wages of Violence: Naming and Identity in Postcolonial Bombay.* Princeton, NJ: Princeton University Press.

———. 2005. "Sovereigns beyond the State: On Legality and Public Authority in India." In *Religion, Violence and Political Mobilisation in South Asia*, edited by R. Kaur, 169–91. New Delhi: Sage.

———. 2009. "Javeedbhai (Mumbai)." In *Muslim Portraits: Everyday Lives in India*, edited by M. Banerjee, chap. 4. Bloomington: Indiana University Press.

Hansen, T. B., and F. Stepputat, eds. 2005. *Sovereign Bodies: Citizens, Migrants, and States in the Postcolonial World*. Princeton, NJ: Princeton University Press.

———. 2006. "Sovereignty Revisited." *Annual Review of Anthropology* 35:295–315.

Hansen, T. B., and O. Verkaaik. 2009. "On Everyday Mythologies in the City." *Critique of Anthropology* 29 (1): 5–26.

Haqqani, H. 2005. *Pakistan: Between Mosque and Military*. Washington, DC: Carnegie Endowment for International Peace.

Hariman, R. 1995. *Political Style: The Artistry of Power*. Chicago: University of Chicago Press.

Harper, T., and S. Amrith. 2012. "Sites of Asian Interaction: An Introduction." *Modern Asian Studies* 46 (2): 249–57.

Harrison, S. 1956. "Caste and the Andhra Communists." *American Political Science Review* 50 (2): 378–404.

———. 1960. *India: The Most Dangerous Decades*. Princeton, NJ: Princeton University Press.

Harriss, J. 2010. "Is Government in India Becoming More Responsive? Has Democratic Decentralisation Made a Difference?" *Simon Papers in Security and Development* 8:3–24.

Harriss, J., and C. Jeffrey. 2013. "Depoliticizing Injustice." *Economy and Society* 42 (3): 507–20.

Harriss-White, B. 2003. *India Working: Essays on Society and Economy*. Cambridge: Cambridge University Press.

———. 2010. "Globalization, the Financial Crisis and Petty Production in India's Socially Regulated Informal Economy." *Global Labour Journal* 1 (1): 152–77.

———, ed. 2015. *Middle India and Urban-Rural Development*. New Delhi: Springer India.

Harriss-White, B., and E. Jannakarājann. 2004. *Rural India Facing the 21st Century*. London: Anthem Press.

Harriss-White, B., and L. Michelutti. Forthcoming. *Wild East? Criminal Political Economies in South Asia*. London: UCP.

Hartmann, B., and J. Boyce. 2013. *A Quiet Violence: View from a Bangladesh Village*. *Dhaka:* Create Space Independent Publishing Platform.

Harvey, D. 2003. *The New Imperialism*. Oxford: Oxford University Press.

———. 2005. *A Brief History of Neoliberalism*. Oxford: Oxford University Press.

———. 2006. *Spaces of Global Capitalism: Towards a Theory of Uneven Geographical Development*. London: Verso.

Hasan, A., N. Ahmed, M. Raza, A. Sadiq, S. ud Din Ahmed, and M. Sarwar.

2013. *Land Ownership, Control and Contestation in Karachi and Implications for Low-Income Housing*. International Institute for Environment and Development (IIED), March. http://pubs.iied.org/10625IIED.html.

Heath, O. 2015. "The BJP's Return to Power: Mobilisation, Conversion and Vote Swing in the 2014 Indian Elections." *Contemporary South Asia* 23 (2): 123–35.

———. 2016. "Does Multiparty Competition Increase Ethnic Security Fears? Evidence from North India." *Party Politics* 22 (6): 746–57.

Herrenschmitt, O. 2009. "A propos de Tirupati: Les présidents du TTD Board of Trustees. Religieux et politique. Collusions vendettas Mafias." Unpublished manuscript.

Herring, R. J. 1983. *Land to the Tiller: The Political Economy of Agrarian Reform in South Asia*. New Haven, CT: Yale University Press.

Herzfeld, M. 1997. *Cultural Intimacy: Social Poetics in the Nation-State*. London: Routledge.

Heyman, J. 1999. *States and Illegal Practices*. Oxford: Berg.

Hill, P. B. E. 2006. *The Japanese Mafia: Yakuza, Law, and the State*. Oxford: Oxford University Press.

Hirsch, J. S., H. Wardlow, D. J. Smith, H. M. Phinney, and C. A. Nathanson. 2010. *The Secret of Love*. Nashville, TN: Vanderbilt University Press.

Hobsbawm, E. 1969. *Bandits*. New York: Delacorte Press.

Hoek, E. 2013. "Blood Splattered Bengal: The Spectacular Spurting Blood of the Bangladeshi Cinema." *Contemporary South Asia* 21 (3): 214–29.

Hoffman, Kasper, and Tom Kirk. 2013. "Public Authority and the Provision of Public Goods in Conflict-Affected and Transitioning Regions." JSRP Paper 7, August. https://assets.publishing.service.gov.uk/media/57a08a49e5274a27b200050f/JSRP7-HoffmannKirk.pdf.

Hoque, A. 2014. "The Political Mercenary: The Emergence of the *Mastan* in Bangladeshi Politics." Working paper presented at Democratic Cultures Workshop, Arundel, Sussex, June.

Hoque, A., and L. Michelutti. 2014. "Brushing with Organized Crime: *Jugaad* as Democracy." Working paper presented at Annual Conference on South Asia, University of Wisconsin, Madison, October 19–22.

Hull, M. S. 2012. *Government of Paper: The Materiality of Bureaucracy in Urban Pakistan*. Berkeley: University of California Press.

Humphrey, C. 1997. "Exemplars and Rules: Aspects of the Discourse of Moralities in Mongolia." In *The Ethnography of Moralities*, edited by S. Howell, 25–47. London: Routledge.

———. 1999. "Traders, 'Disorder' and Citizenship Regimes in Provincial Russia." In *Uncertain Transition: Ethnographies of Change in the Postsocialist World*, edited by M. Burawoy and K. Verdery, 19–50. Lanham, MD: Rowman and Littlefield.

———. 2004. "Sovereignty." In *A Companion to the Anthropology of Politics*, edited by D. Nugent and J. Vincent, 418–36. Oxford: Blackwell.

Ibrahim, A. 2015. "The Not-So-Happy Ever After: Crime as Moral Corruption in the Family in Hindi Television News." *Contributions to Indian Sociology* 49 (3): 344–68.

Islam, Mohammad Mozahidul. 2013. "The Toxic Politics of Bangladesh: A Bipolar Competitive Neopatrimonial State?" *Asian Journal of Political Science* 21 (2): 148–68.

Jaffe, R. 2012. "The Popular Culture of Illegality: Crime and the Politics of Aesthetics in Urban Jamaica." *Anthropological Quarterly* 85 (1): 79–102.

———. 2013. "The Hybrid State: Crime and Citizenship in Urban Jamaica." *American Ethnologist* 40 (4): 734–48.

Jaffrelot, C. 2002. "Indian Democracy: The Rule of Law on Trial." *India Review* 1 (1): 77–121.

Jaffrelot, C., and S. Kumar, eds. 2009 *Rise of the Plebeians? The Changing Face of the Indian Legislative Assemblies*. Delhi: Routledge.

Jahan, R. 1976. "Members of Parliament in Bangladesh." *Legislative Studies Quarterly* 1 (3): 355–70.

———. 2005. *Bangladesh Politics: Problems and Issues*. Dhaka: UPL.

———. 2015. "The Parliament of Bangladesh: Representation and Accountability." *Journal of Legislative Studies* 21 (2): 250–69.

Jahan, R., and I. Amundsen. 2012. *The Parliament of Bangladesh: Representation and Accountability*. Report in External Series. CPD-CMI Working Paper series CPD-CMI WP 2012:2. Dhaka/Bergen: Center for Policy Dialogue (CPD) and Chr. Michelsen Institute (CMI). https://www.cmi.no/publications/4422-the-parliament-of-bangladesh.

Jalal, A. 1995. *Democracy and Authoritarianism in South Asia: A Comparative and Historical Perspective*. Cambridge: Cambridge University Press.

Jauregui, B. 2014. "Provisional Agency in India: *Jugaad* and Legitimation of Corruption." *American Ethnologist* 41 (1): 76–91.

Jayawardena, K., and M. de Alwis, eds. 1996. *Embodied Violence: Communalizing Women's Sexuality in South Asia*. New Delhi: Kali for Women.

Jeffrey, C. 2001. "A Fist Is Stronger Than Five Fingers: Caste and Dominance in Rural North India." *Transactions of the Institute of British Geographers* 26 (2): 217–36.

———. 2010. *Timepass: Youth, Class, and the Politics of Waiting in India*. Stanford, CA: Stanford University Press.

Jeffrey, C., P. Jeffery, and R. Jeffery. 2008a. "Dalit Revolution? New Politicians in Uttar Pradesh, India." *Journal of Asian Studies* 67 (4): 1365–96.

———, eds. 2008b. *Degrees without Freedom? Education, Masculinities and Unemployment in North India*. Stanford, CA: Stanford University Press.

Jeffrey, C., and S. Young. 2012. "Waiting: Youth, Caste and Politics in India." *Economy and Society* 41 (4): 638–61.

Jeffery, P., and A. Basu. 2012. *Appropriating Gender: Women's Activism and Politicized Religion in South Asia*. London: Routledge.

Jodhka, S. 2004. "Sikhism and the Caste Question: Dalits and Their Politics in Contemporary Punjab." *Contributions to Indian Sociology* 38 (1): 165–92.

———. 2014. "What's Happening to the Rural? Revisiting Marginalities and Dominance in Northwest India." In *Persistence of Poverty in India*, edited by J. Parry and N. Gooptu, 317–43. Delhi: Social Science Press.

Jones, G. A., and D. Rodgers, eds. 2009. *Youth Violence in Latin America: Gangs and Juvenile Justice in Perspective*. New York: Palgrave Macmillan.

Jones, J. 2010. "Nothing Is Straight in Zimbabwe: The Rise of the Kukiya-kiya Economy 2000–2008." *Journal of Southern African Studies* 36 (2): 285–99.

Joshi, V. 2009. "Economic Resurgence, Lop-Sided Performance, Jobless Growth." In *Continuity and Change in Contemporary India: Politics, Economics, and Society*, edited by A. Heath and R. Jeffery, 73–106. Delhi: Oxford University Press.

Kakar, S. 1996. *The Colours of Violence: Cultural Identities, Religion and Conflict*. Chicago: University of Chicago Press.

Kane, P. C., and S. C. Parnell, eds. 2003. *Crimes' Power: Anthropologists and the Ethnography of Crime*. New York: Palgrave Macmillan.

Kapferer, B. 1998. *The Feast of the Sorcerer: Practices of Consciousness and Power*. Chicago: University of Chicago Press.

Kaplan, D. E., and A. Dubro. 2003. *Yakuza: Japan's Criminal Underworld*. London: Robert Hale.

Kapur, D., and M. Vaishnav. 2013. "Quid Pro Quo: Builders, Politicians, and Election Finance in India." Working paper 276, Center for Global Development, updated March 29. http://www.cgdev.org/publication/quid-pro-quo-builders-politicians-and-election-finance-india-working-paper-276-updated.

Kasturi, M. 2013. "The Bandit as King." In *Crime through Time*, edited by A. Rao and S. Dube, 20–48. Delhi: Oxford University Press.

Kaur, R. 2010. "*Khap Panchayat*, Sex Ratio and Female Agency." *Economic and Political Weekly* 45 (23): 14–16.

Kaur, R., and T. B. Hansen. 2016. "Aesthetics of Arrival: Spectacle, Capital, Novelty in Post-reform India." *Identities—Global Studies in Culture and Power* 23 (3): 1–11.

Kaviraj, S. 2000. "Modernity and Politics in India." *Daedalus* 129 (1): 137–64.

Kennedy, A. 1993. "Of Dacoits and Desperados: Crime Reporting in Pakistani English." In *The English Language in Pakistan*, edited by R. J. Baumgardner, 69–79. Karachi: Oxford University Press.

Khan, M. 2011. "The Politics of Public Interest Litigation in Pakistan in the 1990s." *Social Science and Policy Bulletin* 2 (4): 2–8.

Khan, M. H., and K. S. Jomo, eds. 2001. *Rents, Rent-Seeking and Economic Development: Theory and Evidence in Asia*. Cambridge: Cambridge University Press.

Khan, N. 2010. "Mosque Construction or the Violence of the Ordinary." In *Beyond Crisis: Re-evaluating Pakistan*, edited by N. Khan, 482–518. London: Routledge.

Kochanek, S. A. 1993. *Patron-Client Politics and Business in Bangladesh*. Thousand Oaks, CA: Sage Publications.

———. 2010. "Corruption and the Criminalization of Politics in South Asia." In

Routledge Handbook of South Asian Politics: India, Pakistan, Bangladesh, Sri Lanka, and Nepal, edited by P. Brass, 364–81. London: Routledge.

Kohli, A. 1991. *Democracy and Discontent: India's Growing Crisis of Governability*. Cambridge: Cambridge University Press.

Kooistra, P. 1989. *Criminals as Heroes*. Bowling Green, OH: Popular Press.

Kumar, A. 2007. "The 2007 Punjab Elections: Exploring the Verdict." *Economic and Political Weekly* 42 (22): 2043–47.

———. 2014. *Criminalisation of Politics*. Delhi: Rawat Publications.

Laidlaw, J. 2000. "A Free Gift Makes No Friends." *Journal of the Royal Anthropological Institute* 6 (4): 617–34.

———. 2013. *The Subject of Virtue: An Anthropology of Ethics and Freedom*. Cambridge: Cambridge University Press.

Lama, T. 2001. "The Hindu Goddess and Women's Political Representation in South Asia: Symbolic Resource or Feminine Mystique?" *International Review of Sociology* 11 (1): 5–20.

Leeds, E. 1996. "Cocaine and Parallel Polities in the Brazilian Urban Periphery: Constraints on Local-Level Democratization." *Latin American Research Review* 31 (3): 47–83.

Lempert, M., and M. Silverstein. 2012. *Creatures of Politics: Media, Message, and the American Presidency*. Bloomington: Indiana University Press.

Levien, M. 2011. "Special Economic Zones and Accumulation by Dispossession in India." *Journal of Agrarian Change* 11 (4): 454–83.

Lewis, D. 2011. *Bangladesh: Politics, Economy, and Civil Society*. Cambridge: Cambridge University Press.

Lieven, A. 2011. *Pakistan: A Hard Country*. London: Penguin.

Lindquist, J. 2015. "Of Figures and Types: Brokering Knowledge and Migration in in Indonesia and Beyond. In "The Power of Example: Anthropological Explorations in Persuasion, Evocation, and Imitation." Special issue, *Journal of the Royal Anthropological Institute* 21 (S1) :162–77.

Lund, C. 2006. "Twilight Institutions: An Introduction." *Development and Change* 37 (4): 673–84.

Lyon, S. 2002. "Power and Patronage in Pakistan." PhD diss., University of Kent.

Maccaglia, F., and M. Matard-Bonucci. 2014. *Atlas des mafias: Acteurs, trafics et marchés criminels dans le monde*. Paris: Autrement.

Machiavelli, N. 2003. *The Prince*. Translated by George Bull. London: Penguin.

Madsen, S. T. 2011. "Ajit Singh S/O Charan Singh." In *Trysts with Democracy: Political Practice in South Asia*, edited by S. T. Madsen, K. B. Nielsen, and U. Skoda, 73–102. London, Anthem 2011.

Madsen, S., and K. Nielsen. 2011. *Trysts with Democracy*. London: Anthem Press.

Major, A. J. 1999. "State and Criminal Tribes in Colonial Punjab: Surveillance, Control and Reclamation of the 'Dangerous Classes.'" *Modern Asian Studies* 33:657–88.

Malhotra, I. 2003. *Dynasties of India and Beyond: Pakistan, Sri Lanka, Bangladesh*. New Delhi: HarperCollins.

Malik, S. M. 2009. "Horizontal Inequalities and Violent Conflict in Pakistan: Is There a Link?" *Economic and Political Weekly* 44 (34): 21–40.

Mallick, A. 2014. "Class Politics in the Era of Neoliberalism: The Case of Karachi, Pakistan." Master's thesis, York University.

Mandelbaum, S. J. 1965. *Boss Tweed's New York*. New York: Wiley.

Mankekar, P. 2013. "'We Are like This Only': Aspiration, 'Jugaad,' and Love in Enterprise Culture." In *Enterprise Culture in Neoliberal India: Studies in Youth, Class, Work and Media*, edited by N. Gooptu, 19–34. London: Routledge.

Manor, J. 2000. "Small-Time Fixers in India's States: 'Towel over Armpit.'" *Asian Survey* 40 (5): 816–35.

———. 2007. "Changing State, Changing Society in India." *Journal of South Asian Studies* 25 (2): 231–56.

Martin, N. 2009. "The Political Economy of Bonded Labour in the Pakistani Punjab." *Contributions to Indian Sociology* 43 (1): 35–59.

———. 2015a. *Politics, Landlords and Islam in Pakistan*. Delhi: Routledge.

———. 2015b. "Rural Elites and the Limits of Scheduled Caste Assertiveness in Rural Malwa, Punjab." *Economic and Political Weekly* 50 (52): 37–52.

Martin, N., and L. Michelutti. 2017. "Protection Rackets and Party Machines: 'Mafia Raj' across Western Uttar Pradesh and Punjab." *Asian Journal of Social Science* 45:6.

Marwah, S. 2014. "Mapping Murder: Homicide Patterns and Trends in India, an Analysis from 2000–2010." *Journal of South Asian Studies* 2 (2): 145–63.

Mascarenhas, A. 1986. *Bangladesh: A Legacy of Blood*. London: Hodder and Stoughton.

Mauss, M., and H. Hubert. 1993. "Esquisse d'une théorie générale de la Magie." In *Sociologie et anthropologie*, by M. Mauss. Paris: PUF.

Mazzarella, W. 2003. *Shoveling Smoke: Advertising and Globalization in Contemporary India*. Durham, NC: Duke University Press.

Mbembe, A. 1992. "The Banality of Power and the Aesthetics of Vulgarity in the Postcolony." *Public Culture* 4 (2): 1–30.

McCartney, M. 2015. "From Boom to Bust: Economic Growth and Security in Pakistan 2003–2013." In *Democratic Transition and Security in Pakistan*, edited by S. Gregory, 76–101. London: Routledge.

Mehdi, R. 2013. *The Islamization of the Law in Pakistan*. London: Routledge.

Mehta, S. 2004. *Maximum City: Bombay Lost and Found*. New York: Vintage Books.

Menon, K. D. 2010. *Everyday Nationalism: Women of the Hindu Right in India*. The Ethnography of Political Violence. Philadelphia: University of Pennsylvania Press.

Menon, R., and K. Bhasin. 1998. *Borders and Boundaries: Women in India's Partition*. New Brunswick, NJ: Rutgers University Press

Michelutti, L. 2008. *The Vernacularisation of Democracy*. Delhi: Routledge.

———. 2010. "Wrestling with (Body) Politics: Understanding 'Goonda' Political Styles in North India." In *Power and Influence in South Asia: Bosses, Lords, and Captains*. Delhi: Routledge.

———. 2013. "Sons of Krishna and Sons of Bolivar: Charismatic Kinship and Leadership across India and Venezuela." *Focaal—Journal of Historical and Global Anthropology* 67 (Winter): 19–31.

———. 2014a. "Circuits of Protections in Western Uttar Pradesh." Working paper presented at Democratic Cultures Workshop, Hyderabad, India, March.

———. 2014b. "Kingship without Kings." In *Patronage as Politics in South Asia*, edited by A. Piliavsky, 283–302. Cambridge: Cambridge University Press.

———. 2017. "'We Are All Chavez': Charisma as an Embodied Experience." *Latin American Perspectives: A Journal on Capitalism and Socialism* 44 (1): 232–50.

Michelutti, L., and O. Heath. 2013. "The Politics of Entitlement: Affirmative Action and Strategic Voting in Uttar Pradesh, India." *Focaal—Journal of Historical and Global Anthropology* 65:56–67.

———. 2014. "Cooperation and Distrust: Identity Politics and Yadav-Muslim Relations in Uttar Pradesh, 1999–2009." In *Development Failure and Identity Politics in Uttar Pradesh*, edited by R. Jeffery, J. Lerche, and C. Jeffrey, 128–64. New Delhi: Sage.

Michelutti, L., and D. Picherit. 2015. "Myth Scripting and Gangsters." Working paper, "Democratic Cultures" Project, Paris Nanterre University.

Migdal, J. 1988. *Strong Societies and Weak States*. Princeton, NJ: Princeton University Press.

Mines, M. 1996. *Public Faces, Private Voices: Community and Individuality in South India*. Delhi: Oxford University Press.

Mines, M., and V. Gourishankar. 1990. "Leadership and Individuality in South Asia: The Case of the South Indian Big-Man." *Journal of Asian Studies* 49 (4): 761–86.

Mitchell, T. 1990. "Everyday Metaphors of Power." *Theory and Society* 19 (5): 545–77.

———. 1991. "The Limits of the State: Beyond Statistic Approaches and Their Critics." *American Political Science Review* 85 (1): 77–96.

Moatasim, F. 2015. "Making Exceptions: Politics of Nonconforming Spaces in the Planned Modern City of Islamabad." PhD diss., University of Michigan.

Mohiuddin, K. 2007. *Asthaminchani Ravi: Oka Udymaveeruni Oppiri Yatra*. Dharmavaram: Narayanamma Publications.

Mosse, D. 2011. "Uncertain Networks: NGOs, Dalit Rights and the Development Agenda in South India." Paper presented at the Caste out of Development conference, Chennai, December. https://casteout.files.wordpress.com/2013/07/david_uncertainnetworks.pdf.

———. 2015. "Caste and the Conundrum of Religion and Development in India." In *The Routledge Handbook of Religions and Global Development*, edited by E. Tomalin. 200–214. New York: Routledge.

Murthy, P., and E. de La Fuente, eds. 2014. *Aesthetic Capitalism*. Leiden, Netherlands: Brill.

Nadeem, A. H. 2002. *Pakistan: The Political Economy of Lawlessness*. Karachi: Oxford University Press.

Narayan, B. 2005. *Women Heroes and Dalit Assertion in North India: Culture, Identity and Politics*. Delhi: Sage.

Nelson, M. 2011. *In the Shadow of Sharia*. London: Hurst.

———. 2016. "Informal Agencies of Influence in Pakistan: The Interdependence of Social, Religious, and Political Trends." *Special Report of the National Bureau of Asian Research* 55:60–70.

Newell, S. 2012. *The Modernity Bluff: Crime, Consumption, and Citizenship in Côte d'Ivoire*. Chicago: University of Chicago Press.

Nilsen, K. B., and P. Oskarsson, eds. 2016. *Industrialising Rural India: Land, Policy and Resistance*. London: Routledge.

Nisar, M. A., and A. Masood. 2012. "The Nostalgic Detective: Identity Formation in Detective Fiction of Pakistan." *Pakistaniaat: A Journal of Pakistan Studies* 4 (3): 33–60.

Nonstrom, C. 2000. "Shadows and Sovereigns." *Theory Culture and Society* 17 (4): 35–54.

Oldenburg, P. 1992. "Sex Ratio, Son Preference and Violence in India: A Research Note." *Economic and Political Weekly* 27 (49/50): 2657–62.

Olivieri, E., and S. Sberna. 2014. "Set the Night on Fire! Mafia Violence and Elections in Italy." SSRN Working Paper 37.

Omvedt, G. 2005. "Women in Governance in South Asia." *Economic and Political Weekly* 40, (44/45): 4748.

Orsini, F. 2004. "Detective Novels: A Commercial Genre in Nineteenth-Century North India." In *India's Literary History: Essays on the Nineteenth Century*, edited by S. Blackburn and V. Dalmia, 435–79. New Delhi: Permanent Black.

———. 2009. *Print and Pleasure: Popular Literature and Entertaining Fictions in Colonial North India*. New Delhi: Permanent Black.

Ortner, S. B. 1995. "Resistance and the Problem of Ethnographic Refusal." *Comparative Studies in Society and History* 37 (1): 173–93.

Osburg, J. 2013. Meeting the "Godfather": Fieldwork and Ethnographic Seduction in a Chinese Nightclub. *PoLAR* 36 (2):298–303.

Osella, C., and F. Osella, eds. 2006. *Men and Masculinities in South Asia*. London: Anthem South Asian Studies.

Paoli, L. 2003. *Mafia Brotherhoods: Organized Crime Italian Style*. Oxford: Oxford University Press.

Pardo, I. 1996. *Managing Existence in Naples: Morality, Action, and Structure*. Cambridge: Cambridge University Press.

———, ed. 2000. *The Morals of Legitimacy*. Oxford: Berghahn Books.

Parry, J. 2000. "'The Crisis of Corruption' and 'the Idea of India': A Worm's Eye View." In *The Morals of Legitimacy*, edited by I. Pardo, 27–56. Oxford: Berghahn Books.

Peabody, N. 2009. "Disciplining the Body, Disciplining the Body-Politic: Physical Culture and Social Violence among North Indian Wrestlers." *Comparative Studies in Society and History* 51 (2): 372–400.

Pemberton, J. 1999. "Open Secrets: Excerpts from Conversations with a Javanese Lawyer, and a Comment." In *Figures of Criminality in Indonesia, the Philippines, and Colonial Vietnam*, edited by V. Rafael, 193–209. Ithaca, NY: Cornell University Southeast Asia Program.

Picherit, D. 2015. "Dalit Mobilisation and Faction Politics in Rural Andhra Pradesh: Everyday Life of a Dalit NGO and Agricultural Labour Union." *Economic and Political Weekly* 50 (52): 74–82.

———. 2016. "Rural Youth and Circulating Labour In South India: The Tortuous Paths towards Respect for Madigas." *Journal of Agrarian Change* 18 (1): 178–95.

Piliavsky, A. 2014. "Introduction." In *Patronage as Politics in South Asia*, edited by A. Piliavsky, 1–39. Cambridge: Cambridge University Press.

Pine, J. 2012. *The Art of Making Do in Naples*. Minneapolis: University of Minnesota Press.

Pingle, G. 2011. "Reddys, Kammas and Telangana." *Economic and Political Weekly* 46 (36): 19–21.

Pipyrou, S. 2014. "Altruism and Sacrifice: Mafia Free Gift Giving in South Italy." *Anthropological Forum* 24 (4): 412–26.

Prasad, N. P. 2015. "Agrarian Class and Caste Relations in 'United' Andhra Pradesh, 1956–2014." *Economic and Political Weekly* 50 (16): 77–83.

Prasad, N. P., K. Laxminarayana, V. Vakulabharanam, and S. Kilaru. 2012. "Mining in Tribal Habitats of Araku Valley: Tragedy of the Commons Revisited (II)." *Economic and Political Weekly* 47 (42): 14–17.

Prasad, N. P., V. Vakulabharanam, and K. Laxminarayna. 2012. "Tragedy of the Commons Revisited (II): Mining in Tribal Habitats of Araku Valley." *Economic and Political Weekly* 47 (42): 14–17.

Price, D. H. 2008. *Anthropological Intelligence: The Deployment and Neglect of American Anthropology in the Second World War*. Durham, NC: Duke University Press.

Price, P. G. 1989. "Kingly Models in Indian Political Behavior: Culture as a Medium of History." *Asian Survey* 29 (6): 559–72.

———. 1996. *Kingship and Political Practice in Colonial India*. Cambridge: Cambridge University Press.

———. 2006. "Changing Meanings of Authority in Contemporary South India." *Qualitative Sociology* 29 (3): 301–16.

Price, P., and A. E. Ruud, eds. 2010. *Power and Influence in South Asia: Bosses, Lords, and Captains*. Delhi: Routledge.

Pritchett, L. 2009. "Is India a Flailing State? Detours on the Four Lane Highway to Modernisation." HKS Faculty Research Working Paper Series RWP09-13, John F. Kennedy School of Government, Harvard University.

Rafael, V. L., ed. 1999. *Figures of Criminality in Indonesia, the Philippines, and Colonial Vietnam*. Ithaca, NY: Cornell University Press.

Raheja, G., and A. G. Gold. 1994. *Listen to the Heron's Words: Reimagining Gender and Kinship in North India*. Berkeley: University of California Press.

Rais, R. 1985. "Elections in Pakistan." *Asian Affairs: An American Review* 12 (3): 43–61.

Ram, R. 2007. "Social Exclusion, Resistance and *Deras*: Exploring the Myth of Casteless Sikh Society in Punjab." *Economic and Political Weekly* 42 (40): 4066–74.

Rancière, J. 1999. *Disagreement: Politics and Philosophy*. Translated by Julie Rose. Minneapolis: University of Minnesota Press.

Rao, A., and S. Dube, eds. 2013. *Crime through Time*. Delhi: Oxford University Press.

Rashiduzzaman, M. 1978. "Bangladesh in 1977: Dilemmas of Military Rulers." *Asian Survey* 18 (2): 126–34.

Reddy, M., K. Gopinath, Rao T. Anil Kumar, and O. Springate-Baginski. 2011. "Issues Related to Implementation of the Forest Rights Act in Andhra Pradesh." *Economic and Political Weekly* 46 (18): 73–81.

Reddy, R. G., and G. Haragopal. 1985. "'The Fixer' in Rural India." *Asian Survey* 25 (11): 1148–62.

Rediker, M. 2004. *Villains of All Nations: Atlantic Pirates in the Golden Age*. Boston: Beacon.

Rege, A. 2016. "Not Biting the Dust: Using a Tripartite Model of Organized Crime to Examine India's Sand Mafia." *International Journal of Comparative and Applied Criminal Justice* 40 (2): 101–21.

Reuter, P. 1987. *Racketeering in Legitimate Industries: A Study in the Economics of Intimidation*. Santa Monica, CA: RAND.

Richter, L. K. 1990. "Exploring Theories of Female Leadership in South and Southeast Asia." *Pacific Affairs* 63 (4): 524–40.

Robben, A. 1996. "Ethnographic Seduction, Transference, and Resistance in Dialogues about Terror and Violence in Argentina." *Ethos* 24 (1): 71–106.

Robbins, J. 2013. "Beyond the Suffering Subject." *Journal of the Royal Anthropological Institute*, n.s., 19:447–62.

Rodgers, D. 2001. "Making Danger a Calling: Anthropology, Violence and the Dilemmas of Participant Observation." Working Paper No. 6, Development Research Centre, LSE.

———. 2006a. "Living in the Shadow of Death: Gangs, Violence and Social Order in Urban Nicaragua, 1996–2002." *Journal of Latin American Studies* 38 (2): 267–89.

———. 2006b. "The State as a Gang." *Critique of Anthropology* 26:315–30.

Roitman, J. 2004. *Fiscal Disobedience: An Anthropology of Economic Regulation in Central Africa*. Princeton, NJ: Princeton University Press.

Rollier, P. 2014. "The Vanishing Wrestler: Illegality and Criminal Mediation in Urban Pakistan." Paper presented at Democratic Cultures Workshop, Cambridge, UK, September.

Roy, R. 1996. "State Failure: Political-Fiscal Implications of the Black Economy." *Bulletin, Institute of Development Studies* 27 (2): 22–31.

Ruud, A. E. 2000. "Corruption as Everyday Practice. The Public-Private Divide in Local Indian Society." *Forum for Development Studies* 27 (2): 271–94.

———. 2003. *Poetics of Village Politics: The Making of West Bengal's Rural Communism*. Delhi: Oxford University Press.

———. 2010. "To Create a Crowd: Student Leaders in Dhaka." In *Power and Influence in India: Bosses, Lords and Captains*, edited by P. Price and Ruud, 70–95. London: Routledge.

———. 2011. "Democracy in Bangladesh: A Village View." In *Trysts with Democracy: Political Practice in South Asia*, edited by S. T. Madsen, K. B. Nielsen, and U. Skoda, 45–70. London: Anthem.

———. 2014. "The Political Bully in Bangladesh." In *Patronage as Politics in South Asia*, edited by A. Piliavsky, 303–25. Cambridge: Cambridge University Press.

Ruud, A. E., and M. M. Islam. 2016. "Political Dynasty Formation in Bangladesh.. *South Asia: Journal of South Asian Studies* 30 (2): 401–14.

Ryter, L. 2012. "Privateers, Politicians, Prowess and Power in Indonesia." In *Southeast Asian Perspectives on Power*, edited by L. Chua, J. Cook, N. Long, and L. Wilson, 107–18. New York: Routledge.

Sahlins, M. 1963. "Poor Man, Rich Man, Big Man, Chief: Political Types in Melanesia and Polynesia." *Comparative Studies in Society and History* 5 (3): 285–303.

———. 2002. *Waiting for Foucault, Still.* Chicago: Prickly Paradigm Press.

Sanchez, A. 2015. *Criminal Capital. Violence, Corruption and Making of Class in an Indian Steel Town.* Delhi: Routledge.

Sánchez-Jankowski, M. 1991. *Islands in the Street: Gangs and American Urban Society.* Berkeley: University of California Press.

Santoro, M. 2011. "Introduction: The Mafia and the Sociological Imagination." *Sociologica* 2:1–36.

Sarkar, T., and U. Butalia, eds. 1995. *Women and the Hindu Right: A Collection of Essays.* New Delhi: Kali for Women.

Saviano, R. 2015. *Zero Zero Zero.* London: Penguin.

Scheper-Hughes, N., and P. Bourgois. 2003. *Violence in War and Peace.* Hoboken, NJ: Wiley-Blackwell.

Schmitt, C. 1985. *Political Theology: Four Chapters on the Concept of Sovereignty.* Cambridge, MA: MIT Press.

Schneider, J. C., and P. T. Schneider. 1999. "Is Transparency Possible? The Political-Economic and Epistemological Implications of Cold-War Conspiracies and Subterfuge in Italy." In *States and Illegal Practices*, edited by J. Heyman, 169–98. Oxford: Berg.

———. 2003. *Reversible Destiny: Mafia, Antimafia, and the Struggle for Palermo.* Berkeley: University of California Press.

———. 2007. "Mafias." In *A Companion to the Anthropology of Politics*, edited by D. Nugent and J. Vincent, 303–18. London: Blackwell Publishing.

———. 2008. "The Anthropology of Crime and Criminalization." *Annual Review of Anthropology* 37:351–73.

———. 2011. "The Mafia and Capitalism: An Emerging Paradigm." *Sociologic* 2:1–22.

Scott, J. 1969. "Corruption, Machine Politics, and Political Change." *American Political Science Review* 63 (4): 1142–58.

Seal, G. 2009. "The Robin Hood Principle: Folklore, History, and the Social Bandit." *Journal of Folklore Research* 46 (1): 67–89.

Searle, G. L. 2013. "Constructing Prestige and Elaborating the 'Professional': Elite

Residential Complexes in the National Capital Region, India." *Contributions to Indian Sociology* 47 (2): 271–302.

———. 2014. "Conflict and Commensuration: Contested Market Making in India's Private Real Estate Development Sector." *International Journal of Urban and Regional Research* 38 (1): 60–78.

Sen, A. 2007a. "Everyday and Extraordinary Violence: Women Vigilantes and Raw Justice in the Bombay Slums." In *Global Vigilantes: Anthropological Perspectives on Violence and Vigilantism*, edited by P. David and A. Sen, 69–92. London: Hurst.

———. 2007b. *Shiv Sena Women: Violence and Communalism in a Bombay Slum.* Bloomington: Indiana University Press.

———. 2011. "Surviving Violence, Contesting Victimhood: Communal Politics and the Creation of Child-Men in an Urban Indian Slum." *South Asia: Journal of South Asian Studies* 34 (2): 276–97.

Sennett, R. 1980. *Authority.* London: Faber and Faber.

Shah, A. 2006. "Markets of Protection: The Terrorist Maoist Movement and the State in Jharkand, India." *Critique of Anthropology* 26 (3): 297–314.

Sharma, L. 1999. "The Organized Crime in India: Problems and Perspectives." In *Resource Material Series No. 54*, 82–129. Tokyo: UNAFEI. https://www.peacepalacelibrary.nl/ebooks/files/UNAFEI_no54.pdf#page=85

Shulman, D. 1986. *The King and the Clown in South Indian Myth and Poetry.* Princeton, NJ: Princeton University Press.

Siddiqa, A. 2007. *Military Inc.: Inside Pakistan's Military Economy.* Karachi: Oxford University Press.

———. 2013. *The New Frontiers: Militancy and Radicalism in Punjab.* SISA Report No. 2-2013. Centre for International and Strategic Analysis, February 4. http://strategiskanalyse.no/publikasjoner%202013/2013-02-04_SISA2_The_New_Frontiers_-_Ayesha_Siddiqa.pdf.

Siddique, O. 2013. *Pakistan's Experience with Formal Law: An Alien Justice.* Cambridge: Cambridge University Press.

Sidel, J. 1999a. *Capital, Coercion, and Crime: Bossism in the Philippines.* Stanford, CA: University of California Press.

———. 1999b. "The Usual Suspects: Nardong Putik, Don Pepe Oyson, and Robin Hood." In *Figures of Criminality in Indonesia, the Philippines, and Colonial Vietnam*, edited by V. Rafael, 70–94. Studies on Southeast Asia, No. 25. Southeast Asia Program Publications. Ithaca, NY: Cornell University Press.

———. 2004. "Bossism and Democracy in the Philippines, Thailand, and Indonesia: Towards an Alternative Framework for the Study of 'Local Strongmen.'" In *Politicising Democracy: The New Local Politics of Democratisation*, edited by J. Harriss, K. Stokke, and T. Olle, 51–74. International Political Economy Series. Basingstoke, UK: Palgrave Macmillan.

Siegel, J. 1998. *A New Criminal Type in Jakarta: Counter-revolution Today.* Durham, NC: Duke University Press.

Simmel, G. 1968. "Sociological Aesthetics." In *The Conflict in Modern Culture and Other Essays*, edited by P. K. Etzkorn, 68–80. New York: Teachers College.

Singh, G. 1996. "Punjab since 1984: Disorder, Order and Legitimacy." *Asian Survey* 36 (4): 410–21.

———. 2014. "Class, Nation and Religion: Changing Nature of Akali Dal Politics in Punjab, India." *Commonwealth and Comparative Politics* 52 (1): 55–77.

Skoda, U. 2004. "The Politics-Kinship Nexus in India: Sonia Gandhi versus Sushma Swaraj in the 1999 General Elections." *Contemporary South Asia* 13 (3): 273–85.

Slocum, W. L., J. Akhtar, and A. F. Sahi. 1960. *Village Life in Lahore District: A Study of Selected Sociological Aspects*. Lahore: University of the Panjab, Social Sciences Research Centre.

Sluka, J. 1990. "Participant Observation in Violent Social Contexts." *Human Organization* 49 (2): 114–26.

Smith, D. 2007. *A Culture of Corruption: Everyday Deception and Popular Discontent in Nigeria*. Princeton, NJ: Princeton University Press.

Spencer, J. 2003. "Appalling Fascination: The Emerging Anthropology of 'the Political' in Postcolonial South Asia." *Journal des anthropologue* 1–2 (92–93): 31–49.

———. 2007. *Anthropology, Politics, and the State: Democracy and Violence in South Asia*. Cambridge: Cambridge University Press.

Spencer, J., J. Goodhand, S. Hasbullah, B. Klem, B. Korf, and K. Silva. 2014. *Checkpoint, Temple, Church and Mosque: A Collaborative Ethnography of War and Peace*. London: Pluto Press.

Springer, S. 2013. "Violent Accumulation: A Postanarchist Critique of Property, Dispossession, and the State of Exception in Neoliberalizing Cambodia." *Annals of the Association of American Geographers* 103 (3): 608–26.

Srinivas, S. V. 2013. *Politics as Performance: A Social History of the Telugu Cinema*. Delhi: Permanent Black.

Srinivasan, K. 2007. "Money Laundering and Security." In *Controlling Arms and Terror in the Asia Pacific*, edited by M. Vicziany, 21–44. Northampton, UK: Edward Elgar.

Srinivasulu, K. 2002. *Caste, Class and Social Articulation in Andhra Pradesh: Mapping Differential Regional Trajectories*. Working Paper 179. London: Overseas Development Institute.

———. 2009. "Y S Rajasekhara Reddy: A Political Appraisal." *Economic and Political Weekly* 44 (38): 8–10.

Srivatsan, R. 2015. *Seva, Saviour and State: Caste Politics, Tribal Welfare and Capitalist Development*. London: Routledge.

Standing, A. 2003. *The Social Contradictions of Organised Crime on the Cape Flats*. ISS Paper 74. Pretoria: Institute for Security Studies.

Stiglitz, J. 2002. *Globalisation and Its Discontents*. New York: W. W. Norton.

Still, C. 2014a. "Dalits in Neoliberal India: An Overview." In *Dalits in Neoliberal India: Mobility or Marginalisation?*, edited by C. Still, 1–44. London: Routledge.

———. 2014b. *Dalit Women: Honour and Patriarchy in South India*. Delhi: Social Science Press.

Stokes, S., T. Dunning, M. Nazareno, and V. Brusco. 2013. *Brokers, Voters, and Clientelism: The Puzzle of Distributive Politics*. New York: Cambridge University Press.

Strange, S. C. 1996. *The Retreat of the State: The Diffusion of Power in the World Economy*. Cambridge: Cambridge University Press.

Strathern, A. 1971. *The Rope of Moka: Big-Men and Ceremonial Exchange in Mount Hagen, Papua New Guinea*. Cambridge: Cambridge University Press.

Strathern, M. 2012. "Gifts Money Cannot Buy." *Social Anthropology* 20 (4): 397–410.

Suchitra, M. 2012. "Cheated for Bauxite." Down to Earth, January 31. http://www.downtoearth.org.in/content/cheated-bauxite.

Sukhtankar, S. 2012. "Sweetening the Deal? Political Connections and Sugar Mills in India." *American Economic Journal: Applied Economics* 4 (3): 43–63.

Suri, K. C. 2002. *Democratic Process and Electoral Politics in Andhra Pradesh, India*. Working Paper 180. London: Overseas Development Institute. https://assets.publishing.service.gov.uk/media/57a08d3240f0b649740016e0/wp180web.pdf.

Suri, K. C., and C. V. Raghavulu. 1996. "Agrarian Movements and Land Reforms." In *Land Reforms in India: Andhra Pradesh—People's Pressure and Administrative Reforms*, edited by B. N. Yugandhar, 28–56. New Delhi: Sage.

Suud, N. 2014. "The Men in the Middle: A Missing Dimension in Global Land Deals." *Journal of Peasant Studies* 41 (4): 593–612.

Taussig, M. 1991. *The Nervous System*. London: Routledge.

———. 1997. *The Magic of the State*. London: Routledge.

Tejpal, T. J. 2010. *The Story of My Assassins*. New Delhi: HarperCollins.

Telugu Desam Party (TDP). 2004. *If a Factionist Becomes Chief Minister*. Hyderabad: Telugu Desam.

Tilly, C. 1985. "War Making and State Making as Organised Crime." In *Bringing the State Back In*, edited by P. Evans, D. Rueschemeyer, and T. Skocpol, 169–91. Cambridge: Cambridge University Press.

Tripathy, S. 2014. *The Colonel Who Would Not Repent: The Bangladesh War and Its Unquiet Legacy*. New Delhi: Aleph.

Turner, V. 1969. *The Ritual Process: Structure and Anti-structure*. London: Routledge.

Upadhya, C. 1997. "Social and Cultural Strategies of Class Formation in Coastal Andhra Pradesh." *Contributions to Indian Sociology* 31 (2): 169–93.

Vaishnav, M. 2011. "The Market for Criminality: Money, Muscle and Elections in India." Working draft, August 31. https://casi.sas.upenn.edu/sites/casi.sas.upenn.edu/files/iit/Market%20for%20Criminality%20-%20Aug%202011.pdf.

———. 2012. "The Merits of Money and 'Muscle': Essays on Criminality, Elections and Democracy in India." PhD diss., Columbia University.

———. 2017. *When Crime Pays: Money and Muscle in Indian Politics*. New Haven, CT: Yale University Press.

Van Schendel, W. 2009. *A History of Bangladesh*. New York: Cambridge University Press.

Van Schendel, W., and I. Abraham, eds. 2005. *Illicit Flows and Criminal Things: States, Borders, and the Other Side of Criminal Things*. Bloomington: Indiana University Press.

Varese, F. 2001. *The Russian Mafia: Private Protection in a New Market Economy*. Oxford: Oxford University Press.

———. 2011a. *Mafias on the Move. How Organized Crime Conquers New Territories*. Princeton, NJ: Princeton University Press.

———. 2011b. *Organized Crime: Critical Concepts in Criminology*. Vol. 1. London: Routledge.

Varma, P. K. 2004. *Being Indian: Inside the Real India*. Delhi: Arrow.

Varshney, A. 2001. "Ethnic Conflict and Civil Society: India and Beyond." *World Politics* 53 (3): 362–98.

———. 2002. *Ethnic Conflict and Civic Life: Hindus and Muslims in India*. New Delhi: Oxford University Press.

Verdery, K. 1996. *What Was Socialism, and What Comes Next?* Princeton, NJ: Princeton University Press.

Verkaaik, O. 2001. "The Captive State: Corruption, Intelligence Agencies, and Ethnicity in Pakistan." In *States of Imagination: Ethnographic Explorations of the Postcolonial State*, edited by T. B. Hansen and F. Stepputat, 345–64. Durham, NC: Duke University Press.

Verniers, G. 2014. "The Root of the Goonda Raj: Why There Is So Much Violence in Uttar Pradesh." *Daily Brief*, June 7. http://scroll.in/article/666450/The-roots-of-Goonda-Raj:-Why-there%27s-so-much-violence-in-Uttar-Pradesh/.

Vidal, D., G. Tarabout, and E. Meyer, eds. 2003. *Violence/Non-violence: Some Hindu Perspectives*. Delhi: Manohar.

Vigh, H. E. 2006. *Navigating Terrains of War: Youth and Soldiering in Guinea-Bissau*. London: Berghahn.

Vohra Committee Report. n.d. Delhi: Government of India, Ministry of Home Affairs.

Volkov, V. 2002. *Violent Entrepreneurs: The Use of Force in the Making of Russian Capitalism*. Ithaca, NY: Cornell University Press.

Wade, R. 1985. "The Market for Public Office: Why the Indian State Is Not Better at Development." *World Development* 13 (4): 467–97.

Wagner, K. A. 2007. "Thuggee and Social Banditry Reconsidered." *Historical Journal* 50 (2): 353–76.

Waseem, M. 1994. *The 1993 Elections in Pakistan*. Lahore: Vanguard Press.

Wasti, T. 2009. *The Application of Islamic Criminal Law in Pakistan: Sharia in Practice*. Leiden, Netherlands: Brill.

Watson, J. L., ed. 1997. *Golden Arches East: McDonald's in East Asia*. Stanford, CA: Stanford University Press.

Weber, M. 1978a. *Economy and Society*. 2 vols. Edited by Guenther Roth and Claus Wittich. Berkeley: University of California Press.

———. 1978b. "Politics as a Vocation." In *Weber: Selections in Translation*, edited by

W. G. Runciman, translated by Eric Matthews, 212–25. Cambridge: Cambridge University Press.

Weiner, M. 1963. *The Politics of Scarcity*. Chicago: University of Chicago Press.

Weinstein, L. 2008. "Mumbai's Development Mafias: Globalization, Organized Crime and Land Development." *International Journal of Urban and Regional Research* 32 (1): 22–39.

West, D. M., and J. M. Orman. 2003. *Celebrity Politics: Real Politics in America*. Upper Saddle River, NJ: Prentice Hall.

Wheeler, M. 2013. *Celebrity Politics: Image and Identity in Contemporary Political Communications*. Cambridge: Polity Press.

Whitehead, J. 2008. "Rent Gaps, Revanchist and Regimes of Accumulation in Mumbai." *Anthropologica* 50 (2): 269–82.

Wilce, J. M. 2004. "To 'Speak' Beautifully in Bangladesh: Subjectivity as Pāgalāmi." In *Schizophrenia, Culture, and Subjectivity: The Edge of Experience*, edited by J. H. Jenkins and R. J. Barrett, 196–213. Cambridge: Cambridge University Press.

Wilkinson, S. 2004. *Votes and Violence: Electoral Competition and Ethnic Riots in India*. Cambridge: Cambridge University Press.

Wilson, E., ed. 2009. *Government of the Shadows. Parapolitics and Criminal Sovereignty*. London: Pluto Press.

Wilson, I. D. 2015. *The Politics of Protection Rackets in Post–New Order Indonesia: Coercive Capital, Authority and Street Politics*. London: Routledge.

Witsoe, J. 2009. "Territorial Democracy: Caste, Dominance and Electoral Practice in Postcolonial India." *Political and Legal Anthropology Review* 32 (1): 64–83.

———. 2011. "Rethinking Postcolonial Democracy: An Examination of the Politics of Lower-Caste Empowerment in North India." *American Anthropologist* 113 (4): 619–31.

———. 2011a. Corruption as Power: Caste and the Political Imagination of the Postcolonial State. *American Ethnologist* 38, (1): 73–85.

Worsley, P. 1968. *The Trumpet Shall Sound: A Study of "Cargo" Cults in Melanesia*. New York: Schocken Books.

Yadav, Y. 2000. "Understanding the Second Democratic Upsurge: Trends of Bahujan Participation in Electoral Politics in the 1990s." In *Transforming India: Social and Political Dynamics of Democracy*, edited by F. R. Frankel, 120–45. New Delhi: Oxford University Press.

Zaidi, S. A. 2014. "Different Governments, Same Problems: Pakistan's Economy 1999–2013." In *South Asia in Transition: Democracy, Political Economy and Security*, edited by B. Chakma, 109–26. London: Palgrave Macmillan.

Zaidi, S. M. A. 2016. "Reconstituting Local Order in Pakistan: Emergent ISIS and Locally Constituted Shariah Courts in Pakistan." Brookings Institution, *Local Orders Paper Series* 4:1–28.

INDEX

Page numbers in italics indicate material in figures and tables. See also glossary, 261–263.